The Lochsa Story

Land Ethics in the Bitterroot Mountains

Bud Moore

Mountain Press Publishing Company
Missoula, Montana 1996

Second Printing, July 1997

Photos not otherwise credited are by the author.

Maps drawn by Bob Siloti

Library of Congress Cataloging-in-Publication Data

Moore, Bud, 1917–

The Lochsa story : land ethics in the Bitterroot Mountains / by Bud Moore.

p. cm.

Includes bibliographical references and index.

ISBN 0-87842-341-9 (cloth : alk. paper). —ISBN 0-87842-333-8 (pbk. : alk. paper)

1. Lochsa River Region (Idaho)—History. 2. Lochsa River Region (Idaho)—Historical geography. 3. Land use, Rural—Idaho—Lochsa River Region—Moral and ethical aspect. 4. Land use, Rural—Bitterroot Range (Idaho and Mont.)—Moral and ethical aspects. 5. Bitterroot Range (Idaho and Mont.)—History. 6. Bitterroot Range (Idaho and Mont.)—Historical geography. 7. Selway-Bitterroot Wilderness (Idaho and Mont.)—History. 8. Moore, Bud, 1917– —Homes and haunts—Idaho—Lochsa River Region. I. Title.

F752.I2.M66 1996 96-27228

978.6'8—dc20 CIP

PRINTED IN THE U.S.A.

Mountain Press Publishing Company

P. O. Box 2399 • Missoula, MT 59806

(406) 728-1900 • 1-800-234-5308

*To the men and women who discovered the Lochsa country
and to the people of today who would learn from the experiences
of those early-day participants in the life of the natural earth.*

Contents

Maps

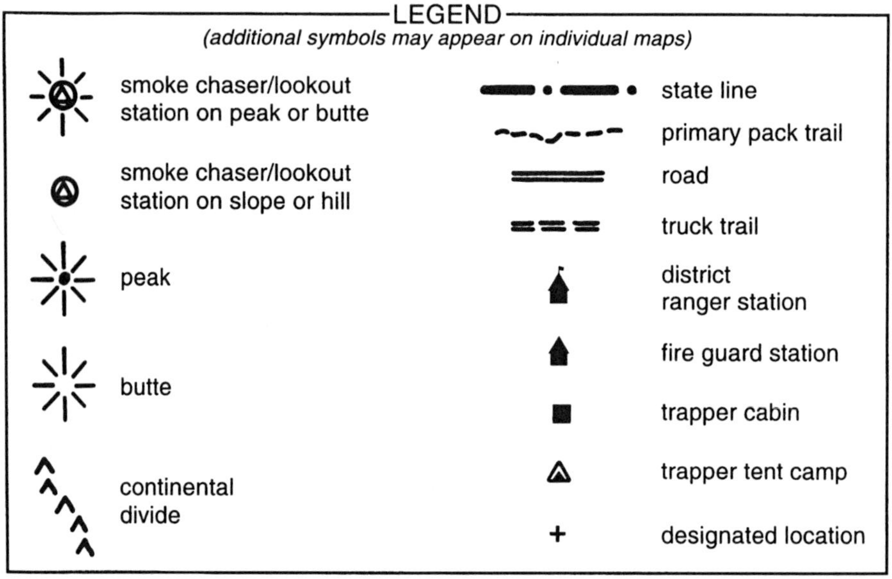

LEGEND
(additional symbols may appear on individual maps)
smoke chaser/lookout station on peak or butte
smoke chaser/lookout station on slope or hill
peak
butte
continental divide
state line
primary pack trail
road
truck trail
district ranger station
fire guard station
trapper cabin
trapper tent camp
designated location

Acknowledgments

If this book turns out to be a valuable contribution to land ethics and history, it will be due in large part to several people who believe that public value can be gained from considerate care of the land and its resources. In retrospect, it is clear to me that without their help, I would have never laid down my pack long enough to write the story, much less attempt to evaluate the meaning of the Lochsa's heritage.

Noted teacher and author, the late Norman Maclean took care of my inclination to put outdoor pursuits first, desk work last. Every time I dropped my pencil and looked at my fly rod, he would show up in some form or another. He even threatened to write the story himself, which he was capable of doing because, by the time I was two years old, he was already at work for the Forest Service in the Lochsa country. How does one deal with a guy like that? The best I can offer is: "Thanks, Norman."

Thanks also to my wife, Janet, for launching and picking me up at the end of several wilderness explorations and for companionship on two of such trips. She became so excited about the story that she began marketing my work while the outline and first three chapters were still in draft—and also before I had any sure idea that a book would ever emerge from the Lochsa's history. But I slowed her down by mailing a prospectus to a publisher who sent us back to the story board. Her faith never wavered.

I write in a longhand scrawl that few people besides Janet can interpret well enough to type into manuscript form. Nonetheless, several courageous women have done their best, and I am grateful to Janet, my daughter Vicki, Ronda Underwood, Cindy Jette, Michele Potter, and Suzanne Vernon for their editing, typing, and encouragement.

After long deliberation and two pack trips into the wilderness, I raised enough willpower to ask five critics to read my second draft. Retired professor of Wildlife Management, the late Les Pengelly, furnished invaluable advice on historical accuracy, scientific soundness, and writing style. Thanks, Les. Neighboring Swan Valley homesteader Mike Stevenson contributed the viewpoint of a modern-day mountain man who appreciates the wisdom of those who have lived close to the earth in the past. Here's what Mike said: "That's one helluva story. But it sounds like you were lecturing some ranger in chapter 25." That's what I *was* doing, but, just the same I rewrote the chapters, and the lessons of the Lochsa are much better said because of Mike's attention.

Dick Potter is a capable businessman, an outdoorsman, a perceptive writer and editor, and an emigrant from California who knows nothing about the Lochsa. To say that his critique separated the wood from the slash is an incomplete statement. He hammered away on organization, too many adjectives, too many testimonials, and not enough bear stories. Dick should know that I used his advice, together with detailed editing contributed by my daughter Vicki for major revisions of content and style. Thanks, Dick and Vicki, for helping to blaze the trail through the Lochsa's wilderness of words.

The comments of Wayne A. "Butch" Harmon, an eager reader of my earliest drafts, come packaged differently from all the rest. Outdoorsman Butch is a logger, trapper, and past president of the Montana Trappers' Association who has a hang-up with spelling and won't write anything down. So, whenever Butch assembled a mind full of comments, he would show up at our cabin where, over steaming cups of black coffee, his suggestions would emerge for discussion. The outcome of this neighborly evaluation of my work had much to do with the quality of the Lochsa Story.

After reviewing chapters 2 and 3, Nez Perce Tribal Council member Allen Pinkham would like to have seen more written about his people. I agree with Allen, who also understands why I couldn't present more details in this historical overview of the Lochsa. His reaction was : "If you feel comfortable with it, go ahead and publish." Thanks, Allen.

Nor could this story have been written without the contributions of seventy-nine people who shared their experiences in interviews during which it became obvious that, for some, the Lochsa association had been the high point of their lives. I also found clues to the Lochsa's past in the works of several writers and interpreters of western, national, and world history. And but for the contributions of old-timers who wrote the four volumes of *Early Days in the Forest Service*, the support of archivist Beverly Ayers and science librarian Irene Evers, and the historical writings of Ralph S. Space, Louis Hartig, and Neal Parsell, the Lochsa story would be shallow indeed. Also, the cooperation of personnel of the Idaho Fish and Game Department, the Nez Perce County Historical Society, the Nez Perce National Historical Park, and the Nez Perce Tribe is much appreciated, as are the open-file policies of the Clearwater National Forest, the Lolo National Forest, the Lochsa and Powell ranger stations, and the Region One Headquarters of the Forest Service at Missoula, Montana. Carol Maier, Judd Moore, and Joyce Pritchard were especially helpful in locating information from the Regional Office files, as were Dennis Elliott, Linnea Keating, and Jeff Fee from the files of the Clearwater National Forest.

David H. Jackson and Alan G. McQuillan, professors at the University of Montana School of Forestry, guided me to the scientific literature and legal interpretations of applicable laws I needed to study to update my ten-year-old draft to 1994. Professor James M. Peek and Dean John C. Hendee, of the University of Idaho College of Forestry, Wildlife, and Range Sciences, provided cutting-edge information on forest management conditions in Idaho. When the manuscript was nearly finished, a critical review by Paul W. Hirt, assistant professor of history at Washington State University, furnished much-needed advice. And copyediting by Debra Donahue, assistant professor of law at the University of Wyoming, disclosed deficiencies in the work that I was too involved to discover. These data and counsel were invaluable, and so is the time of those busy people. Thanks, friends. You pointed me in the right direction.

Clearwater supervisor Jim Caswell, Powell district ranger Margaret Gorski, and Lochsa district acting rangers Gerald Beard and Gary Manning welcomed me home to the Lochsa in 1994. They shared their scientific knowledge, creative thoughts, and feelings about the past and future of the Lochsa's land. Drawing from some twenty years experience as ranger in the Lochsa country, Jon Bledsoe added a one-of-a-kind perspective. It is from the attitudes of these men and women and their staffs that I discovered the flavor of the government land ethics of today and tomorrow. Thanks for sharing. Thanks also to those old-time members of the Powell district with whom I worked in earlier days. We formed a good team. Your contributions extend far beyond this book, for it was our working together that set the standards governing much of my personal life.

And finally, I feel privileged to have shared the Lochsa with mountain men of an earlier generation and to have heard their stories of a generation before that, thereby inheriting some of their respect for the natural earth. It has been good to know them in life and again in narration. Wherever their spirits might be, I hope they are not disappointed with this story.

Preface

This is a story about the Lochsa country—the place in the Bitterroot mountains of Idaho where I spent most of my life from boyhood to near middle age and which, since then, has never for long been absent from my thoughts (see map 1). To acknowledge the work of those who discovered, used, and protected the country, and to examine the idea that the history of the Lochsa has implications far beyond its local environs, have been my objectives throughout. It seemed from the outset that something of lasting value could be drawn from the Lochsa by combining literature, study of the land, the adventures of people who created the history, and my own experiences in search of ideas useful for the present and future.

Preparation for writing this story began sometime during the early 1920s when the Lochsa's mountain men brought their inescapable enthusiasm to our home situated in the valley of the Lolo Fork of Montana's Bitterroot River. No one so exposed could avoid catching their contagious wonder at the mystery of that wild land of rivers, tributaries, mountains, and wildlife. I thought then, and still think, they were the greatest people on earth. And I hope my writing has captured some of their vitality as well as the spirit of the land of the Lochsa, because these are entwined together in a man-land association that fosters a great deal of respect for the natural earth.

After describing the geographical setting, this story continues with a brief history of Indian occupation of the land and then traces the historic milestones of European occupation of the Lochsa from the time of Lewis and Clark's expedition until 1994. Significant land management laws, policies, and decisions are included as history, and I present these within the frame of knowledge and cultural mores of that time. I have endeavored to make the story historically accurate, scientifically sound, and interesting. To lend a sense of reality to some past events, on occasion I have departed from historical narrative and assumed in a "surely-they-would-have" manner that the characters acted in certain ways. I resort to this method only in instances where I have visited the locations involved and have seen and felt the power of the place. In those instances it is my own experience I project to help bring the story alive. I have also tried to add realism to history by visiting many historical sites, then relating these to information gathered during several interviews with old-timers.

Due to its long remoteness from settlements, much early-day lore of the Lochsa, especially during the period from Lewis and Clark's time until the late 1880s, remains obscure. Nonetheless, this book includes some heretofore unrecorded events and assembles additional information previously available only from scattered sources. It is an overview of historical milestones, not a comprehensive coverage of history. And I hope it will prompt informed persons to add more information to the historical record of the Lochsa.

Although much has been recorded, a rich treasure of undiscovered history of Native American occupation and use still hides in the land of the Lochsa. I apologize for dedicating but one chapter to the Indian people when their historical activities in the area deserve much more. But that is another story that should one day be written by someone who better understands the culture of the Indian nations involved.

This story is not limited to a chronology of happenings within the environs of the Lochsa. To draw meaningful conclusions from the Lochsa story, I show how the culture and politics of America affected the people and the land and, in turn, how events in the Lochsa influenced the course of the nation. In the last three chapters, I depart from historical documentation to report what seems to me to be the most significant findings of this, my first journey by pad and pen through the Lochsa's remarkable history.

This book, then, is a story of people and land, of achievements and failures, and of lessons learned that have value in shaping America's future.

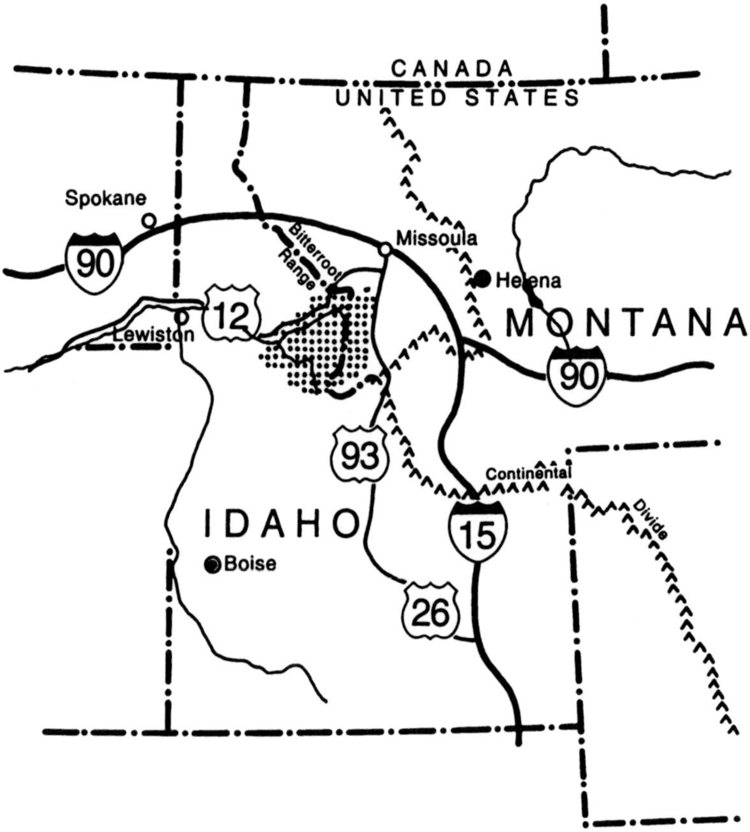

Map 1. *The Lochsa country and environs*

1

Over the Hill, That's God's Country

At noontime on a cold day in January 1930, Homer, Shorty, Dad, and I gathered for lunch around an open fire near the old Indian "road" that led from Montana's Bitterroot Valley across the mountains into Idaho's Lochsa Fork of the Clearwater River. During those times of America's Great Depression, we earned our livelihood by trapping furs in winter and peddling firewood to the people of the towns on the outskirts of the mountains. Beyond that we lived much like the Indians before us, by hunting, fishing, and preserving produce grown on the land.

We skewered Mom's frozen mule deer steak sandwiches on willow sticks, then thawed them near the fire's glowing coals. And while coffee sizzled in a sooty can, talk turned to the wild expanse of mountains extending far to the west from our valley of the Lolo Fork of the Bitterroot River. That wilderness was for us an adventurous place, a land whose wild landscapes surely held secrets not yet discovered by humans. To dream of finding its gold, trapping its furs, and confronting its great peaks and rivers provided a welcome break from the labor of cutting wood.

Of the four of us, only Homer had journeyed deep into the Lochsa country. A stocky, muscular man, he had probably seen sixty winters, but his features were so ageless one couldn't tell for sure. As he chunked half-burned pine limbs into the dying flames, he said, "There's nothin' in this wood cuttin' fer a man. Next spring I'm goin' over the hill and next winter I'm gonna stay there. That country over the hill, that's God's country."

In about 1924, Bill Moore and part of his family leave the Chickaman Mine cabin en route to their homestead about one mile away. Author Bud Moore closes the gate, with his sister Clarine standing nearby, while sister Sylvia stays close to their father. —Clara Hollopeter

Blue wood smoke drifting through the firs and pines spiced our glade's frosty air, while the harnesses rattled as the skidding team munched hay. No one responded to Homer's statement. Preoccupied with his own thoughts, each man peered through the smoke at the flames, while I watched them with the curiosity of twelve-year-old youth and wondered what promise Homer's God's country might hold for Dad, Shorty, Homer, or me.

Because they were the heads of growing families, neither Shorty nor Dad would likely find time to explore the wilds of the Lochsa, but I, like Homer, was eager to journey over the hill because I had already searched out most of the topography of the Lolo Fork's drainage. I had killed two bears. Shooting a mule deer buck behind the shoulders had become for me a common necessity for survival in the mountains. But perhaps most compelling, the mystery of the Lolo Fork's wilds was shrinking. I was growing. And I needed room to expand outside our valley—not to the cities, like Missoula, Butte, or Hamilton, but over the hill where the Lochsa rumbled out of the mountains to join the other great rivers of the Clearwater country.

Snow-dusted Lolo Peak shines in the background of the small meadow (upper left center) where the Moore family's log cabin home stood during the 1920s.

I wanted to go, but it was hard to break away from a family like ours. We had long depended on each other for economic and emotional support. Although the Lochsa was calling, I tarried at home. As always, there was the garden to tend, hay to cut and stack, wood to chop, hams to smoke, and big trout to catch from the Lolo Fork. Besides that, substantial security enriched our humble life there in the forty-acre clearing with its two-room log cabin, chicken pens, pig pens, smokehouse, barn, and root cellar, all clustered in the meadow near a cold spring.

So it was late August before I left. To see more country, I climbed into the high mountains south of our homestead equipped with a battered .30-30 Winchester, light tarp, one blanket, fish line and hooks, and salt, bacon, flour, and oatmeal to supplement berries and game. I followed the timbered ridge behind our log cabin to the alpine moraine beneath Lolo Peak and camped that first night near timberline on the shores of Mill Creek Lake.

The second night out I slept in Frank Bretschneider's trapper cabin near where the cascading waters of Falls Creek joined the south branch

Here is all that remained in 1969 of Frank Bretschneider's cabin on the south fork of Lolo Creek.

of the Lolo Fork. At dusk on the third day, smoke from my campfire drifted across the Snowslide Meadows high up in the cirquelike canyon of the South Fork. The late-day sun of waning summer warmed the crests of the peaks, while at my shaded camp in the valley the nip of fall warned of winter close at hand. I shivered and edged nearer to the crackling fire.

Evening shadows crept over the land. It was lonely, especially when the flames flickered low and darkness surrounded the feeble fire, leaving me outside its light. The day creatures had surrendered the woods to the prowlers of night. So I wrapped in my blanket and stretched out on the bed I had fashioned from the boughs of a spruce tree. Although reassured by the blanket's warmth, I thought of home—of the fragrance of newly mown hay, of Mom's bubbling sourdough jug, of hot oatmeal and cow's cream, and of the family banter around the breakfast table. A rock rattled down the mountainside and crashed into a nearby thicket. Perhaps a grizzly was digging for marmots. Other wildlife heard it, too, for high on the mountain to the west an elk bugled. The wild notes suspended in the still night air until they penetrated every nook within the basin.

Camping alone in the mountains was not new to me, but the ties to home had always been stronger than the call of the wilds. No matter the solitude, I had never before been truly alone. Dad always knew, give

During the late summer and fall, the grizzlies of the Bitterroot mountains dug big holes in the rock slides to catch hoary marmots like this one.

or take a canyon or two, where I was. He trusted my ability to care for myself, but, should he sense something wrong, I knew he would strike out on my trail with his rifle and pack. Much of my self-confidence had its roots in that emotional bond.

But that night on the South Fork, home was fading; in its place the wildness of unknown land tugged at my future. Each sound in the night held fresh meaning. Tomorrow I would climb up past where the bull elk bugled its challenge and for the first time get an expansive look at the land of the Lochsa. Tonight was the eve of my departure from the waters of the Lolo Fork and the security of home. For some time, excitement defied sleep. But the murmur of the stream soothed my senses until at last I slept—while the bull elk tended his harem on the mountain and the grizzly dug for food among the granite boulders.

By daybreak the grasses of the meadow had stiffened beneath white frost, but sunlight soon crept down from the crest to warm the mountainsides. I climbed up through the shaded forest until the sun and I met a quarter of a mile above the valley's floor. By late morning I neared the summit, where white plumes of beargrass in full bloom nodded in the Lochsa-borne breeze. Two hoary marmots scrambled up on a boulder. Their whistles of alarm shattered the silence as I gained the last five yards to the top of the Bitterroot mountains.

There it was. The Lochsa country: an expanse of mountains and forests extending westward from an alpine lake one-half mile beneath my feet to where haze and the curvature of the earth combined to render

A glimpse of the Lochsa country as seen from the crest of the Bitterroots in 1930.

all things indistinct. The Lochsa River's valley carved a deep slice through the center of that landscape, and its ridges and draws reached down from the crest and then vanished into the canyon's shadow. Beginning somewhere far to the south the river flowed northward, formed a great hook around an island of granite in that mountainous ocean, then plunged westward to fade from view, like the mountains, where the peaks and saddles joined the pale Clearwater sky. Tributary canyons and hanging valleys stretched from the Lochsa's bosom out toward the high country, and dozens of those streams drained sparkling water from landscapes far larger than the Lolo Fork (see map 2).

Such space far exceeded my expectations. Homer's hill turned out to be a massive wall of granite peaks and rubble whose precipitous bulk protected the Lochsa from exploitation by the people of the bustling Bitterroot Valley. It divided the states of Montana and Idaho. When the buffalo flourished, it fenced them out of the Columbia country. Sea-run salmon and trout spawned on the gravel bars in the Lochsa, but that wall of granite confined them to the waters flowing down its western slopes. Homer's hill controlled two climatic regions. Its crest, nine thousand- to ten thousand-feet above sea level, hoisted

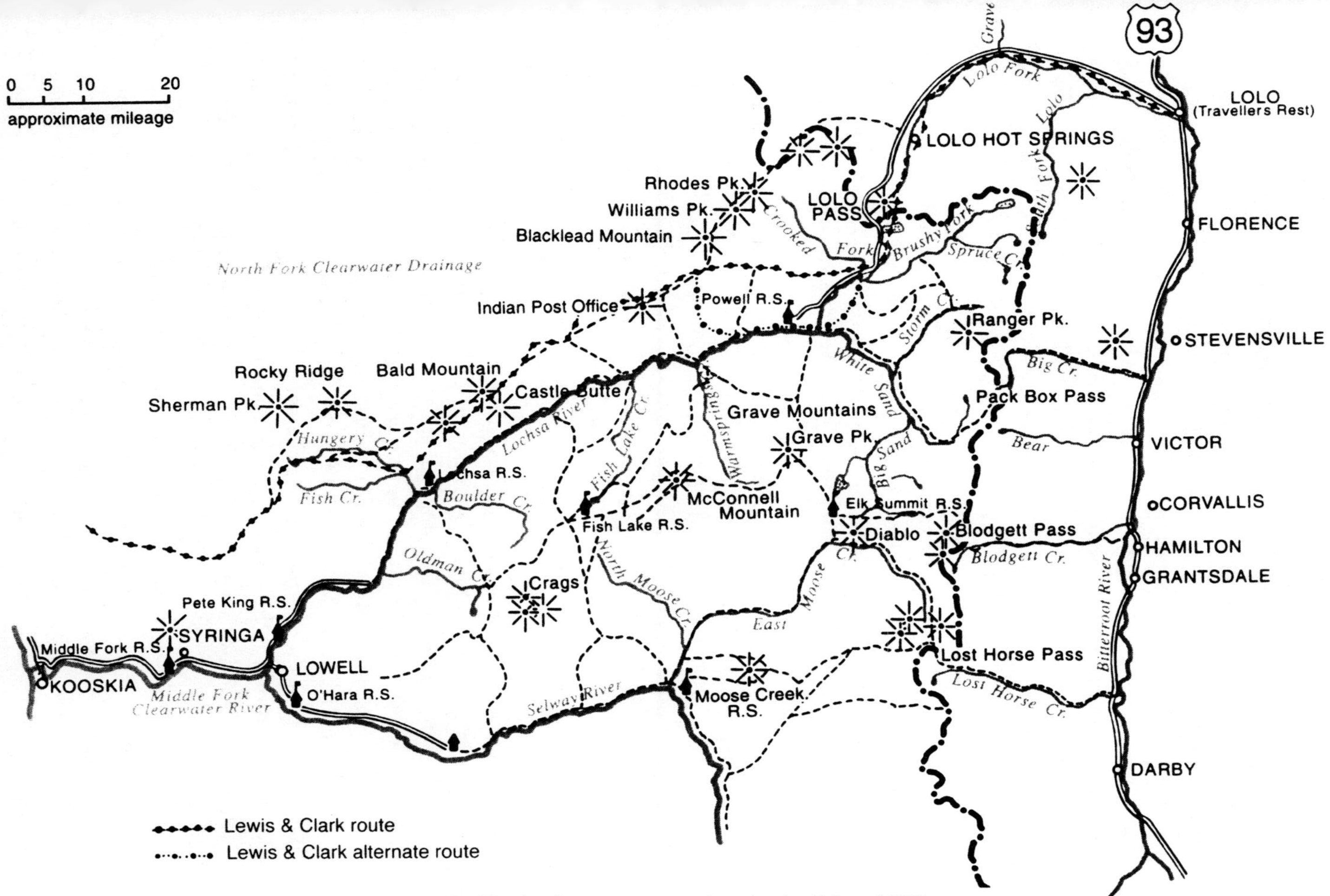
0 5 10 20
approximate mileage
93
LOLO
(Travellers Rest)
FLORENCE
STEVENSVILLE
VICTOR
CORVALLIS
HAMILTON
GRANTSDALE
DARBY
LOLO HOT SPRINGS
LOLO
PASS
Rhodes Pk.
Williams Pk.
Blacklead Mountain
North Fork Clearwater Drainage
Indian Post Office
Powell R.S.
Ranger Pk.
Pack Box Pass
Rocky Ridge
Bald Mountain
Sherman Pk.
Castle Butte
Grave Mountains
Grave Pk.
Lochsa R.S.
McConnell
Mountain
Fish Lake R.S.
Elk Summit R.S.
Diablo
Blodgett Pass
Crags
Pete King R.S.
SYRINGA
Middle Fork R.S.
KOOSKIA
LOWELL
O'Hara R.S.
Moose Creek
R.S.
Lost Horse Pass
Grave
Lolo Fork
Lolo
South Fork
Crooked
Fork
Brushy Fork
Spruce Cr.
Storm Cr.
White Sand
Big Sand
Big Cr.
Bear
Warmsprings
Fish Lake Cr.
Lochsa River
Hungery Cr.
Fish Cr.
Boulder Cr.
Oldman Cr.
North Moose Cr.
Moose Cr.
East
Selway River
Blodgett Cr.
Bitterroot River
Lost Horse Cr.
Middle Fork
Clearwater River
Lewis & Clark route
Lewis & Clark alternate route

Map 2. *The Lochsa country and major facilities, 1930.*

moisture-laden storms bound inland from the Pacific so they dumped their loads on the Lochsa basin, leaving near-empty clouds to travel across the more arid Bitterroot Valley. For centuries the Bitterroot crest limited east-west transportation routes primarily to three Indian roads.[1] Except for the expedition led by Meriwether Lewis and William Clark, the western pioneer movements detoured to the north and south, leaving the Lochsa alone, locked in wildness, a mysterious land that cast its spell on pilgrims who would rather join with the grizzly bears than follow the trails blazed by the earlier-day explorers of the West.

A breeze whipped through the rocky saddle where I had gained the crest, then died just as suddenly. A striped chipmunk climbed a beargrass stalk, his weight bending the plant's stem while he hung on and chiseled seeds from the nutritious blossom. The mountains brightened, then dimmed, hidden momentarily in the shadows of clouds. The land was alive.

And I too was alive, born again into the spirit of the Lochsa, a partner to the bears, mountain goats, moose, and great rivers. Homer's God's country was good for the wild creatures, and it was a good place for me to reach out from boyhood to seize a sense of worthiness from life. It felt like that land was going someplace, and I wanted to go with it. So I tightened the straps on my pack for downhill travel and proceeded to expand my perception of life from the Lolo Fork's familiar landscapes to the larger world of the Lochsa.

I hiked down toward the lake, avoiding the steep inclines of slippery granite to gain sure footing where clumps of beargrass grew in shallow soil between the rocks. The slope smelled dry—grass curing, blossoms ripening, needles dehydrating, light gray granite reflecting sunshine in shimmering waves toward the sky. I was thirsty, but not for long, for I soon drank from the stream that flowed from the lake, cascaded over the cirque dike, then vanished into the spruce forest at the head of the valley. About four miles beyond, the stream broke out into a large glade called Elk Meadows where small but tasty trout could be caught from deep pools. That's where I wanted to camp for the night.

Distant skylines disappeared behind the nearby ridges as I descended. With each downward step my surroundings grew more intimate, until but a short distance below the lake the day-lighted subalpine forest merged into the twilight of dense spruces and firs. There well-worn game trails led in several directions. Sometime that morning a band of elk had nipped buds from the snowbrush and grazed several small meadows.

Their marble-shaped dung had not yet dried in the sun, and the smell of their urine still hung in the air. A big bull had polished his horns on a pine sapling, peeling the bark to a height of six feet and scattering branches on ground trampled by saucer-sized hoofs.

The peeled sapling, the grazed meadows, the tracks on the trail—all made it plain that I had found a summertime paradise for elk, and more. One elk trail led down into the shadows past the base of a talus slope to an excavation that looked like a prospector with dull tools had been mining for gold. Granite rocks the size of washtubs lay moss side down. Fresh dirt covered the sedges and huckleberry bushes, and tree roots had been chomped into chunks and then flung into the forest out of the digger's way. Judging from the tracks (as big as steak platters) in the dirt, the diggings looked about two weeks old. That hole in the talus had been dug by one of the greatest of all marmot hunters, a powerful grizzly bear.

I pressed on. The game trail passed among dark spruce trunks where shoulder-high snowbrush blocked the way. I parted the brush with my hands to get through, and it sprang back to close the way behind as I moved ahead. I was alone, yet the air smelled of life. Because I couldn't see very far, the unknown lurked everywhere; it hammered at my senses until I felt my heart pounding hard against my ribs.

I crossed several noisy little brooks flowing down from their origins in springs and lakes near the crest of the mountains. Once I unslung my load, stretched out on my belly, and gulped the cold water. Spray splashed up in my hair, and the earthy smell of ferns, moss, and rotted logs hovered beside the stream in the darkening woods. The brooks rambled on, each an artery to be joined by another and another, until at length the song of a larger current announced that I had found the Brushy Fork of the Lochsa River. No precise point in the forest marked its beginning. Rather, small streams of clear water joined, coalescing the lifeblood of the land into its main artery, the Brushy Fork—an able host to trout, mink, and otters. Long, pointed tracks showed that moose also lived in those bottomlands. Their coming and going had stirred wet places into muddy bogs, which I skirted by stepping on hummocks firm enough to carry my weight.

A long-used trapline followed the game trail. Old blazes led from set to set, and each tree on the line was blazed twice, once about six feet above the ground and again ten to twelve feet up the bole, above the deep snows of the Lochsa winters. Three closely spaced hacks on

Old notches record snow depth where a fur trapper raised his marten and ermine sets following wintertime storms.

a tree indicated a set nearby; from notches and pegs in the trees I could tell that the trapper had been after marten and ermines.

Hiking in the spell of the old trapline chased the loneliness from the pit of my stomach, for I had already caught the fever of fur trapping from Dad back in the Lolo Fork's mountains. Now here was a real wilderness trapline. Because the growth of the trees had nearly covered the blazes, I could tell that the trapline was old. But it had also been used recently. Number one sized traps hung from the sets on the trees, sprung the past spring by the trapper, then left in place to be reset when the fur primed again in the fall.

Twilight darkened the mountains. I hurried through woods broken here and there by avalanche paths that extended from the crest of the Bitterroots down the mountainsides and across the Brushy Fork. Piles of broken tree trunks demonstrated the power of sliding snow. I discovered a "bear tree" at the edge of one path. Claw and teeth marks scarred its trunk. Scales from the tree's bark littered the forest floor, and one pile of bear dung—a mixture of huckleberry blue wired together with hoary marmot hair—lay where it fell as recently as the day before.

I hiked in silence softened by the murmur of the stream. Each twist in the game trail disclosed sudden new vistas; miniworlds they were, each different from the last, expanding ahead then closing behind a huge boulder or towering spruce as I ambled on through the evening hush. This was the time of day for mountain animals to be on the move, when one expects to meet an elk or moose or great bear. Anticipation tuned my protective instincts like a mule deer alert to the stalk of a lion. My Winchester felt so companionable that I almost spoke to her. Old guns are like that, especially on mountain trails when night begins to overlap the day.

Then muddy water in a bog hole drew my attention, and I watched the gray mud settle from the water into the four-inch-deep print left by a giant's paw. It seemed to me that the bushes on the trail must have barely closed behind him. The long, flat claws of the digger left unmistakable marks in the mud. I was no longer alone! Somewhere between me and the meadow prowled a big grizzly bear. The pulse of life still throbbing in the wake of the great bear's passing overwhelmed my emotions and my senses. As I walked along the trail, I hardly noticed that it led past an old cabin standing on the bank of the Brushy Fork; or that one corner of the roof had rotted and broken; or that the trapper of old had chosen a homesite in one of the most beautiful places on earth.

From the cabin, the trail left the streamside and led me over a low ridge into a rocky draw where I could no longer hear the sounds of

Silvertip grizzlies were common in the upper tributaries of the Lochsa during the 1920s and early 1930s. —Chuck Bartlebaugh

water flowing in the Brushy Fork. Twilight deepened. Then something moved in the shadows ahead. He came toward me, not more than thirty feet away. His head swung back and forth near the ground; I saw the short nose, the broad flat face with rounded ears set nearly a foot apart, the big hump on his shoulders, the black hair luminous in the twilight and peppered with gray on his head, neck, and hump. Grizzly.

There was no chance to move out of his way. I raised the Winchester halfway to my shoulder, cocking the hammer in the same swift motion. The metallic click shattered the silence and broke the spell of wildness gripping me and the bear and the valley of the Brushy Fork.

The bear's head stopped swinging. His body rose slowly, huge fore-paws armed with long claws held out like a boxer's fists. At half stance his hump topped the trailside boulders and kept on rising, nose searching, the patchlike hollow of his eyes peering at my form ahead on the trail.

For a long moment we faced each other, a scared kid with a cocked Winchester and a grizzly bear with senses sharpened by centuries of evolution in the Bitterroot mountains. Suddenly the bear dropped from its upright stance to all fours and vanished. I could hardly believe that a bear of such size could disappear without a sound.

I was alone again, alone with shattered nerves and trembling knees. Glad to have postponed a showdown, I walked on from near darkness in the forest into the welcome half-light of the open meadow. The forest belonged to the bear, but the meadow was mine; so I camped at its edge beneath thick-limbed spruces that would shield my blanket from frost falling in the night.

Except that my boot prints mingled with grizzly tracks on the trail, my introduction to the Lochsa country in 1930 was insignificant to the land and its life. Yet the moment at the meadow was great for me and the bear in the forest. It had something to do with the past and much to do with the future. Had I possessed the insight to phrase the questions, I surely would have asked what had happened in the past to create such rich land and life. And, perhaps more important, I would have wondered what might become of that land—with its grizzlies, great forests, and abundant other natural life—and its power to influence the future of us people as well.

2

The Nez Perce Indians' Ethic

There was a great stirring of life in the mountains when light from the east announced the dawn of a new day on the Brushy Fork. Wakened when a pileated woodpecker hammered two-inch-long chips from a resonant snag, I threw off my blanket and heard a white-tailed doe blow its alarm at my sudden move. Two gray jays landed on a log near camp. A squirrel chattered. It was morning, a remarkable time for me at my first campsite alone beside the headwaters of the Lochsa River.

Mornings like that must have been similarly inspirational for those early dwellers, the Nez Perce Indians, who sought adventure, food, and fulfillment in these mountains. They camped in the glades beside the streams for centuries, and at the first hint of dawn each band's crier would announce the birth of another virgin day: "I wonder if everyone is up. It is morning. We are alive so thanks be! Go see the horses lest the wolf have killed one! Thanks be that the children are alive!"[2]

The Lochsa, the whole Clearwater, the waters of the Salmon below the mountains, the beautiful Wallowa—all land between the Blue Mountains and the crest of the Bitterroot mountains was once Nez Perce country (see map 3). Their ways of life and livelihood depended on its beauty and its productivity. Yet, they did not own the land in the sense recognized by Europeans; in their view the land owned them. Dwelling as they did in nature's places, no middle men stood between their tepees and the bounty and the harshness of the land. They were children of the mountains, the rivers, and the prairies, and they held allegiance to their mother, the wild, natural earth.[3]

By the early 1800s the Nez Perce numbered nearly 6,000 souls. They measured their wealth primarily in numbers of horses, spiritual fulfillment

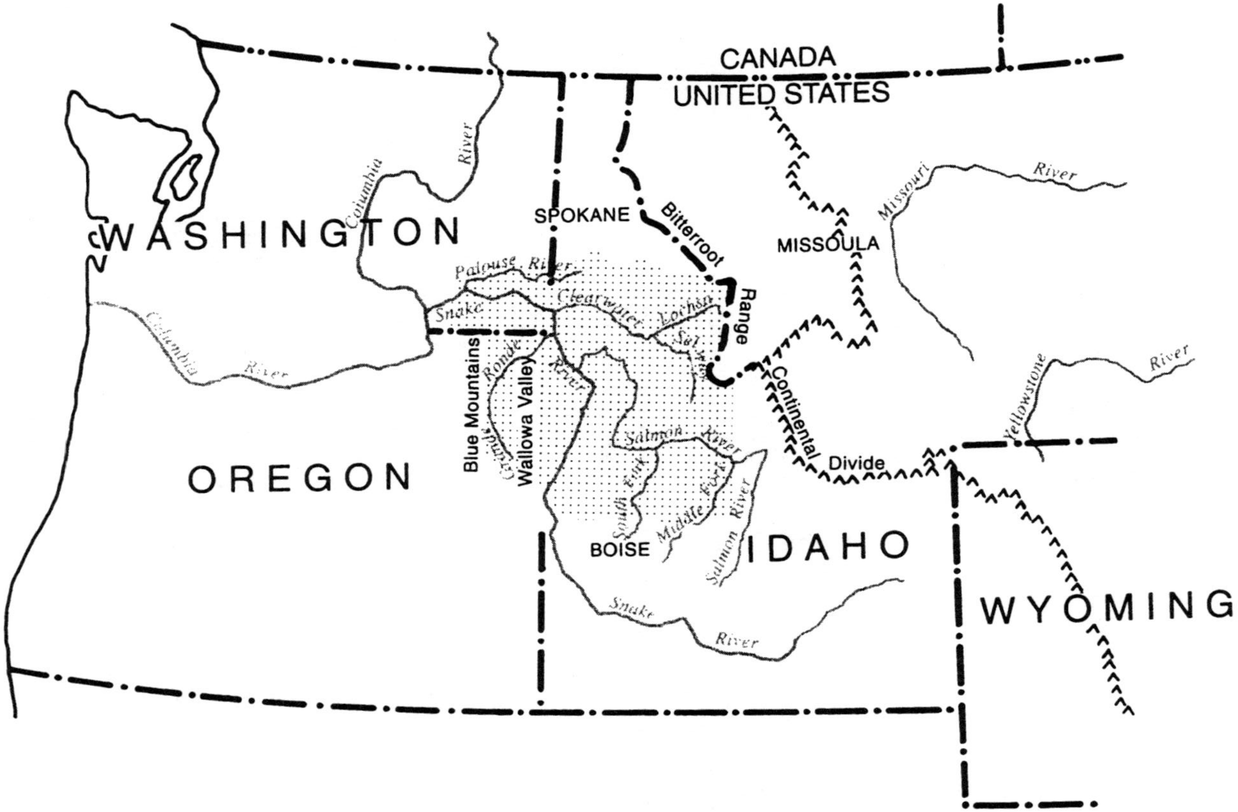

Map 3. *Traditional Nez Perce territory*

in their faith, and the natural bounty available from the land. The men stood tall, upright, and lean; the women, fair in form and feature. Prominent among the greatest of all Indian nations, they called themselves the Ni-me-poo, or "the real people."[4]

Because there is no written record of their history, nobody knows when the Ni-me-poo first found the land of the Lochsa and the Clearwater country. One theory suggests that they originated from a group of people who came south from Alaska over 10,000 years ago.[5] Legends of uncertain origin, passed on through generations, tell of their people dwelling year-round in mountain places long before the acquisition of horses provided the mobility necessary to expand their activities out onto the plains and along the rivers. Two of those early dwelling places are located close to the Lochsa country and are described by the Nez Perce War singer Camille Williams: "There are a few remote mountain places where the long-ago Nez Perce lived the year around. Kakayohneme Creek, at the head of the Clearwater River, the region known by whites as Three Forks, is one of them. It is in Idaho, west of Hamilton, Montana. Another place is known as Nekeulaketh, up the south fork of the Three Forks, known as the Pettibone Ranch. Those long-ago Nez Perce used to come to Kamiah or Clearwater every year to trade for camas and kouse roots."[6] (See map 4.)

Those ancient Ni-me-poo at times must have also journeyed to the land of the Lochsa, at first carrying big loads on their backs and later followed by provision-laden dogs as they hiked along trails worn only by wild game and Indian moccasins. History suggests that sometime during the early 1700s the Nez Perce acquired horses from the Shoshone Indians,[7] and not long after that the hooves of many ponies established three roads across the Bitterroots from the prairies in the west to the buffalo country in the east (see map 4).

Beginning at the edge of the Camas Prairie, the southern road (We-sa-iss-kit, or Camping Trail) crossed the upper reaches of the Clearwater's South Fork, then progressed eastward close to the divide between the waters of the Salmon River and the Selway Fork of the Clearwater, cresting the Bitterroot mountains at Nez Perce Pass. The northern route, their main Road to the Buffalo (Ku-sey-ne-iss-kit),[8] followed the hundred-mile-long divide separating the Lochsa and North Fork of the Clearwater drainages. It crossed the Bitterroots near Lolo Pass. Beginning near the junction of the Lochsa and Selway forks of the Clearwater, the center road, also a camping

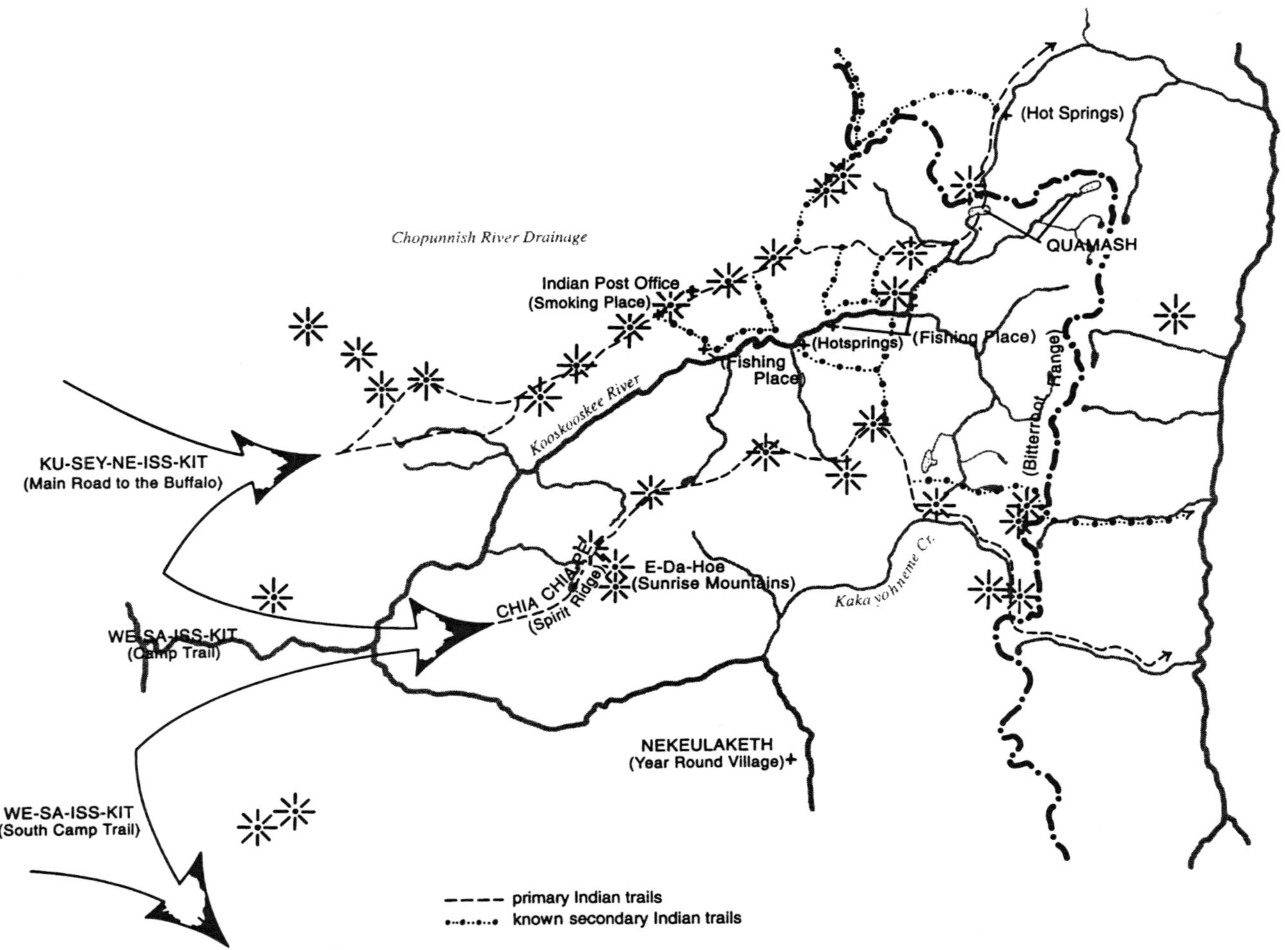

Map 4. *The Lochsa and environs before Lewis and Clark.*

trail, traced a course eastward along or near the divide separating those two rivers.

Travelers following the southern road passed through the mountains forty miles south of the Lochsa region. But those using the northern Road to the Buffalo either passed through or sought destinations in the heartland of the Lochsa. Several side roads led the Ni-me-poo, and to a lesser extent their eastern neighbors, the Flatheads, to hunting, fishing, and spiritual grounds along the way, thereby providing a variety of choices for Indians who traveled the northern route. Depending on their mood or mission, they could journey to and from the buffalo country, go north for high-alpine hunting, or take one of several routes to fish, hunt, bathe at hot springs, or enjoy the spirituality of the Lochsa deep in the canyon below.

The short summers of the Lochsa's high lands left scant time to play and at the same time prepare for winter. Meat had to be cured, roots and berries dried, lodges repaired, and broken weapons replaced with sharp points chipped from flint. Although their earth mother was generous, she demanded full efforts from each that all might live. So, by necessity, their work, play, and worship blended fully with the natural earth. "Everything about them, the inanimate objects as well as the creatures that lived, was bound like themselves to the earth and possessed a spiritual being that was joined through a great unseen world of powers to the spirit within an individual Indian."[9]

Thus, the Road to the Buffalo served many functions, but of the three routes across the mountains, the Ni-me-poo probably found the center road offered the most exciting journey of all. This was the Ni-me-poo's mountain hunting road—or perhaps more aptly termed their living road, for during the heat of summer the men, women, children, dogs, and all would ascend it to escape from the heat of the valley and to drink cold water from the springs along the Chia Chia-Pe (Spirit Ridge).[10]

The air was cool up there. Wherever fires had opened the forests, fields of huckleberries ripened to juicy blue in early summer. The Ni-me-poo found abundant game, and their horses grew fat nipping the blue-stemmed grass growing in the alpine meadows along the divide between the Lochsa and Selway forks of the Clearwater. Gentle highland terrain stretched eastward to lure the Ni-me-poo through this summertime land of natural and spiritual plenty. Each summer for centuries they would move their camps progressively from glade to glade

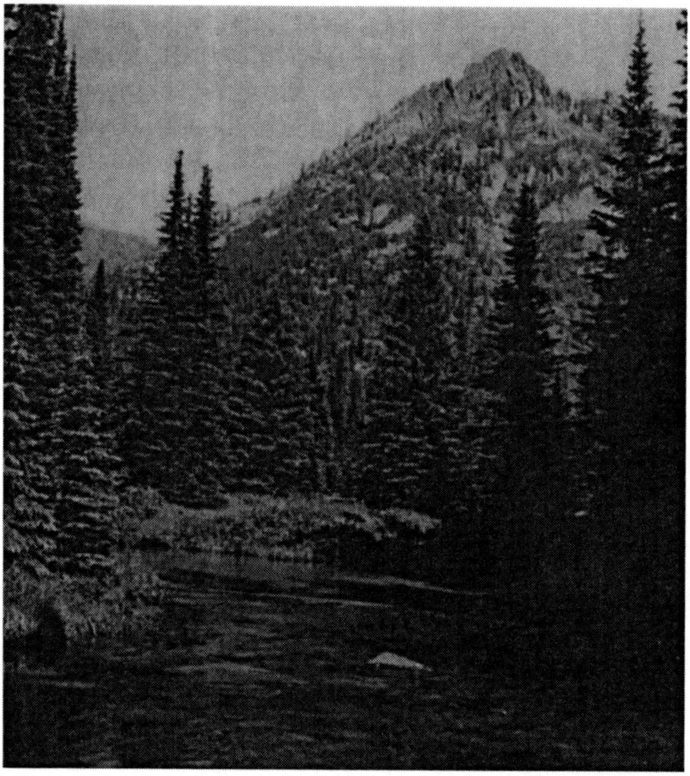

Old Man Creek flows through good camping country near the base of the Crags mountains.

along the hunting road until the bulk of the Crags mountains blocked their way (see map 2).

The treeless peaks of that jumbled rubble rise 7,800 feet above the level of the sea. Steep granite walls reach down from the crests in all directions, and they touch the cirques, the lakes, and the ridges extending into the Lochsa to the north and the Selway to the south. Thrust up in ancient times from the bowels of the earth, the Crags stand there, a thirty-mile-square island of pale granite in a sea of forests, sinister barriers to travelers on an otherwise hospitable divide stretching eastward toward the distant Bitterroot crest.

Since the Crags were too rough to cross with loaded horses, the Ni-me-poo located their hunting road in a deep valley to the north, camping where a clear stream wound through meadows overshadowed by peaks that seemed to reach from earth to sky. They called this sparkling tributary of the Lochsa "Old Man Creek" because, according to legend, the old men and women and children tarried there while the more vigorous braves pushed on to explore and hunt in the lands of the Lochsa and

Selway.[11] Old Man Creek flowed gently through big glades lush with grass, ferns, and hellebore plants that by mid-July reached to the withers of the Indians' ponies. The creek's riffles connected deep pools where hungry trout grabbed any unfortunate bug that lit on the surface of the clear water. How the young must have thrilled to the mystique of those mountains! And the cascades rumbling down from the Crags surely stirred the old to reminisce of vision quests and days when they too climbed the walls in search of adventure beyond the valley's rim.

New days burst quickly over the mountains in summertime. And lest they miss the splendor of the morning, the Ni-me-poo likely built their breakfast fires while the Crags loomed indistinct against a moonlit sky. Stars still winked as the first wisps curled up from the sooty smoke holes of the tepees and shadows from the flickering flames wrinkled the tepee's walls. Then a pika would squeak from the rubbled slope beside the camp. Then another. Like the Ni-me-poo, they too sensed that a new day with new life drew near.

When the light turned pink, the Crags stood clear against the heavens. Such skylines were important to new days because they made the mountain walls feel close and cast a sense of eternity throughout the basin. First light touched the crest of the peaks, and as the sun rose the Indians could watch its descending rays glow on the cliffs and in the basins. The sun-bathed summits foretold a good day for the people camped in the shade of the valley. And they believed. They had seen the new awakening. The mountain crest had shown the beauty and the life. The great Crags had spoken, and they were the Ni-me-poo's "E-da-hoe," that is, their Sunrise Mountains.[12]

Whenever I go to Old Man Creek, it is easy to imagine that the young braves left camp armed with advice from the old ones who had long before confronted great bears along the trails leading deep into the mountains to the east. Dust would surely fly and rocks rattle as they urged their ponies up the head wall. It would be summertime in the valley, but, during August, they would find springtime 2,000 vertical feet above the tepees. While ferns grew three feet tall below, glacier lilies barely poked their buds through snowbanks melting on the rim.

Looking eastward from there, the mountains and valleys form waves in a great ocean of geologic creation. Ridges vanish into shadows, peaks lean on peaks, and the sky descends on such a jumble of knolls and canyons that all landscapes lose continuity in all others and one cannot tell where any individual part of that mountain universe begins or ends.

The hunting road and its byways led the Nez Perce people to and through the most commanding uplands of the Lochsa.

It flows in disorganized unity to vanish at the Bitterroot crest whose light-colored granite peaks shape a distant skyline to be replaced beyond by another, and another, beyond.

Did the mountains move? Or was that an illusion cast by the sun rising in haze above the skyline? A pony would shake his rawhide hackamore and paw the dusty trail, while his rider peered eastward with eyes narrowed to shield out the sun. The rider would surely glance back at the valley camp now bustling with activity around the smoky tepees on the banks of Old Man Creek far below. Blue campfire smoke would drift up toward the hunters, and the voices of the women, the children, and the old would echo in the canyon.

A thump of a moccasined foot against a pony's ribs, and the band would move east. Somewhere out amongst those mountains the hunting road led to the upper lands of the Lochsa. There was game out there. But more important, there was space out there. Wild, natural space needed by the young Ni-me-poo to grow from boys into men.

To the extent the broken topography permitted, the hunting road followed the divide between the waters of the Lochsa and Selway Rivers to where the grassy meadows sprawled across the deep saddle at Elk Summit. From that summertime example of Indian heaven, the main

The Nez Perces left these Crags mountains behind as they traveled east on their hunting road toward the crest of the Bitterroots.

road descended to the east fork of Kakayohneme Creek (Moose Creek), then up that stream to gain the Bitterroot crest at Lost Horse Pass. Little-used yet significant side roads led from Elk Summit into the hidden valleys of the Lochsa. One road connected the highlands of the Grave Mountains[13] to the fisheries along the upper Lochsa River.

With much of their summertime life spent along roads leading through such beautiful creation, it is not surprising that the Ni-me-poo revered the perfection of nature. In earlier times, they sent their young to contemplate alone in the solitude of the mountains. In that way, all youths, both boys and girls, sought their "Wyakin," which would in time speak to them through symbols of nature. Not all youths were able to develop a "Wyakin," but those who did believed that the voice of the wind made their bodies invulnerable to bullets and arrows. Thunder and lightning furnished prowess in battle. The appearance of a coyote gave them cunning in approaching their enemies. And apparitions of other animals, birds, and natural phenomena delivered special powers.[14]

Their God Hunyahwat, creator of earth, was above all; but his spirit was everywhere on earth—in the mountains, the rocks, the animals, the fish, the birds, the streams, and the people. When he made the earth Hunyahwat had provided for every need of the Indian, so there was no thought that humankind could improve on the works of nature.

Like the Nez Perces of old, a modern-day hiker is preoccupied with the spirit of Horse Heaven Meadows at Elk Summit.

Hunyahwat was their God, the earth, their sacred mother, to be respected and, above all, not degraded in any way by the acts of the Ni-me-poo.

Hunyahwat had two countries, the earth for this life and the Ahkinkenekia, or happy hereafter. If one of the Ni-me-poo had been more good than bad during his life on earth, at death his soul would be flown on the back of a small bird directly to the happy hereafter. The souls of bad Indians could also gain entrance to the Ahkinkenekia, but their journey would be difficult. No bird would carry their spirits. They would be lost in huge deserts with little water. Many snows would come to pass before they reached their destination, and along the way they would have to cleanse themselves again and again. But because even bad Indians could, with persistence, eventually join their friends who had been good, no Indian feared death.[15]

The Ni-me-poo's Ahkinkenekia was loaded with natural splendor. The finest streams rumbled from the mountains through thick forests and spewed their clear waters on green meadows and lush prairies. Cold springs bubbled up from alpine basins and deep valleys. Ahkinkenekia was a place where the mountains drew close at night for reassurance but receded in daytime to create extensive vistas sparkling to the eye, their snowy crests displayed sometimes both high in the sky and upside down in the lakes beside their camps. The Ni-me-poo would share the natural paradise of their happy hereafter with fish and birds and animals of the same species that they had known and loved on earth. The Ni-me-poo at death would, upon reaching the happy hereafter, join with other living creatures in perfection of the same nature they revered throughout their life on earth.

That others might not agree with this vision was foretold by an Indian prophet named Swopscha, who predicted the coming of white men to the land of the Clearwater and adjacent Ni-me-poo country. They would be kind and friendly at first, Swopscha said, then things would change for the worse. "Dispossessed of their lands the tribes would become broken and scattered. There would be wasting sicknesses and diseases would be brought by the invaders with which the medicine men could not cope, sweeping away not only villages but entire tribes."

Passed from one generation to another in dream songs, Swopscha's prophecies warned that the Indians' names would be picture painted

Bud's second wife, Janet Moore, is captured by the wildness of this reflection somewhere in the Selway-Bitterroot Wilderness.

(recorded), that the chiefs would be troubled and disagree with each other; that all creation would be overthrown, the buffalos gone, elk and deer fenced in, eagles caged, Indians confined, happiness broken, their earth mother ripped open where the life lies hidden. Beautiful, naturally rough places would be smoothed and straightened. Flowers would no longer bloom. Forests would vanish, game would disappear, rivers would be held back, and the salmon would become too scarce to feed the tribes.[16]

A proud, spiritual people, the Nez Perce revered their homeland, the land that had provided a stable and rich past, a wholesome interaction between few people and abundant earth. But Swopscha predicted that inconsiderate, even destructive, hordes would come. Troubled times, he said, loomed ahead for the land of the Lochsa, the whole Clearwater country, and its sons and daughters, the Ni-me-poo.

This 1995 view from US 12 along the Clearwater River is typical of the present-day Nez Perce Reservation.

3

A Tough Trip for Lewis and Clark

N***obody knows, nor will anyone ever know,*** when the first pilgrim crossed the mountains via the valley of the Lolo Fork and the Lochsa country. Whoever he was, his tracks began to wear a trail that, in time, became the Road to the Buffalo for the Ni-me-poo (Nez Perce) and the route to the salmon for the Flathead Indians who lived in the

Located near present-day Lolo, Montana, a stone-faced woman overlooks the Travellers Rest valley where the Lewis and Clark expedition camped in 1805 and 1806.

Bitterroot Valley. A stone-faced woman stands on the foothills near where the trail enters the plains of the Bitterroot, facing west toward the mountains. Her bust is twenty feet tall; her perfume is sage warmed by the summer sun; her voice the whisper of winds in pines growing close at her side. She rose some 12,000 years ago from the subsiding waters of ancient Lake Missoula to become a visible Native American whose association with the United States began in 1792, when American sea captain Robert Gray claimed the land drained by the waters of the Columbia.[17]

Surely by the nineteenth century the Indians had passed the stone-faced woman for hundreds of years when, on Monday, September 9, 1805, the first Euro-American explorers straggled down the Bitterroot Valley. Could her stony eyes have seen, she would have watched through the needles of the pines while they unpacked their horses, pitched tents, and kindled their cooking fires.

Lewis and Clark's party camped near the banks of the Lolo Fork. The valley was wide and beautiful, game was plentiful, and the Indians were friendly. Here's how Captain Lewis described that day: ". . . we continued our rout down the W. side of the river about 5 miles further and encamped on a large creek which falls in on the West. as our guide inform me that we should leave the river at this place and the weather appearing settled and fair I determined to halt the next day rest our horses and take som scelestial Observations. We called this Creek Travellers rest."[18] (See map 2.)

A routine entry to be sure. But that was no ordinary expedition preparing to journey over the hill through the Lochsa and Clearwater country and on to the Pacific Ocean.

Until May 1792, all United States territory lay east of the Mississippi River. But after Captain Gray claimed the Columbia River drainage for the United States, the nation also became interested in the lands that lay in between. The vast region known as Louisiana territory had been claimed by France until 1762, when it ceded its holdings west of the Mississippi to Spain. It was a long way for the United States's ships to sail from East Coast harbors around the horn of South America to the Columbia River country. The country needed an overland route across the continent, and Thomas Jefferson took a personal interest in organizing an expedition.

In 1800 Spain secretly decided to return Louisiana to France, then ruled by the bellicose Napoleon, but the transaction would not take effect until 1803. Jefferson's expedition, formed under his private secretary

Meriwether Lewis and with Napoleon's approval, would explore the upper reaches of the Missouri for a route to the Pacific Ocean. Lewis chose William Clark as his partner and cocaptain. However, before the expedition began, Robert R. Livingston, American minister to France, and James Monroe, United States minister extraordinary and plenipotentiary, achieved the astounding purchase of all Louisiana territory. With a stroke of Napoleon's pen, the United States nearly doubled its territory. Though title to much of the lands remained in dispute, the United States claimed land all the way across the North American continent.[19] As a result, President Jefferson broadened the mission of Lewis and Clark: they were to find a route to the Pacific *and* strengthen the claim of the United States to the Columbia country and to the Louisiana territory as well.

Prior to their departure President Jefferson instructed Captain Lewis: "The object of your mission is to explore the Missouri river, and such principal stream of it, as, by its course and communication with the waters of the Pacific Ocean, may offer the most direct & practical water communication across this continent, for the purpose of commerce."[20] Beyond that, all Indian tribes encountered had to be notified that the Great Father now lived in Washington, not across the ocean in France. Thus instructed, on Monday, May 14, 1804, Captain Clark set out from St. Louis up the Missouri with an advance party, while Captain Lewis tended unfinished business and then followed.

Now, one year and four months later, they camped at Travellers Rest at the foot of the mountains and were about to become the first white men known to journey across the Bitterroots on the Indian road. Captain Lewis chose the Lolo Fork route after learning from the Shoshone Indians that the Salmon River was too rough for travel either by boat or horses. While trading for horses in the Salmon River valley, Shoshone Chief Cameahwait informed Lewis of the route used by the Nez Perce Indians. The Nez Perce had told Cameahwait that the road was bad, there was no game, and the mountains were broken, rocky, and so thickly covered with timber that people could scarcely pass. Nonetheless, Lewis was convinced that if the Indians could travel across mountains then his party could make it, too.

During his party's day of rest and preparation, Captain Lewis dispatched all hunters in different directions to kill game for the trip. John Colter hunted up Travellers Rest Creek, where he met three well-mounted Indians who at once prepared for battle with their bows and arrows.

But Colter laid his gun on the ground and walked toward them. That calmed their fears. They accompanied Colter back to Travellers Rest, where they explained that they were pursuing two Snake Indians who had stolen twenty-three horses from their camps on the Kooskooskee (Clearwater) River across the mountains. Two of these Indians continued pursuit of the thieves. But one remained to help guide Lewis's party to his numerous relations who, he said, lived on the plains below the mountains and along the Columbia River. He said that it would require five sleeps, or six days travel, to reach his relations. Lewis and Clark mistakenly thought that these Indians were Flatheads.[21]

The explorers broke camp on the morning of September 11, 1805. Captain Clark describes their departure from Travellers Rest and their first day's journey:

> The loss of 2 of our horses detained us unl. 3 o Clock P.M. our Flat head Indian being restless thought proper to leave us and proceed on alone. Sent out hunters to hunt in advance as usial. we proceeded on up the Creek on the right Side thro a narrow valie and good road for 7 miles and Encamped at Some old Indian Lodges, nothing killed this evening hills on the right high & ruged, the mountains on the left high & Covered with Snow. The day Verry worm[22]

Although their first day on the Lolo Fork went well, it is ironic that the explorers who searched for a practical route to carry on commerce had chosen one of the most difficult of all roads through the mountains to the waters of the Columbia and the Pacific Ocean. According to Clark, they passed the "most intolerable road on the Sides of the Steep Stoney mountains, . . . Several Springs which I observed the Deer Elk & c. had made roads to, and below one of the Indians had made a Whole to bathe, . . . I found this water nearly boiling hot at the places it Spouted from the rocks."[23]

The road led them from the hot springs to the Bitterroot crest about one mile east of Lolo Pass, where they skirted a large meadow tinted with frost-nipped pygmy willows, Labrador tea, and quamash plants. A small stream flowed through the meadow, its serpentine course so near the crest of the mountains that its waters barely flowed into the Lochsa drainage instead of the Lolo Fork. The meadow and stream must have looked to their horses and lone mule like a good place to drop those heavy packs. But the impatient explorers followed the road through forests broken by small meadows for two more miles before they camped near the banks of the creek.

Packer Meadows in 1805 would have looked to Lewis and Clark much like this view in late summer 1994.

They called the stream Glade Creek, and it thus became the first geographical feature in the Lochsa to be named by an ambassador of the United States. And while the packers unhitched the loads from the saddles, scouts reported that high snow-covered mountains stood in full view twenty miles to the west.

The Lochsa welcomed Lewis and Clark's party with cold rain and wet snow. Next morning wisps of fog hung on the mountainsides as the men and loaded animals climbed through soaked snowbrush over a ridge and then descended to the place where Glade Creek joined the stream now known as the Crooked Fork of the Lochsa. From there they pushed on through a jungle of fallen timber, climbed a high ridge south of the Crooked Fork (they called it a continuation of Glade Creek), and then descended to where Glade Creek joined "a large fork from the left which appears to head in the Snowytoped mountains Southerly and S. E."[24] They crossed Glade Creek (Crooked Fork) above its mouth where the Indians had built two weirs to catch salmon. Since they saw no fish in the stream and all the grass had been eaten by the Indians' horses, they proceeded one and one-half miles downstream and camped near where a small island parted the waters of the eighty-yard-wide Kooskooskee River. By the time I first looked west from the headwaters of the South

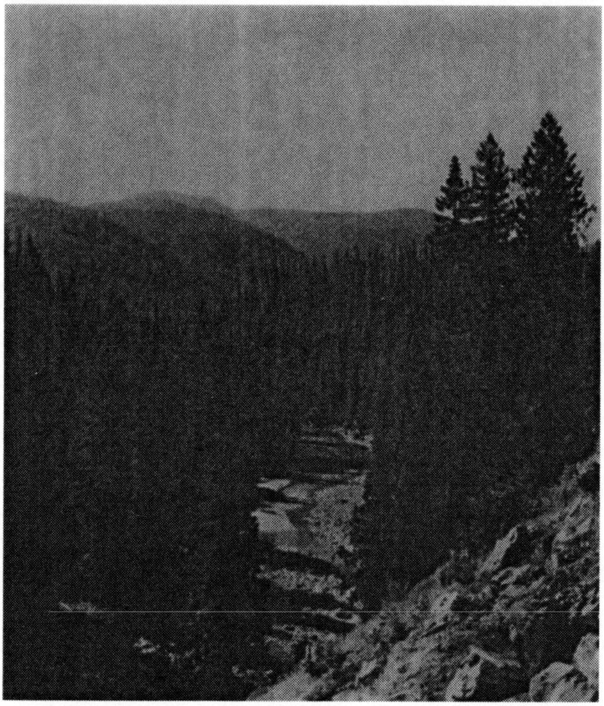

The Lewis and Clark party on September 14, 1805, crossed Glade Creek (present-day Crooked Fork) at an Indian fishing site near the left center of this photo.
—Leland Prater,
U.S. Forest Service

Branch of the Lolo Fork, that stream had been renamed the Lochsa. And the entire drainage of the great river to the west (the Kooskooskee) was known as the Clearwater, and the Lochsa considered one of its several branches.

That flat along the Lochsa was a good place to camp, but food was scarce. Accustomed as they were to hunting on the prairies, their hunters shot little game in that mountainous region. The men were tired and hungry. Here's how Sgt. Patrick Gass described their situation on September 14, 1805: "None of the hunters killed any thing except 2 or 3 pheasants; on which without a miracle it was impossible to feed 30 hungry men and upwards, besides some Indians. So Capt. Lewis gave out some portable soup, which he had along, to be used in case of necessity. Some of the men did not relish this soup, and agreed to kill a colt, which they immediately did, and set about roasting it, and which appeared to me to be good eating".[25]

This journal entry suggests that Sergeant Gass was not yet hungry enough to eat horse meat but that many of his companions were. This could have been the first colt killed for food on the journey, thus explaining why they named the Lochsa's south branch "Colt Killed Creek," a stream now called "White Sand Creek." (See map 2.)

This 1965 aerial view of the Powell Ranger Station shows the island in the river near Lewis and Clark's camp of September 14, 1805. —W. E. Steuerwald, U.S. Forest Service

Early next morning they followed a road downstream along the river's north bank through forests of pine, fir, and spruce and over steep points of rock. After four miles of slow travel they passed an Indian fishing place where a small stream entered the Lochsa from the north. The fishery was located near the center of a forested flat extending for at least a mile along the north bank of the river. The forest was broken only by a small, grassy glade at the fishing site and by a shallow pond, about five acres in size, situated against the foothills a short distance to the north. A canyon one-half mile below the fishery made safe horse travel doubtful; there, the road turned northward.

Captain Clark describes their climb up what is now called Wendover Ridge:

> . . . here the road leaves the river to the left and assends a mountain winding in every direction to get up the Steep assents & to pass the emence quantity of falling timber which had falling from dift. causes i e. fire and wind and has deprived the Greater part of the Southerley Sides of this mountain of its gren timber, 4 miles up the mountain I found a Spring and halted for the rear to come up and to let our horses rest and feed, about 2 hours the rear of the party came up much fatigued & horses more so, Several horses Sliped and roled down Steep hills which hurt them verry much The one which carried

my desk and Small trunk turned over & rolled down a mountain for 40 yards & lodged against a tree, broke the Desk the horse escaped and appeared but little hurt Some others verry much hurt.[26]

They pushed on from the spring to camp that night near a snow bank on the divide between the Lochsa and North Fork of the Clearwater (called "Chopunnish" by the Nez Perce) River. The hunters had killed two pheasants which, along with remnants of their colt, provided modest fare. Captain Clark recorded their situation: ". . . evening verry cold and cloudy. Two of our horses gave out, pore and too much hurt to proceed on and left in the rear— . . . From this mountain I could observe high ruged mountains in every direction as far as I could see."[27]

Three hours before daylight the next morning, September 16, 1805, snow began to fall. By morning it blanketed the mountains four inches deep. It continued to fall all day long, covering the road and loading the branches of the firs, pines, and hemlocks until the lightest touch dumped avalanches of snow onto the buckskin clothing of the explorers. That they traveled in misery is witnessed by Captain Clark's journal: "I have been wet and as cold in every part as I ever was in my life, indeed I was at one time fearfull my feet would freeze in the thin Mockirsons which I wore, after a Short Delay in the middle of the Day, I took one man and proceeded on as fast as I could about 6 miles to a Small branch passing to the right, halted and built fires for the party agains their arrival which was at Dusk, verry cold and much fatigued. . . . Killed a Second Colt which we all Suped hartily on and thought it fine meat."[28] Finding "the most direct and practical water communication across this continent, for the purpose of commerce" must have seemed an unattainable goal to Lewis and Clark and their companions as they huddled for warmth around Clark's campfires and gnawed at their flame-seared colt meat.

Their route followed on or near the divide between the Lochsa and North Fork of the Clearwater Rivers, a giant among the several ranges extending westward from the crest of the Bitterroot mountains (see map 2). Sergeant Gass likely sums up the feeling of most of the party in his journal entry of September 18, 1805: ". . . except on the sides of hills where it has fallen, the country is closely timbered with pitch and spruce pine, and what some call balsam-fir. We can see no prospect of getting off these desert mountains yet, except the appearance of a deep cove on each side of the ridge we are passing along."[29]

And Captain Lewis adds: "this morning we finished the remainder of our last coult. we dined & suped on a skant proportion of portable soupe, a few canesters of which, a little bears oil and about 20 lbs. of candles form our stock of provision, the only resources being our guns and packhorses."[30]

That corps of discovery had fallen on hard times in rough country. So on the morning of September 18, Captain Clark set out ahead with six hunters to "try and find deer or Something to kill & send back to the party." Captain Lewis stayed with the main party, forcing the march as much as the weary horses' condition would permit.

Captain Clark's hunters "Killed nothing in those emence mountains of stones falling timber and brush" on September 18, 1805. But twenty miles from camp, from atop present-day Sherman Peak, Clark "had a view of an emence Plain and leavel Countrey to the S. W. & West at a great distance." Captain Clark and the hunters made thirty-two miles that day and camped on a "bold running creek," draining to the Lochsa River, which Clark called "Hungery Creek." They had nothing to eat.

Captain Clark, his attention centered on killing game to feed the party, gave little space in his journal to the view of the plains from

'his contemporary view of the Clearwater's camas prairies resembles what Lewis and Clark saw from present-day Sherman Peak.
—Henry Eide, U.S. Forest Service

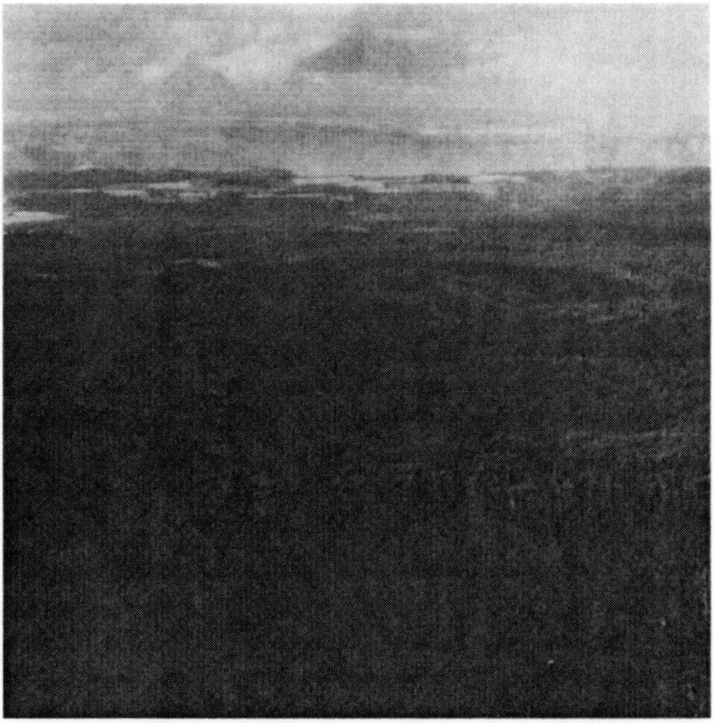

Sherman Peak. But when Captain Lewis saw the same view on September 19, he wrote:

> Set out this morning a little after sun rise and continued our rout about the same course of yesterday or S. 20 W. for 6 miles when the ridge terminated and we to our inexpressable joy discovered a large tract of Prairie country lying to the S. W. and widening as it appeared to extend to the W. through that plain the Indian informed us that the Columbia River, in which we were in surch run. this plain appeared to be about 60 miles distant, but our guide assured us that we should reach its borders tomorrow the appearance of this country, our only hope for subsistance greatly revived the sperits of the party already reduced and much weakened for the want of food.[31]

While their escape from the Lochsa's confining topography seemed assured, some of their roughest travel still loomed ahead. Sergeant Gass gives an example in his journal entry of September 19, 1805:

> We again went on; and descended a steep mountain into a cove on our left hand, where there is a large creek, which here runs towards the east. The hills on each side along which the trail passes . . . are very steep. One of our horses fell down the precipice about 100 feet, and was not killed, nor much hurt: the reason was, there is no bottom below, and the precipice, the only bank which the creek has; there fore the horse pitched into the water, without meeting with any intervening object, which could materially injure him.[32]

On September 19 Captain Clark and the hunters found a lost horse, which they killed, in a small glade in Hungery Creek. They ate part of it and hung up the remainder for the rear party. On September 20 they passed through "Country as ruged as usial" for twelve miles, then descended the mountain and traveled through a "leavel pine Countrey" for three miles to a "Small Plain" where they discovered the lodges of the Nez Perce.

At first encounter the Indians panicked and ran. It is said that, but for an old woman, Wat-ku-ese, who lay dying in her tepee, the frightened people would have tried to kill the explorers. Wat-ku-ese heard the excited chatter and said, "White men, did you say? No, no, do not harm them. They are the crowned ones who were so good to me. Do not be afraid of them. Go near to them."

Captured by a war party years before, Wat-ku-ese, then a young girl, had been taken east over the Road to the Buffalo to a distant land where white men lived. She called them "So-yap-po," the crowned ones, because they wore hats. One day she escaped with her infant and, be-

Hewn from a large pine log, this replica of the canoes built and used by the Lewis and Clark party on their journey westward from the mouth of the North Fork of the Clearwater to the Pacific Ocean is on display at the Nez Perce National Historical Park.

friended by white traders, made her way to the Flathead country where her baby died. From there, a band of Nez Perce eventually brought her home, weak, sick, and dying, back over the Road to the Buffalo in time to help her people greet Lewis and Clark and begin a long friendship with the United States government.[33]

The Lewis and Clark party built canoes near present-day Orofino, Idaho, then paddled seaward to the mouth of the Columbia River where they camped for the winter of 1805–6. Springtime greening of the prairies found the explorers eager to recross the Bitterroot mountains and descend the Missouri with news of their discoveries. But the Lochsa's winter, unlike the prairies, yields slowly to spring. When on May 7, 1806, the homeward-bound party again viewed the mountains, even the spurs of the Bitterroots remained snowbound.

They waited for more than a month for the snow to melt, during which time they explored the surrounding country and bartered with the Nez Perce for supplies. They also drew a map of the continent and described the American nation to the Indians. They told the Nez Perce

Most years it takes until late spring or early summer to melt the wintertime snowfall from the long ridges extending west from the crest of the Bitterroots.

leaders that they wanted to establish peace among all of the warring tribes so that they could establish trading posts where the Indians could acquire the white men's goods. After holding a council, the chiefs recommended to their band "confidence in the information they had received." There was not a dissenting vote among the men, although many of the women feared that they had placed too much trust in the intentions of the explorers.[34]

Thanks to the goodwill of the Indians, Lewis and Clark's party retraced their westward route with each member mounted on a strong horse and leading a lightly loaded second horse. Several extra horses trailed along to be used in case of accident or need for food.

Their eagerness to recross the Bitterroot mountains shows in Captain Lewis's journal of June 14, 1806:

> We had all our articles packed up and made ready for our departure in the morning. our horses were caught and most of them hubbled and otherwise confined in order that we might not be detained. from hence to Traveller's rest we shall make a forsed march; . . . We have now been detained near five weeks in consequence of the snows; a serious loss of time at this delightful

> season for traveling. . . . every body seems anxious to be in motion, convinced that we have not now any time to delay if the calculation is to reach the United States this season; this I am detirmined to accomplish if within the compass of human power.[35]

When on June 15, 1806, they left the base of the mountains to begin their climb, the quamash bloomed in such profusion that from a distance each glade resembled the blue waters of a mountain lake. They departed the foothills in driving rain, and by Monday afternoon, June 16, 1806, their ponies' hooves chopped into the surface of hard-packed snow in places eight to ten feet deep. By the afternoon of June 17 they reached a place on present-day Willow Ridge near the divide between the North Fork and Lochsa Rivers, where twelve to fifteen feet of snow hid the Indian road from their view.

They considered it "madness" to proceed farther into the mountains over such snow without a guide. So they cached most of their luggage, instruments, and food ("roots and bread of cows"), and the dejected party returned to the foothills. Of their situation, Captain Lewis wrote in his journal: "this is the first time since we have been on this long tour that we have ever been compelled to retreat or make a retrograde march. it rained on us most of this evening."[36]There was nothing they could do except wait for the snow to melt enough to expose more grass for their horses to eat.

The time seemed right to set out again on June 24, 1806. Accompanied by three Nez Perce guides, they left the Quamash Glade to retrace their steps of the past September over the Indian Road to the Buffalo across the mountains to Travellers Rest. They journeyed much of the way over hard-packed snow, which provided good footing for the horses. The weather was sunny and warm, possibly because the spirits of the Lochsa responded favorably to the ceremony of fire conducted by the Indians on June 25. Clark described the event as follows:

> last evening the indians entertained us with Setting the fir trees on fire. they have a great number of dry limbs near their bodies which when Set on fire create a very sudden and emmence blaize from bottom to top of those tail trees. they are a boutifull object in this Situation at night. this exhibition remide me of a display of firewoks. the nativs told us that their object in Setting those trees on fire was to bring fair weather for our journey.[37]

No matter the deep snow, their Nez Perce guides followed the Road to the Buffalo along the Lochsa–North Fork divide with unerring ac-

The smoking place and part of the "Stupendous Mountains" viewed by Lewis and Clark, June 27, 1806. —Ralph Space

curacy. Captain Lewis said of their skills: "these fellows are most admireable pilots; we find the road wherever the snow had disappeared though it be only for a few hundred paces."[38] At the first high point west of present-day Indian Grave Peak, they halted for a few minutes at the request of the Nez Perce guides and smoked the pipe. The Indians had raised a conical mound of stone about eight feet high at this site. They explained that, when traveling through the mountains with their families, some of the men were usually sent ahead on foot to the Colt Killed Creek fishery to catch salmon, and then rejoined the main party at the Quamash Glade (present-day Packer Meadows) at the head of the Kooskooskee (Lochsa) River (see map 4).

That the Lochsa's geography impressed those explorers shows in Captain Clark's journal entry written at the Smoking Place on Friday, June 27, 1806: "from this place we had an extencive view of these Stupendeous Mountains principally Covered with Snow like that on which we stood; we were entirely Serounded by those mountains from which to one unacquainted with them it would have Seemed impossible ever to have escaped, in short without the assistance of our guides, I doubt much whether we who had once passed them could find our way to Travellers rest."[39]

On June 28, 1806, the explorers passed their camp of last September 15 but did not descend to the fisheries of the Lochsa. Instead they followed a road along the divide and camped near good horse feed on the ridge east of present-day Papoose Saddle. Next day the road led them over present-day Rocky Point, down across the Crooked Fork and back to the road that they had followed westward via the fisheries. They retraced their westward route past the Hot Springs, arriving at Travellers Rest on June 30, 1806.

Except for eight days of waiting for the snow to melt or harden, fortune smiled on the party while it recrossed the mountains. In seven days they traveled 156 miles from the Quamash Glade to Travellers Rest without losing a man or horse in the land of the Lochsa—truly cause for rejoicing.

So they camped at Travellers Rest for two days, and during that time they hunted, dried meat, put all rifles in prime order, and rested men and horses. They talked at length with their Indian guides, who told them many white buffalo (mountain goats) lived in the high mountains to the south. One of the Nez Perce chiefs exchanged names with Captain Lewis who became "Yo-me-kol-lick," which means "white bear skin foalded."[40] Horse and foot races went on between the Indians and the white men except for Goodrich and McNeal, who suffered from pox

While camped at Travellers Rest, the Nez Perce Indians told Lewis and Clark that many white buffalo (mountain goats) populated the rocky cliffs of the Bitterroot mountains. —Danny On

contracted from the Chinook women while wintering on the Columbia River. It must have been a happy time for those pilgrims who had come so far and seen so much.

Although Lewis and Clark did not find a "most direct and practical water communication across this continent," they did discover something of the theretofore unknown immensity of the Rocky Mountains, including the land now known as the Lochsa country. They traced a road by land and water from the Mississippi River across Louisiana to the Pacific Ocean. During their homeward-bound descent of the Missouri in 1806, they met eleven well-equipped parties already coming up.[41] The trappers were coming. The prospectors were coming. The settlers were coming. The lives of the Nez Perce and other western Indians were going to change, as was the land in which they lived. And even the most remote corner of the mountains would, in time, be found by pilgrims trudging over the hill from the valley where the stone-faced woman faces west.

4

Pioneer Occupation of the Indians' West

After Lewis and Clark crossed the mountains via the Lochsa, subsequent exploration of the new territories of the United States detoured around the rugged Bitterroots; those lands remained in possession of the Indians for another seventy years. Nevertheless, westward migration of pioneers during that time gave rise to events that would decide the future of people and land and life in the Lochsa and Clearwater country, as well as in the rest of the Rocky Mountain West.

By 1807 Manuel Lisa had built the first American fur trading post on the upper Missouri, at the confluence of the Yellowstone and Big Horn Rivers. During late August 1812, American Fur Company trader Donald McKenzie established a short-lived trading post near where the Clearwater River joins the Snake. Three years earlier, David Thompson had erected Saleesh House for the Canadian North-West Company on the Clark Fork River. And by 1810 white trappers and Indians were trading furs caught in the valleys that drained the eastern slope of the Bitterroot mountains. In like manner, fur trappers from Canada's North-West and Hudson's Bay Companies probed toward the Bitterroot mountains from the northwest. Hudson's Bay Company trader Alexander Ross wintered in the upper Bitterroot Valley in 1823–24, but, as far as is known, none of his men climbed over the crest into the Lochsa region.[42]

After the peace treaty ending the War of 1812 was signed, boundary commissioners were appointed to settle areas of dispute. They recommended the forty-ninth parallel as the dividing line between the United States and Canada from Lake of the Woods to the crest of the Rockies, putting the headwaters of the Mississippi and Red Rivers firmly in U.S. hands. But the negotiators could not agree on the ownership of the

It took traders and trappers only 38 years to catch and market most of the fur-bearing beavers from the valleys of the West.

Oregon country. So in 1818 they granted citizens of both the United States and Great Britain equal rights to settle and trade in the Pacific Northwest for ten years. Postponing settlement of this land dispute left the entire Oregon country open to the highly competitive fur men of both nations.[43]

In 1828, the United States and Great Britain extended joint occupancy for another ten years. By 1843, only thirty-eight years after their discovery, trappers had reduced the once-abundant beaver populations of the western mountain valleys to scattered remnants that were no longer profitable to trap. During that time trappers also found the best routes through and around the mountains—mostly well-used Indian trails—which would be followed by many emigrants responding to the U.S. government's invitation to settle the West contained in the Preemptive Act of 1841. That act allowed United States citizens to claim up to 160 acres of nonmineral land by living on it and paying $1.50 per acre.

Some displaced trappers hired on as guides for emigrant wagon trains headed west. Others signed on with explorations led by government agencies. In 1843 veteran trapper Jim Bridger built a trading post on a tributary of the Green River. It was the first post established beyond the Mississippi, with the purpose of providing supplies and services to emigrants passing through.[44] A few trappers left the once-profitable beaver streams to seek long-haired furs in the rougher ranges bypassed in the beaver trapping rush. Although not as well known as the beaver men, those who took trapping to the higher mountains, like

Trapper Andrew Erickson, pictured here at Lolo Pass, came to the Lochsa about 1914. He demonstrated the hardiness required to trap furs in the mountainous interior. —Henry J. Viche, U.S. Forest Service

the Lochsa's, pioneered a new and poorly documented frontier in the history of the fur trade.

Soon after the trappers came the missionaries, who sought to enlighten the Indians in the ways of the white man's God. There is no record of any missionaries entering the Lochsa country—possibly because there were so few souls in there to be saved. Furthermore, despite their high ranking among God's great creations, the Lochsa's landscapes were too rough for the missionaries and an inconvenient setting to begin Christianizing those first Americans. The missionaries had in mind an obedient people who would, once they heard the Word, rearrange their lifestyles in the interests of humanity as viewed by the whites. The Indians would first be taught to revere God and to drop any rebellious or warlike tendencies. After that they would learn to plow fields, grow gardens, raise domestic livestock, and generally abandon their culture to adopt the white man's way of life.

Both the Flathead people to the east and the Nez Perce to the west of the Bitterroot mountains wanted missionaries in their midst. They had heard of the white man's God from Christian Indian trappers brought west by the Hudson's Bay and North-West Company traders. As early as 1825, some Indians from Oregon country and Canada were already attending the Church of England Missionary Society School at the Red River settlement near present-day Winnipeg, Manitoba. Two of these (one a Spokan and the other a Kutenai, both in their early teens), named "Spokan Garry" and "Coutonais Pelly," attended the school for four years, where they were taught reading, writing, history, and geography. They also learned how to plant and tend crops and became knowledgeable of the scriptures. On returning home in 1829, Garry, then eighteen, actively spread the word of God and Jesus to various tribes, including the Nez Perce and the Flatheads. He spoke enthusiastically about heaven and hell, the Ten Commandments, the need to observe Sundays, and to pray each morning and before meals. Many Indians intuitively trusted God and sought the counsel of his disciples—so much so that they sent delegates from the Bitterroot Valley to St. Louis in search of a "black robe" to join them.[45] Although the Indians at that time regarded the teachings of Garry and Pelly as supplemental to their own spiritual beliefs, the missionaries and many other pioneers considered them ready for conversion to Christianity. Eventually both Indian nations, for better or worse, inherited the service of missionaries. Presbyterians Henry H. Spalding and Marcus Whitman built missions in Nez Perce and adjacent Walla Walla and Cayuse country; Catholic Father Pierre Jean De Smet established his mission in the Bitterroot Valley among the Flatheads.

In 1836 Reverend Henry Spalding and his wife, Eliza, located their original mission two miles up Lapwai Creek but later moved it to this vicinity where the creek flows into the Clearwater River.

Congregationalist Samuel Parker, the first missionary to reach the homeland of the Nez Perce, went west in 1835 searching for suitable locations to establish one or more missions. He recruited a thirty-three-year-old Presbyterian physician named Marcus Whitman as an assistant. The two traveled west with the American Fur Company supply caravan and joined the rendezvous on the Green River on August 12. There they observed among the Indians great need and acceptance for missionary work. Thus encouraged, Whitman returned to the States to organize an expedition while Parker continued westward looking for desirable mission sites.[46]

While in the East, Whitman married Narcissa Prentiss, herself accepted by the American Board of Commissioners for Foreign Missions, and convinced Reverend Spalding and his wife, Eliza, to join them in the venture. The two couples left New York in February 1836 to establish a mission somewhere in the little-charted Indian land west of the Continental Divide.

Traveling in company with fur trader Tom Fitzpatrick's supply caravan, they reached South Pass on July 4, 1836, and Narcissa and Eliza became the first known white women to cross the Continental Divide. The two families could not get along with each other, and by the time they reached Fort Walla Walla on the Columbia River and went on to Fort Vancouver for supplies, they had decided to establish separate missions.

On October 6, 1836, Spalding and Whitman located a place for Whitman's mission about twenty-two miles from the fort up the Walla Walla River. The site belonged to a band of Cayuse Indians and was known by them as Waiilatpu, "place of the rye grass."

On October 8, Spalding and Whitman, accompanied by head man Tackensuatis leading a group of Nez Perce, journeyed up the Columbia and Snake Rivers to the mouth of the Clearwater River, which Parker thought would be a good location for a mission. But Tackensuatis had another location in mind and led them about twelve miles farther up the Clearwater to a small stream that flowed into the Clearwater from the south. This was Lapwai Creek, "place of the butterflies." They chose a site about two miles up Lapwai Creek for Spalding's mission, then returned downriver to get supplies and bring up the rest of their party.

Reverend Spalding and Eliza arrived to work among the Nez Perce on November 29, 1836. With the help of the Indians, they had by December 23 constructed "a log hut divided by a partition into two

The Spalding Presbyterian Church, near Spalding's permanent mission site, held its first services in January 1886 and today remains an active Nez Perce congregation.

sections—a living quarters for Eliza and himself, and an assembly and classroom for the Indians."[47]

The Nez Perce tried from the beginning to understand the white man's religion. But there were many conflicts between their Hunyahwat and God. Hunyahwat had two countries—earth and the happy hereafter—while God had three—earth, heaven, and hell. Because the Indians believed in the perfection of nature, they respected all life forms. But the white man poisoned the wolves and coyotes and killed any other creature that competed with him or interfered with his immediate gain. The earth's mantle was to the Nez Perce their mother's blanket, but the whites ripped gold from her bosom and plowed the prairies wrong side up. Where their Hunyahwat was incapable of cruelty, the white man's God burned bad people in perpetual fire.

To make matters worse, would-be missionaries, particularly Isa B. Smith and his wife, Sara, and William H. Gray, undermined the credibility of the Spaldings in every way they could, at first behind their backs, later, out in the open. Even the Whitmans joined periodically in opposing Spalding. Much of the open fighting took place in front of the Indians, who were either confused or contemptuous, and many of the Nez Perce began to regard the missionaries as ridiculous and childish.[48] Spalding received much of the blame for the decline of the missions because his personality was ill-suited to deal with the Indians and he was seen by the old Nez Perce as a tyrant who enslaved Indians willing to work for the Lord. He made frequent use of the lash on those who failed to conform to his interpretation of the Lord's will or who disobeyed his personal orders. In cahoots with Indian agent Dr. White, he imposed on the Nez Perce a code of laws, some to be enforced by the hangman's noose.[49]

Given such treatment, it is no wonder that discontent mounted among the Nez Perce. However, it must be said of Spalding that he foresaw that white settlers would populate the West and the buffalo would vanish. His objective, then, was to prepare the Nez Perce for this American Manifest Destiny by converting them to a nation of farmers, "no longer anxious to leave their homes to chase buffalo on the plains, but settled happily around him and accessible to his religious instruction the full year." Spalding's intent may have been good, yet he did not understand either the similarities (and there were many) or the differences between the Indians' native spirituality and Christianity. He wanted to convert the tribes to the Christian way and had no inclination to include their beliefs in the process. Moreover, despite Eliza's efforts to help him stay calm, his sudden bursts of anger often undermined his sincere efforts to better the lot of the Nez Perce.[50]

The coming of Catholic priests to the area worsened the situation for the Protestant missionaries, in some respects giving them a vicious dose of the same manners they used in ministering to the Indians. In 1838, at the request of Hudson's Bay Company's resident governor, George Simpson, two Canadian-born priests—Father Francis Norbert Blanchet and Father Modeste Demers—crossed the continent with the fur men to Fort Walla Walla. The two priests talked to the Indians there, and the Catholic interpreter told the Indians that the spiritual powers of the priests differed from and were more effective than Whitman's and Spalding's. Confusion increased among the Indians, who now had two white man's religions to deal with. So began a period of intense animosity between the Protestant missionaries and the Catholic priests, involving numerous accusations and counter charges and leading to further resentment among the Indians against the Protestant missions.[51]

Father Pierre Jean De Smet began construction of the St. Mary's Mission in 1841. St. Mary Peak and the Bitterroot Range fill the background. —K. D. Swan, ca. 1934, University of Montana Library

The Catholics also established themselves east of the mountains in the Bitterroot Valley. In response to the request of the Flatheads' fourth delegation to St. Louis, Father Pierre Jean De Smet traveled west in 1840 and met with the Indians. He returned to St. Louis in late summer of that year, assembled supplies and personnel, and in September 1841 began constructing the St. Mary's Mission near the site of present-day Stevensville, Montana (see map 2).[52] In marked contrast to Spalding's lash and noose, De Smet's rules included a kinder framework for learning "(1) with regard to God, (2) with regard to our neighbor, (3) with regard to one's self, and (4) with regard to the means (schools, subjects to be taught, confine to knowledge of their own language, flight from contaminating influences, etc.)." He viewed the Flatheads as "the elect of God," and compared one of his early converts, Chief Big Face, to Moses.[53]

Father De Smet began what turned out to be about five years of amiable missionary work among the Flatheads. The Fathers converted many disciples from their "savage" ways to Catholic worship, yet, for little-understood reasons, commitment to Christianity did not prosper.

By 1850 the settlers had lost so much credibility among the Indians that continuing missionary work was not worthwhile. So Father De Smet abandoned the mission and sold the buildings to pioneer merchant Maj. John Owen.

The dangerous competition between the Protestants and Catholics climaxed in 1847 when Whitman learned of the Catholics' plans to establish a station among the Cayuses. According to Reverend John Baptiste Brouillet, who was to establish the station, Whitman "made a furious charge against the Catholics, accusing them of having persecuted Protestants." Nonetheless, faced with such aggressive competition, a shaken Whitman grew more doubtful that he could continue his mission.

The natives grew still more discontent. That year 4,000 to 5,000 emigrants passed Waiilatpu, bringing with them a devastating form of measles. Almost the entire Cayuse Nation caught the disease. About half of them died. The Indians were desperate. Then Joe Lewis, a half-blood emigrant from Maine who hated white settlers, spread the story that he had overheard Spalding and Whitman plotting to poison the Indians so that they could take their land sooner. Locally known Joseph Stanfield and Nicholas Finlay helped spread the treacherous story.

What happened next is described by author Alvin M. Josephy Jr. in *The Nez Perce Indians and the Opening of the Northwest*, pages 241–43:

> November 29, 1847, was the last day on earth for Marcus and Narcissa Whitman. They were both tired and defeated. . . .
>
> The following day was a bleak and cold Monday. About two in the afternoon the neighboring Cayuse Chief, Tilokaikt, who had offered land to Bishop Blanchet and then withdrawn the offer, entered the Whitman home and asked the Doctor for some medicine. While Whitman's back was turned, a second Indian named Tomahas struck the missionary on the head with a pipe tomahawk. In the struggle that followed, Whitman was hit several times, and his face was slashed and mutilated. Other Cayuses, by signal, joined the attack, shooting and butchering whites inside and outside the buildings. While the doctor was still alive, Narcissa was shot in the arm. Later, weak from loss of blood, she was carried outside the house on a settee, shot again and again by frenzied Indians, dumped in the mud, and beaten with a leather quirt. The enraged bloodletting paused, went on, and paused once more over a period of several days. By the time it ended, the Whitmans and eleven other whites had been slain. Three more persons, including Joe Meek's daughter, Helen Mar, had died, unattended, of illness, or while trying to escape, and forty-seven were being held captive. The rest of the people at the station had escaped

or, like Joe Lewis, were not considered enemies by the Indians. The Cayuses looted and burned the mission buildings, then started looking for Spalding.

What a tragic end to such a well-intended venture. Spalding barely escaped with his life. He blamed the Catholics for inciting the Indians to murder, and he and Eliza fled from the Lapwai Mission; he did not return for over twenty years. Although he converted two-thirds of the Nez Perce to his view of Christianity, the remainder refused to submit to his doctrine of religion. His division of the tribes into Christian and "heathen" factions set the Nez Perce people against each other. And therein lay the seeds of potential war with the Indians.[54]

Meanwhile, as more settlers began to occupy more lands around the mountains, the government of the United States established reservations where the Indians were to live without interference from the pioneering whites. Three such reservations—the Umatilla, Yakima, and Nez Perce—were defined in 1855 at a joint council held by Washington territorial governor Isaac I. Stevens and Oregon Territory's superintendent of Indian affairs, Joel Palmer. The agreed-upon boundaries of the Nez Perce Reservation included all of Lochsa country, left most of their original territorial homeland in possession of the Indians, and provided that no white man, except those employed by the Indian Department, would be permitted to reside on the reservation without permission of the Indian tribe.[55]

But that pact did not last long. Though he had no business prospecting on Indian lands, experienced California miner Capt. Elias D. Pierce invaded the Clearwater country and struck gold at Orofino Creek in 1860. Nez Perce scouts turned him back, but Pierce found ways to circumvent the scouts and confirm his discoveries. Some tribal leaders became concerned that the discovery of gold would flood their reservation with whites, their towns, and their associated clutter. So Pierce spread a false story that his discovery lay outside the reservation, then he aroused the pioneers and the leaders of Walla Walla in a town meeting held about July 20, 1860. Backed by strong support from the whites and with permission from duped Indian agent A. J. Cain, Pierce then led a group of miners into the reservation where they found large quantities of gold near the site of present-day Pierce, Idaho.[56]

The rush into Nez Perce country was underway. Some Nez Perce resisted, but many Indians willingly joined with thousands of miners in the search for gold. They prospected eastward toward the crest of the Bitterroot Range and in 1861 found rich deposits of gold along the Salmon

River–Clearwater divide. There they established the mining towns of Elk City, Florence, Dixie, and the Hump.

So in the 1860s, on the edges of the land of the Lochsa, thousands of miners shoveled gold-bearing muck into sluice boxes; and the yellow metal lodged behind the riffle boards, and muddy water blackened the streams and choked the fish. Inevitably, the strikes played out. Some miners, like their trapper predecessors who had wiped out the beavers, explored deeper into the Lochsa country, believing that Pierce's strike and the Salmon-divide mines, rich as they were, lay at the fringes of a great mother lode. They prospected theretofore unexplored valleys and ridges and crossed the crest into the Bitterroot Valley. Although they found little gold in the Lochsa region, they would be back again and again because, after those few rich discoveries, neither the Indians, the government of the United States, nor the topography of the Clearwater could stay the tide of trespassers converging on the Indian lands of the Bitterroot mountains.

By that time, the farmers and ranchers coveted the Indians' prairies, too. What good is it, they reasoned, to the towns along the Columbia if only a handful of Indians hold those lands to graze ponies and dig roots? Far better to open the prairies to the settler with his plow, that he might begin to order the land, raise crops, populate the foothills with cattle and sheep, and in other ways "Be fruitful, and multiply and replenish the earth and subdue it."[57]

So a new treaty was hatched in 1863, which required the Indians to relinquish all lands ceded to them in 1855 not included within a redesignated reservation. The tribe was to move to the new reservation and would be paid $262,500 for giving to the United States government most of its ancestral territory, including the lands of the Lochsa and all other major forks of the Clearwater River (see map 5).

A Nez Perce known as Lawyer served at that time as "head chief," a position in a system of centralized government, which Indian agent Dr. Elija White had inveigled the several independent tribes of the Nez Perce Nation to accept. Lawyer signed the treaty, as did most of the Christianized Nez Perce tribes. Chiefs Joseph, Looking Glass, White Bird, and Eagle-from-the-Light refused to sign the treaty or comply with its mandates. They remained in their homelands in defiance of the pact. This treaty, called by some the Crime of 1863, finished the divisive work of Spalding's mission and separated the once interdependent tribes of the Nez Perce Nation.[58]

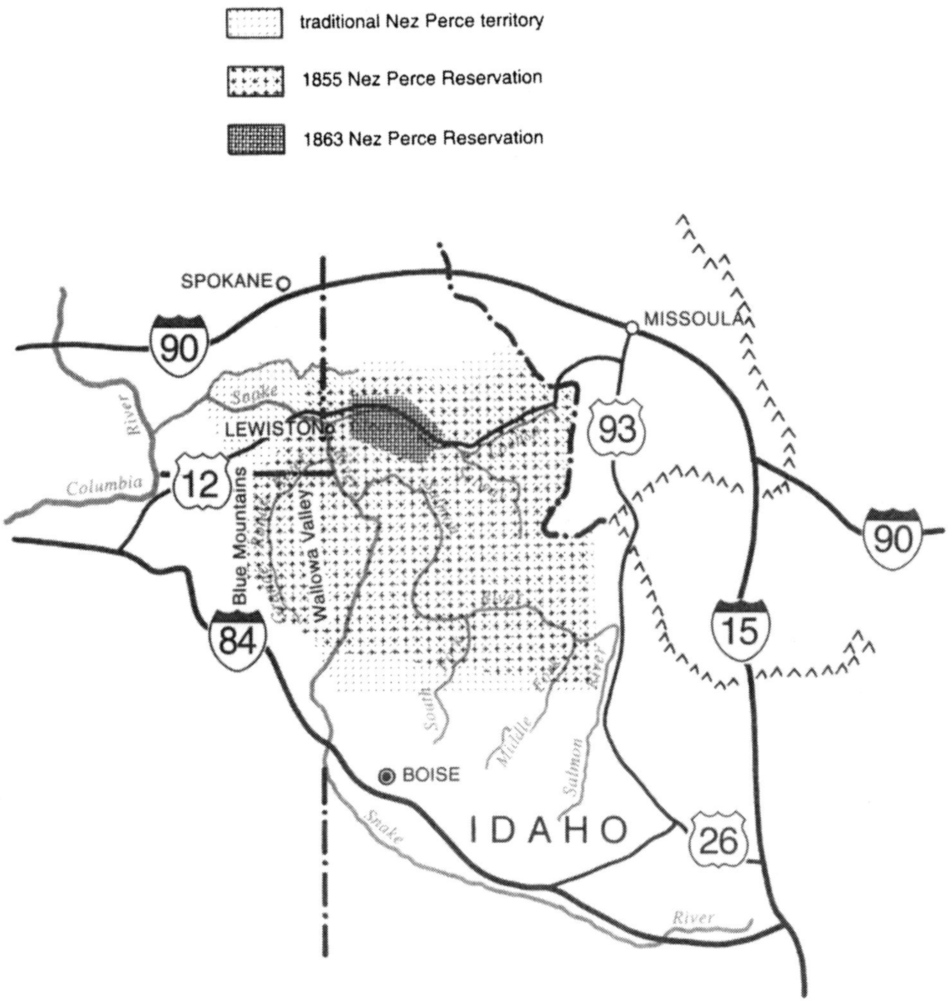

Map 5. *Approximate Nez Perce Reservation boundaries following the treaties of 1855 and 1863.*

In 1853 and 1854, Lt. John Mullan chose the Coeur d'Alene route across the Bitterroots as the best for wagon or railroad construction. He rejected the Lolo Pass-Lochsa option as too "difficult a bed of Mountains."
—University of Montana Library

When it came to seizing wealth from the land, neither most of the advancing whites, the missionaries, nor the United States government respected the Indians' ancestral ways of life. Nor were any of them satisfied for long with Indian roads as routes by which to extract treasures from the mountains, prairies, and rivers. By the 1850s, Isaac I. Stevens, governor of the Washington Territory, had already envisioned the need for three railroad lines across the mountains: a northern route through the Coeur d'Alene country; a southern route along the Salmon River; and a central route across the Bitterroot mountains via the Clearwater River drainage.[59]

In 1853 Governor Stevens assigned Lt. John Mullan of the United States Army to explore potential routes across the Bitterroots. Mullan established headquarters at Cantonment Stevens, south of Fort Owen in the Bitterroot Valley. Armed only with maps drawn by Lewis and Clark, he sent parties into the mountains from this base and at length determined the Coeur d'Alene route most feasible for a railroad or wagon road. In September 1854 the lieutenant led an exploratory expedition through the Lochsa country over the Road to the Buffalo. He concluded:

> In September, 1854, my party having been ordered in from the field, I determined to proceed to the coast by a new route, and the only one then left unexplored, namely, via the Lo-Lo Fork Pass; not that I felt or believed it to be practical for wagons, but more with a view to arm my judgment with such facts as would not leave a shadow of doubt behind which should cause us to err in the final conclusion in so important a matter. This route I found the most difficult of all examined. After eleven days severe struggle with climate and country we emerged into the more open region where "Oro Fino" now stands, glad to leave behind us so difficult a bed of mountains."[60]

Like the Lewis and Clark party in 1805, Lieutenant Mullan had his fill of the Lochsa's mountains after just one trip.

Construction of Mullan's wagon road, intended to connect water transportation at Fort Walla Walla on the Columbia with Fort Benton on the Missouri, began at The Dalles on the Columbia River on May 15, 1859. By the fall of 1860 the road was passable to Fort Benton.[61] In less than two years Mullan built 624 miles of road, which allowed westward emigrants to haul themselves and their supplies on wheels across the northern Rocky Mountains.

Mullan's timing was good. The first steamboat reached Fort Benton in the spring of 1860, while west of the Lochsa's mountains Capt. Ephraim Baughman, of the Oregon Steam Navigation Company, ran the steamer *Colonel Wright* up the Clearwater River to Big Eddy in 1861. Far to the south, the Union Pacific and Central Pacific companies joined their tracks at Promontory, Utah, completing the first transcontinental railroad in 1869.[62] Meanwhile, Congress liberalized its land grant policies by passing the Homestead Act of 1862. It enabled a citizen to obtain 160 acres of public domain by living on it for five years and making certain improvements. He need no longer pay by the acre. The great settlement of the West was underway, and nothing was going to stop it. Even the powerful Blackfeet Indians, once a strong nation of warriors and a threat to settlers, had by that time been reduced by smallpox epidemics to a sparse band struggling for survival against the white man's disease.

The buffalo herds also vanished before the great pilgrimage. Once numbering an estimated eighty million head, they were slaughtered indiscriminately by whites and Indians alike. Scarce by 1867, those "wild cattle of the prairies" were all but gone in the 1870s. And once gone from their prairie hunting grounds, there remained little reason for the

Nez Perce to travel from their homes on the Clearwater across the mountains over the Road to the Buffalo.

The prairies were repopulated with domestic animals brought in by the settlers. In 1833 Charles Larpenteur drove four domestic cows and two bulls into Montana from the Green River country. A conservative count in 1880 showed 48,287 horses, 1,632 mules, 249,888 sheep, and 274,321 cattle in Montana territory.[63]

All Indians grew restless. Responding to pressure from white settlers, the United States government ousted the Flatheads from the Bitterroot Valley in 1871. The Flatheads left reluctantly but peacefully. One deposed chief said:

> Yes, my people, the white man wants us to pay him. He comes in his intent, and says we must pay him—pay him for our own—for the things we have from our God and our forefathers; for the things he never owned and never gave us. What law or right is that? . . . No, no; his course is destruction; he spoils what the spirit who gave us this country made beautiful and clean. But that is not enough; he wants us to pay him besides his enslaving our country. Yes, and our people, besides, that degradation of a tribe who never were his enemies. What is he? Who sent him here? We were happy when he first came. We first thought he came from the light; but he comes like the dusk of the evening now; not like the dawn of the morning. He comes like a day that has passed, and night enters our future with him.[64]

With the Flatheads out of the Bitterroot and the Christian Nez Perce confined to a shrunken reservation, only the bands led by Chief Joseph, Looking Glass, White Bird, Eagle-from-the-Light, and Toohoolhoolzote remained threats to white exploitation of the Indians' birthright. Acting on orders from his superiors, Indian agent John B. Monteith, who had served at Lapwai since February 1871, warned Joseph to bring his people from their Wallowa homeland onto the reservation by April 1, 1877. Joseph replied to Monteith's messengers: "The country they claim belonged to my father, and when he died it was given to me and my people, and I will not leave it until I am compelled to." Joseph thus exposed as a sham the government's peaceful negotiations, leaving the government no alternative but to use force to move the Indians. At a council with the Indians at Lapwai on May 3, 1877, a one-armed army general, Oliver O. Howard, said to the nontreaty Nez Perce chiefs: "I am the man to tell you what you must do. You will come on the reservation within the time I tell you (30 days). If not, soldiers will put you there or shoot you down."[65]

When the Lapwai Council ended, the nontreaty chiefs knew that their homelands were gone and there was no way to recover them short of war. So Joseph, White Bird, and Toohoolhoolzote agreed to move their people to selected locations on the reservation; Looking Glass's band already lived within the reservation. But Howard created an impossible situation, especially for Joseph's band, by ordering them to complete their move within thirty days.

The dejected Indians could not persuade Howard to allow them more time. Accordingly, on May 15, 1877, they returned to their homes and undertook to follow his orders. For Joseph's and Toohoolhoolzote's bands, this required crossing the snowmelt-swollen channels of both the Snake and Salmon Rivers. They lost many possessions and livestock while fording the powerful flood-stage waters. Yet, with twelve days remaining before they were due to enter the reservation only a few miles away, they succeeded in joining the other nontreaty bands at an ancient rendezvous site about six miles west of present-day Grangeville, Idaho. Some 600 resentful Nez Perce camped there at the Camas Prairie beside Tolo Lake for their last peaceful gathering in freedom.

They talked of injustices imposed on them by the white people and their government—of broken promises, unpunished murders of their people, the loss of their homelands, and the haughty orders of General Howard. Tensions mounted as each day passed. The young men wanted to fight, but the chiefs wanted to avoid war because they knew they could not win. They attempted to restrain the bellicose youths. Yet, in the end, it was not the chiefs but the young men who decided the fate of the last of the free Nez Perce. On June 13, 1877, three vengeful young members of White Bird's band attacked and killed several settlers living in isolated locations near the Salmon River. Thus ended seventy-two years of peace between the Nez Perce and the whites who followed Lewis and Clark.[66] War was on.

Until this point in their history, the Nez Perce people had never been warlike in their relations with the United States government. Firm in their convictions, patient in their negotiations, true to their promises—yes; but not truculent. The whites and their government, not the Nez Perce, were the aggressors, pushing the last free Indians from their land and creating resentment and hostility that finally led to war.

Though their warriors probably numbered less than 200, and surely not more than 300, they fought determinedly to preserve something of the life they once had. They fought not for their homelands—those were already lost—but to protect their people and their people's spirit, that they might some day return or find another happier place to live. They routed Captain Perry's U.S. Cavalry and citizen volunteers at White Bird Canyon.[67] Yet, except for their initial scattered and vengeful attacks, their war was a defensive retreat from a nation determined to get the Nez Perce out of the way of American Manifest Destiny. Despite their determination, their small, unsupplied force—burdened as it was with women, children, and possessions—could not last. They knew they must leave the bosom of their mother, their homelands. So they cached their most treasured belongings, defended their last camp along the Clearwater as long as they could, and then crossed the great river. On the evening of July 15 they held council at Weippe Prairie, the same place where their people had befriended the starving Lewis and Clark expedition seventy-two years earlier. The next morning, July 16, 1877, the Nez Perce broke camp. About 200 men and almost 550 women, driving 2,000 horses plus pack animals carrying their possessions, began their last trip as a free nation over their Road to the Buffalo.[68]

No buffalo hunt, that, but a people torn by grief, leaving their ancestral plains, valleys, mountains, and rivers behind them forever. Ahead lay the Bitterroot Valley and unknown hazards. At a narrows in the valley of the Lolo Fork, Capt. Charles C. Rawn's Fort Missoula-based detachment barred their way. To decide how to deal with Rawn's threat to their passage, the Nez Perce halted two miles above the barricade, not far from where the Lewis and Clark expedition had camped on its westward journey on September 11, 1805. So it was that where white men bent on expanding a free nation first camped on that road, free Indians for the last time unsaddled their ponies, pitched tepees, and gathered wood for their cooking fires.

After an unsuccessful attempt to negotiate a peaceful entry into the Bitterroot Valley, the Indians bypassed Rawn's barricades by crossing the mountains to the north. Then they journeyed southward through the Bitterroot Valley, to avoid crossing Flathead country, and on toward safety in Canada. But the way was long and difficult, and many of them were slain on August 9 by Col. John Gibbon's troops and volunteers in a surprise attack at the Big Hole River. Two months later, on October 5, 1877, weary from their flight and surrounded by the army, Chief Joseph surrendered to Gen. Nelson Miles in the Bear Paw Mountains.

When Joseph rode up the hill to surrender his rifle, his hair hung in two long braids on either side of his face. He wore a simple gray blanket with a black stripe and moccasin leggings; he held his rifle across the pommel of his saddle. After dismounting, he pulled his blanket closer about him and walked to General Howard and offered him the rifle. Howard waved him on to Miles. Joseph then walked to Miles and handed him the rifle. Then he stepped back, adjusted his blanket to leave his right arm free, and said:

> Tell General Howard I know his heart. What he told me before I have in my heart. I am tired of fighting. Our Chiefs are killed. Looking Glass is dead. The old men are all killed. It is the young men who say yes or no. He who led the young men is dead. It is cold and we have no blankets. The little children are freezing to death. My people, some of them, have run away to the hills, and have no blankets, no food; no one knows where they are, perhaps freezing to death. I want time to look for my children and see how many of them I can find. Maybe I shall find them among the dead. Hear me, my Chiefs. I am tired: my heart is sick and sad. From where the sun now stands, I will fight no more.[69]

On that day in October, Joseph surrendered 87 men, 184 women, and 147 children. Except for those who escaped to Canada, these were all who remained of the free Ni-me-poo, who numbered 6,000 strong at the time of Lewis and Clark's expedition. For more than seventy years after discovery of this country by white men, its formidable mountain topography under Indian stewardship had detoured the great western migration around most of the Clearwater and all of the Lochsa. After 1877, with the Indians no longer a significant deterrent, only topography stood in the fortune seekers' way.

Chief Joseph of Wallowa, a statesmanlike leader of the Nez Perce people before, during, and after their war with the government of the United States.
—Nez Perce County Historical Society

5

Fur Trappers Claim the Lochsa

I ***n 1890 the U.S. Superintendent of Census reported that,*** except in Alaska, unbroken areas of unsettled, unexploited wilderness had ceased to exist. But it didn't seem that way to me in 1930 as I hiked from Elk Meadows down along the Brushy Fork to where the remnants of Pete Thompson's lean-to cabin decayed in the forest beside the stream (see map 2).

Though nearly destroyed by weather and time, the ridge pole still stood, supported by two ten-foot-high posts. One wall had collapsed to reveal the rubble of a small stone fireplace, a bunk made of poles, several ermine and marten stretchers, and a few rusted pots and pans. Pete built the lean-to sometime during the late 1880s. It served as one of several line camps on a trapline leading from his homestead on the Lolo Fork over the hill into the Lochsa wilderness.

I poked around in the rubble, and the excitement of times past rose from the ruins. I envisioned a tall mountain man snowshoeing through the spruces, chopping the ice on the Brushy Fork to dip for water, or skinning prime furbearers by candlelight while smoke from the lean-to's chimney curled up through the crowns of the snow-laden trees.

Pete trapped alone. He sought no permanent ownership of the land, but simply used the land to trap animals with valuable long-haired furs. Signs of their presence in the Lochsa's woods showed that other trappers had come and gone before Pete built his shelter beside the Brushy Fork. Deadfalls built on stumps atop the snow had caught martens before steel traps were in plentiful supply. Axe blazes so overgrown that they showed only as dark spots on tree trunks marked ways through the forest; trappers had followed them from cabin to cabin as they tended their

Part of an early-day deadfall, this notched stump hinged one end of a heavy log while its other end, supported on a similar stump by a figure-four trigger, was set to drop the log on any furbearer that seized the bait.

deadfalls, traps, and snares. By 1930, though, only outlines of the oldest cabins' original shapes remained where once-sturdy walls had long ago rotted and returned to earth.

The Lochsa's forests offered the marten—sometimes called the American sable—as the trapper's greatest prize, along with mink, lynx, fishers, otters, wolverines, ermines, coyotes, and foxes. More than a wealth of furs could be harvested, however, by trappers who seized each day's adventure with their senses attuned to the Lochsa's creations of nature. The silence of winter, the water ouzel's song, echoes of cascades rumbling in the basins, the smell of freshly cut wood, a cabin's warm haven when blizzards smothered the mountains—all these and similar treasures could be enjoyed by those who held a degree of reverence for the Lochsa country. Small wonder that they, as I, marveled at it all.

Trapper Lawrence was one who abandoned the near-empty beaver ponds to search for furs in the mountains. He traded skins with David Thompson in 1810, then disappeared from recorded history for forty-two years. It is said that he spent those years living with his Nez Perce wife near the edge of the big meadow in the Grave Creek branch of the Lolo Fork (see map 2). The Indians called this first white settler Lou

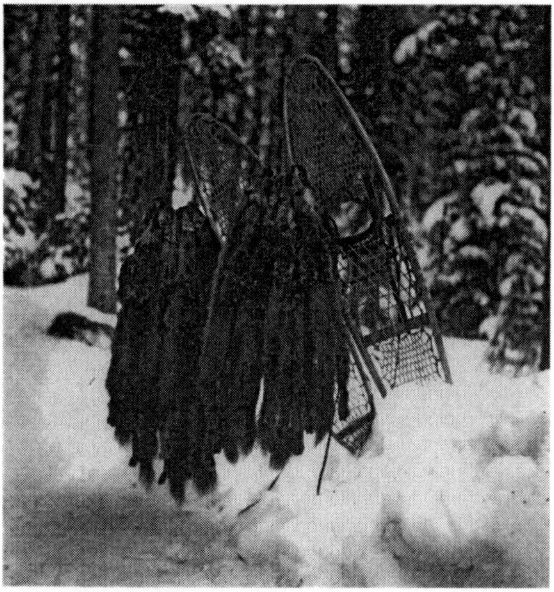

The presence of valuable furs like these marten pelts drew trappers into the Lochsa and similar unexplored mountain ranges.

Lou, later modified to Lolo. Sometime during this period the stream became known by Lawrence's Indian name, even though explorers Lewis and Clark had called it Travellers Rest. In time, even the Road to the Buffalo took the name of the obscure trapper, an apt tribute to Lawrence and his successors who established traplines in the Lochsa country.[70]

Early-day settlers referred to Lawrence as Chief Lolo, suggesting that he may have been adopted into one or more tribes. Nobody knows for sure how long he lived on the Lolo Fork, but it seems certain that the blazes on his traplines must have led from the edge of the glade near his cabin into the Lochsa region, because no serious trapper would overlook that land's wealth of furbearing animals. Thus, Lawrence likely was one of the first, perhaps *the* first, white man to harvest fur, or any other commercial bounty for that matter, from the Lochsa basin.

As trapper Lawrence grew old, time dulled his instincts. One day in about 1852, along the road near his home in the meadow, Lawrence and an Indian friend came upon a grizzly bear at close range. Lawrence fired but only wounded the bear. The Indian, armed with a bow, climbed a tree while the bear mauled Lawrence, nearly tearing off his leg. By firing arrows from his perch in the tree, the Indian drove off the bear. But it was too late. Lawrence, a pioneer who had helped close one great trapping era and open another, died as he had lived, in wildness beside the road that now carries his name.[71]

Here's all that remained of the Alberys' cabin near Storm Creek by 1974.

Other early trappers included the Albery brothers, who were among the first long-line trappers in the Lochsa's Crooked Fork, Brushy Fork, and White Sand drainages. Little is known about them except that they operated around the turn of the twentieth century out of a home cabin located on the west bank of the Crooked Fork near where the Lolo Trail crossed and began its ascent to Packer Meadows.[72] Something of the character of their operations can be learned from the ruins of another of their cabins, which was located near Storm Creek where a stand of lodgepole pines provided wood for the fireplace and logs to build the cabin's walls and roof. A lush meadow nearby assured summertime feed for the horses necessary to pack supplies into the mountains. And nearly hidden by grasses on the meadow's edge, a cold brook delivered water close to the cabin's axe-hewn door. The twelve-foot by fourteen-foot interior was sheltered by a puncheon roof split from straight-grained lodgepole pine. Built entirely with an axe, the cabin's tight-fitting corners demonstrated the work of master axmen. There was no window; cabins, after all, were used mostly during the night by trappers who spent the daylight hours tending their traplines. From this tight cabin in its prime location, with all the necessities of life in the mountains close at hand, the Alberys could concentrate on pursuing the long-haired furs.[73]

Except for artifacts like blazes, remnants of trap sets, and the ruins of their cabins, the trappers left few visible records of their tenure. But in a tradition similar to that of the prophets of the Nez Perce, they preserved some of their history through stories told and retold around campfires and at cabin hearths. For example, one story passed down through the years explains that on an April morning in about 1905, Frank Kube (a trapper we shall hear more about later) kindled his breakfast fire in a cabin on the banks of the Lochsa River near the place where Lewis and Clark camped on September 14, 1805 (see Powell R. S. on map 2). As he turned his bacon, he heard a rifle shot echo across the valley.

Kube opened the cabin door to behold a barrel-chested man on the opposite bank of the snowmelt-swollen Lochsa. To his amazement, the big stranger signaled by swinging his arms that he planned to swim the river. Neither Kube's warning shouts nor all the negative sign language he could muster had the slightest deterrent effect. Apparently intending to swim to the small island near the river's center, the man hiked upstream a bit, pulled off his shoes and heavy mackinaw, tied them securely around his waist, and plunged into the swift waters of the Lochsa.

This island, near present-day Powell Ranger Station and mentioned by Lewis and Clark in 1805, is where "the Russian" swam across the Lochsa about 1905.

Kooskia, Idaho, 1975. The Middle Fork of the Clearwater River flows in the foreground. The South Fork flows through the town from the distant right. —Freeman Mann

He drove toward the island with powerful overhand strokes, head low and half submerged like an otter chasing a salmon. Strong currents swept him past the island, and he swam for the shore where Kube's breakfast scorched unattended in the cabin's fireplace. Kube scrambled through alders and willows along the stream bank opposite the powerful swimmer, and a quarter-mile downstream he waded into the shallows, grasped the near-exhausted man by his arms, and hauled him to safety on the bank.

Kube had fished "the Russian," an early-day trapper, from the icy waters of the Lochsa. For years the Russian's trapline had followed close to the Nez Perce's hunting road on the divide between the Lochsa and Selway Rivers, from the vicinity of Fish Lake across the Grave Mountains to near the headwaters of the Lochsa at Elk Summit. Little was ever known of his activities or cabin locations except what he told Kube

Pack train leaving Kooskia about 1907. —U.S. Forest Service

about a headquarters cabin near Hungry Rock, one of the Grave Mountains' granite peaks.[74]

No one, not even Frank Kube, knew when the Russian first entered the Bitterroot mountains. But he left in 1906 or 1907 with a big catch of fur and never returned. That same spring two trappers, Martin Stanley and Beaver Jack, failed to come out of the mountains from their traplines located farther west on the same divide worked by the Russian. Beaver Jack was never seen again in the Lochsa area, and Martin Stanley's remains were reportedly found near the peak that bears his name. His skull was separated from his body by a considerable distance. Only the spirits of the mountains know what fate befell Beaver Jack and Stanley, but as the shadows of history pass along the ridges, one wonders if perhaps the Russian also knew.

The earliest of the Lochsa's trappers had no contact with established towns, so they bartered their furs at distant trading posts for provisions to sustain themselves another year in the mountains. Later on, settlement of the Clearwater prairies to the west and the Bitterroot Valley to the east created villages that served as outposts from their chosen home ranges at the edges of civilization, places where they could sell furs, buy supplies, and for a brief time reexperience such essentials as comradeship, soft beds, whiskey, and women.

Urban guests gather at the road's end, Lolo Hot Springs hotel, in 1904. —Louise Gerber Gilbert

Kooskia, Idaho, became the trapper's western outpost town. Mountain men of the Lochsa seldom spoke of going "out (of the mountains) to Lewiston" or Orofino or Syringa. It was always "out to Kooskia." Kooskia began in 1889 when F. P. Turner established a post office at his ranch on Sutter Creek, seven and one-half miles east of the confluence of the middle and south forks of the Clearwater River. In 1895 the town of Stuart sprang up nearby, and as this town expanded it claimed the name of Turner's original post office, Kooskia.[75]

Centered on the peninsula between the Clearwater River's south and middle forks, the town extends along both rivers to form a vee-shaped village. Open, grassy slopes—lush green in spring, parched brown in summer—stretch from the river's bottomlands to the benchlands above the river-carved canyons. Scattered fir and pine forests follow the draws leading up to the prairies; here and there a rocky outcrop frowns down on the streets below.

Lochsa trappers like the Russian, Beaver Jack, and Martin Stanley sold their furs and bought supplies in Kooskia. They cargoed packs and loaded their mule and horse trains on Main Street, while the townspeople watched, wondered, and perhaps at times even envied those men

Trappers of the Lochsa display furs at Lolo Hot Springs. Left to right: Fred Schott, Andrew Erickson, Jim Sullivan, Frank Smith, Carl Erickson, and owner of Lolo Hot Springs, Herman Gerber. —Louise Gerber Gilbert

caught up in the spell of the wilderness. Kooskia was indeed a fitting outpost of civilization for the men of the Lochsa's mountains.

But it was a long ways from Kooskia to the uplands of the Lochsa. Consequently, many of the earliest fur takers—Lawrence, Pete Thompson, and others—laid their traplines from closer locations on the Lolo Fork over the hill through the Lolo Pass and the several nearby saddles in the mountains to the north and south. Strategically located only six miles below the Lolo Pass, the quamash meadow and hot springs on the upper Lolo Fork were, from the arrival of the white man, destined to become another major gateway to the Lochsa country.

In his journal entry for June 29, 1806, Capt. William Clark describes the virtues of this meadow and the springs:

> Those Worm or Hot Springs are Situated at the base of a hill of no considerable hight, on the N. Side and near the bank of travellers rest Creek which is at that place about 10 yds wide. these Springs issue from the bottom and through the interstices of a grey freestone rock, the rock rises in irregular masy clifts in a circular range, arround the Springs on their lower Side. imediately above the Springs on the creek there is a handsom little quawmash plain of about 10 acres. the principal spring is about the temperature of the Warmest baths

Blodgett Pass, one favored entry of trappers from the distant Bitterroot Valley to the Big Sand Lake region of the Lochsa.

> used at the Hot Springs in Virginia. in this bath which had been prepared by the Indians by stopping the river with Stone and mud, I bathed and remained in 10 minits it was with dificuelty I could remain this long and it causd. a profuse swet. two other bold Springs adjacent to this are much warmer, their heat being so great as to make the hand of a person Smart extreemly when immerced. we think the temperature of those Springs about the Same as that of the hotest of the hot Springs of Virginia.[76]

Captain Clark's statement, perhaps the first real estate promotion in the Bitterroot mountains, described the kind of place sought for development by certain enterprising people. By the mid-1880s, the hot springs, the quamash glade, and substantial acres of surrounding terrain had been claimed. Thereafter Lolo Hot Springs became a rendezvous point for trappers who worked their lines in the Lochsa country. It was their contact with the outside, their post office, their source of woman-cooked grub, and their place to call the roll each spring to see if the Great Spirit had claimed any of their comrades during the winter (see map 2).

Paul Gerber bought the Lolo Hot Springs in 1903, and for years afterward the Gerber family, primarily Herman and Sarah, operated the place.[77] Access was by a twenty-mile-long wagon road from the Bitterroot Valley. By the early 1900s the facilities included a hotel, swimming plunge, store, hay barn, and several cabins, all used by guests from the cities and by the Lochsa's trappers and other mountain men during their brief journeys out of the wilderness. People of the wildest of mountains mingled with dudes from the city in a homespun environment created by Herman and Sarah. Surely, the association must have been good for all.

The waters of the Lolo Fork babbled close to the cabin doors where, during winter and in the cool of summer evenings, clouds of steam rose from the hot springs, the plunge, and the pool in the hotel. During late winter talk at "the Springs" would turn from weather and politics to trappers. When would they come out of the mountains? Would each of them make it safely to the Springs? How much fur would they have? Trappers were important people at the Lolo Hot Springs outpost because money could be made in trade for the fur they brought to market. But more than that, their coming assembled an exciting breed of men much like those who followed Lewis and Clark some one hundred years before.

Located within a few miles of each other, the Bitterroot Valley towns of Hamilton, Darby, and Victor also became important centers for trappers who worked the major tributary streams flowing into the Bitterroot River. Those trappers crossed the most rugged sections of the Bitterroot Range to reach the Lochsa region. They improved the Indians' trails and in some places hacked new trails in order to deliver supplies by horses and mules to their cabins in the mountainous interior. Though there were several secondary passes, Lost Horse, Blodgett, and Packbox were the passes used most often by the trappers in the early days.

In later years, mostly after 1900, trappers also entered the Lochsa from homesteads on the Selway River in Idaho, Fish Creek in Montana, and the remote North Fork of the Clearwater. But the three major outposts for those white men who first claimed the Lochsa's bounty continued to be Kooskia on the west, Lolo Hot Springs to the northeast, and the Bitterroot Valley towns of Hamilton, Darby, and Victor to the east (see map 2).

Seasonal activity patterns of the early trappers were as predictable as the annual migrations of elk to their winter range. During summer they repaired cabins, cut wood, and some prospected for minerals. In late summer and early fall they packed provisions into their home cabins and line camps. Winter was trapping time. Then in early March they headed out of the mountains to market their furs. Some trappers passed up the outpost towns for big towns like Missoula, Lewiston, or Spokane, where they could find liquor and whores. Others stopped at the

This 1969 photo shows the cabin Andrew and Carl Erickson built near Packer Meadows in about 1914.

outposts, content to barter their furs, visit briefly, and then return to the Lochsa's basins to hunt and trap bears during April and May.

So turned the annual cycle of the fur takers as they established, consolidated, and held their claims for trapping rights in the Lochsa's landscapes. The lone trappers disappeared so thoroughly into the wilds that, for a time, they encountered each other far less frequently than they did grizzly bears. But more trappers came. And still more. Competition for the land's bounty increased.

Consider, for example, the eighty-mile-long Brushy Fork–Beaver Ridge trapline. On its northernmost flank, this line skirts the Road to the Buffalo and Lolo Pass; thus, trapper Lawrence could have been the first to reach it. The Albery boys' traplines crossed the lower Brushy Fork, then went up over Beaver Ridge into Storm Creek. During the 1880s and 1890s, Pete Thompson trapped along the divide from Lolo Pass up into the high country where I met the big grizzly in 1930. From his home cabin, near the junction of the Brushy and Crooked Forks, prospector-trapper Joe Eberle worked the lower Crooked Fork and White Sand Creek around 1900. He was followed by Charley Powell who, in about 1905, established a headquarters cabin on the banks of the Lochsa near the fishery where Lewis and Clark had camped one hundred years before. Meanwhile, soon after the turn of the century, master trapper Fred Schott laid claim to the heartland—Beaver Ridge and the Brushy and Spruce Fork basins—of this fur-rich region.

Fred built his main cabin below the cascades near where Spruce Creek joins the Brushy Fork. He called his Lochsa home "Big Cabin," and from that isolated headquarters he blazed traplines to small cabins near Elk Meadows, Beaver Meadows, and the old Indian fishery on the Brushy Fork.

That's the way it was when the Erickson brothers, Carl and Andrew, showed up in the Brushy Fork–Beaver Ridge country about 1914. They set traps in all unclaimed regions, and when less aggressive men, like Fred Schott, failed to trap an area for a winter, the Ericksons moved in and claimed the land. Their personalities combined the generosity of Jesus with the territorial tenacity of a grizzly bear. Andrew and Carl claimed and consolidated until they had assembled the Brushy Fork–Beaver Ridge line, known when I entered the area as the Erickson line. Seven sturdy cabins, spaced one day's travel on snowshoes apart, were used at the peak of the trapline's operation. To settle their differences after a quarrel, Andrew claimed their traplines in the Lochsa's wilderness and Carl took over their ranch on the Lolo Fork below Lolo Hot Springs.

The Brushy Fork–Beaver Ridge experience was typical of Lochsa traplines. The historical evolution of each combined adventure, unique

Wes Fales's cabin at Big Sand Lake. —Wes Fales, courtesy of Fay Burrell

When Wes Fales built his cabin at Big Sand Lake in 1899, he had an extraordinary view of the life of the land in the Lochsa from his doorway.

personalities, and man-land associations. During the summer of 1899 the mountainsides echoed the sounds of axe blows as Wes Fales felled timber to construct his trapping headquarters at Big Sand Lake. Nobody knows for sure who trapped the Big Sand Basin first. Surely the Russian from Idaho and Frank Meeks from the Bitterroot Valley must have crossed snowshoe trails long before Wes built his home cabin on the lake's northern shore. For even as Wes fashioned his cabin walls, scarcely a mile upstream an older and smaller cabin had already deteriorated beyond usefulness as a winter shelter.

Wes chose his home cabin site with an eye for natural splendor as well as utility. *Why not* pick a nice view? After all, those early-day pilgrims had unrestricted choice of the finest natural beauty in America. Wes built his cabin lean-to style with the window and door facing Big Sand Lake only thirty yards away. In late summer and fall he could watch the circles widen on the lake as the red-bellied trout grabbed bugs floating on the surface of the water. Moose, sometimes a dozen in number, fed in the shallows. On occasion the forests, mountain peaks, and sky reflected in the lake. At those times the mountains shone upside down beneath its surface while they also reached above timberline to touch the sky, so that the lake and the mountains and the moose and the man joined in a double dose of uncommon wildness.

Not long after his cabin was finished, Wes had worn a trail in the turf from the door to the lakeshore where he dipped water for cooking and washing. Ripples would spread across the lake when Wes dipped his bucket. With each fresh breeze, the water wrinkled, causing the mountains to vanish from the lake and leaving the trapper alone with his cabin and the peaks on the skyline. Wild beauty is often such a temporary miracle. Wes Fales, in 1899, had discovered a priceless part of God's country. And as he carried water from the lake to his new cabin's door, he knew precisely the kind of treasure he had found.

Claims to Lochsa fur led to the creation of still other big traplines. Pioneer trapper Milt Savage snowshoed from the Bitterroot Valley over Packbox Pass and established traplines in upper White Sand Creek. His blazes and his cabins reached to the granite peaks of the Grave Mountains where the claims of the Russian and German-born Frank Kube overlapped in time. West of the Grave Mountains, Martin Stanley and Beaver Jack became prominent figures in two big lines separated by the Crags mountains (see map 2).

Fred Schott and Frank Smith laid a network of traplines and cabins throughout the furbearer habitat drained by the Crooked Fork of the

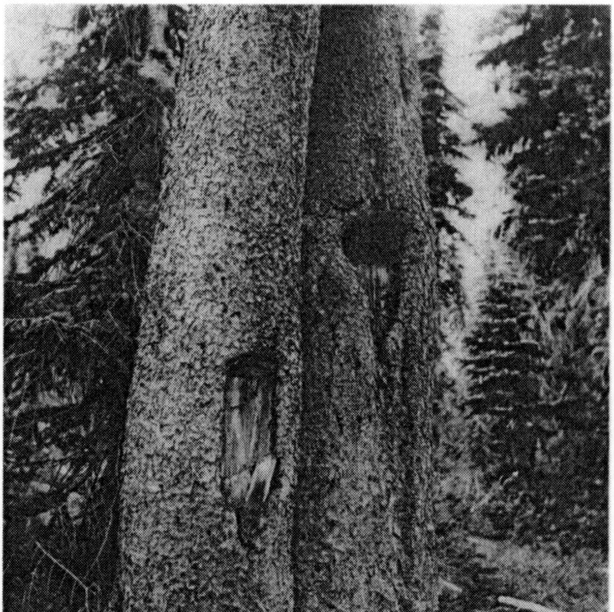

This near-overgrown marten notch set near Stanley Butte was probably used by Martin Stanley sometime around the turn of the century.

Lochsa. About 1913, several traplines in the downriver country were consolidated into one big line by Bert Wendover, a native of Oregon whose doctors had given him less than five years to live. After deciding to spend his remaining life fulfilling a dream of living in the wildest of mountains, he came to the Lochsa. He survived the first winter in a small cabin at Walton Lakes, high in the Grave Mountains. The following summer Bert built a log home at the glade on the banks of the Lochsa where, on September 15, 1805, Lewis and Clark had climbed from the Indian fishery to rejoin the Road to the Buffalo. That trappers had worked the area long before him showed in old notches and peg sets and the rotting remnants of a nearby cabin. Bert stayed for twenty years and left in good health.[78]

Not long after the Nez Perce left their homeland, the Road to the Buffalo became known as the Lolo Trail, and the long ridge separating the Clearwater's Lochsa and North Forks was named the Lolo Divide—probably out of respect for trapper Lawrence who, as we have already seen, was among the first to expand the trapping from the Bitterroot Valley into the Lochsa's mountains. The divide was good fur country. Old sets and cabin ruins reveal that trappers began to operate in the area sometime during the 1880s. Trappers from the Lochsa no doubt met trappers from the North Fork of the Clearwater on this great ridge, but who did what and when remains largely a mystery.

So evolved the traplines, as men with varied backgrounds laid claim to the land for taking the long-haired fur. Although each trapper was as unique as the particular landscape he claimed, collectively they demonstrated many common characteristics in personality and in their relation to the land.

Their love for the land was stronger than their desire to profit from the fur. They believed nature's bounty to be self-sustaining. Somewhere, perhaps over the next ridge, was abundant fur to be harvested, and they began each winter's trapping with the same expectations that accompanied their first penetration into the land. Though there were exceptions, most were loners. Life in the mountains demanded such strong self-reliance that it was a rare pair who could long tolerate each other's will within the demands and freedoms inherent in the Lochsa country. Yet any of them would risk his life without hesitation to aid a fellow mountain man in trouble.

Something in their pasts had caused many of them to reject traditional values of civilization and to seek a primitive life in the Lochsa's wilds. An educated biologist, Frank Kube had trouble with the government of his native Germany and in due time showed up at Lolo Hot Springs, his gateway to God's country. It was said that during Fred Schott's youth in the Midwest, he had been jilted by a girl and never recovered from the blow. In Frank Smith's past lurked a divorce and a daughter. Given only a short time to live, Bert Wendover chose to end it all in the shade of the Lochsa's cedars. Of the Russian and others like him, who knows?

For many of them, from whence they came or where they went remains obscure. Whether in a youthful quest for room to grow or in the backlash of personal troubles, they married the Lochsa's rivers and ridges. Their wedding bands were trapline blazes linking cabins built in sheltered places on the land.

A trapper's cabin at Saddle Camp on the Lolo Divide is nearly buried under eight feet of snow.

Veteran prospector Jerry Johnson searched for precious metals in the Lochsa during the 1880s and 1890s. Jerry Johnson Hot Springs is named after him, as is the campground now located at the site of his cabin. —Montana Historical Society

6

The Legend of Isaac's Gold

G*old! After rich discoveries during the early 1860s at Pierce City,* Elk City, and Florence, prospectors swarmed across the Clearwater's mountainous interior all the way to the Bitterroot crest. No matter that the land belonged to the Nez Perce Indians. The prospectors dug and panned gravel in nearly every tributary, believing those first strikes to be mere satellites of a greater treasure hidden somewhere deep in the Clearwater's heartland, that is, in the basins of the North Fork, the Selway, or the Lochsa.

Prospector Jerry Johnson personified the virtues essential for hunting precious metals. Lean and tough on the trail, his six-foot-tall frame harbored the strength to shovel all day long in the sluice box. Johnson had mastered the crafts of life in the mountains long before he discovered the Lochsa region. Time to acquire wisdom showed in his grizzled beard, and his dark eyes gleamed with zest of the search for the Lochsa's treasure.

One day in late summer during the mid-1880s, Johnson led two companions, another white man and a Nez Perce Indian named Isaac, past a place called "the park" to a small alpine meadow high in the Grave Mountains, commanding an extensive view of the terrain to the north, east, and west (see map 2). They were headed to a secret place where Indian Isaac had gathered gold each summer for many years. Isaac had grown too old and weak to make the trip alone and, realizing his remaining days on earth were few, had offered to take his prospector friend to the hidden source of gold. Johnson was worried because Isaac had become very ill.

As Isaac grew weaker, Johnson and his partner dropped the packs, picketed the horses, and made camp. Fearing Isaac might die, Johnson

Forest scientist Bob Mutch scans part of the Lochsa landscape thought to hide the source of Isaac's gold.

wrapped him in his blanket and then carried him to a ridge top where they could look eastward across the Lochsa's upper basin toward the distant Bitterroot crest.

"Which way is the gold from here?" asked Johnson.

Isaac raised his arm and pointed to a snow-covered peak on the eastern skyline. "See snow," he replied. Then raising one finger, he said, "Sun."[79]

With that, he rolled over on his blanket, exhausted.

Indian Isaac died during the night at their camp, and the location of his gold source died with him. But his journey to Ahkinkenekia launched the legend that would rekindle the waning dreams of the prospectors who had thus far found little gold in the Lochsa's mountains. Johnson and his partner buried Isaac's remains in the shade of a whitebark pine, a fitting place for that Indian who, like all Ni-me-poo, revered the beauty of the land.

One can suppose that, given the solemn finality of Isaac's end on earth, these prospectors spoke little as they broke camp, loaded their pack horses, and rode to the ridge top. Surely they must have paused there to look eastward across the expanse of ridges and tributaries of the Lochsa, extending from the hooves of their horses to the skyline at the crest of the Bitterroot mountains.

Named because of Isaac's legend, Grave Peak is the mightiest mountain in this subrange of the Bitterroots.

As it had done each morning for centuries, a breeze would have stirred the branches of the gnarled pines on the rim. Ridges covered by unbroken forests linked two green-hued lakes in the foreground to the canyons of the Lochsa, and more ridges ranged on to the crest where the peak pointed out by Isaac stood as one among many at the top of the Bitterroot Range. It was a big country, and even the largest gold nuggets were very small by comparison. The gentle breeze would have risen to a vigorous wind and moaned in the stunted pines and snags along the rim. Johnson no doubt glanced back to be sure the loads on the horses were balanced. Then he would have neck-reined his saddle horse and headed east to renew his search for gold.

Named after Isaac's burial place by early prospectors, the Grave Mountains form a geographical hub in the Lochsa country. Tributary canyons and connecting ridges stretch in all directions from the alpine park where Isaac died. And after Johnson rolled Isaac in his blanket for the last time, the Grave Mountains became the navigational center for pilgrims of the great treasure hunt. From there they calculated the direction Isaac would have taken, how far he could have trekked in a day, and how many days he would have traveled. Some even theorized about the evasive tactics he might have used to throw white gold seekers

This map is an example of several used by prospectors who searched for Isaac's gold. Source unknown.

off his trail. Detailed maps were drawn and kept secret lest their strategy be revealed to some rival prospector. Men told and retold the story of Isaac's gold around campfires and in cabins as the search went on.

Two descriptions prevailed about how Isaac had found the gold and the kind of place where he found it. Some said that a band of Indians had been traveling through those mountains when one of them took sick, so they camped and prepared a "sweat bath" to cure the sick man's ills. While gathering rocks to heat to create the steam for the bath, the Indians loosened some white quartz from a nearby outcrop and discovered it to be laced with gold. But this version was rejected by most of the Lochsa prospectors, who reasoned, "How could Isaac alone know of this gold if a whole party of Indians were involved in its discovery?"

It was more commonly held that Isaac had killed a moose during a hunting trip many years before he tried to show Johnson the way to his gold. While dressing the animal, he bloodied his hands and arms. He sought water to wash himself in a nearby streambed. Because the stream had nearly dried up, he scraped a depression in which to collect water. As he dug, his bloody hands scooped up not only gravel but several gold nuggets as well.

Depending on their preference for hard rock or placer mining, prospectors combing the Lochsa might adopt either version of the discovery of the gold. Though Isaac's moose-kill story held the strongest credence, most gold seekers watched for old sweat bath huts, gold-filled quartz, and rich placer gravel alike. No mass rush developed to find the gold, but each prospector went at the search with persistent singleness of purpose. Isaac's gold or some other precious metal had to be out there somewhere.

Using the Indian roads for access, they branched off into nearly inaccessible canyons and crossed little-known passes marked only by blazes of the trappers. Searching the crest of the Bitterroots, they walked on solid granite interspersed with patches of pines and firs dwarfed by the alpine climate of the Lochsa. Sparkling brooklets traced their way from snowfields across the tundra and disappeared into the forests below. It was a mountain goat's paradise. With the bedrock of the earth rarely hidden by soil or vegetation, that high alpine country was, potentially, a prospector's paradise, too.

But no gold was found near the granite peaks of Isaac's "snow." Except for the alpine crests, the land and its geology, and consequently its gold, lay hidden beneath dense forests and brush. The most ambitious prospectors burned the forest in hopes of exposing the treasure. John Lieberg, of the U.S. Geological Survey, reported these activities

Remnants of precious metals, when found in streams like this, could sometimes be traced to their source higher in the Lochsa Mountains.

during his reconnaissance of the Bitterroot mountains in 1897: "For many years the Lochsa Basin has been a favorite field with prospectors hunting 'lost mines,' concerning which all sorts of wild and fabulous tales are extant. In the search for imaginary treasures the timber has suffered enormously from fires that have been set for the purpose of destroying forest covering of the mountains to facilitate the search."[80]

Lieberg held little faith in rumors of lost mines. He went on to record: "The Bitterroot Range is deficient in mineral-bearing areas throughout the granite sections. . . . The regions that appear devoid of mineral-bearing veins are the main range of the Bitterroots and its slopes from near St. Mary Peak southward for a distance of about 50 miles and westward about 40 miles from the summit."[81]

No matter that Isaac died in the northern center of the area that Lieberg excluded. The hope of another rich strike, inspired by Isaac's story, sustained uncommon commitment among the prospectors who had no inclination to read government reports when panning the next creek or exposing an outcrop of quartz that might reveal the precious metal. After all, they were driven by a Lochsa legend, while Lieberg had but a few decades of the study of geology to back his views.

One function of mountains is to drain water from snowpacks at high elevations down to the valleys and then on to the sea. The resulting streams are the arteries of the land, their waters its lifeblood, and the rubble in their bars clues to minerals in each drainage. The force of water plunging seaward had deposited samples of the land's anatomy behind boulders and above the logjams ever since the great ice sheets scoured the Lochsa's upper valleys. The prospectors understood that land-stream association. And like doctors testing blood to assess the health of a patient, they worked the stream courses for indicators of treasure, perhaps a great mother lode hiding somewhere upstream.

Thus, they scoured the Lochsa's tributaries, from bold streams impossible to ford during snowmelt to brooklets so small that undergrowth had to be parted in order to see the water. Few, if any, streams held gold, but all had potential and all were rich in natural beauty. The prospectors dipped their gold pans in clear water flowing over timeworn pebbles, each adding its individual hue to the greens, browns, pinks, whites, yellows, and glistening bits of mica in the streambeds. Surely there would be gold amid such splendor. But, alas, those sparkling pebbles were not gold to be gleaned and sold in some far-off marketplace; instead, like their parent stream, they were there to excite the mind and cause one to wonder at nature's greatness—not to be removed but marveled at, then left undisturbed, taking away only the strength gained from their beauty.

If the Lochsa held treasure of note, it remained hidden in the bosom of that great land. Most pilgrims came, looked, dug, panned, and then left. But the Lochsa's wild mystique combined with Isaac's legend to capture the hearts and souls of the few who stayed. Joe Eberle trapped furs during winter and in summer tunneled into the mountain near his cabin on the Crooked Fork. When Carl and Andrew Erickson weren't trapping, they mined along the Crooked Fork and in Papoose Creek. Even Jerry Johnson built a system of ditches and in springtime caught water from the melting snow to wash the gravel near his cabin on the banks of the Lochsa. Meanwhile, all—trappers, prospectors, and travelers through the country—kept a watchful eye for the spot where Isaac had found his gold.

During the summer of 1886, Jerry Johnson and his partner at the time, Billy Rhodes, and another man extended their search north of the Lolo Trail to the headwaters of Cayuse Creek, a stream whose waters flow into the North Fork of the Clearwater River (see map 2).[82] Huge ice sheets had lain heavily on that land in ancient times, and as the ice receded it had formed cliffs and benches on the mountainsides and had ground millions of yards of gravel into the streams. Though far from Isaac's "snow" and "sun," it seemed a good place to search for placer gold.

They found only slight traces of gold. But a tributary flowing into Cayuse Creek from the north had chunks of heavy, black rock embedded in its gravel bars, and it was easy to follow the trail of broken "float" upstream. Within two days they traced the ore to its source. The dull luster of silver and lead and stains of copper showed in outcrops of rock scattered on a mountain near the head of the drainage.

But Jerry Johnson wasn't interested. Though the heavy ore obviously held a rich mixture of metals, Johnson wanted gold. And unless the nuggets could be handpicked from crushed quartz, he preferred placer gold where he could wash the treasure from the gravel with his sluice box and pan. So Johnson journeyed on into obscurity in Lochsa prospecting annals. Billy Rhodes, however, staked claims and began digging into the outcrops to determine the extent of the ore and whether the lead was richer below the surface of the earth.

Billy Rhodes was big, bony, and part black. In 1860 or 1861, he had joined with Captain Pierce in the first gold discoveries in the Clearwater

Lafe Williams at the cabin built in 1886 by Rhodes, Crane, and Altmiller. From here Williams prospected the Blacklead area during the late 1800s and early 1900s.
—U.S. Forest Service

country and had staked some of the richest claims at the Pierce City prospects. By the time he and Johnson discovered the heavy ore, his once black, curly hair had turned snow white, but he could still swing pick and shovel hour after hour with scarcely a pause. He knew that his quartz claims, situated as they were deep in the wilderness, were a long shot so far as economic returns were concerned. Nonetheless, he journeyed out of the mountains and reported his find to John Silcott and John Risse of Lewiston, Idaho, who had grub-staked his prospecting expedition. The discovery, coupled with Rhodes's reputation for finding gold, created such enthusiasm that his backers sent eighteen-year-old Frank Altmiller and a man named Hass Crane to return with Rhodes and begin developing a mine.[83]

Little time remained to prepare for winter, so they hurried back to the mountains with their pack animals loaded with grub and equipment. Building a cabin had first priority. They selected a site on a small bench near the claims where the red leaves of frost-nipped huckleberry bushes mingled with boulders and pale green clumps of beargrass. Whitebark pines, hemlocks, and firs would shade the spot in summer and thwart the howling blizzards sure to smite the land in winter. Cold spring water was handy, as were dead trees for firewood for cooking their grub and warming the cabin. From the bench, the miners could look out on intimate glades bordered by tall alpine firs; their spire tops shone deep green at midday but stood black against the early morning sun. Lolo peak, Snowy (later renamed Ranger Peak), the Heavenly Twins, Blodgett, and El Capitan, as well as other peaks unnamed at the time, shaped the distant skyline, all old friends of those who had searched for Isaac's gold.

With vigorous pick and shovel work, they leveled a spot big enough to build a cabin with inside measurements of twelve feet by sixteen feet. They cut ten- to twelve-inch-diameter logs from trees on the nearby slopes, and then notched these together securely at the corners until each wall stood seven logs high. Seven ridge logs supported the roof, and these extended to form a porch for storing wood and to make it possible to open the door when their structure was buried in snow. Twenty-four-inch-long shakes split from whitebark pines and nailed to the ridge logs completed the cabin. The floor was dirt, and there was no window.[84] But the cabin was warm and dry. As soon as they had moved in, they began digging their mine.

All went well until sometime in mid-winter when Billy Rhodes took ill and died. Because the snow was fifteen feet deep, Crane and Altmiller could find no place to bury Billy's body. So they stashed it in the snow and, according to some stories, tied it to a tree so that his remains would not slide down the mountain when the snow melted in the spring. When bare ground reappeared in early June, Crane and Altmiller buried Billy

The remains of Beaver Jack's cabin at the site of his Blacklead claims, ca. 1975.

Ernest Hansen, one of five brothers who located Blacklead claims in 1905, at his camp on Cayuse Creek in 1956.

Rhodes in the beautiful land where he had dug the last of his many prospect holes.

Though Billy Rhodes passed into the prospector's hereafter, the adventure of the heavy black outcrops had barely begun. Sometime in the late 1800s, Lafayette "Lafe" Williams, then a cashier in an Idaho bank, staked several claims, which he consolidated in 1904 and called "the Blacklead Group." (The mountain on which the claims were located was thereafter known as Blacklead Mountain. See map 2.) In 1905, the Hansen brothers—Ernest, Julius, Edward, Art, and Kid—moved in. Interest in the discovery ran high, and several other people staked claims, including Beaver Jack, Bill Parry, Fred Bearlock, and the Gerbers,[85] who at that time operated the gateway to the Lochsa at Lolo Hot Springs. There was considerable speculation at Kooskia and Lolo Hot Springs that a railroad might be built over the Lolo Pass; thus, the miners foresaw an opportunity to haul their ore out of the wilderness by rail.

Reflecting their visions of wealth, the miners bestowed the name "Silver Creek" on the stream traced by Rhodes and Johnson, and in summer its basin rang with axe blows, horse bells, and the clatter of picks and shovels. Charcoal smoke drifted from the forges as the miners sharpened their drilling steel. The dull whomps of black powder exploding and shattering rock occasionally smothered the clanging of hammers on anvils. The Hansen brothers, Beaver Jack, and Bill Parry built cabins on their claims.[86] The railroad was coming; Blacklead was booming. There on the northern border of the land of the Lochsa miners had at last found traces of treasure to be dug from the earth.

So they dug and they hoped. During winter the Hansens trapped in the basins where martens, lynx, foxes, and ermines flourished in the boulder patches, glades, and mature forests. Never mind that winter winds piled snow in forty-foot-deep cornices on the ridges. Never mind that several tunnels deep within the earth failed to show pay dirt. Never mind that thirty miles of rocky trails stretched between their cabins and the outpost at Lolo Hot Springs, Montana, or that it took six days of hard travel to pull a loaded pack train from Kooskia, Idaho, to their dreamland on the mountain. The miners considered such hurdles mere stepping stones to prosperity. Their Blacklead mine was going to grow into something big, and they were going to grow right along with it.

But at the peak of its promise, harbingers of the dream's end began to appear. During August 1910, a year of unprecedented drought in the mountains, huge fires roared up from the North Fork of the Clearwater. Except for an isolated patch of forest spared here and there by some twist of nature, the whole country burned, including the alpine forests shading the Blacklead claims. Banded together in common defense, the miners saved the cabin built by Billy Rhodes and later occupied by Lafe Williams. The Hansens' cabin burned.[87] Ironically, the fire spared two giant spruces standing barely twenty feet from the cabin's porch, as the conflagration roared on to the south and east. Flames crowning through the trees reduced the rich habitat of the deer, elk, and furbearers to smoking ruin. The great forces of nature had struck a blow in the Clearwater—1910 was one of those infrequent, dry years when fire destroyed the old and regenerated plant life anew on the land.

It took hours after the flames roared past for the burn to cool. When the smoke lifted, thousands of blackened snags surrounded the Blacklead claims where green forests had covered the earth only the day before. Here and there a smoldering trunk crashed to the ground as its roots let go of the earth. Dust devils spun on the lee side of ridges. The cone-shaped tornadoes scattered ash high in the air, and the ash drifted on the wind, settling back to the blackened earth, and then rising again to cloud the sky. It seemed to the miners that the land would never be the same again, certainly not during their lifetime. The forests were dead and the animals gone, and in the aftermath of that awesome transition, some sensed that they might soon be going, too.

Bill Parry trailed his packstring out to Lolo Hot Springs and engaged mining engineer Charles M. Allen to examine the True Fisher claims in the Silver Creek basin below Blacklead Mountain. Allen's report was negative. Nor could he encourage the others, not even the Blacklead group worked by Williams.[88] Soon after that, the railroad companies gave up the idea of laying tracks along the Lochsa River and over the Lolo Pass, thereby dashing ambitions to ship ore out of the mountains by rail. One by one the miners abandoned their claims, leaving their cabins, humble furnishings, tools, and hopes to rust and decay in the heart of the Clearwater's mountains. Among the last to go, the Hansens abandoned their claims about 1915. Only Williams hung on. Year after year he outfitted at Lolo Hot Springs, then followed an Indian road past Pilot Knob and along the Lochsa–North Fork divide to his Blacklead claims.

Talk at Lolo Hot Springs had it that "somewhere over there old Williams struck."[89] If he did, nobody knows where. But each summer found him on the trail, a handsome old man, erect in the saddle, his snow-white hair and beard shaded by a dusty felt hat. Mounted on a

Fires like those of 1910, though destructive in the short term, left an eerie beauty in their wake.
—Robert W. Mutch

strong horse he trailed four pack animals, each laden with provisions secured to the sawbuck saddles with diamond hitches. Dust puffed up from the trail as Lafe led his pack train through the ghostlike remnants of the great burn of 1910. The stately, fire-killed snags, bleached by wind, sun, and rain, were nearly as white as Lafe's beard. Now and then his battered hat would point back as he scanned his pack train's loads. But mostly he peered ahead, toward his cabin and claims and toward the mountain where the lure of treasure and the beauty of the land, even fire-blackened land, had seized his energy and his soul.

In about 1926, Lafe Williams led his pack train out of the Blacklead country for the last time. Suffering acutely from prostate trouble, he appreciated little of the abundant natural wonders on the way, for it took his full concentration to stay in the saddle and hang on to the lead rope as his horses scrambled up and down the steep trail. He barely made his way out to Lolo Hot Springs. Too sick to ride any longer, he dismounted along Granite Creek and walked and crawled the last mile to Sarah and Herman Gerber's doorstep at the resort hotel. That night Herman took him to a hospital in Missoula, Montana. So far as is known, Lafe Williams never saw his beloved mountains again.[90]

The dream of riches from the Blacklead claims ended shortly after the 1910 fires, though an occasional wandering prospector picked through the old workings. Moreover, no one had found the slightest trace of Isaac's gold in the land of the Lochsa. Most serious prospectors gave up the search, leaving the land to the trappers, several of whom had an eye for metallic treasure as well as for furs.

Tending his traplines in the Grave Mountains, Frank Kube was a long ways from his native Germany but very close to the legend of Isaac's mine. He set traps for marten along the ridge near Isaac's grave, and his home cabin at Sneakfoot Meadows stood in the very basin addressed by Isaac as he pointed and said, "See snow." Fascinated by the legend, Kube watched for signs of Isaac's gold while he trapped.

Late summer 1913 seemed an ordinary time to Kube as he packed in supplies and cut wood at his cabins at Powell's Flat, Kube Park, and Sneakfoot Meadows. After trailing his horses out to Lolo Hot Springs, he returned on foot accompanied by his collie dog, Pete Boy, to hunt elk before deep snow drove the animals down from the vicinity of his high-country cabins. While hunting near one of his cabins, he became entangled in a dense forest of lodgepole pines, the kind of place the mountain men called "dog hair thickets." Finding no game there, Kube

Frank Kube and his dog Pete Boy at Lolo Hot Springs about 1911. —Louise Gerber Gilbert

worked his way downhill toward a little canyon where he could escape the tangle and resume hunting in more open terrain.

Near the bottom he chanced upon a small clearing, and from that vantage point he scanned the canyon's slopes, rifle ready, for signs of elk. Nothing moved. His attention then centered on the opening before him, which he at once recognized as no natural clearing. Someone had made it. He spotted the blackened stones of an old cooking fire and beyond that, bent and broken by deep wintertime snow, an assortment of tepee poles leaning against a fire-killed snag. Kube had chanced upon an old Indian camp in an unusual place. Far from any Indian road, there was no obvious reason for anyone to stay down in that hole, except . . .

With Isaac's moose-hunting story bombarding his mind, Kube strode to the shallow streambed and scooped his drinking cup full of sand and gravel. He knelt there beside the brooklet sifting the gravel through his fingers. Multicolored pebbles, black sand, and mica crossed his palm, and then he saw it: Gold—coarse, yellow, heavy gold! He stroked his blonde walrus mustache and looked at Pete Boy. The collie's tail wagged as his nose sniffed in the mixture of pine resin, sweat, and woolen underwear. His master had found something good, and what was good for Kube was obviously good for Pete Boy, too.

That's the way Kube told the story to Fred Schott and Frank Smith at the Powell's Flat cabin in the late fall of 1913.[91] With supper over and the dishes scrubbed, the trappers gathered near the cabin's crude hearth. Kube threw a chunk of dry lodgepole pine on the fire and hunkered in front of it. Pete Boy likely rested on his stomach at Kube's side, eyes closed, senses dulled by the cabin's warmth, his nose wrinkling to be sure that the smell of wood and smoke and sweat did not go away. In the dim light of the yellow flames, Kube's slightly rounded shoulders trembled with excitement as he told of discovering Isaac's gold. To have found the gold fulfilled a dream; to share the discovery with trusted friends climaxed events of a lifetime.

"This is the last winter we'll have to trap," Kube said. "I've found the gold. It's too late to do anything this fall. But next spring we'll go in and get it."[92]

With that they parted, each to his separate way, after furs and fortunes in the Lochsa's land of winter.

Spring came early in 1914. Day after day warm rains poured down on the snowpack, until by early March the ice had been disgorged and the rivers rose to rumbling torrents. All forks of the Lochsa flooded their banks, but the trappers had to cross them somehow to pack their furs out to Lolo Hot Springs. Frank and Fred teamed up and hiked out together. En route they saw no sign of Kube.

They waited at Lolo Hot Springs until all the trappers, save Kube, had slogged their way out of the mountains. Two weeks passed. Frank and Fred could stand the suspense no longer. Loading packsacks with grub and a blanket each, they snowshoed over Lolo Pass to find their friend. It took six days to reach Kube's cabin buried beneath the snow at the edge of Sneakfoot Meadows. In line with Kube's disciplined habits, the cabin was neat, with all equipment stored securely. A bull moose head hung on the porch. The attached tag showed that Kube had killed and caped it at the request of the Smithsonian Institution in Washington, D.C. On a homemade calendar pinned to the log wall near his bunk, Kube had written a final entry in early March, nearly a month before. The notation read: "Headed out to the Springs with fur."

Frank and Fred reasoned that, with the streams at flood stage, Kube could not have followed the Indian road past Isaac's grave and crossed the turbulent Lochsa River at Powell's Flat. They figured his probable route through the upper reaches of the Lochsa drainage. Following their hunch, they hiked southeast, crossing the White Sand Fork on a log jam. They found a foot log felled across Storm Creek by Kube. Being mountain men of a kind, their instincts led them from there to Big Island on the Crooked Fork of the Lochsa.

Big Island was the natural place to try to cross the Crooked Fork and reach shelter at Joe Eberle's cabin one-half mile upstream on the north bank. Fred and Frank had been gone from Lolo Hot Springs a long time when they stumbled through the rotten snow and found the fresh-cut stump and scattered chips where Kube had fallen a twelve-inch-diameter spruce. The log spanned swift, six-foot-deep water, forming a precarious bridge to the island. A man with good balance could walk across. Kube must have tried to do so and failed; no foot log spanned the channel on the far side of the island to the northern shore. The Crooked Fork of the Lochsa had claimed their friend and, as far as they could tell, Pete Boy had drowned with him.[93]

So ended a mountain man's trail of life. Only two men, Indian Isaac and Frank Kube, had ever seen the elusive Lochsa gold, and both of them had died on the verge of showing the location to someone else. When Kube and Pete Boy plunged into the icy waters of the Crooked Fork, the legend sprang anew.

Legends are important in man's interaction with mountains, especially mountains like those in the land of the Lochsa where wild beauty was everywhere but exploitable treasure seemed to be nowhere. Nobody needed legends at Pierce City or Elk City where the muck was rich in dust and nuggets. There, pilgrims had only to stake their claims and take the gold from the earth. But the Lochsa country boasted no paying mines. The Lochsa's mystique alone was not enough to keep the prospectors going. Men like Jerry Johnson and Billy Rhodes—and even those hooked on the beauty of the land, like Lafe Williams—had to have a dream to spur them on.

After 1912, wildness reclaimed the basins where Kube's axe blows once echoed in the forests. Time and weather and forest fires concealed all signs of Isaac's grave. But purpose remained in the wind, moaning among the weathered snags along the beautiful ridge where Isaac's parting words, "see snow" and "sun," began the legend of Lochsa gold.

Fur trapper and prospector Bob Boyd summed up the theme of the wind's song in the Grave Mountains when he said, "There's a lot out there that ain't found yet."[94]

7

The Government Stakes Its Claims

The pioneer ethics that evolved among the Lochsa's trappers and prospectors expected self-reliance and a sense of fair play from the region's few but hardy pilgrims. It was, for example, unacceptable, indeed dangerous, for a trapper to trespass in the established domain of another. A prospector might covet the claim of a neighbor, but he had better keep his thoughts to himself. Game could be killed for food, even used for baiting traps, but wasting meat was considered a breach of the unwritten code of the mountains. A person's past was not pried into. Each person earned either respect or disrespect from others for who and what he was, not for what he had been at some prior time. As an expression of hospitality and a demonstration of trust in others—friends, strangers, even enemies—cabin doors were never locked. Lochsa dwellers also expected each other to do their best to protect the lives of their wilderness neighbors. As they figured it, they could do everything for themselves and all that was necessary to help each other; the less they had to do with any kind of organized government, the better.

Nevertheless, two political events in Washington, D.C., in the 1870s would have much to do with the future of the Lochsa's mountain men. Concerned about widespread exploitation of federal timber lands, the Congress of the United States authorized the commissioner of agriculture in 1876 to appoint a competent person to study the forestry situation. Dr. Franklin B. Hough was chosen.[95] Two years later Congress passed the Timber and Stone Act, permitting a citizen to purchase from the public domain up to 160 acres of nonmineral land, chiefly valuable for timber and stone, at a cost of not less than $2.50 per acre.

Dr. Hough's appointment seemed to set the stage for controlling the use of the nation's public forests for the general welfare, but ironically in the Timber and Stone Act lay opportunity for individuals to acquire land and then pass it on to the lumber industry. Many persons, often financed by big corporations, bought land one day and deeded it to the same corporation the next. Congress began to fear that unbridled, fraudulent exploitation would destroy the western forests; consequently, in 1891 it repealed the Timber and Stone Act.

On March 3 of the same year Congress passed "an act to repeal timber-culture laws and for other purposes," section 24 of which gave the president of the United States authority to set aside federal forest reserves as public reservations.[96] By this time, the buffalo were gone from the prairies, the beaver had been trapped out of the valleys, men had ripped open the earth in search of gold, and people without a land conscience had begun to strip the forests from the mountains. In providing authority to set aside the reserves, the federal government for the first time seriously considered the destiny of the big mountain ranges bypassed by early settlement of the West. The Clearwater country with its Lochsa basin in the center was among the largest, most rugged, and least settled of all the wild country left to be grabbed by the pioneers.

President Benjamin Harrison established the first reserves, and Grover Cleveland followed his example by creating thirteen more on George Washington's birthday in 1897. Over four million acres in size, the Bitterroot was the largest among those new reserves. It included the mountainous land west of the Bitterroot Valley from the Lolo Fork to the Bitterroot River's headwaters, part of the Salmon River drainage, all of the Lochsa basin, and the remainder of the Clearwater country except the North Fork of the Clearwater River.

With a stroke of President Cleveland's pen, the United States had staked out the land of the Lochsa and much of its neighboring territory, to be held in public ownership for the common, conservative use of all the people. And on June 4, 1897, Congress, as part of "an Act making appropriations for sundry civil expenses of the Government . . . and for other purposes," allocated funds for surveying the boundary line between Idaho and Montana and for surveying the forest reserves. This act later became known as the Organic Administration Act because it also provided for protecting the forests against fire and destruction, authorized the appraisal and sale of timber, gave free use of timber and stone to settlers and miners, and generally authorized administration according to the reserves' stated purposes. The act provided: "No public forest reservation shall be established, except to improve and protect the forest within the reservation, or for the purpose of securing favorable conditions of water flows, and to furnish a continuous supply of timber for the use and necessities of the citizens of the United States; . . . but it is not the purpose or intent of these provisions, or of the Act providing for such reservations, to authorize the inclusion therein of lands more valuable for mineral therein, or for agricultural purposes, than for forest purposes."[97]

Responsibility for protecting and managing the reserves was assigned to the General Land Office; the surveying and mapping were to be done by the U.S. Geological Survey. Both were bureaus within the Department of Interior. In marked contrast to the lethargy demonstrated earlier by the government in protecting the rights of the Indians, those bureaus moved swiftly to implement their new missions.

Nonetheless, it took a long time for Washington politics to appear in the western mountains. Except for the scratching of prospectors, line blazing by trappers, and the guns of hunters, the pioneers had thus far brought nothing new to the Lochsa. Seen from the viewpoint of the land there was no good or evil, only a great system of climate, geology, and life flowing into the future from an ancient past. It was the injection of human values, including those of the newcomers, that led to labeling parts of the natural environment as bad or good. The 1897 act was a significant step in that human, political evolutionary process.

In 1898 the General Land Office began assigning rangers to patrol the Bitterroot Reserve, while the U.S. Geological Survey launched exploratory surveys of the uncharted territory. John Lieberg, a keen observer of nature and resources useful to civilized people, took charge of these explorations.

An early report by Lieberg reveals how the Timber and Stone Act had been employed in corporate land-grabbing schemes. He wrote that "the disposal of these lands under the Timber and Stone Act furnishes good arguments for the repeal of that act. The lands were originally purchased by individuals who, upon acquiring ownership, immediately transferred their holdings to lumber corporations. It is a matter of common report that the purchase money was supplied by these same corporations, and a bonus besides to cover the value of the individual's purchasing right under the law."[98]

Lieberg noted a variety of activities in and around the Bitterroot Reserve. He found a few rangers in the Bitterroot Valley fighting fires

To conserve water for irrigation in the valley below, settlers dammed this outlet from Big Creek Lake before forest rangers began patrolling the Bitterroots in 1898.

and examining claims to lands on the edges of the reserve. He also noted extensive logging underway. Ninety percent of the accessible, merchantable timber below Grantsdale already had been cut; above Grantsdale, five thousand acres at the mouth of Lost Horse Creek had been logged. All yellow pines had been harvested from Tin Cup Creek, and the valley bottom of the lower West Fork was logged off clean (see map 2).

But the settlers had been occupied with more than logging. Lieberg observed that trails had been constructed up Big Creek and Mill Creek and small dams built on their headwaters for the purpose of providing water to irrigate crops in the valley below. All of the major creeks flowing into the Bitterroot River from the west had been named by the settlers.

Such was the bustling situation on the eastern edge of the reserve near the turn of the century. Lieberg spent two summers exploring the Lochsa region. His observations and reports were colored by the cultural values of the day. The forests, he said, were indispensable in regulating snowmelt and water flows. He explained how the alpine fir served as nature's primary regulator of water on high and intermediate terrain: Its tall, conical shape permitted most of the wintertime snow to fall to the ground. Yet it provided ample shade to slow the snowmelt, thus prolonging the runoff and sustaining steady flows in the streams below.

He found substantial volumes of commercial-sized timber and described these in detail by species and lumber quality. He devoted much of his report to discussing how these trees might, at some time in the future, be harvested and transported to market.

Lieberg discovered that much of the area had been burned over by both ancient and recent fires. He blamed the Indians and the prospectors for starting fires and calculated that the area burned had increased three hundred percent per year since the prospectors swarmed across the mountains in the early 1860s. It did not occur to Lieberg that many fires might have been started by lightning. He viewed fires, regardless of their cause and without exception, as an enemy to be brought under strict control: "The after effects of fires in this region are various, but are always evil, without a single redeeming feature. They are far-reaching and lasting in their consequences, affecting the economic interests not alone of the communities situated adjacent to the burned districts, but even those in more remote localities. The primary interests involved are those of timber and water supply, and through them there is not a single industry which is not more or less affected."[99]

Explorer John Lieberg considered alpine firs to be important watershed trees because their conical shape shed snow to the ground and at the same time provided shade to delay snow melt.

The undisturbed condition of mountain meadows is needed to sustain water flow and regulate run-off into the streams of the Bitterroot mountains.

Lieberg reported that the high mountain meadows were water reservoirs of such importance that they could not be grazed or otherwise disturbed without serious adverse consequences to sustaining the water flow. He marked the southern extent of the range of two tree species, white pine and mountain hemlock. And, though others must have been present, he found only one cabin, Jerry Johnson's, in the entire Lochsa drainage.

Boom times prevailed to the west of the Bitterroot Valley as well. In the southwestern portion of the reserve and far distant from the Lochsa, the placer mining camps of Dixie, Florence, Elk City, and Warren still buzzed with activity, and new quartz lode discoveries near Buffalo Hump showed promise. The railroad reached the western gateway of Stuart, later called Kooskia, in 1899. Lieberg was excited about the possibility that the railroad would be extended up the Lochsa River and across Lolo Pass, thereby opening up the timber resources of the region adjacent to the line. Upriver from Kooskia, two farms had twenty acres under plow at Syringa, and two more farms of fifteen acres each were being worked at the junction of the Lochsa and Selway Rivers. From that point eastward, however, the works of the settlers remained practically unnoticeable throughout the Lochsa's wild interior.

Lieberg also recorded the natural resources that could be extracted from the land and sold in the marketplace, primarily water, timber, and minerals. He recommended measures to assure that these resources would be protected until the country could be made accessible by roads or a railroad. Unsurprisingly, he made only passing mention of the attributes of the land so cherished by the trappers—the solitude, the wildness, and the wildlife. After all, what possible good could a handful of trappers and a few cranky old grizzly bears contribute to a civilized society?

Perhaps most important, Lieberg's report confirmed the rugged character of the mountain barriers that had thus far shielded that natural land from the white settlers populating the West and their chopping, digging, and clamor. Lieberg, like Lewis and Clark before him in 1805 and 1806, viewed these peaks and canyons as obstacles to transportation and to development of the resources. Even the rangers assigned by the General Land Office had not reached the Lochsa interior by 1898–99, the time of Lieberg's survey. Consequently, Lieberg reported that the Bitterroot Reserve, especially the Idaho portion, was a difficult region to patrol effectively. Further, he said, "A much larger force of rangers than was stationed there last summer will be needed."[100]

The way the rangers came to the Lochsa country was no different than that of the arriving trappers or prospectors. At first the rangers

Rangers Than Wilkerson and Hank Tuttle at their new Alta Ranger Station southwest of Darby, Montana. These men built this first Forest Service ranger station in the United States in 1899.
—U.S. Forest Service

As it had for earlier pioneers, Kooskia, Idaho, became the headquarters for forest rangers who explored the Bitterroot interior from the west. —U.S. Forest Service

nibbled around the region's edges, and then, after establishing a foothold, they probed the interior. Only six rangers were appointed to the entire reserve in 1898, and four of those were based in the Bitterroot Valley. Pope Catlin and Mr. Veeder patrolled the South Fork of the Bitterroot River, while Ed Buker and Ben Lancaster worked out of the central valley town of Stevensville. During 1899 J. B. Weber was supervisor of the Montana portion of the reserve, and eight rangers patrolled from bases in the Bitterroot Valley. Two of these, H. C. Tuttle and Than Wilkerson, that same year built the first ranger station in the United States at a place called Alta on the West Fork of the Bitterroot River.[101]

Meanwhile, in 1898, the secretary of interior placed James Glendinning in charge of all reserves in Idaho. In 1899 ten rangers were assigned to patrol the Idaho portion of the Bitterroot Reserve. These men operated out of the town of Grangeville, Idaho, and they spent most of their time attempting to control timber cutting around the boom-and-bust mining camps of Elk City, Florence, Warren, and Buffalo Hump.[102]

Also in 1899 the highly respected Maj. Frank Fenn was assigned as supervisor of the Bitterroot Reserve and its headquarters, established

George Ring (back row, third from right) opened the Lolo Trail in 1902.
—U.S. Forest Service.

at Kooskia, Idaho. Kooskia thus became the gateway to the mountains for the rangers as it had been for the trappers, miners, and pilgrims before. More personnel were appointed on both sides of the mountains in 1900, and the rangers began extending their patrols deeper toward the Reserve's interior and the Lochsa country.

Appointed from the ranks of the frontiersmen, many of those first rangers possessed characteristics similar to those of the trappers and prospectors before them. The rangers' approach to the land and the people, however, was significantly different. Where the trappers and prospectors personified individuality and free choice, the rangers represented federal law and regulations written by a secretary of the interior far removed from the Lochsa's mountains. The tools of the trappers were traps, snares, and deadfalls; the prospectors', pick, pan, and shovel. But each ranger carried a book. Indeed, rangers may have introduced the first book to the land of the Lochsa, for the Bible of the missionaries was not commonly found in the packsacks of the trappers and prospectors.

The book of these first rangers was small—five by eight inches—with ninety-seven pages bound between its reddish brown covers. Its no-nonsense instructions began:

> The object of these reserves is to maintain forests on lands where they are needed for two principal reasons:
>
> 1. To furnish timber, a valuable and much-needed product, from lands which are unfit to produce a more valuable crop, such as corn and wheat.
>
> 2. To regulate the flow of water. This they do—
>
> (a) By shading the ground and snow and affording protection against the drying and melting action of the sun.
>
> (b) By acting as wind breaks, and thus protecting the ground and snow against the drying action of the wind.
>
> (c) By protecting the earth from washing away and thus maintaining a "storage layer" into which the rain and snow soak and are stored for the dry seasons, when snow and rain are wanting.
>
> (d) By keeping the soil more pervious, so that water soaks in more readily and more of it is thereby prevented from running off in time of rain or when the snow is melting.[103]

Regulate water flows, act as wind breaks, protect the earth from washing away, keep the soil pervious—seemingly redundant instructions for the functioning of the Lochsa forests. Had not the great forests always done these things, and more? Of course they had, at least before the coming of the whites and their exploitative ways. And the whites continued to come. They were chopping and digging around the edges of the Lochsa country, their attention riveted on the wealth to be gained from those resources hidden deep in the Lochsa's mountains.

The book's instructions continued: "Keeping in mind the object and purposes of the reserves and their forests, it is clear that the first and foremost duty of every forest officer is to care for the forest, and every act, every decision he is called upon to make should be guided by the thought, will it improve and extend the forest?"[104] Armed with their brown book, the rangers set out to demonstrate that the U.S. government was going to defend the land from gross misuse by individuals and corporations and in that way protect the people and the nation from long-term damage. There was no need to govern the natural systems of the Lochsa; rather, man was going to have to govern himself.

Since the reserves were to be open to use by the people, the ranger's book detailed procedures for him to follow in permitting activities. Prospecting and mining were not to be interfered with. Timber could

The first rangers to reach Fish Lake found a plentiful nook in the Lochsa mountains. They also confirmed that the Nez Perces had traveled there hundreds, perhaps thousands, of years before.

be sold, and in some cases settlers could obtain timber and stone free of charge. The book detailed procedures for making agricultural entries; building roads and trails; allowing grazing and other common activities; conveying rights of ways for ditches, canals, pipelines, reservoirs, railways, and telegraph and telephone lines; and making available building sites for schools, churches, hotels, and other business enterprises.

Fires, the book directed, were to be controlled at reasonable cost. Anyone caught setting or carelessly leaving a fire to burn was to be prosecuted. The rangers' prescribed duties included stopping trespasses on the reserves, assisting state authorities in protecting game, managing timber sales, planting trees, examining land claims, supervising livestock grazing, surveying land and timber, and constructing trails, bridges, cabins, and other improvements.

The book left no doubt that the reserves were to be used by the people and that the rangers were to regulate that use according to instructions from Washington. The trouble was, any decision of consequence had to be approved by the secretary of interior. The central government not only wrote the rules, it retained the authority to direct their enforcement. That kind of centralized control would never be understood or accepted by the free-spirited frontiersmen—nor, indeed, by some of the rangers themselves.

Native cutthroat trout from Fish Lake, 1975.

By 1902 the General Land Office's rangers began reaching into the Lochsa from the west. Ranger George Ring opened the Lolo Trail that year.[105] While the axe blows of his crew echoed in the saddles crossed by Lewis and Clark, other rangers hacked logs to reopen the Indian hunting road, whose tracks were fast growing indistinct where the road wound past the cool springs along Spirit Ridge to the south.

By 1904 rangers E. H. Clark, Dan Dunham, and James Stuart had reached the beautiful Fish Lake Basin (see map 2).[106] Situated in a hanging valley beneath the divide separating the Lochsa and Selway Rivers, the one-hundred-acre lake gleams as a rare gem even in the water-rich Bitterroot Range. Since the lake and its tributary streams host thousands of trout, it was then, as now, a place impossible to overlook by mountain men in search of a campsite. Like those early-day rangers, I too have camped many times at Fish Lake. There, captured by the thoughtful mood of a summer evening, it is easy for me to imagine ranger Jim Stuart, in the prime of life at age 32, catching fish for supper.

Those trout were hard to see in the water. But when one rose from the depths to strike Stuart's hackled fly, his red throat would flash in the evening sun, thrashing clear water into a spray of droplets. Ultimately, Jim would haul the red-bellied trout ashore and string him on a forked branch cut from the pigmy willows bordering the stream. He fished upstream, stalking the trout from their rear, until he caught enough to feed himself and his partners at suppertime. Then, squatting on a sandbar, he would clean the trout, all the while smearing his face and neck with slime and sweat as he brushed away the bloodthirsty mosquitoes.

With the sun gone the mountains cooled, and smoke from the campfire would drift with the settling air down along the meadow and over the lake. Ranger Stuart had fish in the frying pan and a book in his pocket. The book, written in far-off Washington, told him how to conduct himself and how to manage the land that was once the birthright of his Nez Perce ancestors. At times like that he must have wondered at the future of it all.

Meanwhile, the forestry activities launched in the United States Department of Agriculture by Dr. Franklin B. Hough had gained both political recognition and professional capability. Gifford Pinchot, America's second educated forester (Bernhard E. Fernow was first), was prominent among the staff of the USDA's Forestry Division. Born to a family of social prominence and wealth, Pinchot had graduated from Yale in 1889 and, following the advice of his father, enrolled in the Nancy Forest School in France on November 13 that same year. He studied silviculture, forest organization, and forest law, concepts quite foreign to the contemporary frontier practices in the United States.

Gifford Pinchot rides in the Inaugural Parade in Washington, D.C., March 4, 1925. —U.S. Forest Service

While studying forestry in France, Pinchot received two pieces of advice that were destined to have great influence on his life and, therefore, the future of forestry in the United States. First, his father wrote: "It seems to me that you may fairly depend on this, that in a very short time there will be something to do in this country for the man best prepared to decide upon forestry matters." And, second, his respected teacher at the Nancy School, Professor Lucien Boppe, told him: "When you get home to America you must manage a forest and make it pay."[107]

Pinchot became acquainted with the Bitterroot mountains in 1896. In July and August, while scouting locations for forest reserves with Lt. George P. Ahren and Henry S. Graves, the country's third educated forester, Pinchot crossed the mountains from Hamilton, Montana, and spent three weeks exploring the Clearwater country.

Having learned a great deal about forestry, Pinchot in fact soon became the man who, in his father's words, was "best prepared to decide upon forestry matters." On Friday, July 1, 1898, Gifford Pinchot replaced Bernhard E. Fernow, then chief of the Forestry Division in the U.S. Department of Agriculture.

In his new job Pinchot assumed federal responsibility for forestry education, research, and extension. However, all was not well in bureaucracy. Pinchot himself described the problem this way: "But at this time all 43 million acres of forest reserves and several times more million acres of unreserved timber lands were in charge of the U.S. Department of Interior without a single forester to look after them."[108] In other words, the forestry skills of the nation in 1898 resided in the Department of Agriculture, while the government's forest lands were under the control of the Department of Interior. Gifford Pinchot was not going to let that situation prevail for long.

Meanwhile, many citizens of the West resented the government curbing their exploitation of the woods. To make matters worse, the General Land Office appointed supervisors and rangers from the ranks of political favorites. Though some good men were hired, the many incompetents among them eroded the public trust.

Pinchot was outspoken in his criticism of the USDI's management. Following a trip through the western reserves in 1899, he said, "It was awful." Later, in his autobiography, he wrote: "However lightly the western men of those days may have held the land laws, they had high standards of personal courage and hardiness, and they were not lazy. Such men could have nothing but contempt for a service manned by the human rubbish which the Interior Department had cheerfully accepted out of the eastern and western political scrap heaps and dumped into the forest reserves."[109]

On September 14, 1901, an assassin shot President William McKinley at the Pan American Exposition in Buffalo, New York. When, on that same day, outdoorsman Theodore Roosevelt took the oath as president of the United States, the wild country that remained, like the land of the Lochsa, gained a friend in the nation's highest office. Roosevelt made this clear in a presidential message delivered on December 2, 1901: "The fundamental idea of forestry is the perpetuation of forests by use. Forest protection is not an end in itself; it is a means to increase and sustain the resources of our country and the industries which depend upon them." Regarding the administration of the forest reserves, he added: "These various functions should be united in the Bureau of Forestry, to which they properly belong. The present diffusion of responsibility is bad from every stand point."[110]

Pinchot had made his point with the new president; even Secretary of Interior Ethan A. Hitchcock agreed to the transfer. On February 1, 1905, Congress passed an act transferring the administration of the forest reserves from the Department of Interior to the Department of Agriculture, thus sowing the seeds of a new United States Forest Service. The forest reserves were not designated by Congress as national forests, however, until March 4, 1907.

Bitterroot National Forest headquarters at Kooskia, Idaho, about 1907. Left to right: Summer Rachliff, Jack Fitting, Lou Harrington, Major Frank Fenn, and a Forest Service clerk.
—Elmer Walde, U.S. Forest Service

Pinchot and his men were ready; indeed, they chafed at each political delay in passing the Transfer Act. By July 1, 1905, they had distributed a new book to the field men titled *Use of the National Forest Reserves*, which on July 1, 1906, was replaced by *The Use Book*. And it was no accident that its title emphasized "USE" in large capital letters. Pinchot was a master politician. The mood of the frontiersmen was to *use* the bounty from the reserves. Pinchot's education in France emphasized use, especially commercial use. Already he had managed the Biltmore Estate, a large private forest near Asheville, North Carolina, and, as instructed by Professor Boppe, had made it pay.

The Bureau of Forestry's new green *Use Book* included instructions similar to the General Land Office's brown book. It reserved most decisions of consequence for headquarters in Washington and required a system of reports to provide decision-making intelligence to Pinchot and his staff. But the *Use Book* also included some new ideas. It incorporated a letter written by Gifford Pinchot and signed by Secretary of Agriculture "Tama Jim" Wilson, directing, among other things: "In the administration of the forest reserves it must be clearly borne in mind that all land is to be devoted to the most productive use of the permanent good of the whole people and not for the temporary benefit of individuals or companies."

In a statement tending on the contradictory, however, Wilson's letter left no doubt that he viewed the industrial good as synonymous with the public good: "The continued prosperity of the agricultural, lumbering, mining and live-stock interests is directly dependent upon a permanent and accessible supply of water, wood and forage, as well as upon the present and future uses of these resources under business-like regulations, enforced with promptness, effectiveness and common sense." After directing that the needs of the dominant industries would be considered first, he capped his policy statement by stating: ". . . where conflicting interests must be reconciled, the question will always be decided from the stand point of the greatest good of the greatest number in the long run."[111]

This was to be the bureau's long-term policy. There would be many conflicting interests to reconcile, and it was going to take some competent men and women to do the job. By the presidential order of December 17, 1904, all persons employed on the forest reserves were classified under the federal Civil Service and were required to pass qualifying examinations.

The *Use Book* established the following qualifications for rangers:

> To be eligible as a ranger of any grade the applicant must be, first of all, thoroughly sound and able-bodied, capable of enduring hardships and of performing severe labor under trying conditions. Invalids seeking light out-of-door employment need not apply. No one may expect to pass the examination who is not already able to take care of himself and his horses in regions remote from settlement and supplies. He must be able to build trails and cabins, shoot, ride, pack, and deal tactfully with all classes of people. He must know something of land surveying, estimating and scaling timber, logging, land laws, mining and the live stock business.[112]

Though they posed nothing new to many frontiersmen, requirements like these would weed out most of the incompetents appointed under the General Land Office administration. The *Use Book* further required the assignment of expert forest inspectors who would assure that the book's provisions were carried out by the supervisors, rangers, and assistant rangers responsible for each reserve.

Forest rangers hired under the Bureau of Forestry (Forest Service) policies patrolled large areas and supervised assistant rangers assigned to get the needed work done in designated locales. In 1908 Gifford

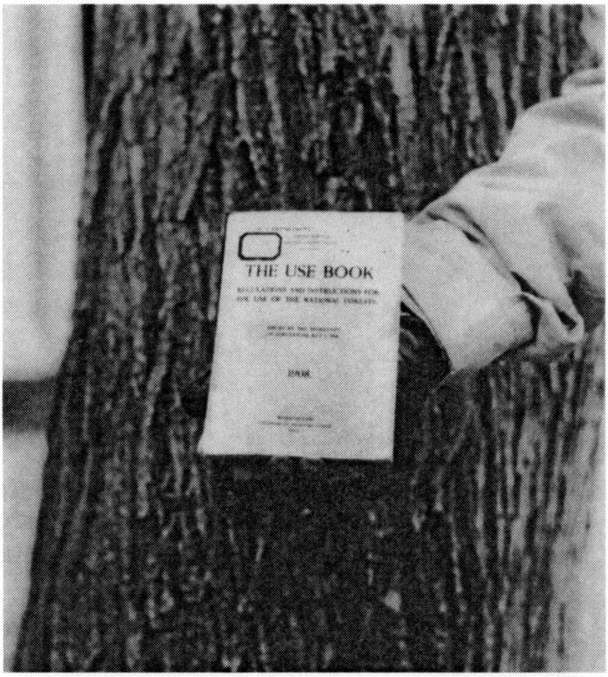

First published in 1906, the early issues of The Use Book *represents the beginning of the present-day Forest Service manual system.*

Pinchot's staff revised the *Use Book* to require that "ranger districts be established and rangers who are qualified by training and experience will be placed in charge of them. As a rule, assignment will be to permanent districts rather than specific lines of work."

Following this direction, the Forest Service divided the Idaho portion of the Bitterroot Reserve into fourteen districts.[113] Until then, the mountain men of the isolated upper Lochsa had rarely seen a ranger. But the establishment of ranger districts set the stage for their multiplication. The great powers of Washington had spoken through the *Use Book*, and more specific territorial lines were drawn around the domains of the prospectors, trappers, and grizzly bears.

8

The Coming of the District-Based Rangers

Sometime near the turn of the century Charley Powell, probably already in his late fifties, laid claim to the flat beside the Lochsa River where the Lewis and Clark party had camped and killed a colt for food on September 14, 1805. Charley filed no papers, nor did he mark the boundaries of his claim. Instead, using logs cut from the nearby forest, he simply built a one-room cabin about twelve by fourteen feet in size. He dug a ditch across the flat to divert water from the nearby stream so it would flow past the cabin's porch to supply his kitchen and irrigate

Ranger Frank Smith and Jay Turner at Charley Powell's cabin about 1910. —U.S. Forest Service

Supervisor Major Fenn, his staff, and rangers gather at Station Number One on April 1, 1911. Elk Summit ranger Adolph Weholt is number 9 in the photo. Powell ranger Frank Smith is number 17. —U.S. Forest Service

a small vegetable garden. The waters of the ditch also flowed through Charley's cooler, a small log structure he fashioned to protect vegetables, meat, butter, and lard from the heat of summer.

Charley trapped furs during winter. In summer he lived in a kind of natural theater created by the surrounding forests and mountainsides, whose acoustics spread the song of the river throughout the valley and into his heart. In springtime fifteen-pound steelhead trout spawned on the gravel bars, and, until the ice locked the riffles in the fall, both rainbow and cutthroat could be taken at will from the river's pools. That's why, years before Charley's time, Indians from both east and west of the mountains often camped there. They had constructed a weir to catch fish in the channel a short ways upstream from the spot where Charley's cabin stood. The trappers and prospectors called the site Powell's Flat, in recognition of Charley's occupancy.

There, during summer afternoons, Charley would tend his garden while the sun fell toward the horizon down river to the west. Banded together in the shade of a lodgepole pine, the horses dozed, now and then one switching a horsefly from his rump or stomping to dislodge another from his legs. It was too early in the evening for the night hawks to scoop mosquitoes in mouth-open dives through the sky, or for the small owls

Forest Service Station Number One, thought to be the first in the Middle Fork area, was the take-off point for rangers and pack trains probing into the interior of the Lochsa and Selway country. —Carl Weholt, Lou Hartig collection, Clearwater National Forest

to screech their delight at the end of day and beginning of night. Except for the Lochsa's song, the scraping of Charley's hoe, and a soft westerly breeze whispering in the pines, it was quiet there on the flat. Charley lived alone with his cabin, his garden, his mountains, and his river.

Then one evening in late June 1909 he heard voices followed by the pounding of hooves resonating in the surface of the earth. While the sounds of men and stock grew louder, Charley closed the gate in the pole fence surrounding the garden and strode out on the flat to meet the newcomers as they rode into the clearing.

A wiry, slight of build, dark-haired man with a walrus mustache rode ahead on a strong gray horse, leading eight heavily laden pack horses. Four more mounted men followed. It was a big outfit. Excited by the sudden invasion, Charley's horses nickered and milled around the loaded pack train. In swirling dust, the dark-haired leader dismounted, dallied one rein around his saddle horn, dropped the other to the ground, and, with a stiff gait borne of days in the saddle, walked up to Charley. He introduced himself as Frank Smith, forest ranger, and said that he intended to set up camp there that summer. Charley would respond, "Glad to have ye." Then, in the custom of the mountains, add, "While you tend them horses, I'll boil up a pot o' coffee."

This mule team hauled supplies from Kooskia to Station Number One in 1917. Driver is unknown. —Carl Weholt, Lou Hartig collection, Clearwater National Forest

Ranger Smith's expedition into the Lochsa's interior had begun seven days earlier at Station Number One (Middle Fork R. S.), road's end on the Clearwater River twenty-five miles upstream from Kooskia, Idaho (see map 2). Middle Fork district ranger Joseph McGhee had helped him assemble and cargo equipment for the journey. The first ranger ever assigned with headquarters at Powell's Flat, Smith led a crew of competent woodsmen, all experts in using an axe or crosscut saw. They had loaded the pack train while dew still clung to the grasses at Station Number One, then followed the trail eastward over gentle terrain along the Middle Fork of the Clearwater River. By the time they reached the settlement of Lowell, the packs had settled snugly into the sling ropes.

First night out they stayed in a new cabin on the bar near where Pete King Creek flows into the Lochsa. Next morning they climbed the ridge east of the creek to reach the Lolo Trail. They found much of the mountains still covered with snow, but the firm snow supported their horses' weight. So Smith's party turned east and followed the trail toward the crest of the Bitterroots, much as Lewis and Clark had done during their return from the mouth of the Columbia River 103 years earlier.

The Lolo Trail bustled with activity in 1909. Several parties of miners had already passed en route to the Blacklead claims. The pack trains of

The log Pete King Station at right center was new when Frank Smith stayed there en route to Powell in 1909. By 1921, the time of this photo, roads and automobiles had arrived. —U.S. Forest Service

the Northern Pacific and Oregon Railroad and Navigation (Union Pacific) companies—competing to finish the first railroad surveys up the Lochsa and over Lolo Pass—followed close on Smith's heels. A railroad was coming. Forest fires had to be controlled. Haste ruled the times, yet much of the Lochsa's wilderness remained unknown, frequented only by trappers and prospectors who mattered little in comparison with the great industrial development expected to impact the land. Ranger Smith had much to do in little time to assure that the resources of the Lochsa achieved the greatest good for the greatest number.

Smith's party followed the Lolo Trail past the Devil's Chair, a prominent tower of granite shaped like a giant's throne. Each night their cooking fires gleamed at or near the same campsites used by General Howard as he pursued Chief Joseph's band across the mountains in 1877. On the fifth day of their journey, the party topped the ridge at Indian Post Office, and Frank Smith got his first expansive view of the land he was to bring under government control in line with instructions in his brand new *Use Book*.

There seemed no end to it. At close foreground he could tell the firs from the pines and that the beargrass had not yet bloomed and that the tracks in the trail leading east had been left by a mule deer only the night before. But that detail faded in the distance until the mountains all looked

The Devil's Chair, a prominent landmark along the Lolo Trail.

alike. Nothing stood out of the hazy mass except a patch of white fog in the valley and the snowfields gleaming along the Bitterroot crest. Fires, both old and new, had scarred the slopes of the Lochsa River to the south and also the mountains beyond. But to the east, the Lochsa's upper basin consisted of dark landscapes of mature forests broken only here and there by the architecture of random fires, most of them less than three hundred acres in size. Halfway to the Bitterroot crest and deep in the hazy center of Smith's universe, the Lochsa's valley forked and two great tributaries reached out into the distance—Crooked Fork to the north and White Sand (named Colt Killed Creek by Lewis and Clark) to the south. Smith was going down there to the center of the Lochsa world, two days travel from his vista on the high divide at Indian Post Office. He had never been there, but he had heard that Powell's Flat would be a fine headquarters for his ranger district. His instructions from Supervisor Fenn gave high priority to clearing trails, fighting fires, and building phone lines eastward to connect with Lolo Hot Springs, gateway to the Bitterroot Valley.

The big gray horse would paw impatiently and nudge Frank's back with his nose. Gripping mane and reins in his left hand and the pack train lead rope in his right, Smith would step up on the stirrup, ease

The immensity of the Lochsa region is apparent in this partial view of what ranger Smith saw from Indian Post Office while en route to his district headquarters at Powell's Flat in 1909.

into the wear-polished saddle seat, and ride along the ridge marked by ancient Indians with cairns of stone. Half turned in the saddle, he would assure that the diamond hitches held tight and that the packs on all eight horses rode in balance. Then his attention would again center on the maze of ridges and canyons in the Lochsa where he was supposed to govern the land and what the people did with the land.

Meanwhile, near the headwaters of the White Sand Fork of the Lochsa, another pioneer ranger, Adolph Weholt, climbed up from the canyon lands of East Moose Creek (the Nez Perce's Kakayahneme Creek) toward the 7,560-foot-high summit of Diablo Mountain.[114] He picked his way through granite slab rock that had tumbled down during the Cretaceous period 135 million years before, when pressure from deep within the earth thrust the massive peak skyward. He could hear the saws and axes down in the canyon where his four-man crew were cutting logs to widen the old Indian hunting road leading toward Lost Horse Pass. The echoes of their lusty blows, mingled with the roaring East Fork Falls, faded as he climbed and then fell silent altogether when the shoulder of the mountain cut Weholt off from both the canyon's sight and sound.

This stone cairn and others nearby were thought by early-day travelers of the Lolo Trail to be ancient message centers used by the Indians.

Like Ranger Smith, Weholt had launched his expedition into the wilderness from Station Number One at road's end on the Middle Fork of the Clearwater. His instructions from Supervisor Fenn: "Go find the Elk Summit district, select a place for a headquarters, and begin opening the Indian trails."[115]

It had taken all of July and part of August to get to East Moose Creek Falls at the base of Diablo Mountain. After leaving Station Number One in early July, Weholt's group forded the Lochsa at Lowell—no easy task in early summer—then trailed up the Selway River to Three Links Creek, detoured the Selway's then-trailless gorge by climbing up over Sixty-two Ridge, then traveled down a long, steep ridge to reach Moose Creek a short ways above its confluence with the Selway. From there they followed Indian and trapper trails, cutting logs and grading a roadbed with their mattocks and shovels to get their loaded pack train safely through the wilderness. When near the falls, Weholt calculated Elk Summit to be somewhere to the north. While his crew worked on the trail, he climbed up onto the divide between the Lochsa and Selway Rivers to locate a site for his ranger station (see map 2).

Diablo Mountain stands in the heart of the Bitterroots. When Ranger Weholt gained its summit he saw the treeless alps of the Lochsa standing guard over forested basins where nothing, least of all the whims of hu-

Here is a portion of Ranger Weholt's view from Diablo Mountain while searching for Elk Summit in 1909.

mans, hurried or slowed the land's natural processes. There was no end to that landscape within his power to see. No roads, no towns, no farms. Only mountains so extensive that he knew of nothing to which their vastness compared. Immensities of granite, that's what they were, at a standstill in human history yet flowing like a vast ocean in geologic time.

A humbling sense of integration with all creation must have possessed the ranger who had come to rule the land. Surely he knew it was good for the soul to be dwarfed by eternity. But he was supposed to be in charge of the place, to bring government regulations to the mountains, its men, and its errant bears. Momentarily thrust by the overwhelming scene into the maelstrom of geological oblivion, he must have wondered how one person could hope to regulate such an overpowering natural region.

His gaze would have followed the valley of the White Sand northward across the Lochsa basin's lush forests to its turn around the shoulder of the Grave Mountains. Somewhere out there near the big bend,

Fish Lake Ranger Station, ca. 1909. —U.S. Forest Service

Smith and his crew were also establishing a ranger district. Weholt knew that, and he was glad. Though the spell of the mountains transcended the rules in his *Use Book*, the work of the government had to be done. He was only a speck, but he was a significant speck; and with Smith out there someplace in that wilderness, at least he was not alone.

From Diablo's summit Weholt saw his headquarters site—hundreds of acres of lush meadows gleaming in a saddle on the Lochsa-Selway divide only three miles to the west. A sparkling brook threaded through the meadows, and young trees were beginning to reforest the adjacent land following a recent fire. Where old forests had once stood, thousands of fire-killed snags were scattered ghostlike across the landscape. The snags, he reasoned, would provide dry logs for building cabins and wood for fueling cooking and heating fires. Their horses, lean from the demanding trip up the Selway, could fatten in the knee-deep grass of the meadows. Ranger Weholt had heard that trout populated the stream. And the map, prepared by John Lieberg during his survey of the reserves in 1898–99, revealed that the stream had its source in a small lake hidden from view behind the shoulders of a mountain.

Elk Summit was the headquarters he had been searching for. He returned to his crew camped in the canyon of East Moose Creek. The next day they retraced their steps for four miles, then followed the old

Indian hunting road up a steep ridge to the small lake situated barely on the Lochsa slope of the divide. After considering a wide choice of campsites, they selected a location a short ways—perhaps an eighth of a mile—below the lake where an elevated bench of decomposed granite overlooked Elk Summit's Horse Heaven Meadows.

As far as Ranger Weholt and his crew were concerned, when they pitched their tents at Elk Summit and cut the first snag for wood, they were pioneering the Bitterroot mountains. But ten years before their horse bells rang in the meadows, Wes Fales had built his trapping headquarters cabin at Big Sand Lake only eight miles away. Milt Savage had for many years run traplines on the ridges and in the valleys of the White Sand. And the ghosts of the Russian and Frank Meeks, other unknown trappers, and the Indians lurked in the hazy recesses of historical time.

By the time fall's chill daubed the mountain shrubs with red and yellow in 1909, the forest rangers had established territorial districts in all of the land of the Lochsa. Ranger Joe McGhee supervised the lower end of the Lochsa from his headquarters at Station Number One. Ray Fitting's district, with headquarters at Fish Lake, adjoined Adolph Weholt's, and together their two districts included the wild country in the head of the Lochsa and much of the Selway drainage as well. Ranger Smith's domain encompassed the Lochsa's great center and all of its north-central tributaries.[116] On Smith's border to the north, ranger John Durant had charge of the land where the water flowed to the North Fork of the Clearwater.

The district-based rangers in 1909 considered the region of the Lochsa an unclaimed landscape of public domain whose resources were to be protected for use by the people, whatever such uses might turn out to be. The trappers and prospectors had not claimed fee title to land. Though Charley Powell wanted to stay, he had filed no claim. Nevertheless, long before the rangers arrived the United States government had allocated much of the area in Smith and Weholt's districts to corporate ownership.

The 1850 Congress authorized the first land grants, in addition to rights-of-way, to corporations and states to help build railroads. The idea was that the railroads would finance construction by selling the land. Such land grants gave capitalists incentive to incorporate and invest. By 1857 grants had been made to extend railroads to the western boundaries of Louisiana, Arkansas, Missouri, Iowa, and Minnesota. Both the settlers of the West and the federal government wanted to hook the East to the West by one or more transcontinental railroads.

To this end Congress passed the Pacific Railroad Act of July 1, 1862, and on July 2, 1864, passed legislation that liberalized the original act. Of four companies chartered, two completed transcontinental railroads. One of these, the Northern Pacific Railroad Company, built the road that influenced land ownership in the headwaters of the Lochsa.

President Abraham Lincoln approved the incorporation of the Northern Pacific Railroad Company on July 2, 1864, for the purpose of building a railroad via the northern route from Lake Superior to Puget Sound. He granted a right-of-way 400 feet wide plus every "alternative section of public land, not mineral, designated by odd numbers to the amount of twenty alternative sections per mile, on each side of said railroad line, as said Company may adopt, through the Territories of the United States and ten alternative sections of land per mile on each side of said railroad whenever it passes through any State." Since only odd-numbered, alternate sections could be chosen, this primary grant reached out forty miles on each side of the right-of-way through the territories and twenty miles through the states. In order to compensate the railroad for mineral lands (to which it was not entitled) or lands already claimed, an in-lieu area of ten additional miles on each side was provided; and in 1870 Congress added a second ten-mile area to that.

So began the longest railroad in America—2,128 miles—with an estimated land grant of 45 million acres, 131,990 acres of which were situated in the heart of the Lochsa's uplands.

The company finished building the railroad in 1883, thereby qualifying for the land grants. But conveyance from public domain to the company could not be done until the land was surveyed, and surveyors did not reach the remote Lochsa until after the rangers came.[117]

So dawned a new day in the history of people and land in the Lochsa country. For four thousand years the Indians had come in summer and departed in winter; their hunting, fishing, camping, and travel barely scratched the earth. By 1864 President Lincoln had bartered Lochsa land for a cross-country railroad. Then in 1877 the Indians fled their homeland, pursued on that last trip through their mountains by General Howard and the United States Army. For a brief thirty-two years after that, trappers and prospectors roamed free, constrained only by the forces of nature and the codes of the hills respected among them. All that ended when the rangers took charge of their districts. It had to be, for throughout history nations have conquered or otherwise acquired land and then proceeded to govern the inhabitants (at best, in the interest of all; at worst, in the interest of the few holding money and power).

In the policy "the greatest good of the greatest number in the long run" lay the reason to govern the activities of some for the benefit of all—and "all" meant all citizens of the United States. From the moment Charley Powell welcomed Ranger Smith to Powell's Flat, the men of those mountains would never be so free again. The Nez Perce chiefs were gone and, for better or for worse, the United States government was ruling in their place.

9

The War of the Railroads

A *quarter century before the rangers established districts* in the Lochsa region, settlers from both east and west of the Bitterroot mountains wanted a more direct route from the gold discoveries of 1863 at Bannack and Virginia City, Montana, to water transportation at Lewiston, Idaho. Mullan's Road went too far to the north, and the shorter Indian routes were unsuitable for transporting heavy freight. Spurred by demands from the people of Lewiston, the U.S. government in 1865 appropriated $50,000 to locate and construct a wagon road across the Bitterroot mountains through Lolo Pass. The secretary of interior hired Wellington Bird, an engineer from Iowa, who organized a big outfit at Lewiston, including engineer George Nicholson; scientist Oliver Marcy; surveyor Maj. Sewell Traux; Idaho's first white settler, Col. William Craig; Nez Perce guide Tahtutash; and fifty laborers, cooks, teamsters, and blacksmiths.[118]

They left Lewiston on May 24, 1866. After scouting the area, Bird realized that the road could not be built with the money available. He decided instead to relocate and improve the most difficult sections of the Lolo Trail. Bird's crew eliminated many steep and dangerous portions of the trail by building new trails on contour grades between saddles and constructing switchbacks where the Indian trail led over the tops of the steep mountains. They cut back the brush and cleared fallen timber from the route. When they reached the Bitterroot Valley in October, 130 miles of improved trail lay behind.

But nobody maintained the new Lolo trail except occasional travelers who would chop a windfall here and there to get their horses through. While pursuing Chief Joseph in 1877, General Howard described the problems encountered in reopening the trail: "At half past five A.M., Spurgin, with his axeman, was already on the trail, working hard to get ahead of the command, so that it might make, to-day, the utmost distance over this terribly rough and obstructed pathway. He cleared away the fallen trees, made bridges across chasms, and when there was time, by side digging or walling with fragments of rock, he improved portions of the break-neck trail."[119] Only ten years after Bird's party had done its work, the Lolo trail was clearly in bad shape.

But the people who had wrested so much of Idaho's Clearwater country from the Nez Perce were not ready to discard their dreams of the economic growth that a road through the mountains could generate. This time they promoted a railroad to haul the commerce of industrial America back and forth over the mountains. In 1879 several prominent citizens of Lewiston organized an expedition into the interior in hopes of finding and publicizing an attractive route for the transcontinental railways then laying track across the United States. On loan from the Northern Pacific Railway Company, Engineer H. M. McCartney was placed in charge of an all-out attempt to bring the railroad builders into the Clearwater region.

After extensive exploration, McCartney reported that the elevation of Lolo Pass was 7,500 feet, that the Lochsa–Lolo Pass route was practical, but that construction of a railroad would take too long.[120] Consequently, the railroad companies chose to lay the first track across the mountains through Lookout Pass far to the north, leaving the Lochsa's landscapes undisturbed.

Nevertheless, the notion that those mountains could block the flow of prosperity from the east remained unacceptable to Idaho's people. So another group of citizens in Lewiston organized the Idaho, Clearwater, and Montana Transportation Company for the purpose of exploring the mountains and promoting a railroad if it found a feasible route. Widespread belief held that a low pass, located somewhere south of Lolo Pass, would provide an excellent crossing for a wagon road or railroad. That pass was said to be known only to a few Indians and trappers, and it was supposed to be so hidden from view that detailed exploration would be necessary to find the place.

In the summer of 1881 the company sent an expedition, headed by Alfred J. Beall, to look for the hidden pass. Beall returned on September 22 and reported finding a pass only 4,550 feet in elevation and ideally suited for the construction of a railroad. His discovery generated great excitement in the towns along the lower Clearwater. Surely a railroad would at last breach that cussed mountain barrier. The Northern Pacific Railway Company, however, dispatched Major Traux, Beall's report in hand, to validate the discovery. Major Traux's search disclosed no theretofore undiscovered pass. He did, however, report the elevation of Lolo Pass to be less than 5,000 feet instead of 7,500 feet as reported by McCartney in 1879. Like McCartney, he said a railroad could be built along the Lochsa and through Lolo Pass, yet he also agreed that tremendous cost and too much time would be required. The Northern Pacific Railway Company, he said, would not be interested in building over Lolo Pass.[121]

The rough geography of the Bitterroot Range remained protective of the region's solitude.

But populations and businesses were growing along the lower Clearwater and in the Clark Fork and Bitterroot Valleys to the east. And it was a long way around those mountains either to the north or south. How convenient it would be to go straight across. Thus, the idea of a shortcut route via Lolo Pass between Missoula, Montana, and Lewiston, Idaho, continued to gain momentum. But despite energetic promotion by citizens and several exploratory surveys, all they had at the turn of the century was the Lolo trail, and even it had fallen into disuse. The natural systems of the Bitterroot mountains were already reclaiming the works of the earliest pioneers.

Meanwhile, the railroads extended into the prairies and lowlands from the west, and that activity generated vicious competition between the Northern Pacific Railway Company and the Oregon Railroad and Navigation Company. In 1899 these two adversaries declared a truce and agreed to construct some railroads jointly. But that plan didn't last long. The depth of their enmity can be seen in a statement made by a high official of the Oregon Railroad and Navigation Company during an interview with a correspondent of the *Spokesman Review*. He said, "For the present there can be no open collision because the Northern Pacific has its lines east of Lewiston to complete and the Oregon Railroad and Navigation Company has its Ryparia-Lewiston line to build. When these are constructed, unless by that time a traffic arrangement has been agreed upon, the fight between the two companies will begin in earnest, and a fight of no mean proportions it will be."[122]

E. H. Harriman of the Union Pacific (Oregon Railroad and Navigation Company) and James J. Hill of the Northern Pacific had long

Men of the Northern Pacific Rairoad Company's survey crew raft supplies down the Lochsa River near present-day Powell Ranger Station in 1909. —C. I. Harrison

fought to gain power for themselves and advantage for their companies.[123] The shortcut through the Lochsa looked to Harriman like a good place to build a railroad. When he set out to do that, Hill counterattacked, and the war was on again. By 1908 they were locked in a contest to complete surveys up the Clearwater and the Lochsa over Lolo Pass, and down the Lolo Fork to connect with the railroad in the Bitterroot Valley. The company to finish first would gain control of key locations along the way. Neither the bears, the trappers, the prospectors, nor the rangers had ever seen the likes of the activity that went on in the land of the Lochsa during that war of transits.

In order to follow grades negotiable by locomotives, both companies confined their surveys to the bottom of the trailless Lochsa canyon. The Oregon Railroad and Navigation Company supplied their camps by pack train, but the Northern Pacific sought to gain advantage by hauling supplies up the Lochsa by boat. Ten or twelve men towed each boat while one man held the craft out in the current by use of a long pole. After swamping its boats in a big rapid where the Black Canyon confines the Lochsa River between steep cliffs, the Northern Pacific quit this strategy, and it too began hauling its camps in by pack trains.[124]

En route to the Lochsa with supplies for the surveyors. This pack train crosses the West Fork of Lolo Creek just above Lolo Hot Springs. The packer rides in front. The assistant packer follows behind. —C. I. Harrison

Both companies launched survey parties east from Kooskia, Idaho, and west from Lolo Hot Springs, Montana. They hired packers and pack stock wherever they could find them until at least one hundred pack animals worked on the Idaho side alone. Trails were needed for the loaded pack trains to get into the riverbottom camps. So the companies assigned crews to clear out the game and Indian trails leading down the ridges from the Lolo Trail into the Lochsa's canyon. The packers led their loaded pack trains from Pete King on the Lochsa, up the long ridge followed by Ranger Smith in 1909 to the Lolo Trail, and then down low standard trails to campsites on the river far below. Working from the east, the Northern Pacific crews built a good trail from the mouth of the Brushy Fork, down the south side of the Crooked Fork, then along the north side of the Lochsa River. Wherever possible they built the trail close to the river, but at each canyon narrows—and they were many—their route climbed above the bluffs to circumvent the obstacle, and then descended again to the river.

When either company built a trail, it tried to prevent its rival's use of it. After bridging a stream, the Oregon Railroad and Navigation

Northern Pacific surveyors pitched this camp beside the Brushy Fork of the Lochsa in 1908 or 1909. —C. I. Harrison

Company would station a guard to keep the pack trains of the Northern Pacific from crossing. So the Northern Pacific crews built their own bridges. There, deep in the Lochsa's wilds, pack trains crossed parallel bridges much like the big engines ran on parallel tracks in the valleys outside the mountains.[125]

While the competition was mutual, the Oregon Railroad and Navigation Company was especially ornery. It hired a man with a pack horse whose main job was to linger on narrow stretches of trail and slow down the Northern Pacific Company's pack trains or stop them altogether at places where they couldn't pass each other. Dean Harrington of Kooskia, Idaho, and Forest Service guard George Trenary once accompanied a Northern Pacific pack train over the narrow trail along the Lochsa River. At one place Oregon Railroad and Navigation Company crews had built a trail around a sheer ledge by drilling holes in the cliff, leaving their drill steel sticking out of the holes, and then placing logs on the protruding steel to form a trail. Harrington, Trenary, the packer, and his loaded train made it across that precarious shelf, but the makeshift trail had been dynamited into the river before their return trip. They found the man who had done the blasting nearby, and Trenary arrested him. They called him "Johnny Behind the Rock."[126]

The competing surveys created boom times in Kooskia, Lolo Hot Springs, and the town of Lolo near where Lewis and Clark camped in the land of the stone-faced woman. Many pack trains and saddle horses crossed Lolo Pass all winter long in 1908–9, and they packed a road through snow that at times was twelve feet deep. (When an animal stepped off the packed track it would flounder in soft snow until the

Northern Pacific Railroad survey operations at Lolo Hot Springs, Montana, about 1909. Buildings include a barn, bunkhouses, and a hospital. —Louise Gerber Gilbert

packers could get him onto the road again.) The Northern Pacific built bunkhouses, barns, and a hospital at Lolo Hot Springs, and in 1908 the company extended a wagon road along the Lolo trail to within two miles of Lolo Pass where it constructed a log warehouse and camp buildings. Northern Pacific pack trains heading into the Lochsa country used that outpost as a jumping-off point.

To demonstrate its will to beat Harriman, the Northern Pacific in 1909 began building grade west from the Bitterroot spur line. Cochran, Winters, and Smith had the construction contract, and it subcontracted sections of the job along the Lolo Fork. Four-horse teams pulled rattling wagons hauling grub to the camps as well as hay and grain for the hundreds of horses and mules used to scrape the dirt out of the cuts and tunnels and into the fills across the creek bottoms. As Vic Miller, then a young man growing up in the town of Lolo, described the robust situation: "Jesus! There was some activity here then."[127]

Although many routes had long been used by the Indians to reach favored places, trails built by the railroad companies provided the first access for horses and pack trains into much of the Lochsa country. Transporting supplies in and out of the interior proved a boon to the packing industry. Just as new weapons are invented in time of war, in-

Northern Pacific workers assemble in 1909 at the end of their wagon road, about two miles east of Lolo Pass. —C. I. Harrison

novations in the modes of moving cargo by horses and mules became important by-products of the antagonistic railroad survey operations. Among the most significant developments was a new pack saddle and associated system for handling loads.

Prior to that time, most pack saddles used in the Clearwater country resembled miniature sawhorses and were called sawbuck saddles. As men prepared to haul cargo into the mountains, there would be veteran packers like Bill Parry, at first hint of summertime dawn, currying the dust and loose hairs from the backs of his horses or mules.[128] Such men would grab a blanket in one hand and one of those sawbuck saddles in the other and walk up to the lead animal's left side. Depending on the animal's disposition, he might announce his intentions gently—You'd better whoa now—or with a militant Stand still! punctuated by an expletive. Then standing near the animal's shoulder, where he was least likely to get kicked by a vicious hind foot, he'd ease the pad and blanket into place on the curried back. Next, he'd hoist up the saddle and settle it snugly on the blanket, then reach under the animal's belly, grab the cinch hanging down on the opposite side, run the latigo strap through the cinch ring, and pull. If the animal humped and bucked, the packer had to hang on until the beast settled down. Then he'd tie the latigo with a flat hitch, work the breeching under the tail—often a sensitive operation—and finally snap the breast collar in place.

With all animals saddled, the packer was ready to load the string—essentially a two-man job when using the sawbuck saddle with top packs.

A railroad survey pack train crosses Packer Meadows in 1909. The diamond hitches and loose pack stock are typical of the pre-Decker pack saddle era. —C. I. Harrison

During loading, the packers tied each animal securely to a strong post or tree. Then they hoisted the panniers (boxes) first to their knees then up to hook the leather straps onto the saddle's forks (or sawbucks). When properly loaded, the panniers distributed weight evenly on each side of the animal, and the packers piled additional gear on top of the boxes. After covering the top load with a square piece of canvas, the packer would grab a fifty-foot length of rope with a cinch attached to one end and, with the help of an assistant, secure the whole load by means of a diamond hitch.

Tying the diamond hitch was a time-consuming operation, but the knot effectively held gear on the pack animals under the roughest conditions. After loading, each pack animal was turned loose; most of them quietly accepted their fate as beasts of burden. With a nod to his assistant and a "Heyaah" to announce departure, the packer would rein his saddle horse up the trail along the Clearwater River. The pack animals followed, each in his place in the train, while the assistant packer brought up the rear, hazing the laggards along the hoof-chopped trail leading in to the Lochsa country.

Bill Parry's operation was typical of pack trains hauling cargo into the mountains. But one packer, McDaniels, was different. Instead of trailing his pack animals loose on the trail he tied them together to form a linked train. He removed the sawbucks from the saddle trees and replaced their wooden forks with horseshoes and in that way formed

Decker pack saddles in use at Powell Ranger Station in 1955.
—W. E. Steuerwald, U.S. Forest Service

iron loops on which to tie his cargo.[129] McDaniels wrapped his side packs in heavy canvas, then lashed them to the iron loops with a tie called a squaw hitch—possibly because the Indians had long before fashioned a similar saddle tree by steaming and bending the horns of an elk. There were no awkward top packs or complicated diamond hitches involved in McDaniels's packing system. His operation was fast and simple, and one man could handle the job.

McDaniels's idea caught on. The Decker brothers, who packed out of Kooskia, Idaho, adopted and improved the system in cooperation with a creative blacksmith, Oll Robinette, who had his home and shop along the Clearwater River near Three Devils rapid. Oll built the new saddle's tree from the soft wood of the riverbottom cottonwoods, and he replaced McDaniels's horseshoe forks with round iron. Robinette patented the invention, and every saddle made by him was stamped on top of the tree "O.P.R."[130] Meanwhile, the Decker brothers designed a leather and canvas cover (called a half-breed) to fit over the saddle tree. This new innovation in transportation took the name Decker pack saddle. Thus, competition spawned by the war of the railroad surveys, together with the resourcefulness of the Indians, the creativity of an excellent blacksmith, and the needs of the packing industry, revolutionized the saddle and packing systems used in the Bitterroot mountains. As far as the mountain men of the Lochsa were concerned, after 1909 the time-tested sawbuck saddle and diamond hitch were on their way out.

Packer Johnny Decker at Lolo Hot Springs about 1915.
—Victor J. Miller

Oll Robinette's stamp, O.P.R., identifies the Decker saddle tree. The historical sawbuck tree is on the left. Both trees are displayed at the Lochsa Historical Ranger Station.

Harriman died at the peak of the railroad activities, and the determination of the Oregon Railroad and Navigation Company to penetrate the Lochsa's wilderness died with him.[131] With its adversary gone, the Lolo Pass railway idea held little appeal for the Northern Pacific Company. Almost certainly, Northern Pacific had been motivated more by the quest for power and profit than a desire to serve the people. Another truce was hatched in some executive command post far to the east. Both companies ceased operations in the area as abruptly as they had begun.

More by corporate default than by virtue of their own indomitability, the natural systems of the Lochsa had once again avoided subjugation by the people of the times. But the railroad war had left more marks on the land than had all the people, white and Indian, who had marched through it until then. New trails penetrated the Lochsa's theretofore inaccessible canyons. Cliffs had been drilled by sweating men swinging double-jack hammers, who turned steel, tamped the drill holes full of black powder, and exploded the whole works to make way for men and pack stock to pass. With each blast the earth trembled, and the wild game moved deeper into the wilderness. The railroad companies' warriors cut clearings in the forests for campsites and dug gaping holes to bury their garbage. After the surveyors left, the bears returned, reopened these pits, and scattered the cans and stinking refuse on the beautiful bars and riverbanks. For the first time ever, many tributary streams of the Lochsa were bridged, indeed, as we have seen, frequently spanned by two bridges side by side.

Competition within nature was nothing new in the Lochsa country. What was new was the malicious mischief of man against man who, at least in the Christian tradition, was supposed to be the wise one, intellectually a notch above the bears and the wolves. But the men of the railroad companies fought each other like coyotes snarling over a fallen deer. They demonstrated to the rangers, the trappers, the prospectors—all those whose world centered inside the last frontier—that their mountain-locked habitat could not for long resist the will of corporate America. The death of Harriman was the end of the railroad idea, and it seemed then that the naturalness of the Lochsa might last a long time. But in 1916 a proposed highway up the Lochsa and across the Lolo Pass was included in the federal highway system.[132] The concept of a shortcut route through the mountains would not die; too many people of both Montana and Idaho were determined to keep it alive.

10

Their Common Enemy Was Fire

The government's new rangers soon found that protecting the land required confrontation with a powerful force of nature: fire in the forests. Since practically no rain fell after April during the summer of 1910, by mid-August the sun had parched the woods to tinder, ripe for ignition by lightning strikes or careless acts of people. Inevitably, it happened—smoke filled the canyons as big fires scorched the mountains in full view from the Bitterroot Valley, where hundreds of men fought to keep the flames from destroying the homes of the settlers. The whole land darkened, even at noonday, as huge columns of smoke billowed over the crest of the Bitterroots from fires burning in the Lochsa and Selway drainages. There, the Lochsa's rangers, like the people of the Bitterroot Valley, were trying to order nature in the interests of the settlers and the nation by controlling the fires.

Lightning storms had ignited many small fires throughout Ranger Smith's district, several with the potential to spread before his limited manpower could suppress them. A conflagration threatened to sweep into the Lochsa from the mountains drained by the North Fork of the Clearwater River. To make matters worse, about August 15 a fire broke out on the south side of the Lochsa River near the mouth of Warm Springs Creek, eleven miles below Powell's Flat. To control that fire, Smith had to get at least twenty men there quickly, along with equipment and food to last for several days. Fortunately, sixty-five men were camped at Packer Meadows (Glade Creek), only twenty-five miles away, but by the time Smith's saddle-horse–borne request for help arrived, the fire had begun spreading into dense forests southward toward the Selway River. Meanwhile, Smith dispatched twelve men equipped with axes, saws,

Standing in the blackened aftermath, this observer ponders the natural fury of the 1910 fires in north Idaho and northwestern Montana. —U.S. Forest Service

and shovels to build trails so that pack trains could haul equipment from Powell's Flat to Warm Springs Creek. This job took two days, and by then the fire had generated an eight-mile-wide front. That night a message from Forest Service headquarters in Missoula instructed him to bring his outfit out to Packer Meadows; fires were so bad in other places that the service could not spare men to fight the fire on Warm Springs Creek.

By that time the fire had spread east and south—no one knew how far. And still another big fire roared across the mountains and into the Lochsa from the north. How big the land, how awesome the power of nature, how futile the efforts of the ranger and his crew.

Ranger Weholt had his troubles that summer, too. While Smith stalked flames at Warm Springs Creek, lightning struck the ridge above the cedar groves at Elbow Bend on Moose Creek. The fire crowned through the forest and soon became too big for Weholt and his men to handle. Weholt called for help, using an emergency telephone line strung that year from Hamilton, Montana, over Blodgett Pass to Elk Summit.

Deputy supervisor Ed Thenon responded by leading a crew of thirty men, accompanied by a pack train loaded with grub and fire-fighting equipment, from the Bitterroot Valley over Lost Horse Pass to Weholt's aid.

After a long journey across the Bitterroots, Thenon's crew camped in a grove of large cedars beside the East Fork of Moose Creek. They could see no flames, but smoke obscured the sun and drifted through the forest while the men cooked supper, pitched tents, and prepared their beds for the night. Because the trunks of those cedars—some eight feet in diameter at the base—stood close to each other, daylight, even in brighter times, was always dim beneath their crowns. On that smokey day in August 1910 the grove was dark by four o'clock in the afternoon. The men retired early, but Thenon couldn't sleep. The still night air was oppressive, even ominous.

Something rattled on the tent's roof. Thenon sprang from his blankets and went outside to find the stillness broken by the sound of wind from the west. Dislodged from the tree crowns by the gust, needles and cones spattered the tent like drops from a summertime shower. But no moisture rode on that wind, only smoke and dry needles and the smell of parched woods. Thenon spoke aloud to himself: "Damn! Why couldn't it just as well be rain?"

From out of the darkness came the voice of his foreman, Lou Fitting:

"Come out here. I just saw a star fall on the hillside across the creek and it started a fire."[133]

Both men studied the small fire for a moment. A pink glow in the sky to the west caught their attention, and they realized that the fire-starting star was a flaming brand sucked high in the air by the convection of a big fire and then dropped to ignite the dry forest ahead of the holocaust. The fire was coming fast, and their camp was directly in its path.

Thenon awakened the men. In the light cast by the approaching flames he found a place to make a stand in a bend of the stream near camp. The creek there ran eight feet wide and six to eight inches deep; it was flanked on one side by a strip of sand. Not much of a sanctuary, but that cool water could mean the difference between living and burning to death. Thenon didn't like the looks of the big log jam that plugged the stream channel just above the bend. Should it catch fire, they could be roasted between the burning jam and the flames crowning through the trees above. With the fire so close upon them, however, there was no time to look for a safer haven.

Some men wanted to escape by running away. But Thenon convinced them that their best chance to live was to stick together. So they piled their grub and equipment on the sand bar and soaked it with water. Then they jumped into the creek, held wet blankets over their heads, and doused each other while fire roared through the forest around them. Two men went insane. It took three firefighters to hold one of them in the creek. Thenon pushed the other into the deepest water, and there the afflicted man sat, a soggy blanket over his head, singing a lullaby tune. The whole canyon burned. Smoke boiled skyward. Tongues of flames licked high into the churning clouds, where exploding gases rumbled across the mountains. Thirty men fought for their lives inside that conflagration. The creek, the sand bar, their individual selves—all seemed so very small compared to the massive inferno.

Suddenly, the grub and camp pile were ablaze. The log jam, too. In desperation Thenon dashed a bucket of water on the grub, but heat from the flames in the crowns blasted his breath away. He dropped to his knees in the ash-filled creek, the empty bucket dangling from his hand. Unable to breathe, he felt sure his time on earth had ended. On impulse he jammed the bucket over his head. It worked—he could breathe! He knew then he was going to live. Meanwhile, everybody else soaked in the creek, and the lullaby boy kept right on singing his tune.

In late afternoon of the same day, fire swept over ranger Ray Fitting, who was scouting along the North Fork of Moose Creek. At a point about one mile below that creek's major fork, a dense mass of gray smoke closed in on Fitting from every direction. The mountain air grew hot and sultry; the sun became a red ball and then vanished into the thickening pall.

A big fire was coming. The trapped ranger headed down the mountain to seek safety in the waters of North Moose Creek, but the drought of 1910 had reduced the once-bold stream to a trickle. Dismayed by the stream's small size, he followed it down to where it flowed under an eight-foot cliff and formed a pool of water about two feet deep. Not an ideal place to ride out the fire, but time had run out for Ranger Fitting. Even as he soaked his coat in the water, the fire was casting burning brands into the forest around him. He could feel the earth vibrate as huge cedars burned along the stream and flames roared and flashed from one canyon wall to the other.

Fitting hugged the cliff and immersed himself in the water. The air got so hot that steam rose from his sodden clothes whenever he

Ray Fitting, extreme right, poses with a Forest Service trail crew at Lost Knife Meadows about 1911. —Lou Hartig, U.S. Forest Service

raised his head to breathe. As the stream warmed, dead fish floated past, and he thought water hot enough to kill fish would surely kill him, too. But he managed to survive the night. In the smokey dawn he made his way down the canyon to his cabin at the forks of North and East Moose Creeks. Of that trip, he said, "Not a green leaf, not an unburned twig, or any sign of wildlife was visible for approximately the first eight miles."[134]

Small wonder that the people of the Bitterroot, the Clark Fork, and other settled valleys near the wilderness viewed the smoke and drifting ash with apprehension. The woods had grown drier all summer. Parched crops produced such feeble yields that the railroad companies had laid off hundreds of workers. Jobless men sometimes set fires for spite or to gain work fighting the blazes. Clouds formed over the mountains on hot afternoons, their cumulus empty of rain but loaded with the electrostatic impulses that bred lightning storms. Each lightning strike, each careless or incendiary act of man, added new fires to swell the growing threat.

By mid-July, three thousand men were fighting fires in the Bitterroot mountains. On August 8, President William H. Taft authorized the regular army to help Forest Service personnel control fires. But on August 10, despite their combined efforts, many fires escaped. They burned from the Clearwater, St. Joe, and Coeur d'Alene River basins, up the western

Unless aided by some factor in nature such as fuels, weather, or topography, the awesome power generated by a blow-up fire cannot be controlled by human effort.
—Ernest Peterson, U.S. Forest Service

slopes of the Bitterroots, and over the top through saddles in the crest of the mountains.

Redoubling their efforts, firefighters had built control lines around most fires by August 19, but the dry gale that swept the mountains on August 20 destroyed all hopes that nature's maelstrom could be brought to heel by man. Those caught in the fire's path, like Thenon and Fitting, abandoned any hope of controlling the flames and concentrated instead on saving their lives. When the winds finally died, two days later, five towns had burned; eighty-five men, most of them firefighters, had died; and three million acres of forest had gone up in flames and smoke. More fortunate than their neighbors to the north, the rangers in charge of the Lochsa country lost much of their forests but came through their trial by fire alive.

This blown-down forest demonstrates the power of the winds that created the conflagration of 1910.
—J. B. Halm, U.S. Forest Service

While rangers of the U.S. Forest Service were wholly occupied with the 1910 fires, with no time to spare for other forestry matters, University of Idaho professor of forestry C. H. Shattuck was studying "forestal" conditions in the Selway and Lochsa Forks of the Clearwater River. Professor Shattuck considered the eventual best uses of that wild land to be lumbering, livestock grazing, and agriculture. After examining the mountains around Ranger Weholt's headquarters at Elk Summit, he wrote: "The burns from the White Sand Lake to Grave Peak have been numerous and severe. In many places natural seed regeneration, mostly of lodgepole pine, is taking place in a proper manner, but there are thousands of acres unfit for either agriculture or grazing, where no regeneration is now occurring and where nature must be aided in order to again establish a forest cover."[135]

During his study, Professor Shattuck journeyed from Elk Summit via the old Indian road leading past Grave Peak to the fishery near Powell's Flat. While high in these mountains he described the potential commercial lumber value of the timberline trees—alpine larch and whitebark pine. But for the smoke of the fires he could have looked north and east across the forested basins that form the headwaters of the Lochsa. He could have seen the great peaks of the Bitterroot crest and the tiny saddle at the head of the Brushy Fork where, as a youth, I climbed the crest and first saw the Lochsa country. He could have seen

Fires smoldering in Wallace, Idaho, one of five towns burned in the northern Rocky Mountains by the fires of 1910. —R. H. McKay

the ridges and canyons that hid Isaac's gold from Jerry Johnson, the basins that drew trappers after fur, and the land's immensity that humbled Lewis and Clark and seized the souls of rangers Smith and Weholt.

Had the smoke cleared, what he probably would have seen with greatest clarity was the potential commercial value of the lumber in that expanse of forests. They stretched as far as topography allowed the eye to see, unbroken except for the near-treeless crest of the Bitterroots, a few meadows and lakes, and patches here and there marking old, small burns. In 1910 it had been many years since large fires had visited much of the upper half of the Lochsa basin.

The Indian road led Professor Shattuck from the high country toward the Lochsa River through "excellent" stands of both young and mature spruce. As he descended, the spruce gave way to lodgepole pine, fir, and larch, stands so dense that Shattuck could not see out of them to view the adjacent terrain. Further diminishing the visibility, smoke from the fire that had escaped Ranger Smith's control efforts at Warm Springs Creek drifted through the trees. Except when hot afternoon winds occasionally stirred the branches, the air was oppres-

As professor Shattuck noted, fires leave blackened forest in their wake. But fire in the northern Rocky Mountains also helps recycle the old forest and regenerate the new.

sive and still. Professor Shattuck's objective was to determine the size and extent of that valuable forest, but the sultry air, drifting smoke, and falling ash warned that fire was near and on the move. So he hastened down the trail through the white pines and cedars near the canyon bottom, forded the Lochsa River, and joined Ranger Smith and his crew at Powell's Flat (see map 2).

Two days later Professor Shattuck viewed the ridge he had descended from a vantage point on the north side of the Lochsa River. He described it thus: "We saw a sheet of flame, sometimes 200 feet in height, sweep over the region leaving only blackened and mostly dead trunks in its wake." No wonder that Professor Shattuck later opined, "Fire has produced on this reserve far greater losses than all other agencies combined and is today the most dreaded and dangerous forest enemy with which we must contend."[136]

No astute observer of the times disagreed with Shattuck's conclusion. Lieberg had previously expressed a similar view. And, writing in retrospect years later, the 1910 supervisor of the Lolo National Forest, Elers Koch, said, "The 1910 forest fire in the Northern Rocky Mountain Region is an episode which has had much to do with the shaping of fire policy not only of that region but the whole United States. The tragic and disastrous culmination of that battle to save the forests shocked the nation into a realization of a better system of fire control."[137] After surviving in the heart of the fire on Moose Creek, Ray Fitting summed up his feelings and those of his neighboring rangers, Smith and Weholt, when he said, "I was bewildered and confused as I tried to grasp the enormity of the catastrophe."[138]

Fire, then, became the people's common enemy, its control their central purpose. After 1910 the rangers declared war on this great natural force that had for at least ten thousand years shaped the Lochsa's landscapes, uninfluenced by human hands.

This forest burned about 1903; by 1910 its standing dead and fallen trees had created the kindling needed to fuel another intense fire.
—A. Gaskill, U.S. Forest Service

11

Expanding the Indian Trails

We have seen that by 1909 widespread exploration and the railroad surveys had shown the best route across the mountains for commerce to be via the Lochsa River, Lolo Pass, and the Lolo Fork of the Bitterroot River. To enrich the economy of communities east and west, politicians and their constituents promoted first a railroad and then a highway, as auto and truck travel became feasible. Their objective was to get through the mountains. The Lochsa rangers had additional ideas—they wanted access *to* the land, not just a route *through* it. To them the mountains were more than mere barriers between settled valleys. They were sources of bounty to be administered for a continuous supply of wood and water. To do that would require a transportation network far more complex than a single route connecting the Bitterroot Valley's railroad with water transportation at Lewiston, Idaho.

With help from his superiors at Missoula and Washington, D.C., U.S. Forest Service Supervisor Fenn established priorities to guide the work of the rangers. First, they were to build trails and telephone lines connecting each ranger district with headquarters at Kooskia. The next item of business was the fencing of pastures to hold pack and saddle stock at strategic locations. Because the rangers and their crews could be sheltered in tents, the building of cabins was to be delayed until the basic network of trails and telephone lines was complete. Meanwhile, the rangers always had to be prepared to battle their ever-threatening enemy, fire.

As the men of the Forest Service cleared eight-foot-wide swaths through the mountains, sounds of crosscut saws, axe blows, and falling timber mingled with the whisper of summertime winds in the trees. Long

The axman is not identified but is probably Alec McLendon, hewing logs for construction of the original Powell Ranger Station about 1911.
—U.S. Forest Service

shavings, ripped from the wood by saw teeth and rakers, coiled on the earth where each log had been cut in two. Fresh axe chips littered the woods, trampled into the damp earth by the soles of the laborers' caulked boots. Those people were on the move. They dug trails in mountain sides with grub hoes and built bridges so pack trains could be led across powerful streams. The smell of earth and chips and sawdust hung in the air along the new trails, easy to follow because their builders chopped big blazes, visible from one to the other, on the trunks of the trailside trees. Each Forest Service blaze was a long hack with a notch above. It looked like a sole and heel track made by a man walking down the tree heading backward instead of pushing forward, deeper into the trailless woods, like these determined builders.

When it came to trail construction, Ranger Smith hit the jackpot in 1909. During that first season at Powell's Flat, he was surrounded by crews of the Northern Pacific Company and the Oregon Railroad and Navigation Company (Union Pacific) who had more trail-building capacity than the Forest Service would be able to muster for many years. Smith could do little to influence either the locations or construction standards of the trails. But he urged the railroad companies to seek routes useful to the Forest Service, and occasionally his men helped improve mainline trails built by the railroads in 1908.

Ranger Smith soon recognized that the most practical outlet to obtain supplies and establish communication with the settlements was over Lolo Pass to Lolo Hot Springs, not to Kooskia via the Lolo Trail. So during the summer of 1909, Smith and his men concentrated most of their work east of their headquarters at Powell's Flat.

Despite the stated priority given to the building of telephone lines and trails, all rangers stationed on the upper Lochsa built cabins in 1911. Indeed, even as fall rains settled the smoke from the 1910 fires, Frank Smith had a crew cutting and skidding logs at Powell's Flat. In the spring of 1911 Alec McLendon, an expert log man, came to Powell's Flat with Ranger Smith to hew and fit logs for the new ranger station. Seven men formed the crew that year: Ranger Smith, Alec McLendon, Jake Leech, Oro Flynn, Kress, and Ray and Jay Turner.[139]

Charley Powell still claimed his cabin and the flat. His coffee pot was on as usual, but his cool greeting plainly showed that he was troubled inside. Charley liked Frank Smith—everybody did, for that matter—and he knew him to be a fair man. But Charley had no use for the government, and the government wanted his flat. When Smith and his crew began cutting cabin logs in the fall of 1910, Charley knew that the government meant business. Ranger Smith, obviously, had his instructions, and he intended to carry them out.

After opening the mainline trails in 1911, all hands turned to building the log cabin station. While the men finished cutting and skidding the timbers, McLendon laid straight sill logs on sturdy foundation stones. He locked the wall logs together with tenoned corners hewn to precision with his razor-edged axe. Such painstaking carpentry took time. The chip pile grew; the cabin rose slowly. The resinous smell of fresh-hewn lodgepole pine mingled with the fragrance of sourdough bannock, fried trout, and beans wafting from the cook tent.

So much for log walls. What of the floor and roof? Jay Turner and his brother Ray knew how to handle those. Just teenagers, they had become veterans at splitting building materials from the boles of cedar trees while growing up on the Turner homestead along the Middle Fork of the Clearwater. And plenty of cedar grew close to the new station site at Powell's Flat. Jay selected a cedar about four feet in diameter at eye level with a vertical pattern of bark indicating that straight-grained wood would be found inside its trunk. They studied the lean of the tree, then aimed the undercut so that the tree would land in a good location for sawing and splitting into bolts. Felling that big cedar with a crosscut saw and axe was no small task, even for the wiry Turner boys. One can imagine that when the monarch crashed to the ground, Alec McLendon looked up from his work on the cabin's walls and said something like, "Sounds like shakes and puncheons will be coming in soon."

Jay and Ray sawed the trunk into bolts thirty inches long or eight feet long, depending on knots or limbs on the tree. They used a froe and a club hewn from a tough yew to fashion puncheons and shakes from the bolts. Split one-half inch thick and varying in width from six to twelve inches, each shake formed a cross section of the cedar's bole—rich, red heartwood trimmed with two inches of white sap. When nailed in overlapping rows on the ridge logs, the shakes created a beautiful waterproof roof.

To form the floor and overhead loft, McLendon fastened puncheons to pole joists with round pegs hewn from the hard, white wood of the lodgepole pine. The new cabin breathed fresh smells of the Lochsa's woods, and its red and white floors, dotted with white pegs, seemed at first too beautiful to touch. By the time Smith's crew finished the cabin,

Ranger Weholt and his crew whipsaw lumber in 1911 to build the first ranger station at Elk Summit. Left to right: Lou Tisen, Loyd Rupe, Adolph Weholt, and George Eckel. —Loyd Rupe

frost had painted the shrubs and turned the leaves of the cottonwoods gold. Too late to move in that fall, they headed out via the Lolo Trail. All were eager to return in the spring—1911 was the last summer they would live in tents.

With the building of the cabin, the United States government had staked its permanent claim to Powell's Flat. Ranger Smith offered to issue Charley a permit to settle on the next flat down the river. He could stay there, Smith said, at the pleasure of the government, but he couldn't continue to squat on government land at the ranger station site. That lower flat was beautiful, too. A fine creek could be diverted for irrigation, and it would take only minor work to clear a garden and pasture. But Charley would have to fill out papers to validate his new occupancy. He would have to build another cabin. And once settled in the new location, he would forever feel the hand of government on his shoulder.

Charley Powell set no traps in the fall of 1911. Sometime in late October he loaded his meager belongings onto his pack horses and climbed into his weather-cracked saddle. At the edge of the forest he probably reined in his horse and studied the clearing where water sparkled in the ditch as it flowed by the porch of his weathered cabin. Deep snow during the past winter had broken some shakes on the spring house roof, and Charley would have thought about replacing them. His garden fence stood sturdy and strong only fifty yards from the new Forest Service cabin, where the hammers of the builders filled the glade with a different rhythm than Charley had known before at Powell's Flat.

Charley couldn't tolerate government control of his life, and he wouldn't submit to the paperwork required by the Forest Service. So he left and never returned; nobody in the Lochsa knew where he went. In an ironic twist of human events, government surveyors in 1915 and 1916 found Powell's Flat and Frank Smith's ranger station to be located in Section 33, which had been granted to the Northern Pacific Railroad Company by President Lincoln in 1864. Frank Smith and his crew dubbed their new log building Powell Ranger Station, and they called the whole center of the Lochsa highlands the Powell Ranger District—apt tributes to the only man who came close to taking up land for a homestead in the upper Lochsa country.

Meanwhile Ranger Weholt and his crew skidded logs with a saddle horse to build a cabin at Elk Summit. They whipsawed boards from whitebark pine logs and cut shakes from the cedars of Moose Creek, eight miles away, and then hauled them all to Elk Summit by pack train.

The new Elk Summit Ranger Station as it looked about 1912 or 1913. —U.S. Forest Service

Unlike Smith's multipurpose station, their small cabin would serve solely as a warehouse for storing tents, stoves, tools, and other heavy gear, thus enabling them to lighten their pack trains' loads as they returned to the mountains in early summer and left for the settlements each fall.[140]

Like Smith at Powell's Flat, Weholt discovered that the nearest source of supplies was over the crest in the Bitterroot Valley. While it took seven days to reach Kooskia, Idaho, with his pack train he could reach Hamilton, Montana, in two days easily. The trouble was, the trails leading east were so rough that only light loads could be carried by the pack horses. Consequently, improving the trail through Blodgett Pass vied with cabin building for his attention, and his time, in 1911.

During his first trip from Elk Summit to Hamilton for supplies, Weholt's youthful packer, Loyd Rupe, found practically no trail at all around the shores of Big Sand Lake. The first mile of his descent from Blodgett Pass was so steep that the pack horses could barely slide down between the cliffs. Remnants of broken pack boxes and bleached bones of horses left no doubt that troubles had beset travelers who had gone that way before.

In 1911, Loyd Rupe led his pack train over a rough trail through Blodgett Pass to haul supplies from Hamilton, Montana, to Elk Summit Ranger Station.

Forest Service packer Loyd Rupe, third from left, poses in 1911 with other crew members at the Elk Summit corral. —Carl Weholt, U.S. Forest Service

While exploring his district in 1912, Ranger Weholt waters his pack stock in the shallows of Big Sand Lake. —Carl Weholt, U.S. Forest Service

When Rupe led his pack train out of Blodgett canyon he could see the Bitterroot River winding serpentlike through a broad valley dotted here and there with green fields. Four miles from his viewpoint at the canyon's mouth, a train rattled into the village of Hamilton, Montana. The forlorn notes of its whistle reached the mountains, while the stack of its engine spewed a trail of coal smoke, which lingered behind along the track.

The valley was beautiful. But nineteen-year-old Rupe soon discovered that its splendor masked tragedy. Spotted fever, he learned from a homesteader, each spring claimed the lives of several valley residents. Rupe bought his supplies and hurried his loaded pack train out of the valley and over the crest of the Bitterroots. Safely back at Elk Summit he unbuckled his dusty chaps and hung his sweat-stained black Stetson on a peg. He said to his partners, "When I left Kooskia I rode clean through the mountains. And I came out there at Blodgett and I seen that Green Valley and I didn't know what to think."

Without waiting for response, Rupe continued: "Homesteaders was a clearin' brush in there before you cross the river. And that's where they was a gittin' bit with them ticks. I met this old man and he said

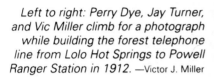

Left to right: Perry Dye, Jay Turner, and Vic Miller climb for a photograph while building the forest telephone line from Lolo Hot Springs to Powell Ranger Station in 1912. —Victor J. Miller

them ticks is thick down there. They killed forty-eight last year. Man! when I heerd that I kept that pack string right in the middle of the road. Never let 'em touch a bush."[141]

Ranger Weholt and packer Rupe took time from cabin and trail construction to explore the country that year. One midsummer morning they saddled horses at Big Sand Lake while mist was still rising from the calm waters. They followed the blazes of trapper Wes Fales across a high ridge into the next basin to the north. After working their way through thick brush and much down timber, they broke out of the forest onto the shores of a lake easily as large and beautiful as the Big Sand. They claimed first discovery by Forest Service people and named the sparkling gem Hidden Lake because it was so difficult to find.

Camped on its shores that night, the wildness of the Bitterroot mountains descended upon them. Weholt and Rupe were far from other humans but certainly not alone. Big black moose splashed as they fed along the lakeshore. When Rupe went down to the lake to wash their bannock pan, foot-long trout swam up from the depths to investigate and then gobbled up the dough. And this was grizzly country, where the great bears' presence magnified the meaning of every sound in the night. In talking about it years later, Loyd Rupe summed up the feeling

Ranger Frank Smith leads his pack train across the newly constructed Brushy Fork bridge in 1913.
—Victor J. Miller

of many who were seized by the wildness in the land of the Lochsa. He said, "My God, that Hidden Lake was purty. I kin jist see it yit."[142]

In the fall of 1912, Ranger Smith brought the first telephone line into Powell Ranger Station. His crew that year consisted of Jake Leech, Jay Turner, Ray Turner, Perry Dye, Fred Schott, McFarland, and Vic Miller. They nailed their first insulator on the corner of the hotel at Lolo Hot Springs and then strung the No. 9 galvanized wire from there through the forests toward Lolo Pass. Although none of the crew had built phone lines before, they learned fast under Smith's supervision. By the time they reached the pass, every man could splice the line. Each could wire the split insulators together on the line and fasten those insulators to staples driven sixteen to twenty feet up each tie tree's bole. Fred Schott was the crew's expert axman. Half of the crew could buckle the iron spurs to their legs, hook an insulator to their heavy leather climbing belts, stick their butts out so as to angle the sharp spurs toward the tree's bole, and then scamper up, bear fashion, in short, choppy steps, carrying the insulator and line high into the air. Vic Miller had even learned how to execute a dramatic descent in three or four jumps. Holding the angled stance of the climber, he would kick both spurs loose, drop four feet or more, jam the spurs into the tree to slow his fall, and then kick loose and drop again, sending bark flying.

While the crew worked, Ranger Smith loaded their camp gear on his gray pack horses and set up a new camp near where each day's line construction would end. One night in October he made camp in a cedar grove alongside the Crooked Fork of the Lochsa River. He had the cooking fire lighted when the boisterous crew hiked into camp. They were good at their work, and all of them knew it. Even soft-spoken Fred Schott showed a flash of pride when he said, "That damn fool kid Miller's gonna kill himself with those spurs someday."

While they bantered, Smith grabbed the coffee pot and headed to the Crooked Fork for water. He returned slowly through the cedars, his stubby pipe clenched between teeth that gleamed beneath his tobacco-stained mustache. The wet pot hissed when he shoved it in the flames. Then he turned toward the men, took the pipe from his teeth and said,

"Come here fellows and look at this."

As the men gathered, Smith held out a frayed leather belt and said, "I found this hanging on a cedar limb at the high water line."

Fred Schott crowded up close and studied the heavy brass buckle. Memories of the foot log at Big Island welled up in his mind. Then he looked at Smith and said:

"That's Kube's belt. He must have tried to strip off and swim for it."

Except for the crackle of burning wood and the sound of the Crooked Fork's rapids, silence descended on their camp in the cedars. The men gathered in the warmth radiating from the fire. The water steamed then boiled. Ranger Smith broke the spell cast upon them by a free spirit lost in the Lochsa.

"Get your cups," he said, "and I'll pour you up a shot o' coffee."[143]

Smith's crew had built a telephone line from Lolo Hot Springs to Powell Ranger Station by late October 1912—five years before phone communication was linked between Lolo Hot Springs and the Bitterroot Valley.

The next year the same crew began building a trail southward to forge a transportation link with Weholt's Elk Summit Ranger Station. The new trail led from the Lochsa River up Walton Hill and through Savage Pass, a 6,000-foot-high saddle named after trapper Milt Savage. By the fall of 1913, the crew reached Colt Creek, then the boundary between the Elk Summit and Powell ranger districts.

From his headquarters at Three Forks on Moose Creek, ranger Ray Fitting was busy building trails in 1913, too. Alec McLendon, who in 1911 had hewn the logs for Frank Smith's ranger station, was Fitting's trail crew foreman. Floyd Newlon, John Van Horn, Lee Hawkins, and Ed Gilroy were the crew members. During July they built a new phone line from the mouth of Three Links Creek up a steep ridge leading from the Selway River to Sixty-two Rock, high in the Crags mountains. From there they moved camp to Fish Lake. After spending a day filling up on red-bellied trout, they began reopening the old Nez Perce hunting road eastward along the divide toward Elk Summit.[144]

Much of that country had burned in 1910, and hundreds of fire-killed trees had fallen to block the trail. In testimony to the love of the Nez Perce for alpine mountaintops, the hunting road climbed to the crest of McConnell Mountain and then dropped abruptly down its eastern side. But Fitting's trail builders sought efficiency, not scenery. They abandoned the alpine route, opting to follow the contour of the mountains on the slope above Moose Creek, and then rejoined the hunting road at a chain of meadows east of McConnell Mountain. The great fires had spared the forest surrounding the meadows, so they camped there in cool shade near fresh water with grass available for their horses to graze.

The government paid the men $75 per month — Foreman McLendon perhaps got a bit more than the others — and each furnished his own bed roll, axe, shovel, food supplies, and two horses. The government supplied two crosscut saws, mattocks for grading trail, and three seven-foot by nine-foot wall tents. The men paired off two to a tent, Ranger Fitting bunking with Foreman McLendon whenever his duties brought him to the trail crew's camp. Unlike Ranger Smith's crew, who bought grub for all at Lolo Hot Springs and shared the costs and the cooking, these men reopening the hunting road cooked morning and night on three separate camp fires. Like housewives in a friendly village, they borrowed and bartered syrup, butter, sugar — whatever was needed to round out their menus. On the trail they worked as an integrated team; but each day while they sawed logs and dug tread, it is likely that individual sourdough jugs bubbled in each of the three tents at the Chain Meadows camp.

At a deep saddle eight miles east of McConnell Mountain, Fitting's crew left the hunting road and built trail into the head of Warm Springs Creek, where they ended their work for the summer. Before returning to Fish Lake, Ed Gilroy and Floyd Newlon climbed to the summit of Grave Peak. They saw no sign of the hand of humans on that pinnacled hub of the land of the Lochsa. The Bitterroot Range stretched in all directions, its forest green broken here and there by patches of granite rubble and alpine lakes. A big, wild country it was. But even in 1913 industrialization was closing in on its wildness. Reordering the Lochsa in the interests of civilization required that forest fires be controlled, and the expanded trail network would help them do that. Telephone lines made it possible for people who dwelt outside the mountains to direct events inside. The Forest Service had a plan for that land, and effective communication was necessary to assure that the rangers got their jobs done in line with the plan.

But the Lochsa breathed freedom, not government control, and it cast its spell over all, including these modern mountain men. Ranger Smith loved that land, and strong currents of its free spirit pulsed through his veins. By midsummer 1914 he had encountered more government regulation than he could tolerate. He quit the Forest Service after a clash with Deputy Supervisor Howell. His crew wanted to leave with him, but Smith urged them to stay and carry on the work of the Forest Service.

Only Smith and Howell knew for sure what happened between them. Of his choice between a free life in the mountains and one smothered by government rules, Smith said, "If Howell can't take my word for it, I ain't writin' any papers for him."[145]

Ranger Smith built sturdy cabins, high quality trails, and phone lines that carried one's voice with the clarity of a coyote's howl in the moonlight. He met the deadlines and priorities established by Supervisor Fenn and set forth in the *Use Book*. He was respected by his crew for his woodsmanship and admired for his competent leadership of mountain men. But to bring lands like the Lochsa under administrative control, the Forest Service needed men who respected the government system of hierarchy and rules at least as much as they answered the call of the natural earth. Some men could tolerate that clash of bureaucracy and spirit while still maintaining allegiance to the land that had captured their hearts and souls. Ranger Smith was one of several whose reverence for nature's freedom could not conform to the rules of the Forest Service.

Nonetheless, those disciples of government who left boot and heel blazes and strung telephone lines beyond the Indian, trapper, and prospector trails were indeed fortunate men. By 1914 they had begun what was to become the trail-building boom of the twenties. They learned from the fires of 1910 that the natural systems of the Lochsa would not yield easily to control by people. They were blessed with clear purpose, something to love, something to fight, something to control, something awesome to surrender to. Those path builders had fires to fight. They had Tama Jim's letter, the act of 1897, and a land so big and wild they couldn't possibly understand it all.

12

Testing the Rangers' Resolve

I ***n late June 1920 Ed Mackay rode a strong black horse*** and led three loaded mules from Lolo Hot Springs westward over the hill to take charge of the Powell district for the United States Forest Service. The new ranger paid scant attention to the ground squirrels squeaking alarm as he skirted the edge of the forest along Glade Creek, nor did he marvel much at the blooming quamash, which made Packer Meadows look like a lake gleaming in late morning sun. With the reins gripped in his left

More than a decade after he took charge of the Powell district, Ed Mackay studies one of the cabins built at Lolo Pass during his tenure at Powell Ranger Station, 1920–1940.—Henry J. Viche, U.S. Forest Service

Bill Bell served as ranger at Elk Summit Ranger Station from 1917 to 1928.
—Pearl Bell McKee

hand, he yanked on the pack train's lead rope with his right, moving the animals along despite their persistent snatching at the lush grasses of the meadow. Ed's purposefulness showed in the square set of his wide-brimmed hat. 1919 had been a bad year for fires in those mountains, and the woods already smelled dry. How to keep that country from burning up in the years ahead was foremost in his thoughts as he rode along the trail.

He knew that the rangers before him had built some facilities needed for protecting the land, but he planned to construct more trails to provide faster access to fires. More telephone lines would be needed, and new cabins should be erected at strategic locations to shelter smoke chasers and store firefighting equipment. Another top priority was to identify the mountain peaks that furnished the best visibility of the Lochsa landscape and to install lookouts on them to enable the discovery and location of fires while they were small. In fact, Ed's primary mission was to banish fires from the forest—a big job in a big land. Backed by outstanding service in World War I and considerable experience in the Bitterroot mountains, Ed Mackay, at age 27, seemed like the man to get it done.

Ed was also backed by his neighboring rangers who held similar resolve. Three years before Ed rode over the hill, veteran mountain man

Bill Bell had taken charge of the Elk Summit district to the south, and rangers on the Fish Lake district to the west had pushed trails and phone lines into the heart of the Bitterroot mountains.

Bell's outpost from God's country was Hamilton, Montana. Like Ranger Weholt before him, Bell found that loaded pack animals got sore backs and sometimes rolled while scrambling over the rocky trails across the mountains. Even with light loads, travel was so slow that it took three days to trail a pack train from Hamilton to Elk Summit Ranger Station. Snow cornices, amassed on the crest by winter storms, also prevented safe crossing by pack trains until the snow melted in early summer. Variations in the topography and climate of the Elk Summit district could generate conflagrations in the lowlands of East Moose Creek while snow still blocked pack trains' passage through Blodgett Pass. To be able to control fires, Bell had to get men to Elk Summit earlier and move supplies more efficiently from outside the wilderness into his ranger station and from there to trail crews, lookouts, and men fighting fires.

So in 1922 he switched his supply base to Lolo Hot Springs, where Ed Mackay and rangers before him had constructed a cluster of log buildings called Mud Creek Ranger Station. By that time the rangers had built a good trail and had established a telephone line between Powell Ranger Station and Elk Summit. Pack trains could now cross Lolo Pass

Lolo (Mud Creek) Ranger Station, located adjacent to Lolo Hot Springs resort, as it looked in 1922. —U.S. Forest Service

at least a month earlier in the spring. Sometime in June 1922 the rangers set out from Mud Creek—Mackay with fifteen men, three packers, and three pack trains; Bell with ten men, two packers, and two pack trains. The men walked while the rangers rode sturdy mountain horses; each ranger led two mules loaded with personal gear and equipment. From time to time Bell or Mackay would dismount and let one of the crew ride awhile. Fifty-six government horses and mules and thirty men led by two of the most self-reliant rangers ever assigned to the Lochsa—that's what went over the hill that day.

At length they neared the joining of the two major streams that form the Lochsa River. They found the White Sand Fork running so high that the roar of its waters smothered the clatter of men and horses and mules. Its onrushing torrents overwhelmed the waters of the Crooked Fork, claiming the Lochsa as its own. Like the rivers, the trail also forked here. To reach Powell Ranger Station, Ed Mackay's outfit would turn right and cross the Crooked Fork, a difficult but possible venture. To reach Elk Summit, however, Bell would have to cross the raging White Sand.

Bell's route via Lolo Pass had detoured the snow cornices of Blodgett, but the melting of that snow along the crest of the Bitterroots had discharged a powerful river across his new way to the Elk Summit Station. But Bell had anticipated floodwater; he had 300 feet of five-eighths-inch cable loaded on one of his mules. And the previous fall Ed Mackay's trail crew had installed a tram on a light cable strung from bank to bank across the White Sand. The next morning one of Bell's men, Joe Alkire, worked the big cable across the river, using the tram as transport, and anchored its end to the base of a sturdy fir that stood on the south bank. To test the power of the water, Alkire dropped his dog, a strong swimmer, from the tram into the center of the river. Powerful currents swept the dog downstream a full quarter mile before he gained the shore.

Working under Bell's supervision, the crew mounted a sixteen-inch-diameter log between two cedars growing on the north bank. They fashioned a crude windlass by boring holes through the log to receive two large crowbars. The cedars provided the frame, the log the spool, and the bars the handles. They wound the cable on this rig until it stretched taut across, and 8 feet above, the 220-foot-wide torrent.

Then they made a raft of dry cedar logs, eight feet wide and fifteen feet long. To prevent cargo from tumbling overboard and to serve as a rack for tying horses and mules, they installed a stout railing around

This bridge, built across the White Sand in 1922, provided a safe crossing for people and pack and saddle stock en route from Lolo Hot Springs to Elk Summit Ranger Station. —U.S. Forest Service

the deck. Two lines hooked to pulleys on the big cable served to angle the craft in the current so that it would glide from shore to shore. That angle proved important. Too much and the raft would turn sideways and swamp. Not enough and the raft would hang motionless in the stream.

After a few trial runs the mountain-men-turned-sailors mastered their task. In two days they had strung the cable, built the raft, and moved twenty-six horses and mules, all their saddles and packs, eleven men, and three dogs across the river. Bell resumed his journey to Elk Summit on the morning of the third day. As Ranger Mackay watched the bobbing packs of the loaded trains vanish into the timber, he told his crew: "Nothin' in these mountains is too tough for that old boy."[146]

Later that same year, Ranger Mackay hired a man named Cross and his partner to build a bridge across the White Sand about four miles upstream from Powell Ranger Station, where cliffs crowding the stream on the south bank narrowed the width of the channel. As was common among craftsmen in those days, Cross carried his personal carpentry tools on a pack horse. Ranger Mackay provided a camp, grub, blasting powder, bolts, spikes, and the like, and a mule with harness to skid logs and haul rocks to anchor the piers. Ranger Bell did all of the blacksmithing work. They built a beautiful bridge, a

Ranger Walde is number six in this group of Forest Service personnel assembled at Kooskia, Idaho, in 1922. —U.S. Forest Service

monument to the self-reliant craftsmanship needed by the government to banish fire from the forests.

While Mackay and Bell built trails and bridges, Ranger Walde moved his headquarters from Fish Lake down to the mouth of Boulder Creek on the Lochsa River where ranger-at-large J. H. Robinson supervised construction of a new station in 1921. In the spring of 1922 ranger Al Kolmorgan hoisted the stars and stripes over a complex of log buildings called the Lochsa Ranger Station. Like Ranger Bell, he and his men had to cross the river to reach much of their district, so they too installed a cable and a ferry.[147]

In 1922 Rangers Mackay and Bell had charge of the upper reaches of the Lochsa country. On January 2, 1923, in the small office where ex-Forest Service supervisor Frank Fenn published the *Kooskia Mountaineer*, energetic forest officer Ralph Hand took the ranger's oath and replaced Ranger Walde on the Lochsa district.[148] Mackay, Bell, and Hand, then, represented the United States government in the entire Lochsa drainage except for part of the canyon country upstream from the Lochsa's junction with the Selway; that region was supervised by ranger Jack Parsell of the Middle Fork district. Those were the frontline men who worked tirelessly, and often went without sleep, to ready themselves for the year when the woods would dry as they did in 1910. While thunderstorms

The Lochsa Ranger Station, across the river from the mouth of Boulder Creek, was built in 1921. Note several new rolls of Number 9 galvanized wire to be used for telephone line construction. —U.S. Forest Service

Forest Service personnel ferry pack stock across the Lochsa River at Boulder Creek in 1921 or 1922. —Rowe Lowary, U.S. Forest Service

Lochsa district ranger Ralph Hand inspects Castle Butte lookout in 1924.
—U.S. Forest Service

rumbled across the ridges, they built trails, phone lines, and cabins and stored tools and grub in the back country ready for use by the men who would attack the fires. Each winter they retreated out of the mountains not to return, except for an occasional patrol, until spring.

The rangers stationed men on the high mountaintops—like Beaver Ridge, Indian Post Office, Rocky Point, Grave Peak, Diablo Mountain, McConnell Mountain, Beargrass Mountain, Castle Butte, Stanley Butte, and Fish Butte—to serve as the eyes of the fire control organization. At first each lookout lived in a tent pitched in some sheltered spot near the summit of his mountain. He would hike each day from his "rag camp" to the peak to watch for smoke. When he spotted smoke he telephoned its location to the district headquarters at Lochsa, Powell, or Elk Summit station, depending on which ranger claimed his lookout. His ranger would then dispatch smoke chasers to squelch the fire before it could spread (see map 6).

By 1925 the rangers had erected observatories on the most important peaks, and the lookouts moved from their rag camps to better quarters at the tops of their mountains. Most of these structures measured about fourteen feet square, with a six-foot-square cupola on top. The lookout lived downstairs and climbed a ladder to the cupola to

Middle Fork district ranger Jack Parsell on duty at Woodrat Mountain cabin during the early 1920s.
—U.S. Forest Service

Indian Post Office Lookout, under construction in 1922, shows the type of construction used at the time.
—U.S. Forest Service

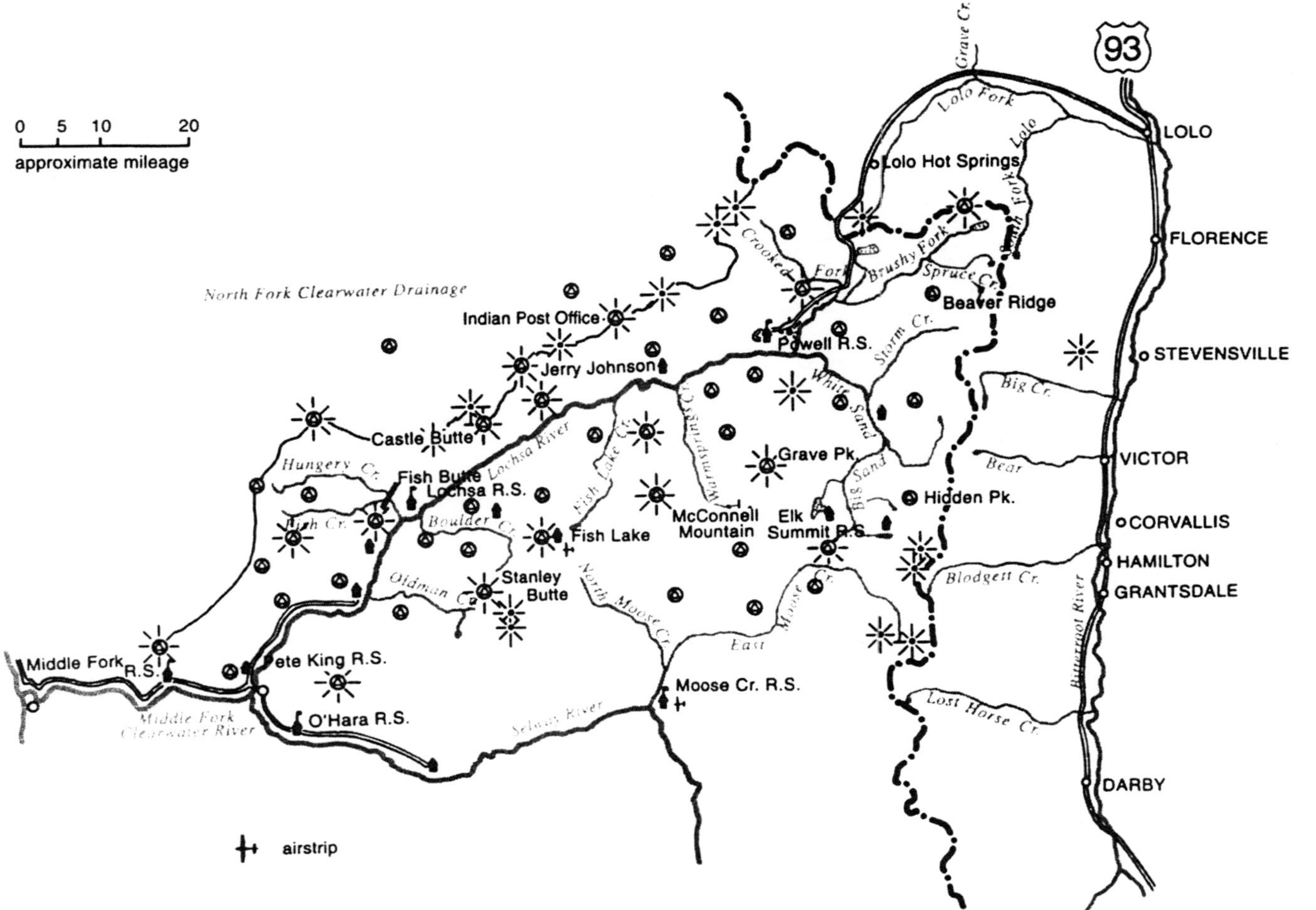
0 5 10 20
approximate mileage
93
LOLO
FLORENCE
STEVENSVILLE
VICTOR
CORVALLIS
HAMILTON
GRANTSDALE
DARBY
Lolo Hot Springs
Beaver Ridge
Powell R.S.
Indian Post Office
Jerry Johnson
Castle Butte
Fish Butte
Lochsa R.S.
Fish Lake
McConnell Mountain
Grave Pk.
Elk Summit R.S.
Hidden Pk.
Stanley Butte
Middle Fork R.S.
Pete King R.S.
O'Hara R.S.
Moose Cr. R.S.
North Fork Clearwater Drainage
Middle Fork Clearwater River
Selway River
Lochsa River
Bitterroot River
Grave Cr.
Lolo Fork
Lolo
Crooked Fork
Brushy Fork
Spruce Cr.
Storm Cr.
White Sand
Big Sand
Warmsprings Cr.
Fish Lake Cr.
Hungery Cr.
Boulder Cr.
Oldman Cr.
North Moose Cr.
East Moose Cr.
Big Cr.
Bear
Blodgett Cr.
Lost Horse Cr.
airstrip

Map 6. *U.S. Forest Service stations, 1934.*

Fine craftsmanship shows in the new Elk Summit Ranger Station under construction in 1925. Note the mitered corners and creative dormer. Part of the original station is at left center. —U.S. Forest Service

observe and locate fires. All structures were grounded to protect against lightning strikes; thus, even during lightning storms, the lookout could work safely in the cupola, spotting smoke and recording the location of lightning strikes. When the forests were dry, the rangers often sent smoke chasers to find individual strikes and confirm that no latent spark lingered to blow up on some hot afternoon. 1910 had taught them that fires roaring through the tree crowns could not be suppressed. The objective, then, was to find fires fast and attack them while small, *before* they left the ground.

Telephone lines connected all of the lookouts with ranger stations by the mid-twenties, and lines extended from each station to the outposts of Kooskia and Lolo Hot Springs. The rangers expanded their headquarters, too. Bell and his men built a new two-story log ranger station at Elk Summit. Mackay added two warehouses for storing equipment at Powell. And by 1925 Ranger Hand had moved his station to a new site at the mouth of Zion Creek, a short ways down river from Boulder Flat. To speed the travel of pack trains, smoke chasers, and large fire crews, the rangers and their men built trails near every place where fire might conceivably gain the upper hand in the Lochsa. Ten- to fifteen-man crews constructed new mainline trails and straightened and widened many of those already in place. Small crews, sometimes

Ranger Bill Bell horse packed the equipment over Blodgett Pass about 1920 and set this mill in Hoodoo Creek a short distance downstream from the Elk Summit Station. —Pearl Bell McKee

only one or two men, extended lower-standard, but nonetheless efficient, trails deep into the mountains.

New trails were churned to dust by packers leading horse and mule trains loaded with supplies to sustain the builders. Since the round trip from Elk Summit to Lolo Hot Springs took five days, Ranger Bell kept one pack train on that route while the other carried supplies from his station to crews in the surrounding mountains. To provide variety, the packers alternated between supplying the camps and pulling the long stretch to Lolo Hot Springs. Packer Heinie Williams liked the camp runs out of Elk Summit best. Of the spell of those mountains, he said, "You talk about Switzerland. We had it all right there."[149]

Ranger Mackay's Powell district pack trains got little rest, either. And trailless canyon country downstream from the Lochsa station made Ranger Hand's supply problems the toughest of all. Hand's crews finally blasted a trail through the cliffs in 1927, but until then the packers had to detour their trains high into the mountains, much like the railroad companies had done in 1908 and 1909.

Since the trails had to be chopped, dug, and blasted through the mountains, dynamite and grub were the main cargoes transported by the packers and their mules. To separate dynamite from detonators, the packers rolled the jar-sensitive blasting caps in their slickers, then tied

Packer Homer McClain, (the old Homer from chapter 1) loads pack horses at Powell Ranger Station in the early 1920s. —U.S. Forest Service

them behind the cantles of their saddles—a risky proposition even on a gentle horse.

Determined men chopped and dug at the Lochsa's mantle. Dynamite blasts shook the canyons as trails probed deeper into the mountains. Elk tangled their antlers in new phone lines, while bears dug up the buried garbage at campsites after the builders moved on. Trees crashed earthward due to forces other than wind and rot. New structures gleamed atop mountain peaks. And the sounds of men and mules and the smells of spent dynamite and grub and garbage signaled the invasion of government order into the land of the Lochsa.

The twenties also saw the fulfillment of a dream of the chambers of commerce of Lewiston, Idaho, and Missoula, Montana. In 1919 the Forest Service surveyed a road from Lolo Hot Springs, Montana, over the hill and down the Lochsa River to Lowell, Idaho. Construction began at Lolo Hot Springs in 1923.[150] Like the trail builders of the interior, those crews used dynamite, horse-drawn scrapers, hand tools, muscle, and sweat to forge their road through the mountains. But their supply lines were much more efficient. With a finished road behind them, cars and trucks could be used to tote supplies from the outposts to the construction camps.

Dynamite explodes near the crest of the Bitterroots as Forest Service crews construct trails to hasten travel of pack trains and firefighters into the Lochsa. —C. H. McDonald, U.S. Forest Service

In 1925 the road crossed Lolo Pass, and motorized vehicles, the likes of which had never before been seen by the wild creatures of the Lochsa, first chugged over the hill. The builders pushed the road on to Powell Ranger Station in 1928,[151] providing a great day for the ranger in charge when the first truck rumbled into the yard. Ed Mackay hosted a picnic to celebrate the event. Forest Service personnel and their families from Missoula, the Bitterroot Valley, and even more distant environs attended the feast, fun, and games. No longer a vague spot on the map of a wilderness, Mackay's Powell Ranger Station now boasted the ultimate in access—it could be driven to by automobile. This meant to some people that the place was civilized; never again would the Powell ranger need to dispatch the packer and his mules to Lolo Hot Springs for supplies.

While developing access and communications, the men of the Lochsa squelched many blazes, though some did manage to get away. In 1917, 1919, and 1926 several fires scorched the forests and headlined the news. Fires that the government was able to control escaped public attention, but they provided evidence of the government's hold on the land. With

Rangers Bill Bell and Ed Mackay examine the new road at Lolo Pass in 1925. —Pearl Bell McKee

Automobiles and roads began replacing pack stock and trails at the Powell district after 1928. —U.S. Forest Service

the extension of each road and trail and phone line, humankind gained an advantage in the war on fire in the woods. Troops attacked each blaze as if it were a major battle. When a fire escaped control they retreated to safety, ordered more men and supplies, and settled in for a long campaign. They lost some battles but never lost heart. They felt sure that, with more men, more equipment, more trails, and more roads, they would eventually prevail.

And no one could shirk his part if they were to vanquish fire. For want of prompt discovery, the smoke chaser might arrive too late to stop the fire. For want of an accurate location, the smoke chaser might search in vain while the fire continued to spread. For want of sharp tools, the line could not be dug with speed. For want of a loaded pack train on the trail, men might go hungry and their strength fail before the flames. For want of competent leadership, the fire could make a mockery of attack strategies. Insuring that no one's failure impaired the work of another became the firefighters' creed. Only the spirits of the mountains and the men themselves knew of their long treks in the night, the interminable hours of all-out effort to keep fires from the crowns, and the numbing sense of failure when a fire escaped, leaving the smoke chaser alone in its wake, his control lines overrun by the power of nature on the loose.

Those firefighters were men committed to a cause. For them the purpose of time was to strike fires harder. They believed in their mission, their supervisors, the Forest Service, and their country. None would get rich from his position on the government's payroll. Since at the time government work was considered less prestigious than private enterprises, those most capable mountain men sometimes yearned to leave the mountains and take up business for themselves. A few tried, but the Lochsa called them back again and again to the dusty trails, the sweat and soot and grime of the fire lines, the vistas high in the mountains, the clear streams, the mystique of the grizzly bear, and the aura that made the Lochsa country in some ways similar to its neighboring rivers, yet different from any place else on earth. They were hooked on that land, and the land was ruled by the government. So if they were going to live and work in the Lochsa, government work was what they had to do.

It took those masters of improvisation twenty years to license trappers, bring their activities under special use permit, and curb unnecessary damage to surface resources by prospectors and miners. And at the

Ex-ranger Bill Bell displays furs at Powell station, ca. 1930.
—Henry J. Viche, U.S. Forest Service

same time, they developed trail access to the wilderness, established telephone communications to ranger stations, and installed equipment and manpower in defiance of the threat from fire. But the conformity inherent in government continued to clash with the free spirits of the best of the mountain men. They could no longer carry the *Use Book* in their saddle bags because the rulemakers in Washington, D.C., and other centralized offices had expanded its directives to fill several thick books. Office bureaucrats tended to burden field men with detailed instructions, while the men of the mountains tried to reduce the complexities of their world to tasks they could understand and accomplish.

As sure as the grizzly was king of the wilderness, Ranger Bell was the master of mountain crafts and a leader among men. He feared no one. He never started a fight, but he never lost one, either. Although Bell spoke very little, his dog, his pack stock, and his men understood his instructions completely. Perhaps the most respected man in the land of the Lochsa, he took great pride in his outfit, in men of his own cut, and in their achievements in the mountains. He considered inspections of his work by higher authorities insults to his personal dependability.

It may have been inevitable that Ranger Bell and supervisor Charles D. Simpson tangled in 1928. Nobody knew what happened, though sev-

Regional forester Evan W. (Major) Kelley at the Forest Service's Nine Mile Remount Station in the mid-1930s.
—U.S. Forest Service

eral had their ideas. Ranger Jack Parsell said, "They tried to put a uniform on him."One of Bell's crew bosses, Bill Samsel, said, "Simpson reckoned Bill had misappropriated money. But there were other things." According to Packer Heinie Williams, "Him and Supervisor Simpson fell out about cuttin' logs out of the trail. Bell had his men cut the big cedars out of the Moose Creek trail. Simpson gave him hell and Bill swore at him."[152]

Bell himself provided little more insight when in the fall he greeted his aged mother and kid sister, Pearl, at their home near Hamilton, Montana. "What happened, Bill?" they asked. "I backed him up agin a tree," Bill said. "I don't know why I didn't kill him."[153]

Ranger Mackay had said of Bell: "There's nothin' in these mountains too tough for that old boy." But the government's regulations and the cut of at least one man who enforced them were more than the normally cool-tempered Ranger Bell could stomach. Furthermore, no one, not even a man as widely respected as Bill Bell, could treat a superior officer of the Forest Service the way Bell dealt with Simpson and get away with it for long. Bill Bell made his last trip out of the Lochsa as ranger in the fall of 1928. He turned in his Forest Service badge, withdrew the money he had deposited for retirement, bought stock and saddles, and took up packing and trapping.

Bell would be missed as ranger. But others in charge of the Lochsa and lands elsewhere in the northern Rocky Mountains gained a strong ally in their war against fire when chief of the Forest Service F. A. Silcox in 1929 assigned Maj. Evan W. Kelley as regional forester in charge of the Northern Region (Region One). Kelley's instructions from Washington were to stop the large fires in Region One. Besides his outstanding personal commitment to the mission, Kelley's major fire-control policies were to (1) deliver manpower, supplies, and equipment to fires faster by extending a network of low-standard roads into the remote areas of the region and (2) set high standards of accountability for people responsible to control fires.

Kelley tolerated no mediocre performance. He weeded the less-than-fully committed personnel out of the organization by requiring investigation of every fire that escaped control. Reasons for the escape were disclosed, individuals were held accountable, and discipline—ranging from letters of reprimand to discharge from the Forest Service—was meted out.

With Major Kelley in charge of Region One, the fire force was more ready than it had ever been before, and motorized access was extending every day. The odds seemed to favor successful control of fires in the Lochsa.

One of those dry years for which the fire-fighting organization had been getting ready came in 1929. On August 1 cumulus clouds, scattered over the prairies west of the mountains, joined to form black storms that rumbled thunder and marched eastward through the hot, blue summer sky toward the parched forests and the waiting rangers.

One big storm struck Ranger Hand's district in early evening. By that time updrafts of moist air in the clouds' interior had transformed the fluffy cumulus of the prairie to generators of electricity. Although light rain fell from the clouds' base, none reached the ground. As thunder shook the mountains, lightning flashed between the positive and negative fields in the clouds' interior. Great bolts carried the charge from cloud to earth, exploding there in flame.

Some bolts struck rocks and started no enduring fires, but others ignited trees whose crowns flamed like giant candles against the storm-blackened sky. From Castle Butte Lookout, observer Larsen and smoke chaser Chenowith saw a powerful bolt ignite a dead cedar snag deep in the canyon of Bald Mountain Creek. Less than five minutes after smoke first puffed out of the forest, Chenowith was headed down the mountain to the fire, confident that he could defuse the menace before it grew too big to handle.

But nature intervened. En route to Bald Mountain Creek, Chenowith discovered another fire, as yet unseen by the lookouts. Fearing it might

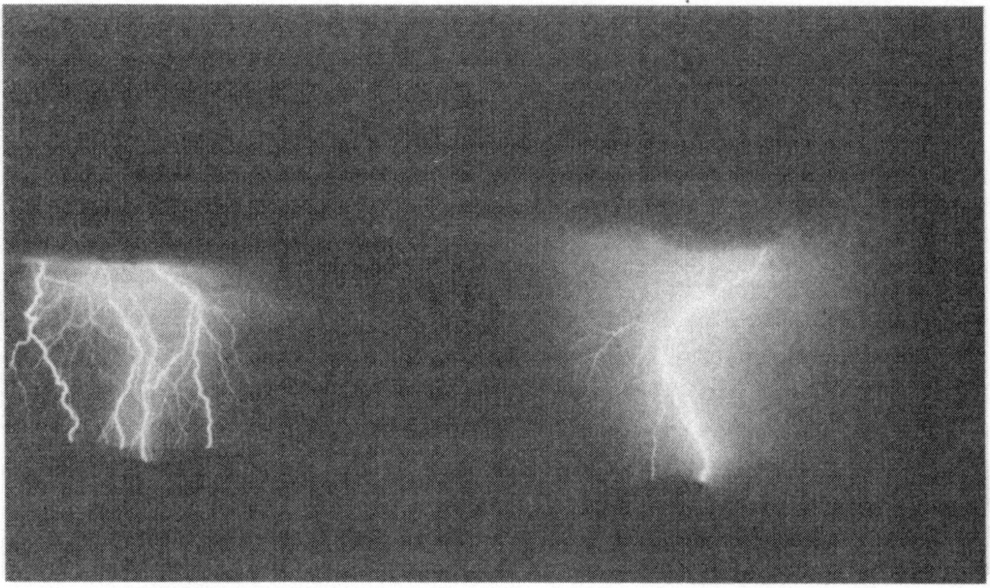

As in all years of drought, lightning bolts in 1929 started several fires in the Lochsa's forests. —William H. Petram, U.S. Forest Service

blow up, he dug a trench around it and cooled the flames with dirt, thus preventing it from spreading.[154] Subduing this threat, however, delayed his attack on the Bald Mountain fire. When he arrived at 6:30 A.M. on August 2 he found large logs and dry snags burning on three-quarters of an acre.

Chenowith stored his forty-one-pound pack, including rations for three days, in a safe spot and then began chopping logs with his axe and digging trench with this shovel and mattock. He attacked first where the flames seemed most likely to escape. By 10:00 A.M. he had stopped the spread of the fire's perimeter, though burning snags still threw flaming brands across his line. For a while it looked like Chenowith would gain control. But a high wind during midafternoon scattered the flames. Black smoke boiled out of Bald Mountain Creek as fire rushed through the forest. Observer Larsen phoned the Lochsa Ranger Station and told Ranger Hand that the fire had escaped Chenowith's control.[155] Hand sent reinforcements from all directions, but, despite their best efforts, the fire burned three-quarters of the Bald Mountain Creek drainage, including the camp of the firefighters, during the afternoon of August 3.

The Bald Mountain fire had forced the rangers onto the defensive. As it burned its way up the Lochsa River ahead of each day's hot afternoon winds, it scorched forests in tributary after tributary.

Hot, dry weather in 1929 dehydrated forest fuels throughout the northern Rockies. Several fires escaped initial attack and became major conflagrations.
—K.D. Swan, U.S. Forest Service

Packer Heinie Williams leads his loaded pack train through the Lochsa's Wendover Canyon en route to the Bald Mountain Fire.
—K.D. Swan, U.S. Forest Service

The Powell district road construction crew poses at their camp near Indian Grave Peak along the Lolo Trail in 1934. —Henry J. Viche, U.S. Forest Service

By August 14 reinforcements from the Clearwater Forest were fighting the fire's northern flank near the Lolo Trail, while Ranger Hand's crews continued their work on its southern perimeter. In what became known as "the retreat of the Lochsa," Lolo Forest Supervisor Simpson and Ranger Mackay with fifty men attacked the head of the fire on the Lochsa River at the mouth of Weir Creek. The fire overran their control lines again and again. Three times the flames forced them to dump their camps into the river and run for their lives. Some people panicked.

At the mouth of Indian Post Office Creek a band of retreating firefighters tried to take over Bill Bell's pack train, so they could ride his mules up the long trail to Powell Ranger Station and safety. Tough miners from Butte, Montana, these men had had enough of the Bald Mountain fire. They gathered around Bell who was mounted on his black horse, and the leader said, "We're taking your pack train."

Bill hauled his long-barreled, single-action .45 pistol from the scabbard on his belt, thumbed back the hammer, and responded, "Ye might take my pack train. But five or six of you ain't goin' out."

Thus ended the miners' idea of a free ride out of the wilderness.

The conflagration grew so large that Major Kelley on August 21 assigned his top assistant, Elers Koch, to take charge of control operations. By that time Mackay and Simpson had retreated from Weir Creek and established camps at Jerry Johnson's cabin and at a place called Beach Camp about three miles farther down the Lochsa.

Fire surrounded the Beach Camp on August 23 and swept up the south side of the river past Jerry Johnson's cabin. Their defenses shattered, control of the fire seemed hopeless. But fortunately for the sooty band, then 160 strong, the hot weather broke on August 25, and a few drops of rain fell in the night, cooling down the fire. By the time Ranger Mackay's crews connected their lines with Hand's to the south and those of the Clearwater Forest to the north, 480 firefighters had built and lost untold lengths of fire line. In the end, rainstorms and ninety-five miles of held line succeeded in stopping the fire (see map 6).

The land of the Lochsa had produced a flaming welcome for Major Kelley, the newly assigned forester in charge of Region One.

Humbled by the fire but with their resolve unshaken, the rangers rehung phone lines on blackened snags and continued to push Major Kelley's long and narrow roads. Having lost much to the fire of 1929, they redoubled their efforts to protect what forest remained on their districts. To keep the Lochsa green remained their mission.

Two major events during the early thirties accelerated achievement of Major Kelley's road-building objective. First, Earl Hall, a creative Forest Service road construction supervisor from California, invented the first angle bulldozer,[156] a device designed to build roads in the mountains and destined to rip up more earth than the processes of natural erosion had done since Columbus set foot in America.

Second, at 4:00 P.M. on March 9, 1933, newly elected President Franklin D. Roosevelt called together his secretaries of war, agriculture and interior, the director of the bureau of the budget, judge advocate general of the army, and the solicitor of the department of interior. The president spoke of the American people's dependence on natural resources and proposed a program for simultaneously reclaiming the country's wasted natural resources and developing America's young men. The meeting ended six hours later with the birth of the Civilian Conservation Corps. The fledgling organization was to train young men to fight fires, build roads, and in other ways help the government develop and rule its domain, including the Lochsa region.[157]

Aided by the foregoing events, a rough road—appropriately called a truck trail—reached Elk Summit Ranger Station in 1934 and stretched on for three miles, terminating on the slopes of East Moose Creek. That same year, the Powell and Lochsa district road-building crews, following closely the route of the Lolo Trail, completed the first road across the Lochsa portion of the Bitterroot mountains. In late September or early October the east-west crews joined near Noseeum Meadows Although the new road was unsuitable for hauling commerce, the horsemen of the Road to the Buffalo were nevertheless yielding to the drivers of cars and trucks.

Trails followed by roads consumed wildness as fast as crews could gouge dirt from the mountains. To hasten delivery of equipment to backcountry fires, Major Kelley established a remount depot at Ninemile, Montana, equipped with trucks specially designed to haul pack trains to road ends adjacent to roadless country. Transport by road and trail, however, would not be enough. Fires would have to be attacked from the air as well. And by 1934 the rangers had airports ready for use at Fish Lake in the Lochsa Basin and at the junction of Moose Creek and the Selway River to the south. That enthusiasm ran high showed in slogans printed on smoke chaser rations like "Minutes count, let's go," and "Stay with them 'til they're out." To be ready is to be armed psychologically, and in 1934 the rangers of the Lochsa felt more ready than ever before.

By early August the forests were so dry that control of a human-caused fire burning near Selway Falls on August 7 demanded the best efforts of then Selway Forest supervisor Clayton Crocker and his men. While they were still engaged with this fire, three dry storms on August 11 hammered lightning bolts into the Lochsa and Selway country, scattering nineteen fires from the Moose Creek district on the Selway to Fish Butte in the Lochsa district.[158]

Fire staff officer McGregor sent smoke chaser Hy Lyman and a crew of five men from the supply base at Pete King Station to attack what seemed the worst threat, a fire burning in dangerous fuels near Tumble Creek north of the Lochsa River. Lyman and his crew were the toughest kind of firefighters, and they ground the Tumble Creek fire into the Lochsa dirt until not a spark remained to threaten the woods.[159]

Determined smoke chasers dispatched by McGregor snuffed out several additional fires. But two fires burning north of the Lochsa River, one on Pete King Creek and the other on McLendon Butte, outmaneuvered all the attack forces McGregor could muster. Though foreman Sink and six Civilian Conservation Corps men struck the McLendon Butte fire only forty-eight minutes after its discovery, they couldn't contain the blaze. The fire blew up and spotted three miles up the Lochsa River; by the evening of August 11 it had burned 1,500 acres, including a 200-acre spot fire across the Lochsa River and a 60-acre spot that scorched the woods within one mile of the brand new Lochsa Ranger Station.

The McLendon Butte fire, one of several that joined into the great Lochsa-Selway fire of 1934, blows up on a hot August afternoon. —U.S. Forest Service

It took four hours and forty minutes for firefighter Brooks Monroe and three other men to reach the blaze near the forks of Pete King Creek. When they arrived, they found the situation hopeless. With two acres of windfalls and snags burning fiercely, the fire blew up before they could attack. By nightfall, flames had consumed five thousand acres of forest, and a long finger of fire extended from high in Pete King Creek clear to the Lochsa River. Winds carried flaming brands, igniting spot fires as much as two miles from the main fire. The magnitude of the conflagration reduced Monroe and his crew from saviors of the forest to four insignificant specks intent on saving their hides.[160]

All this happened on August 11, 1934, a historic day preceded by a routine weather forecast: "Generally fair weather. Little change in temperature and humidity. Gentle, changeable winds." No matter the forecaster's routine report, big fires had again loosed their fury on the land. The Lochsa Ranger Station was itself threatened, and the rangers were on the defensive one more time.

When the fires blew up, Lochsa ranger Roy Lewis had gone to Fish Lake to be sure the new airport was ready to receive its first airplane. Assistant ranger Jack Godwin, Ranger Lewis's wife, Mabel, and a few crewmen remained at the Lochsa station. With the sixty-acre spot threatening the station, Godwin decided he had to get Mabel out of the canyon to safety.

Mabel loved the cool river, the shade of the cedars, the sparkling water that flowed in Zion Creek, the lichen-covered cliffs, their new station, and all the life and landscape that made their headquarters along the Lochsa a wonderful place to work and live. So when Godwin told her to go, Mabel said, "Jack, I can't leave. I've got to tend the switchboard."

But Godwin was firm. "Throw all the switches together," he said. "And get on your horse and get goin'."

Jack helped saddle Babe, Mabel's horse, and she rode in darkness up the long climb out of the canyon toward the Lolo Trail. She could see that Fish Creek, Obie Creek, and all adjacent forks of the Lochsa were on fire and that widespread flames glowed in the nighttime sky. Mabel thumped Babe's ribs with her heel as they hurried through the night to safety before the flames cut off their way.[161]

Big fires burning on all fronts made August 17 a bad day for the firefighters. Forest officers Brandborg, Rice, and Gerard led 100 men in an all-out fight to save the Pete King station, while farther up the river 250 men retreated from the fire lines and made their stand at the Lochsa Ranger Station. At 8:10 P.M. fire surrounded the men. Ranger Lewis and forest officer I. V. Anderson led the fight to save the Lochsa station and their lives.

Walls of flame rolled across the canyon slopes. Black smoke billowed skyward as fire, fed by the resinous forests, transformed green trees to roaring torches. Gasses rose from the seared wood, and heat and sparks reignited explosive fires high in the smoke column. Parched grass began to burn in the pasture. Great drafts tore hunks of flaming bark from the snags, hauled them up into the smoke column, and then dumped the fiery brands among the men and buildings. The barn and corral burned. Roofs caught fire. This time nature's fury seemed sure to do in the firefighters.

Pumps sucked water from the Lochsa River, but the fire burned the hose in two. After that, six men with buckets climbed on each roof. Others dipped and hauled water from Zion Creek. They doused the flames while the fire swirled around them. As Anderson worked, he sang verses of "Good Old Mountain Music." In an hour, the great wall of fire had swept up the Lochsa River, leaving a band of men marooned on a tiny

That forests burn hot in dry times is evident in the aftermath of the burn of 1934 that surrounds the Lochsa Ranger Station.
—U.S. Forest Service

island of government buildings surrounded by an ocean of burned forests and ash.[162]

On September 20 the rains came.

By that time 5,475 men had built 410 miles of fireline, trying to control the blaze. Four hundred seventy-five head of horses and mules and 115 trucks and cars had delivered tons of supplies to the firefighters; 300 men had been transported to Moose Creek airfield by plane. And fire had burned 252,250 acres in the Lochsa and the adjacent Selway drainage to the south (see map 7).[163]

Despite roads, trails, airplanes, phone lines, new ranger stations, and well-equipped men with plenty of guts, much of the land of the Lochsa and Selway lay blackened and scorched. One-fourth of the entire Selway National Forest had burned. The fires finally were halted, not entirely by efforts of men but also by the barrier of scorched earth left by the Bald Mountain fire five years earlier. That burn helped stop the 1934 fire short of the upper Lochsa's expansive forests.

After the rains came in 1934, Mabel rode Babe back to the Lochsa station to find her beautiful world in burned ruins. She cried. Fire-toughened mountain men cried, too, then cussed and gathered their instruction books and tools and took stock of their situation. The Forest

Service abolished the scorched Selway National Forest and divided its territory between the Lolo, Clearwater, Nez Perce, and Bitterroot forests. Chief Silcox and regional foresters across the land drafted a tough new policy: fires were to be controlled, without exception, before the dangerous burning period (10:00 A.M.) began on the day following discovery.

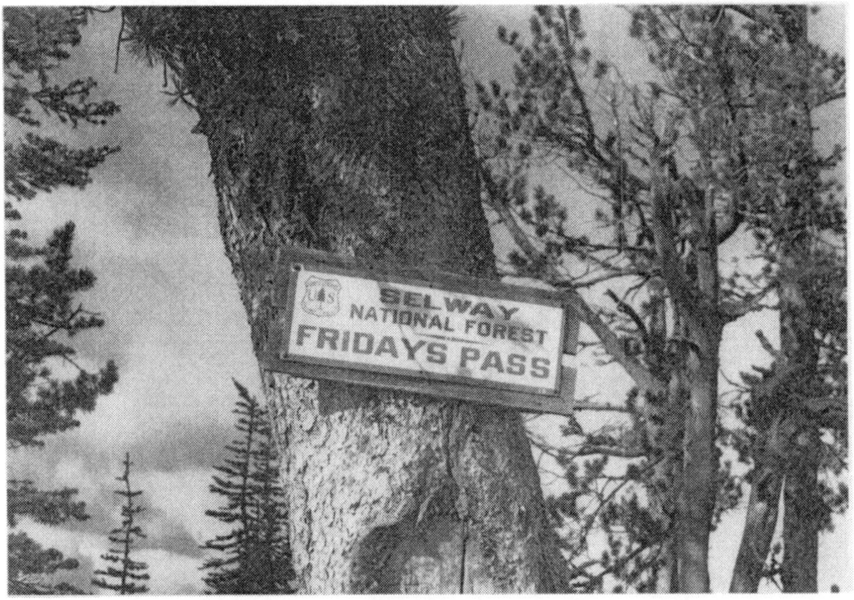

A remnant of the Selway National Forest hangs on a whitebark pine near the summit of the Grave Mountains.

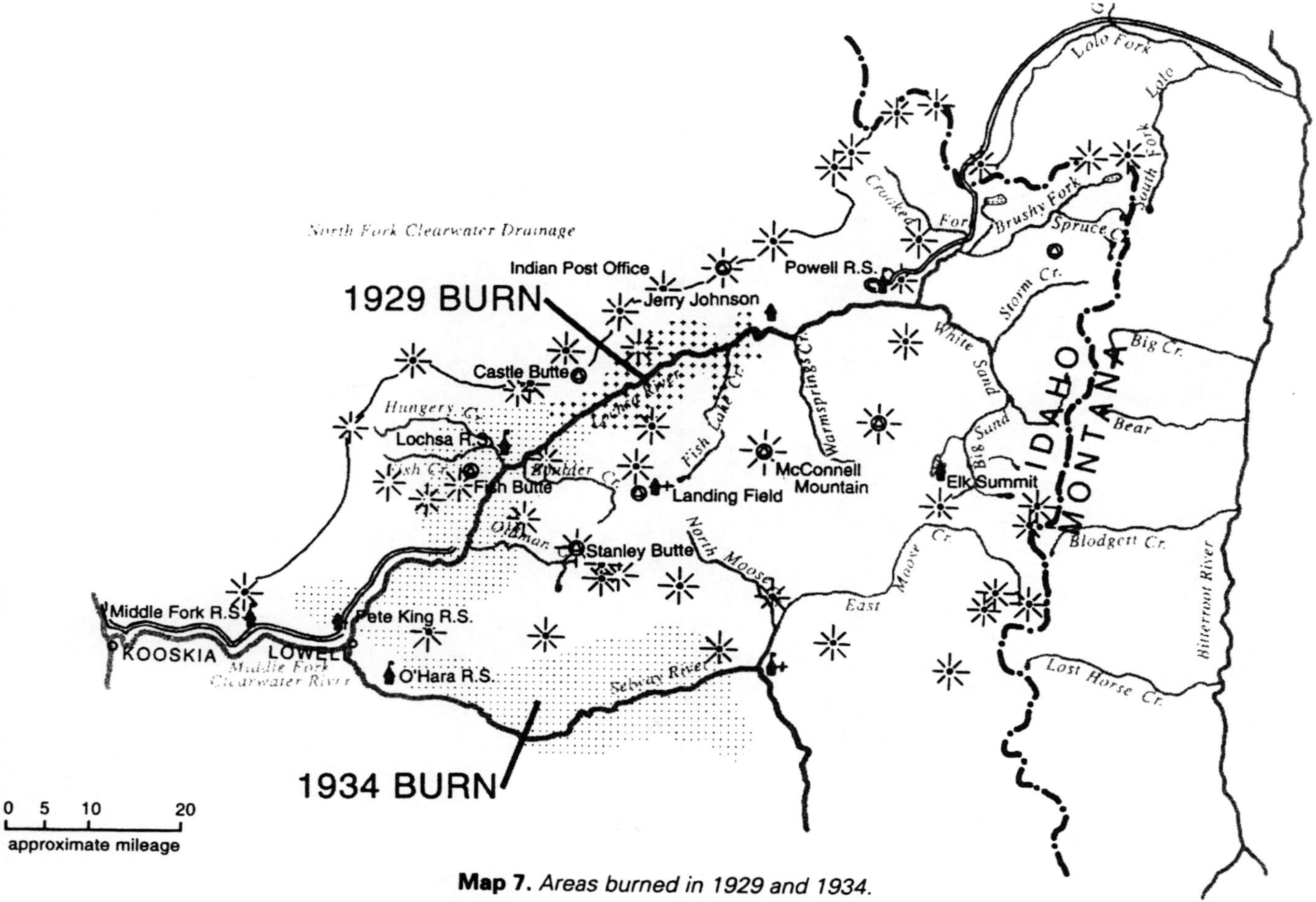

Map 7. *Areas burned in 1929 and 1934.*

Earl Malone repairs Wes Fales's cabin on Blodgett Creek in 1915. —Pearl Bell McKee

13

Lapland and the Fur Poachers

Earl Malone at age eighteen and Fay Burrell at sixteen attended high school in Hamilton and Corvallis, Montana, and on weekends trapped furs in Blodgett Canyon from the edge of the Bitterroot Valley to near the crest of the mountains. The two friends extended their explorations on Thanksgiving Day 1910 by backpacking through knee-deep snow across Blodgett Pass. Descending for the first time into the land of the Lochsa, they discovered Wes Fales's cabin standing near the shores of Big Sand Lake.[164]

After Wes left the mountains in 1912, Fay and Earl took over his trapping territory. By that time Wes had taught them how to improve their sets for marten and that the best bait was mountain goat or horse meat cut in small chunks and dipped in fish that had rotted in a can behind the stove. That they lived in Montana and trapped in Idaho mattered little to Fay and Earl and the other trappers who crossed over the hill through passes in the Bitterroot mountains. They had, after all, discovered the place themselves. They were simply extending a way of life begun by the beaver trappers and carried on in the Lochsa by Lawrence, Alberys, Fales, the Russian, Meeks, and others like them. World War I, however, called the trappers out of the Bitterroots for a short time. The Lochsa's woods, the clear brooks, the mountain passes, the lure of fur, the wildness—from the yeast of all these rose the bread of life for these mountain men. Soldiering was just an interlude. When the war was over, they could hardly wait to get back over the hill to God's country. It was, they now knew, one of the few places in the world where men could roam truly free.

The state line follows the rugged divide between Idaho's Lochsa and Selway drainages and Montana's Bitterroot Valley.

But their freedom to trap unchallenged in the Lochsa country didn't last long. In the early 1900s irresponsible hunters had already begun killing elk and selling their ivory tusks, which at that time commanded good prices. Fearing the elk would be slaughtered like the buffalo, the Idaho legislature in 1919 declared as a game preserve all of the upper Lochsa country south of the river, the Storm Creek Fork, and much of the Selway drainage. There was to be no hunting within the preserve and no trapping except as needed to control predatory animals, such as coyotes or mountain lions, that preyed on elk and deer.

Creation of the preserve threatened the way of life of the trappers, who theretofore had scarcely recognized the crest of the Bitterroots as the border between Montana and Idaho. Nor would they accept the prohibition of their activities by the preserve, which the trappers believed to have been an "unreal bungle" promoted not by the Idaho legislature but by the Forest Service rangers.

So, as in the past, when the needles of the larch turned yellow in the fall, the trappers bought Montana licenses and set traps up the creeks flowing from the mountains into the Bitterroot Valley. When they reached the crest of the Bitterroots, they passed on, as before, deep into Idaho. They didn't worry about the rangers or the preserve or Idaho licenses or Idaho game wardens. They simply moved the border west, claiming territory for their trapping purposes. They called their country Lapland, that is, the place where Montana laps into Idaho.

Charley Powell at the Blodgett Creek cabin in 1919. —Earl Malone

In early November 1919, twenty-year-old Charley Powell (no relation to the homesteader of Powell's Flat) joined Earl Malone for a winter's trapping in the Bitterroot mountains. Six-feet-two-inches tall, 185 pounds, and toughened by a summer's work for the Forest Service, Charley's strength and stamina matched Malone's endurance on the trail. They used pack horses to carry grub and equipment to the cabin located on the south side of Blodgett Creek about one and one-half miles below the foot of Blodgett Pass. From there the two trappers backpacked and sometimes pulled a loaded toboggan over the pass to stock their headquarters cabin at Big Sand Lake.[165]

Blodgett Pass was the only place in the canyon where gnarled trees growing from fissures in the near-solid granite held snow to the steep slopes. They enabled Malone and Powell and trappers before to climb to the pass without being swept back into the canyon by avalanches. That notch on the crest was their gateway to God's country, and to confront its topography energized the adventurous moods of the two young trappers. Buried deep beneath the snow, the trail switchbacked twenty-two times to allow loaded horses and mules to climb the face in summertime. That was fine for pack trains, but the trappers were eager to reach their promised land, west of the divide. The steeper

Earl Malone appreciates the small cabin at Hidden Lake during the wintertime cold of 1919. —Earl Malone

they climbed, the shorter the distance to the crest. So they carved their own trail with snowshoes, crunching the inside bow deep to flatten the tread and angling up and up until they could barely hoist the tips of their snowshoes above the surface of the snow. The topography flattened for a short ways at the summit, then the land receded gently westward from the crest into the forested basins of the Lochsa. There the trappers could take time to wonder at the beauty of the massive peaks that dwarfed their cabins and their snowshoe trails. Once through the pass, it was all downhill to Big Sand Lake. Now they could coast their toboggan, dig into their packs for bait, and begin setting their traps for martens, ermines, and foxes.

Earl and Charley laid traplines in several directions from Big Sand Lake. One line extended to the Moose Creek divide at Jeanette Lake, contoured from there into Dead Elk Creek, then turned back over the Moose Creek divide, returning down a fork of Big Sand Creek to their headquarters. Another reached through a high pass in the ridge to the north and continued on to their small cabin at Hidden Lake. From there they set a spur line into the fur-rich basin of the North Fork of Hidden Creek. They set traps from headquarters over Diablo Mountain to Elk Summit Ranger Station, where they camped in the cabin owned by the government's rangers who were supposed to enforce the laws of the game preserve. After setting traps from Elk Summit to the basins beneath the crest of the Grave Mountains, Charley and Earl would return via the trail from Elk Summit to their cabin at Big Sand Lake (see map 8).

One cold day, while Charley tended the Dead Elk Creek trapline, Earl loaded his pack with traps, bait, grub, and a five-gallon coal oil can to be used as a stove, and then headed for Hidden Lake. He set traps along the way until the temperature became so cold that he could no longer stop or touch the frozen steel. To avoid freezing he had to keep moving, so he mushed on, snowshoe harnesses squeaking in the frozen snow. On arrival, he found that a bear had torn the door from the small cabin standing beside the outlet of the lake. By that time, according to Earl, the cold had settled to forty degrees below zero.

After installing his oil-can stove, he chopped wood from the dead lodgepole pines, the crack of frozen trees sounding like rifle shots in the forest. Even the lake stirred to the cold, its ice banging and hissing in the night as fissures split from shore to shore. Earl stayed awake and stoked the fire all night long. Fortunately, the cabin was easy to heat because it was so small. As Earl put it: "I could set on the bunk and reach everything in the place."[166]

Charley had a better time of it that day. He crossed Jeanette Lake on thick ice and then snowshoed down into the valley of Dead Elk Creek, where he began setting traps upstream toward the creek's source high in the Bitterroot mountains. His pace slowed as the cold drained his energy. Because his body was losing its warmth, it took deliberate concentration to do little things like stroke icicles from his beard or shift his pack. He wanted to stop and gnaw at the frozen sandwiches in his packsack, but he knew that heat generated by exertion was all that kept him from freezing.

Charley needed to get a fire going quickly to thaw sandwiches and warm himself. While searching for flammable wood, he was surprised to come upon a cabin standing in the forest. Like men dying of thirst in the desert, minds numbed by fatigue and wintertime cold sometimes imagine such mirages. But that cabin was no fantasy of a frozen mind. Its thick roof, tight walls, and stone fireplace were a godsend to Charley in that subzero cold.

As was customary among mountain men of those days, the last occupant had left a pile of pine pitch on the hearth, shaved ready for kindling a fire. Already numb in his mittens, intense cold stiffened Charley's hands when he bared them to strike a match against the stone.

Map 8. *Known poacher traplines and cabins, Lochsa portion of the Selway Game Preserve, 1919–1936.*

Fay Burrell and Bob Forbes pause at Elk Summit Ranger Station in December 1922. —Fay Burrell

But flames seized the dry wood. Smoke puffed briefly in the corner, then was sucked up into the flue and drifted out among the pines and firs.

The fire smelled good and felt good. Its warmth soon filled the cabin. A glance at magazines scattered on a rack suspended from the ceiling showed the latest edition to be 1898, one year before Wes Fales had built his headquarters at Big Sand Lake. Charley didn't know who had built the cabin in the thicket along Dead Elk Creek and left dry kindling on the hearth. But on that cold day in December 1919, he was glad that some other mountain man had gone that way before.[167]

A year later Charley was running the spurline from Elk Summit Ranger Station west to the Grave Mountains. It was New Year's Day 1920. Six feet of well-settled snow topped with four inches of powder created excellent conditions for traveling on snowshoes. Scarcely a cloud marred the blue Kooskooskee sky. Moving east to west along its low winter arc, the sun lighted the snow-burdened forest, spreading a holiday spirit across the mountains. Charley climbed from the end of his trapline in the basin to the summit of Grave Peak, where (he said later) he felt alone with God. It seemed to him he could see the whole of creation—plenty of creation, certainly, to keep young men like him and Earl busy at discovery for many years to come.

At Grave Peak, Charley had lapped Montana a long ways into Idaho. He could see several passes notched in the skyline of the Bitterroots both north and south of Blodgett Pass. He knew that other trappers were crossing from Montana into Idaho through the passes at Storm Creek, Maud Creek, Pack Box, Bear Creek, and Lost Horse. As the setting sun lit the mountains with alpine glow, he hurried back to help Earl skin furs and to rest in the comfort of the government's Elk Summit Ranger Station.

Their practice of extending the borders of Montana, however, could not long go unchallenged. Rangers Bell and Mackay could not tolerate their violating the provisions of the game preserve, much less their use of the government's cabins for illegal trapping purposes. In January 1920 the Forest Service sent two expert woodsmen, Jack Clack of the Forest Service and Andy Hjort, an Idaho game warden from Kooskia, to apprehend the poachers who were crossing the mountains at Blodgett Pass.

Malone was in Hamilton for supplies when Clack and Hjort arrived in town and put up at the Hamilton Hotel. Powell and a man named Bernie McGawfin were tending traps in Lapland and living at Elk Summit station. Eager to get back to the mountains and to trapping, Fay Burrell had returned to Hamilton from military service. Though they knew it not, Clack and Hjort would be matching strength and wits with a band of woodsmen as able as any involved in the exploration of the West.

Upon learning of the law's arrival, Burrell and Malone went to the hotel. They watched Clack and Hjort assemble their gear in the lobby and visited with them long enough to learn that the two planned to snowshoe up Blodgett Canyon, cross the pass into the Lochsa country, and then apprehend the poachers wherever they found them trapping furs. Malone didn't want Powell and McGawfin caught at the Elk Summit Ranger Station, so that night Fay Burrell drove Malone to the mouth of Blodgett Canyon.

Darkness swallowed up Malone as he lit out to warn his friends in Lapland. He snowshoed up the canyon, through the pass to Big Sand Lake, and past their headquarters cabin, and still he kept going. With nearly thirty miles of snowshoe trail behind him, he reached Elk Summit to find Powell and McGawfin cooking breakfast. He told them the news, that the law was closing in. Small wonder that Charley Powell said of his stalwart partner, "Earl was good to be in the mountains with. He was tough. Doggone, he was tough."[168]

Instead of tending traplines that day, they packed up their furs and back-tracked with Earl to the headquarters cabin at Big Sand Lake. There they buried the meat of an elk they had killed but a few days before. While the trappers cooked supper, snow fell softly, covering the woods, their tracks, and all signs of the hidden elk. Also that day Clack and Hjort reached the trappers' supply cabin in the canyon on the Montana side of Blodgett Pass.

Malone, Powell, and McGawfin knew that the next day the government men would cross the crest and follow the trail down the north side of the creek to Big Sand Lake. So before daylight that morning they snowshoed toward the pass, holding close to the south side of the valley, intending to pass Hjort and Clack unseen. The whoosh of their snowshoes barely stirred the silence as they mushed through the spruces in single file, now and then shifting position to allow a fresh man to break trail. No one spoke. They never rattled a snowshoe bow. Falling snow covered their packs and piled up on their hat brims until they looked like ghosts of old mountain men drifting through the mystique of that winter-locked land.

Dense forests in the half-mile-wide valley hid them from view of the trail for the first five miles, but the valley narrowed at a place where snow avalanches had stripped all trees from the slopes. Hjort and Clack had not yet crossed this big slide. For the trappers to cross would expose their tracks, thwart their plan to pass the lawmen in the valley, and end with their capture and arrest for poaching furs in the Selway Game Preserve.

So they waited, hidden in the forest, while the arctic air froze their clothes and chilled their bones. At length they heard voices. Soon thereafter, Hjort and Clack crossed the big slide, unaware that the eyes of three trappers watched from the woods across the valley of the Big Sand. That those government men knew what they were doing showed in their steady snowshoe strides along the trail. Frost crystals formed on their beards and shirt fronts. The long tail of Jack Clack's red stocking cap waving among the snowflakes was the last thing the trappers saw as their pursuers disappeared into the forest—first out of sight, then out of hearing, yet hardly out of mind.

Malone, Powell, and McGawfin high-tailed it over the pass into Montana where they were safe from arrest and free to sell their furs. Talking about that experience later, Charley Powell, with a twinkle in his eye, said, "We wasn't exactly wrong. That was the first year we had to have a permit. And we didn't know those furbearers wasn't predators." Earl Malone put it differently. Of Clack, he said, "Nobody liked that Forest Service son of a bitch from England. But we liked the game warden who was with him."[169]

Ruins of a trapper cabin near the Lochsa-Selway divide west of Hungry Rock.

After Hjort and Clack left the mountains, Earl and Charley returned to their cabin, dug up their elk, and rebaited their traplines. They trapped until March that year of 1920, taking 110 marten, many ermines, and a few fox.

Clack and Hjort's unsuccessful expedition made little difference to the men from Montana intent on extracting Idaho fur. Sometime during the winter of 1921–22, Earl Malone was trapping in Lapland, this time alone. As usual he used the log ranger station at Elk Summit as a base from which to extend his lines westward into the Grave Mountains.

Neither snow nor fallen trees had yet disabled the phone line connections from Elk Summit to Ed Mackay's ranger station at Powell, so Earl occasionally talked by phone to Bert Wendover, who was trapping north of the Lochsa River outside of the game preserve. Swapping yarns cheered the two lone trappers during the long winter evenings. But one night ranger Bill Bell overheard their conversation from the telephone at the Forest Service cabin on the Brushy Fork. That Malone had once again appropriated his ranger station for use as a poaching headquarters didn't sit too well with the tall ranger from the Bitterroot Valley.

Bell snowshoed twenty-eight miles to Elk Summit, where he caught Malone at the station. After arresting Malone and confiscating his furs as evidence, the two snowshoed together to Lolo Hot Springs. From

The Forest Service cabin at Fish Lake lies buried under fourteen feet of snow.

there they drove by car to Missoula, where Bell was going to see to it that Malone had his day in court, followed by a few days in jail.

Since ranger and poacher alike held a great deal of respect for each other's honesty, Bell left Malone free until he could arrange for Earl's arraignment the next day. Both took rooms at the Shapard Hotel. The case looked like a winner for the government, but while Bell ate supper that night, Malone stole into his room and took the furs. Nothing wrong with that, he reasoned. After all, he'd worked hard for those furs. They belonged to him. Besides, without the furs as evidence the ranger wouldn't have a legal case against him.[170]

After seventy-five miles of snowshoe travel in the Lochsa's mountains, the ranger had lost his case. And the poachers kept right on crossing the passes to ply their trade in Lapland. Operating from a string of hidden cabins, they extended traplines beyond the Grave Mountains as far west as the Fish Lake Basin. The trappers could handle the Lochsa's topography, its winters, and its wildness. For a time it looked like they could handle the game wardens and rangers as well.

In about 1930, Ranger Mackay began burning or dynamiting all of the trapping cabins he could find within the game preserve. Destroying the cabins struck at the heart of the poachers' supply lines. They retaliated by stealing stoves and dishes from fire lookout stations at Grave Peak, Hidden Peak, Savage Ridge, Diablo Mountain, and other Forest

Service cabins. They lugged this government gear to locations in the best fur country to equip crude shelters fashioned from poles, boughs, bark, split puncheon—any material they could find that was suitable for quick construction.

Only the hardiest poachers persisted after the blasting of the cabins. By that time, Earl Malone and Fay Burrell had left their mountains to pursue more conventional occupations in Montana. Charley Powell had hired on as a forest ranger elsewhere in the Forest Service. Bill Bell had quit the government. Ed Mackay had taken responsibility for the Elk Summit district as well as the Powell. And Bitterroot-born Joe Alkire had become the pacesetter for the poachers of Lapland.

During the depression years of the late twenties and early thirties, Ranger Mackay, like many other law officers in Montana and Idaho's mountains, pursued only the most flagrant violators of game and trapping laws. Of the poachers in Lapland, Ed said, "If they'd leave the government cabins alone, they're better off trappin' those mountains than on the bread lines out in the towns."[171]

But Alkire and others didn't leave the government's cabins alone. So in January 1933 the Forest Service organized to catch Joe Alkire and stop the poaching once and for all. The plan was for Bill Apgar and one other Forest Service man to follow Alkire's tracks up Blodgett Canyon, just as Hjort and Clack had tracked Malone thirteen years before. Ed Mackay would snowshoe via Powell to Elk Summit station and close in from the west. This time there could be no escape like Malone, Powell, and McGawfin had pulled off in 1920.

Apgar and his partner followed Alkire according to plan. But Alkire's tracks vanished in drifted snow where he climbed through the strip of trees from the canyon bottom to Blodgett Pass. His pursuers mushed on and spent a day searching in vain for the pass in the upper end of the canyon. Frustrated by the loss of time and their failure to find a route through the pass, they returned down the canyon and out of the mountains to Hamilton.

Meanwhile, Ranger Mackay snowshoed across Lolo Pass to his Powell Ranger Station. Veteran of the Lochsa's mountains Jay Turner was trapping downriver from Powell station, and Mackay induced him to join in the effort to apprehend Alkire. Together they bucked deep snow in a steady climb from the Lochsa River to Savage Pass.

Those two friends of many years lent contrast to the Lochsa's wintertime landscape. Jay was a small man—he weighed about 150 pounds—

whose strong legs pushed his snowshoes mile after mile in the toughest conditions with barely a pause. Since he wasn't heavy, he skimmed over the snow. On the other hand, Ed's 225 pounds settled deep into the stuff even when Jay was breaking trail. Once Ed said, "Jesus, Jesus, this is tough." But he saved his breath to push on to Colt Creek—a stream flowing east from the Grave Mountains—where they camped for the night.

The weather was cold, and a raw wind blew as they chopped dry wood enough to keep a fire going all night. Then, using their snowshoes as shovels, they dug through six-foot-deep snow to the ground. While Ed kindled the fire, Jay cut boughs from the spruces to thatch a crude shelter to insulate them from the chill of the snow. They ate bacon and hardtack with coffee, then took turns tending the fire while the other slept.

The next day they reached Elk Summit Ranger Station; the day after that they mushed to Big Sand Lake, where they expected to find Joe

Trapper Jay Turner examines his snowshoes at Lolo Hot Springs after hiking out of the Lochsa country.

Alkire. But not a snowshoe track blemished the landscape as they tromped across the frozen lake and up to the cabin's door. A bear had broken a window the fall before, however, and climbed inside, torn up the cupboards, dishes, bunk, and bedding, and even upset the stove. The first order of business, then, was to clean up the place. That done, Ed boiled coffee. He poured Jay a cup and one for himself; steam curled from the brew as they drank. Smells of hot metal, pack rat piss, wet clothes, and strong coffee mingled as the cabin warmed.

Then came a knock at the door.

At Ed's "Come in," Joe Alkire opened the door and, for the first time, ranger and poacher met. Mackay's quarry was a husky man, about five feet, eleven inches tall. Strength showed in his thick arms and legs, and black hair on his barrel chest curled through the open collar of his woolen shirt. Alkire was built for the Lochsa's mountains, and he believed those mountains were built for him. He was accompanied by a young man named Wilhelm. Both were loaded with traps and bait, but they had no fur. All four men stayed together in the cabin that night.

Next morning, Ed said to Joe, "Don't you think you ought to go out with us and quit this renegade stuff?"

Joe said, "Hell! I'm just here. I haven't done anything wrong. But I've been thinking it over. I guess I will go out with you."

So Ranger Mackay, trapper Jay Turner, Joe Alkire, and Wilhelm traveled to Elk Summit and thence to Powell, where Turner returned to tending his traplines. Mackay continued on, escorting Alkire and Wilhelm out of the mountains. After passing the stone-faced woman, they arrived in the town of Lolo. Ed said to Joe, "I'm letting you go. Now don't you go back in there. You'll just get yourself into a lot of trouble."

Joe said, "I won't. I'll stay out."[172]

Then he went up the Bitterroot Valley to Hamilton. He tarried there a few days, then snowshoed up Blodgett Canyon and over the pass back into Lapland. He had a good many traps already set that needed tending. Besides that, Alkire was so hooked on the Lochsa's wildness he couldn't leave that land alone. Joe Alkire never kept his promise to stay out of Lapland, nor did the government have much faith that he would do so. Thus, the Forest Service had assigned a man to watch his movements in Hamilton, and within hours after he headed back up Blodgett Canyon, Ranger Mackay received word that Joe was going home.

Mackay needed evidence to prosecute Alkire, so he waited long enough for Alkire to set traps and catch some fur. Then, accompanied by forest officer Bill Apgar, he set out over Lolo Pass to bring Alkire out of the mountains one more time.

En route from Powell Ranger Station to Lapland, Mackay and Apgar avoided the steep climb to Savage Pass by snowshoeing up the frozen river. With the water imprisoned under thick ice and deep snow, the river's life could be seen and its voice heard at only the most turbulent rapids. At these spots, maybe two or three per mile, rising steam showed the water to be warmer than the wintry air. Otters fished from these openings, climbing out of the dark water after each catch to munch their prey on the snow, then roll and tumble and dive again. Their songs lost in the roar of the rapids, ouzels teetered on the rocks and bobbed in the riffles. Mackay and Apgar took care in passing these lively spots, lest the ice crumble and dump them into the Lochsa along with the ouzels, mink, fish, and otters.

Frozen as it was, their route through the canyon of the White Sand Fork proved good traveling, and by four o'clock in the afternoon they found a snowshoe trail leading west up Colt Creek toward the Grave Mountains. Those fresh tracks had to be Alkire's, so they followed them. Shortly, they discovered Joe's camp hidden in the forest near the creek. A stout pole tied between two firs formed the ridge for the A-frame-type shelter's roof. Poles leaned against the ridge, and half-logs had been placed over the cracks between the poles to seal out the rain and snow. The camp looked like it had been built about two years before. The skinned quarters of a freshly killed moose hung on a limb of a spruce tree not far from the shelter's door.

Compared with the government's ranger stations, Alkire's camp was indeed a humble place. Smells of smoke, cold ashes, and resinous wood drifted out from the eight-by-twelve-foot interior when Ed opened the door. Inside he saw a rusty stove, a bunk filled with dried beargrass, a small table, and a big wood pile. Mountain-man fellowship radiated from the pile of shaved kindling stacked ready for ignition near the stove. Mackay and Apgar went in, cooked themselves a moose steak for supper, and then slept through the night on Alkire's bunk.

Next morning they followed Alkire's tracks up Colt Creek, springing his traps as they went. Near the mouth of Savage Creek the snowshoe trail turned north, leading up the mountainside toward Savage Ridge. Mackay and Apgar climbed in silence, pausing now and then for breath. About two miles up the mountain they heard Alkire coming down the trail. Stepping behind a limby spruce, they waited. Uncertain as to how the encounter might develop, Apgar hauled his .45 Colt from its holster and held it ready.

As he strode down the trail, Alkire whacked wet snow from his snowshoes with a stick like there was no one else but him in Lapland. When he got close, Mackay stepped out and said, "Hello, Joe. You beat us back in. I think we got you this time."

Joe thumped his snowshoe again with his stick and looked south across the Lochsa basins trapped years before by Savage, Kube, Meeks, and others. His gaze turned from the land, and he faced the big ranger.

"O.K.," he said.

It took them three days to snowshoe out of the Lochsa's mountains and reach Lolo Hot Springs. From there Mackay called Forest Service regional law officer P. J. O'Brien at Missoula.

"I got your man, but I don't know what to do with him," he said.

O'Brien answered, "Take him to Coeur d'Alene, Idaho, and turn him over to the United States Marshall."

That's what they did. As the marshall locked Joe in jail, Ed asked, "Have you got any money?"

Joe said, "No. And I don't have any tobacco or papers."

So Ed bought Joe two one-pound cans of Prince Albert tobacco and some papers and gave him $2.50. Then he returned to his ranger station. That was the last time he saw Joe Alkire.

Ed told his boss, forest supervisor Shoemaker, "Joe Alkire's a decent guy. When you catch him he pitches in. Breaks more than his share of the trail. He never squawks."[173]

The freedom of the Lochsa had seized the hearts of those poachers who created Lapland. They would not bow to the government rules, for doing so would mean the end of their free way of life. The rangers loved that land, too, but they represented a government based on law rather than freedom in wildness. That the land of the Lochsa touched both rangers and poachers in different ways can be likened to the adage, As is the receiver so is the gift.

Lochsa ranger Roy Lewis, displaying a great deal of pride, put it this way:

"I thought that country was a man killer. I sweat Lochsa blood over there."

In contrast, poacher (and later, ranger) Charley Powell said, "God, that country back there was wonderful. Back there in 1918 and '19, that was God's country. You know it."[174]

In spite of wrecked cabins, pursuit, and arrests, neither law nor government rangers could close the passes to the men from Montana who loved the Lochsa's wildness and coveted Idaho's fur. Many trapped on until they grew too old to climb over the hill into Lapland.

The call to arms in World War II took several of them out of the mountains. Joe Alkire was among the first to join and among the first to die in service to his country. The wisdom and strength he gained from the Lochsa's wildness served him well at his post in the Merchant Marines. And it is a sure bet that he died in the Pacific as he lived in Lapland, never squawking and breaking more than his share of the trail.

Speaking of his trapping days, the retired Charley Powell told me, "I'd like to do it one more time, but it's too late now." —Freeman Mann

Maple Lake reflects the solitude treasured by people who visit the Selway-Bitterroot Wilderness.

14

The Wilderness Ethic

S*peaking in retrospect of his trapping activities* during the twenties, Earl Malone seemed possessed by something more than trapping furs and outwitting rangers when he said, "I thought . . . I can't express . . . there's something about that country that gives you a feeling you don't get anywhere else. It's just like nature created it. I think it's a wonderful country. And I think we should keep it that way forever."[175]

But to "keep it that way forever" was not what the rangers inside or the growing throng of motorists outside had in mind for the Lochsa country's destiny. Instead, banishing fire from the mountains to save the forests for the sawmills and gaining access for autos and trucks seemed certain to smother the wildness of the Lochsa with roads, dust, the roar of engines, the smell of gasoline, and other manifestations of government order. Neither the rangers, the industrialists, nor the auto-oriented public had room in their definition of progress for Malone's "feeling you don't get anywhere else."

When overrun by "progress" in the past, trappers and others who cherished wild places had no choice but to move out of the way. Yet the inevitability of losing the last of America's frontiers to the road builders was not accepted by all citizens of the United States; indeed, the ranks of men and women who recognized spiritual, recreational, and even economic value in raw nature were growing, too. More than motors and gears and road-building scrapers rattled outside the Lochsa country. A new national movement was underway, and its participants pledged to prevent roads and machines from civilizing many special places. Few, if any, of those who challenged the supremacy of the engine and wheel knew, or cared, how to snap a trap on a marten or lynx. In truth, woodsmanship was uncommon among them. They were, in general, people who enjoyed recreational activities in unroaded mountains, but, more important, many were able activists in matters of politics, science, government, law, philosophy, and the molding of public opinion.

The roots of their convictions were seeded in the cultures of biblical times and grew, always with conflict, to maturity in the wilds of America. Throughout the history of Western civilization, humanity's goal on earth had been to "Be fruitful, and multiply, and replenish the earth, and subdue it," and thereby order nature in the interests of humans. Wilderness and paradise were viewed as physical and spiritual opposites. After Adam ate the forbidden fruit, God sent him and Eve from the Garden of Eden "to till the ground from whence he was taken."[176] Yet wild places had their merits, too. Moses, for example, went into the wilderness and received the Ten Commandments from God on Mount Sinai. From the outset of modern people's interaction with it, wilderness has harbored divergent values; it is at once a place useful only when ordered in the interest of humanity as well as a place to obtain personal freedom and to draw close to God.

The first immigrants to the United States fled Europe to escape oppression, but their tithe for freedom was long hours of labor creating enclaves in the unexplored lands of America. Their food, clothing, shelter, safety, and comfort all depended on conquering the wilderness.[177] Although the pioneers admired nature, their relentless purpose was to order nature and in that way make the wilderness habitable and useful to civilized people.

Henry David Thoreau was among the first to challenge the wisdom of degrading pristine land for materialistic gain. To better understand nature, he built a hut in 1845, at age nineteen, at Walden Pond, Massachusetts, and lived there in solitude until 1847. While at Walden he wrote extensively. Capably expressed in his writing, Thoreau's thinking contributed new values to the American scene then dominated by the quest for money, security, and prosperity. His most revealing statement on nature is found in one of his essays: "The West of which I speak is but another name for the wild; and what I have been preparing to say is, that in Wildness is the preservation of the World."[178] With these words, Thoreau sowed the seed of an idea that natural places were good for, even essential to, fulfillment in life.

By 1877, when Chief Joseph led the free Nez Perce in their last trip over the Road to the Buffalo, a new champion of wild places was expanding the principles set forth by Thoreau. Scotland-born John Muir got a taste of life on the American frontier when in 1849 his family moved to a homestead in central Wisconsin. Though caught up at age eleven in the toil of clearing the wilderness, Muir was happy in wild places and considered the encroachment of civilization arbitrary and cruel.[179]

With spiritual views similar to the Nez Perce's, Muir revered raw nature as God's most perfect creation. He saw no conflict between nature and religion, and he would rather learn of the power of God through contact with natural wonders than from the study of the Bible. Like Thoreau, Muir spoke and wrote persuasively. But to live and philosophize for two years in a cabin on Walden Pond would never do for Muir. Instead, he explored the wild regions of the western United States, especially those in California, and publicized their virtues.

Meanwhile, on March 1, 1872, President Ulysses S. Grant had created the world's first large, wilderness park by signing an act designating over two million acres in Wyoming and Montana territories as Yellowstone National Park. Thirteen years later, the State of New York established 715,000 acres as a forest preserve in the Adirondacks, specifying that it remain forever wild. Citizen support leading to these designations did not dwell on the cultural, spiritual, or recreational value of wild places, but instead was motivated by a desire to prevent the exploitation of natural wonders.[180] These events proved, however, that wild country could be saved even in fortune-hunting frontier America.

By the fall of 1890, Muir was promoting expansion of the national park idea and had argued for establishment of Yosemite National Park. His arguments left no doubt that the prime value of the park was to be its wildness. On September 3, 1890, President Benjamin Harrison signed the bill creating Yosemite National Park, the first preserve designated specifically to protect the values of wilderness.[181]

Creation of Yosemite was a political endorsement of public sentiment—sentiments like those of Earl Malone and Fay Burrell some twenty years later as they pulled their toboggan across Blodgett Pass. Yet greater recognition by the people of the values of wildness was needed, and John Muir worked tirelessly toward that end.

Muir would have been happy to see the forests preserved in their natural state. But he also recognized the material needs of expanding America. He thus sought compromise with Pinchot, Fernow, and other forestry leaders to ensure that the reserves would "be made to yield a sure harvest of timber, while at the same time all their far-reaching (aesthetic and spiritual) uses may be maintained unimpaired."[182]

When Gifford Pinchot developed the notion of conservation, he was thinking about places like this Bitterroot landscape where the national forests extend from farmlands to high alpine country beyond.

Muir's notion that wildness and commercial forestry could coexist on the forest reserves didn't last long. As we have already seen (in chapter 7), on June 4, 1897, Congress passed the Organic Administration Act, declaring that the primary purposes of the reserves were "securing favorable conditions of water flow, and to furnish a continuous supply of timber." The act provided that the forests would remain open to existing uses, such as mining and grazing. There was no mention in the act of the value of wild places. To make matters worse for wild country, Fernow's position, as forester in charge of the reserves, was that "the main service, the principal object of the forest has nothing to do with beauty or pleasure. It is not, except incidentally, an object of aesthetics, but an object of economics."[183]

Convinced that in management of the reserves by the utility-minded foresters lay the sure demise of wild places, Muir withdrew all support for Pinchot and his followers and thereafter labored for official recognition of wilderness. Despite Pinchot's calculated strategy to suppress the idea of preserving wilderness, the national conservation program had split by the time Fay Burrell and Earl Malone discovered Big Sand Lake. The wilderness movement was underway and its leader, John Muir, was saying: "Thousands of tired, nerve-shaken, over-civilized people are beginning to find out that going to the mountains is going home; that wildness is a necessity; and that mountain parks and reservations are useful not only as fountains of timber and irrigating rivers, but as fountains of life."[184] The foresters could not suppress nor would they long ignore the groundswell of citizen opinion supporting Muir's crusade.

The beginning of the idea of multiple use of the national forests came to Gifford Pinchot during the winter of 1907 while riding his saddle horse Jim on the Ridge Road in Rock Creek Park, Washington, D.C. Pondering the relationship between forestry and other natural resources, he struck on the thought that the many questions "fitted into and made up the one great central problem of the use of the earth for the good of man."[185] He called the concept conservation. Though he had no truck with preserving wilderness, his concept of conservation would provide an administrative means to coordinate management of the many forest uses and resources, including wildlife, recreation, and wilderness.

In a move sure to generate competition between government agencies for control of much of the western wilderness, Congress created the National Park Service in 1916. It directed that all national parks were to be managed "to conserve the scenery and the natural and historic objects and the wild life therein and to provide for the enjoyment of the same in such manner and by such means as will leave them unimpaired for the enjoyment of future generations."[186]

The land of the Lochsa and a great many similar jewels of wild country were situated in the national forests, and Muir and his associates had their eyes on those places. So did Stephen Mather, the energetic director of the Park Service. And the Forest Service countered the new agency's thrust by publicizing scenery and outdoor recreation as major amenities available in the national forests. Not long after the turn of the century, public opinion and intragovernmental competition had relegated to history Forester Fernow's pronouncement concerning the utilitarian nature of forestry.

But the true transformation of the foresters began in 1918 with the assignment of landscape architect Arthur Carhart to survey vacation homesites at Trapper's Lake, Colorado. Struck by the beauty and wildness of the place, Carhart recommended to District 2 Forester Carl J. Stahl that the best use of the Trapper's Lake area was for wilderness recreation, not summer homes. Stahl agreed. And by administrative designation, in early 1920 he applied the preservation principle for the first time to a national forest.

Forester Aldo Leopold in neighboring District 3 shared Carhart's vision of preserving some wild places in the national forests as wilderness. At once expressing support for industrial development and protection of wild lands, Leopold said, "While reduction of the wilderness has been a good thing, its extermination would be a very bad one." Due largely to Leopold's efforts, on June 3, 1924, District 3 forester Frank C. W. Pooler designated 574,000 acres within New Mexico as the Gila Wilderness, to be used primarily for wilderness recreation. Late in 1926 chief forester William B. Greeley expressed approval of the Gila Wilderness and encouraged other districts to establish similar reservations. In an article in *Sunset Magazine* in 1927 he called for a new point of view: "[T]he frontier has long ceased to be a barrier to civilization. The question is rather how much of it should be kept to preserve our civilization."[187]

By 1929, the year in which Ranger Mackay led the retreat from the great fires of the Lochsa, the Forest Service had recognized that natural landscapes held value in and of themselves. This recognition was embodied in the agency's L-20 Regulations, which established an official policy of preserving wild places throughout the national forests. But the rangers in the field hadn't yet been informed of this rather startling policy development. Nor could they have anticipated it. After all, the value of the Lochsa's forests for commercial timber had been extolled and mapped by Lieberg in 1897, Shattuck in 1910, and the Forest Service itself in 1915, 1924, and later. Yet no one had even described, much less mapped, the values of the Lochsa's wild country.

In appreciation of wildness lies an irony of American civilization. The trappers, usually a poor lot by economic standards, necessarily joined with nature and thus came to love the freedom and mystery of wild land and to revel in the hardships it thrust upon them. The trappers of the Lochsa, and of the mountain west generally, were the pathfinders who fell so in love with the land as it was that, could they have done so, many would have gated their pathways to bar entry to the pilgrims who were sure to follow their blazes. But most settlers and many foresters wanted the wilderness opened up so that its resources could be available for utilitarian use, as reflected in the purposes and provisions of the Organic Administration Act of 1897. It remained, then, for the more wealthy residents of urban America, people blessed with money but denied nature, to fight hardest for the wilderness cause. Thus, the deepest appreciation for wildness existed at the bottom and near the top of the economic spectrum in American culture. The trappers, few in number and awed by politics, rarely spoke out for their wild land. Those on the other end of the cultural and economic scale often did.

Born of wealthy parents in New York City on January 2, 1901, Bob Marshall was one of those who spoke the loudest and worked the hardest for wilderness. Like trapper Fay Burrell, who discovered Big Sand Lake at age sixteen, Bob Marshall, with his brother George, climbed Mt. Ampersand in the Adirondacks at age fifteen. Climbing mountains and exploring and defending wild places became the principal occupations of Bob's life. By October 1937 he had taken 200 thirty-mile walks, 51 forty-mile walks, and a number of longer walks, including one of at least seventy miles.[188]

Marshall began government service in 1924, and from 1925 to 1928 he worked at the Forest Service's Northern Rocky Mountain Forest and Range Experiment Station at Missoula, Montana, where he was surrounded by some of the largest expanses of unroaded mountain areas in the continental United States. Missoula provided an ideal location for Marshall to explore wild country and promote its protection as wilderness. Moreover, from Missoula Marshall could see the northern crests of the Bitterroot Range, whose western slopes drained into the Lochsa. If any part of that land were to remain wild, it was going to need all the help it could get.

In an article published in *The Scientific Monthly* in February 1930, Marshall tried to define wilderness. He began:

> For the ensuing discussion I shall use the word *wilderness* to denote a region which contains no permanent inhabitants, possesses no possibility of conveyance by any mechanical means and is sufficiently spacious that a person in crossing it must have the experience of sleeping out. The dominant attributes of such an area are: first, that it requires anyone who exists in it to depend exclusively on his own effort for survival; and second, that it preserves as nearly as possible the primitive environment. This means that all roads, power transportation and settlements are barred. But trails and temporary shelters, which were common long before the advent of the white race, are entirely permissible.

He explained that the masses of American motorists already had access to more roads than they could drive in a lifetime. His paper ended:

As first director of the Forest Service Division of Recreation and Lands, Bob Marshall made sure special areas of the national forests would remain forever wild.
—Mable Mansfield, courtesy of The Wilderness Society

"There is just one hope of repulsing the tyrannical ambition of civilization to conquer every mile of the whole earth. That hope is the organization of spirited people who will fight for the freedom of the wilderness."[189]

Such was the creed of Bob Marshall. After leaving his post at Missoula, Marshall continued his crusade for wilderness while serving in Washington, D.C., as director of the Forestry Division of the U.S. Office of Indian Affairs. Recognizing the need for promoting recreation use, Forest Service chief F. A. Silcox in 1937 created the Division of Recreation and Lands in Washington, D.C. He signed Marshall on as the division's first director. From 1937 until his untimely death in 1939, Marshall enjoyed a unique opportunity to create wilderness areas in the national forests.

Probably no one in the United States was as well qualified for that job. Through personal exploration he had acquired firsthand knowledge of many wild areas; his educational background was excellent. During his two-year tenure as chief of the Division of Recreation and Lands, Marshall achieved administrative designation as wilderness of 5.437 million acres in the national forests. He also prepared the U-Regulations, issued in September 1939, which defined several kinds of recreational

From their homes and work places in Missoula, Montana, today's residents can see the same view that inspired Bob Marshall to protect much of the Lochsa country as wilderness.

areas, directed their management, and prohibited road building and logging in all areas designated "wilderness" or "wild."[190]

So by the time the Lochsa's rangers mopped up the fires of 1934, a strong policy to preserve wilderness had developed in the Forest Service, with several areas in the national forests already designated as such. Nonetheless, the thrust for more and better access to the national forests continued. During the winter of 1934–35, Ranger Mackay reported that his Powell district already contained 133 miles of road and 600 miles of trail and that more would be needed for fire control. Still, a different view of the value of nature's creations—distilled from the philosophy of Thoreau, the spirit of Muir, the wisdom of Leopold, and the action of Marshall—was beginning to make its mark on the rangers of the Lochsa.

That Marshall understood the richness of wildness in the Lochsa shows in his journal of a hike he made about 1930:

> It was the last evening of my journey, and I was sitting quietly in the dusk that had gathered in the narrow valley of Big Sand Lake. The somber mountainsides, covered by parallel, overlapping spires of dark green spruce and alpine fir, rose abruptly from the very edge of the water to an indefinite region, where they merged with the fog. The lake was one gray shadow, except for the bright, salmon-colored horns of a giant bull moose, which slowly

The measured movements of this bull moose demonstrate the promise of eternity inherent in wild places. —K. D. Swan, U.S. Forest Service

> wallowed through the lilypads just off the densely wooded shoreline. Everything he did was deliberate and had a dignity appropriate to an environment which measured changes by the century instead of the hour. A gangly-legged calf was splashing in the shallows and looking up every now and then with curiosity. Night birds circled; the last mosquitoes of summer hummed their farewell song; a gentle wind rippled the placid water. The old bull turned slowly and disappeared into the black forest. The calf lingered uncertainly for a few moments, then uttered a queer snort and followed. The trees across the lake lost their identity, and darkness imperceptibly had fallen, no differently than during millions of evenings before the intrusion of man.[191]

Marshall pressed hard for designation of much of the land of the Lochsa as wilderness. He influenced Chief Silcox to stop construction of the truck trails penetrating the pristine mountains south of the Lochsa River. And on June 11, 1936, acting chief Earl H. Clapp designated the Forest Service's largest primitive area—1.875 million acres astride the Bitterroot mountains, including much of the Lochsa and Selway drainages and the canyon country on the slopes of the Bitterroot Valley east of the crest. Known as the Selway-Bitterroot Primitive Area, 1.585 million acres lay in Idaho and 290,000 acres in Montana (see map 9). Several

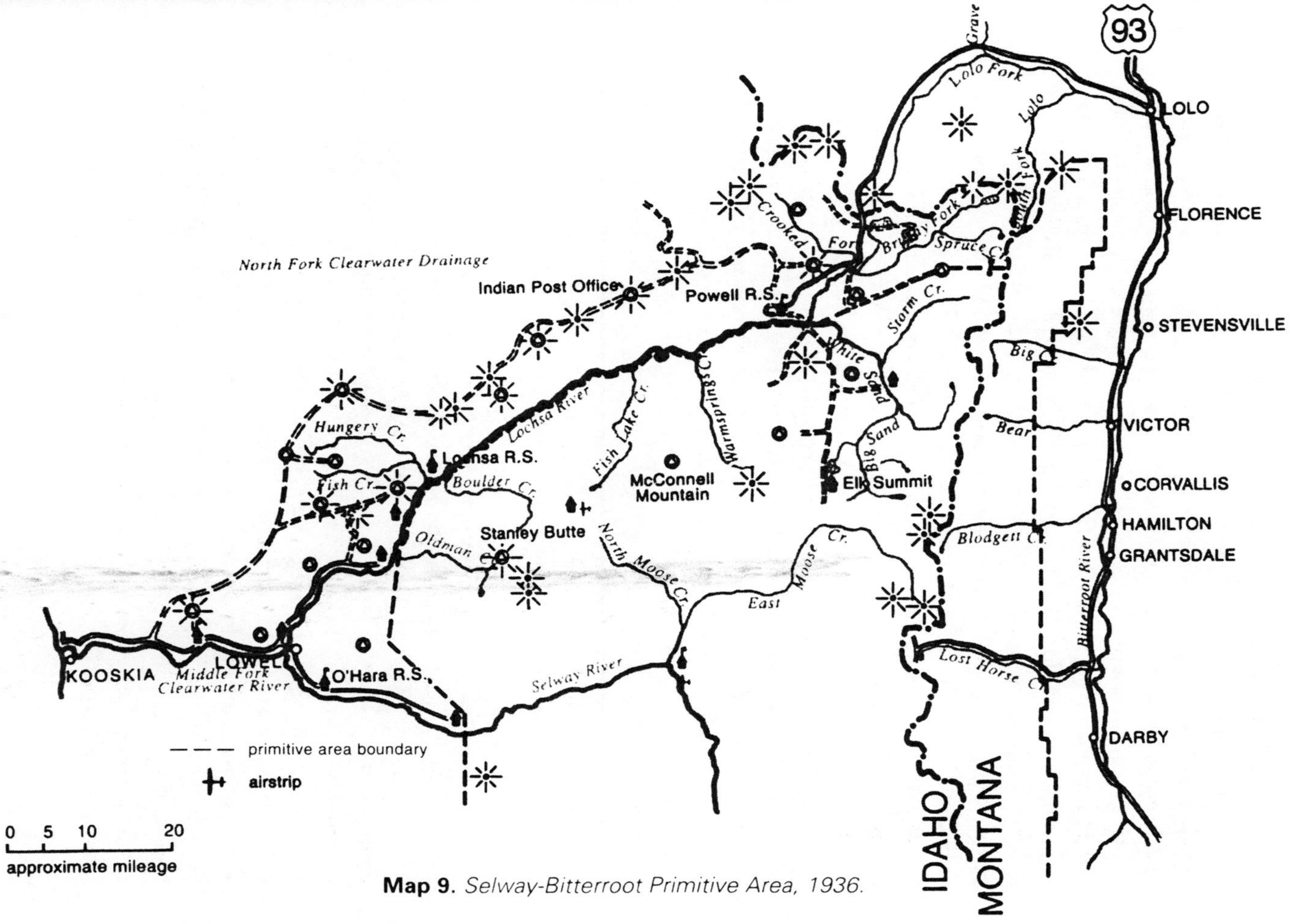
93
LOLO
FLORENCE
STEVENSVILLE
VICTOR
CORVALLIS
HAMILTON
GRANTSDALE
DARBY
IDAHO
MONTANA
North Fork Clearwater Drainage
Indian Post Office
Powell R.S.
Lochsa R.S.
McConnell Mountain
Elk Summit
Stanley Butte
O'Hara R.S.
KOOSKIA
LOWELL
Middle Fork Clearwater River
Selway River
Lochsa River
Lolo Fork
Lolo
Grave
Crooked Fork
Brushy Fork
Spruce Cr.
South Fork
Storm Cr.
White Sand
Big Sand
Warmsprings Cr.
Fish Lake Cr.
Hungery Cr.
Fish Cr.
Boulder Cr.
Oldman
North Moose Cr.
East Moose Cr.
Big Cr.
Bear
Blodgett Cr.
Bitterroot River
Lost Horse Cr.
primitive area boundary
airstrip
0 5 10 20
approximate mileage

Map 9. *Selway-Bitterroot Primitive Area, 1936.*

roads threaded within its boundaries, including the twenty-mile-long truck trail from Powell Ranger Station to Elk Summit. Shearer, Moose Creek, and Fish Lake landing fields remained open to both government and private aircraft. The designation placed no restrictions on several existing uses and activities, including game management projects, hazard reduction projects, controlled burning, snag felling, fire line construction, construction of new landing fields needed for fire control, and irrigation canals or conduits.[192] While striking a blow for wildness, the Forest Service nevertheless retained plenty of options for exploitation that could degrade the natural values of that land.

When in 1939 the strengthened U-Regulations were implemented, the Selway-Bitterroot wilderness was eligible for better protection. To qualify, it had to be reduced in size to exclude roads previously built to control fires. The rangers would continue to fight fires in wilderness, but now there could be no truck trails nor trucks to carry men and equipment in and out of the mountains. Further building of roads was stopped in the protected area, but not in time to save some wild places cherished by those early mountain men.

The new regulations recognized, as many people long had, that wildness dies in the presence of machines. As trapper Fay Burrell put it, referring to the truck trail to Elk Summit: "I was in there so much it was like home. Then after they built that road in there I was blue for a month. That road. It killed it for me."[193]

By designating the Selway-Bitterroot Primitive Area, the government of the United States ratified as a public value trapper Malone's conviction that "There's something about that country that gives you a feeling you don't get anywhere else." In at least a portion of the Lochsa's mountains, humanity and its machinery would no longer "tear at the earth where the life lies hidden." It is unfortunate that, during their fight to keep the country wild, the trappers and Bob Marshall never got better acquainted. Each in his own way—the affluent Marshall, with his knowledge and zeal, and the solitude-rich, dollar-poor trapper, with his homespun philosophy—affirmed the value of wildness in the land of the Lochsa. Henceforth there would always be wild country over the hill from the Bitterroot Valley.

The wilderness idea recognizes that places like Big Creek Lake have in their natural wholeness a greater value to humans than could be obtained by extracting resources for sale in the market place.

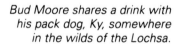

Bud Moore shares a drink with his pack dog, Ky, somewhere in the wilds of the Lochsa.

The youngest child of a pioneer Lolo Creek family, Skookum Woodman lived as a part of, not apart from, nature in the Bitterroot mountains. —Ted and Lil Williams family

15

Hunters and Packers

Prominent among my earliest memories are visits of the mountain men of the Lochsa to our home on the Lolo Fork. They came to leave their horses and mules in our pasture or to visit because they liked Mom and Dad. Mom's warm welcome, sourdough hotcakes, hot bread, and other kitchen creations lured them in. Sometimes they needed a place to bed down for the night before going on to Missoula. Certainly, during the Prohibition days of the twenties, not the least attraction was Dad's reputation for distilling the finest moonshine liquor to be found anywhere in the Bitterroot mountains.

After Mom cleared away the supper dishes, the men would gather around the kitchen table where, in dim light cast by the kerosene lamp, Dad would pour each guest a cupful of clear liquid from the gallon-sized jug in the table's center. Then he'd pour a portion for himself. Each would refill his own cup as needed, and soon after the first taste of the liquor, stories of adventures in the Lochsa country would begin to unfold.

With each cup of Dad's moonshine the bears in their stories grew bigger, and some would, in confidence, share details of their nearness to discovering Isaac's lost mine. Others told stories of fighting the great forest fires. Bert Wendover emphasized marksmanship with his rifle and his understanding of nature. Bill Bell's yarns made heroes of horses and mules. Fred Schott and Skookum Bill Woodman didn't need any moonshine—they never drank the stuff—to recount adventures on their traplines. The stories of each man portrayed his unique view of that remarkable land. These men were in many ways as dissimilar as cougars and lynxes yet, in other respects, as alike as bears of one color. All were accomplished hunters, horsemen, and packers.

Forest ranger Bill Bell displays a sturdy mountain horse. —Pearl Bell McKee

Because the pack train was the only effective means of moving provisions into and bounty out of the Lochsa's mountains, they all had to own, rent, or borrow pack stock. Forest rangers were as much packers as rangers; hunting guides, more packers than guides. And nowhere was the horse-mule-man alliance more crucial than among the outfitters who guided hunters into the Lochsa's mountains after big game trophies and meat. Any good hunter could, with light provisions, hike deep into the mountains and kill game. But getting the hide, antlers, and meat of large game out of the mountains was a task for the mountain horseman, that is, the packer with his horses and mules. With several species of big game growing scarce by the late 1800s, hunters, particularly those in search of trophies, would pay substantial sums for a chance to kill moose, elk, bear, and mountain goats.

Early explorers of the West killed when they needed meat, cut off what they could carry, and left the remainder—which was most of the animal—to the wolves and coyotes. They killed again whenever their supplies ran low. The supply of game seemed to them endless.

And supplies might have lasted, had only these few and widely scattered mountain men been harvesting game. But when their killings were multiplied by the thousands who followed—settlers, military personnel, railroad builders, and others—people began taking far more from the game herds than their reproductive capacity could replenish. The great herds of buffalo, once estimated at eighty million animals, were by the early 1880s reduced to scattered remnants by hunters who shipped the buffalo hides to eastern markets via the new transcontinental railroads. In his works published in 1893, Theodore Roosevelt, himself a tireless hunter, observed: "In all probability there are not now, all told, five hundred head of wild buffaloes on the American continent; and no herd of a hundred individuals has been in existence since 1884."[194]

Although not wantonly killed like the buffalo, elk and deer were hard hit by settlers and trophy hunters until some territories and states tried to slow down the wasteful slaughter of game. Montana, for example, in 1872 prohibited the hunting of buffalo, moose, elk, deer, bighorn sheep, mountain goats, antelope, and bears from February 1 to August 15. Market hunting of game birds was prohibited in 1877. In 1879 Montana authorized bounty payments for predator control. The state's first bag limits for game birds and animals were set in 1895: 3 bull elk, 100 grouse and prairie chickens, 8 deer, 8 bighorn sheep, 8 goats, and 8 antelope. The sale of all game animals and game birds was prohibited in 1897.[195]

Regulations like these, while preventing wholesale slaughter, barely slowed the rate of extermination of wildlife within rifle range of the settlers, sport hunters, and adventurers then populating the West. Indeed, Dr. William T. Hornaday, writing for the New York Zoological Society in 1913, described a situation that had worsened: "The rage for wildlife slaughter is far more prevalent to-day throughout the world than it was in 1872, when the buffalo butchers paved the prairies of Texas and Colorado with festering carcasses. From one end of our Continent to the other, there is a restless, resistless desire to kill, kill!"[196]

Hornaday likened the licensed hunters to a three-million-man army of legalized destruction. To that force he added an unknown but large number of "Guerrillas of Destruction," which he split into two divisions: the "Division of Meat Shooters," including the market gunners, and the "Division of Resident Game Butchers." He considered elk, mountain sheep, and moose threatened species that should not be hunted, and he advocated strict bag limits and buck-only seasons for deer.

In 1909 naturalist-writer Ernest Thompson Seton estimated that, of the probable original population of ten million American elk, only 54,850 remained and 47,000 of those were in or near Yellowstone National Park. American elk had taken a beating at the hands of Americans. By the spring of 1912, elk from the Yellowstone Park herd were being shipped to restock vacant habitat near the western Montana settlements of Deer Lodge, Thompson Falls, Stevensville, and Hamilton. The latter two towns are in the Bitterroot Valley, on the outskirts of the Lochsa country.[197]

In less than a hundred years after Lewis and Clark's expedition, buffalo, grizzly bears, elk, many deer, and nearly all of the antelope had vanished from the prairies and valleys. The turn of the twentieth century looked like the end for the big game of the West and therefore the end of hunting for sportsmen, meat hunters, and commercial operators alike. As we have already seen, however, settlement of the West circumvented the most formidable mountain ranges, leaving them as sanctuaries for game, furbearing animals, and native fish. In these places natural systems remained largely intact, and only a relative few hunted, trapped, fished, panned for gold, or in other ways treaded lightly and impermanently on the land.

The West was settled so fast that by the late 1800s those remaining enclaves of wildness held the last remnants of threatened wildlife and the sole opportunity for experiencing America's vanishing wilderness. Some of those wild places were not big enough to hold out for long against the scourge foretold by Nez Perce Swopscha (see chapter 2). But the land of the Lochsa and its neighboring watersheds was big country, and the game resources it offered to hunters and packers were among the West's most bountiful.

William Wright, an admirer of Grizzly Adams, came west from New England to Spokane, Washington, in 1883 to hunt grizzlies. He packed into the Lochsa country to pursue the big bears for the first time in 1884.[198] Although he killed black bears, elk, deer, and other game, grizzlies evaded his best first efforts. Then one spring in May, in company with a friend, he loaded supplies for an extended trip onto a few pack horses and headed into the Bitterroots, determined to stay until he killed a grizzly bear. The men explored the wilds of the Clearwater all summer without success. Tired of stalking the grizzlies by September, they decided to kill a bull elk as they left the mountains and to pack the head, antlers, and some of the meat home.

While his friend tended camp, Wright found a game lick, concealed himself in some bushes behind a log, and waited for an elk with a trophy-sized rack to appear. The sun dropped behind the mountains, draping long shadows over the glade where the hunter watched for any movement in the forest. Spray from a turbulent stream moistened the freezing air, which chilled Wright's bones as he lay in ambush. He shivered, thinking it probably best to return to camp, but then decided to stay for another five minutes. Here's how Wright described the events that followed: "[J]ust around the point of the hill and out in the bottom about a hundred yards away, I saw what seemed to me to be the old grizzly I had seen in the cage when I was a boy. He had the same carriage and the same big forearms and the gait I would know again any where as long as I live. Best of all the brute was headed straight for my log."[199]

At about forty yards the big bear turned to avoid some bushes, momentarily presenting a broadside view. Wright stood up, drew a careful bead on the point of the bear's shoulder close to the neck, and fired. The grizzly roared "like a mad bull" and rushed in big jumps in Wright's direction. Wright levered his Winchester but the shell jammed in the breech, leaving him defenseless in the path of the charging bear.

With one look at the lumbering giant, Wright dropped his rifle. He sprinted to the creek, jumped back under the bank, and hid there, hoping that the charging bear's momentum would carry him across the creek and that he would keep on going and never look back.

But nothing happened. No maddened bear overshot his hideout. All Wright could hear was the rushing of the creek through the boulders.

Present-day aerial view of Jerry Johnson game licks where I think William Wright killed his first grizzly. —U.S. Forest Service

In a half hour he got so cold that he thought it better to be killed by a bear than to freeze to death. He crawled out onto the bank and inched forward on his belly until he could retrieve his rifle. He extracted the lodged cartridge and reloaded. Armed once again, he rose up from the cold ground. There was the bear, dead, not more than twenty feet from where it had stood when he shot it.

After killing his first grizzly, Wright led many bear-hunting expeditions into the mountains, including the Lochsa country that ranked high among his favored hunting grounds. He described the growth of his outfitting activities in 1889: "I soon found that I had many friends who were anxious to hunt, and who were ready to pay me to take them hunting. Those friends had friends. It was not long before I turned what had been my hobby into a business. Heretofore, I had hunted 3 or 4 months a year. Hence forward I was seldom that long away from the woods."[200]

Trophy hunting was already a genuinely American sport by September 1901, when one of the most enthusiastic hunters in the world, Theodore Roosevelt, became president of the United States. People who believed in conservation of game and protection of wild places from commercial exploitation had no greater champion, anytime, anywhere. Roosevelt likened hunting in the West to development of character:

> In hunting, the finding and killing of the game is after all but a part of the whole. The free, self-reliant, adventurous life, with its rugged and stalwart democracy; the wild surroundings, the grand beauty of the scenery, the chance to study the ways and habits of the woodland creatures — all these unite to give to the career of the wilderness hunter its peculiar charm. The chase is among the best of all National pastimes; it cultivates that vigorous manliness for the lack of which in a nation, as in an individual, the possession of no other qualities can possibly atone.[201]

With promotion like that from the president of the United States, it is small wonder that the hunters and packers had plenty of business guiding dudes into the Lochsa country in pursuit of its game.

So the Lochsa, like similar isolated mountain ranges, served up to the hunters its noblest elk, its biggest moose, a few of its mountain goats, and the best of its grizzly bears. With wildlife still bountiful here, most hunts ended happily. Hunters relished the hardships associated with the chase and the elements, but sometimes nature delivered more clout than either the hunters or their packers and guides were prepared to handle. That's what happened to one unfortunate party hunting the Lochsa in 1893.

Prospector Jerry Johnson and trapper Ben Keeley had begun that year building a cabin on the banks of the Lochsa River. Johnson chose the site with future activities in mind. From the new cabin he could follow an Indian road north to the Lolo trail, then turn east to Lolo Hot Springs, Montana, or west to Kooskia, Idaho, for supplies. Or he could go south on the Indian road, cross the river, and gain access to the Grave Mountains where he had buried Indian Isaac and searched for his gold. In addition, the flat behind the cabin site held traces of fine gold. At snowmelt time in the spring Johnson intended to divert water from the gulches into sluice boxes and wash the gold from the gravel bar.

Thuds and echoes of Johnson and Keeley's axe blows mingled with the song of the river. Each morning crystals of ice formed on the stream's boulders. As the days passed, the arc of the sun fell lower, until its rays no longer warmed the pines, sending their resinous fragrance drifting through the forest. By mid-October the shoulders of the mountains would shade most of the river until springtime returned in March.

It was the end of summer, and Johnson and Keeley were preparing for winter. Other prospectors, hunters, or adventurers had already left the mountains or were making ready to leave, but Johnson and Keeley were staying. After the first substantial snowfall, they would become the sole residents of the land of the Lochsa.

Then on September 26, 1893, they heard the clatter of horses' hooves and the squeaking of saddle leather as a party descended the Indian road on the mountain behind their cabin. A young man riding a powerful, white horse led the party into the clearing. He introduced himself as Martin Spencer, guide and partner of William Wright, the well-known bear hunter from Missoula.

With one exception, Spencer's hunters were a youthful, boisterous gang. They included Will Carlin, the party organizer and son of Brig. Gen. William P. Carlin; Abe Himmelwright, a civil engineer from Connecticut; John Pierce, Carlin's brother-in-law; and the cook and trophy skinner, George Colgate, an older man from Post Falls, Idaho. They had outfitted in Kendrick, Idaho, some 165 miles across the mountains to the west, followed the Lolo Trail to the Indian Post Office, and descended from there to the river. Five pack horses carried their gear, and each man rode a sturdy saddle horse. A grouse-hunting spaniel and two bear dogs named Idaho and Montana flanked the group. It had taken them eight days to travel from Kendrick to Jerry Johnson's cabin (see map 9).[202]

Eager to get on with the hunt, they set up a comfortable camp. Colgate, who had taken sick with swollen legs, failed to join in the camp construction, but the spirits of the others soared during a short spell of bright weather. Too soon, cold rain was pelting their tents and soaking the forests and the land. Since Colgate could not work, the others shared the camp chores. Day after day they hunted in the rain without success as Colgate's illness grew worse.

Early in the morning of their fifth day of hunting, Will wounded a six-point bull elk at the game licks about two miles downriver from their camp. He trailed the bull one-half mile and shot him five times before killing him, hardly an exemplary demonstration of mountain meat hunting. Will, however, was pleased with his trophy though disgusted with the performance of his rifle.

Shortly after that, Abe and Will camped overnight to watch for elk at a game lick one mile up a bold stream plunging into the Lochsa from the south.[203] At dusk the first evening, an old grizzly with two cubs at her side shuffled into the licks. After missing two shots, Abe wounded her with a third. But a long search the next morning failed to show any sign of her carcass. Abe's description of the adventure demonstrates the attitude of that party of hunters and of many other hunters and packers of the times when it came to killing bears. "Just think! A grizzly and two cubs! They came up behind me, passed within fifteen feet of me, crossed the lick, and, by thunder, got away from me. If it had been fifteen minutes earlier, I could have seen my sights and I'd have had the whole crowd. Why, the cubs would have weighed a hundred pounds apiece!"[204]

While searching for the bears next morning, Will wounded another bull elk near the lick. He and Abe shot it six times before bringing it down.

Meanwhile Colgate's condition worsened. Upon observing increased swelling in his legs, feet, and hands, Will forced Colgate to admit the true cause of his illness. Colgate, they learned, had for a long time used instruments as an aid to relieve himself of urine, but he had failed to bring the instruments with him on this trip. He did not like to use them, he said, and thought he could do without them. That's why his illness was going from bad to worse.

Rain kept pouring down with little letup. By October 6, Colgate's legs had swollen to twice their normal size. Spencer urged the hunters to quit so that they could get Colgate out of the mountains as soon as possible. Since John didn't like hunting in the rain, he agreed with Spencer. Abe and Will, expecting an Indian summer, thought it best to

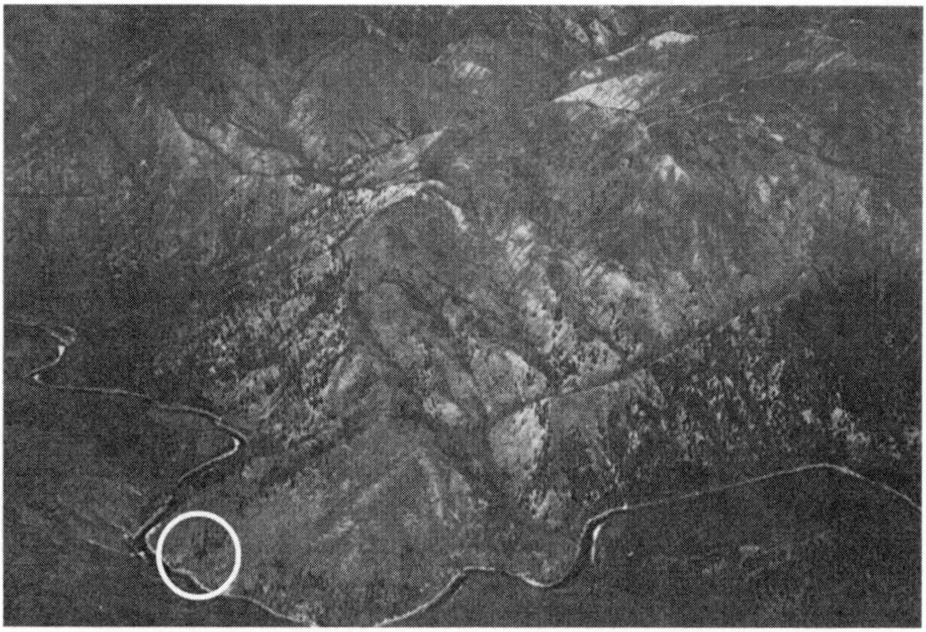

On November 3, 1893, guide Spencer's Carlin Party launched their rafts from the "licks" circled at the lower left in this 1936 photo. Jerry Johnson's cabin stood on the north bank of the river in the lower right.
—Washington National Guard

wait for the rain to stop before moving Colgate. Besides, they wanted to continue the hunt, and Colgate himself preferred to remain until more trophies could be brought to camp.

But snow began to fall on the river, warning the hunters that winter was near. Finally, on October 10, they loaded their camp and trophies, bid Johnson and Keeley good-bye, and strung out on the Indian trail leading up the ridge behind the cabin. Snow deepened as they climbed, until by noon their horses were floundering in three feet of the fluffy stuff. The Lolo Trail remained four miles beyond and two thousand feet higher in elevation; they had no doubt that the snow would be at least four feet deep up there on the divide. Travel by horseback or on foot without snowshoes was now impossible, and by this time Colgate could not walk at all.

The hunters left the snowbound high country and returned to the river. In about fourteen days they constructed two rafts big enough to haul camp supplies, grub, Colgate, and, of course, their trophies. They bought Ben Keeley's grub and hired him to help navigate the rain-swollen river. Using cedars from near the licks below Johnson's cabin, they built

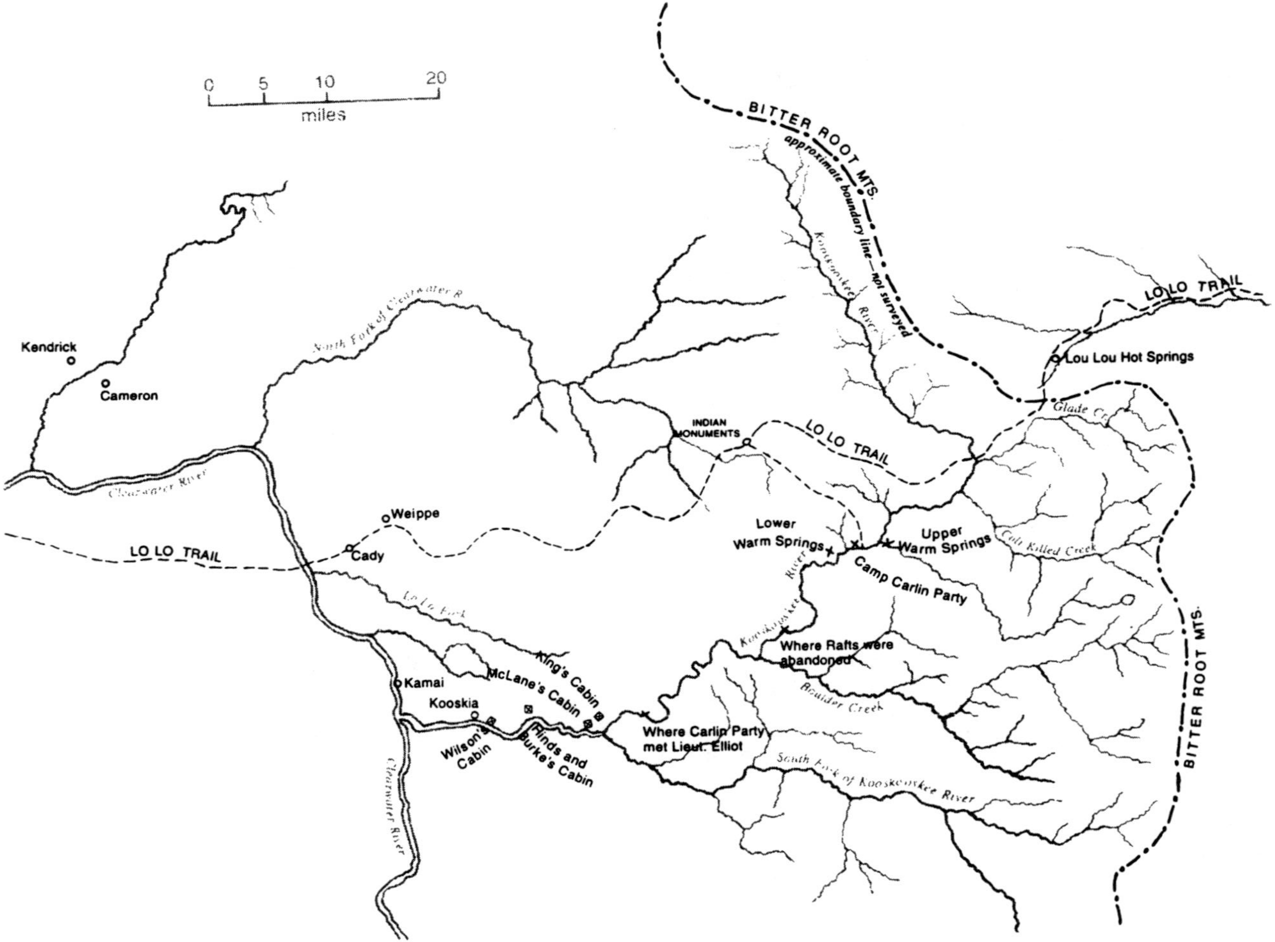

Map 10. *Carlin Party hunting trip, 1893.* —Adapted from a map in Abraham L. A. Himmelwright, *In the Heart of the Bitter-root Mountains: The Story of the Carlin Hunting Party of 1893.* (G. P. Putnam Sons, 1894).

each raft $4\frac{1}{2}$ to 5 feet wide and 26 feet long. They killed more game for meat. From the moment they had forced the reluctant horses to turn around in the snow, their objective had switched from hunting for trophies to fighting for survival.

They launched the rafts on the third day of November 1893. Old Jerry, now facing winter in the mountains alone, hiked down from his cabin to see them off. Eleven days later, at least fifty miles of trackless canyon country still separated them from the most remote homestead on the Clearwater River. Their rafts were battered by white water and boulders, most of their grub and equipment was ruined or lost, and they themselves were approaching exhaustion. After making Colgate, then near death, as comfortable as possible, they shouldered their packs and left him to die alone on the banks of the Lochsa (see map 10).

Meanwhile, concern for the hunters' safety had been spread by Spencer's partner, William Wright. Three rescue operations were launched. Wright guided a military detachment of fifty-three men led by Captain Andrews in a futile attempt to penetrate the mountains from Missoula via Lolo Pass. Lieutenant Overton of the Fourth Cavalry led four troopers and a pack train eastward from Kendrick, Idaho, in an unsuccessful assault on the snowbound Lolo Trail. Lieutenant Elliott, also of the Fourth Cavalry, began an ascent of the Clearwater from Kamiah, speculating that the hunters might attempt an escape from the mountains down the river.

Lieutenant Elliott's detachment made its way by boat some seven miles up the Lochsa River from where it joined with the Selway. While portaging their boats around one of many rapids, Elliott encountered the bear dog Idaho. Then Spencer climbed out of the rocks.

Elliott called out, "Hello. Who in God's name are you?"

Came the reply: "My name is Spencer, the guide of the Carlin Party."[205]

So ended that trophy hunt of 1893. Spencer, Carlin, Himmelwright, and Keeley made it out of the wilderness. Old Jerry wintered safely at his cabin in the wilds and among the wildlife of the Lochsa. Some time after Colgate was abandoned, his spirit fled the earth, leaving his body, the party's trophies, wrecked rafts, and equipment on an unknown gravel bar of the Lochsa River.

For a long time the topography of the Lochsa, not regulation of hunting, saved big game from the muzzle of the hunters' rifles. As we have already seen (in chapter 13), however, the Idaho legislature had

During the summer of 1894, Lieutenant Elliott found Colgate's remains. He carried them upriver to the licks and buried them in this grove of cedars. —C. I. Harrison, ca. 1908

established several game preserves because it feared that the elk would be exterminated like the buffalo. One of these, the Selway Game Preserve, encompassed much of the Lochsa country and some of the Selway River drainage to the south. Unlike the Lapland trappers, packers and hunters did not poach much inside the preserve, partly because their activities created far more notice than did the obscure trappers who could prowl through the mountains as silent as a lynx on the trail of a snowshoe hare. Packers and hunters needed big camps. Rifle shots could not be concealed. Furthermore, few phenomena attract more attention than a meat-laden pack train with trophy elk antlers tied on top of the loads.

The bases used by most packers and hunters consisted of tent camps, which were hauled out of the mountains each fall when the hunting was finished. Some outfitters became so taken by the spell of certain wild places, however, that they wanted a more permanent claim to the land. One such power place lies in a valley shaded by Ranger Peak, a towering cone of granite that thrusts skyward from the crest of the Bitterroot Range. Beginning in the crevasses on the peak's treeless slopes, small streams tumble down toward the canyon, their waters gleaming in dense forests along the way. The many streams join at the base of the mountain to form Storm Creek, which, at one point, is bordered by a meadow where the grass in midsummer reaches to the withers of a tall mountain horse. From the stream side, the meadow slopes to the north, gently at first, then pitches up the steep mountain. At its upper end a

Two hunters pack elk meat and antlers out of the Lochsa's mountains. —K.D. Swan, U.S. Forest Service

These Lochsa hunters seem happy with their camp and trophies. —Pearl Bell McKee

Summertime melting of snow on Ranger Peak discharges clear water into Storm Creek, a tributary of the White Sand Fork of the Lochsa River.

small tributary babbles down, then vanishes from sight beneath such lush grass that one can find it only by parting the tall vegetation and peering through its leaves to see the water.

The ten-acre meadow is the only open space in an otherwise unbroken forest of firs, spruces, and pines. A pilgrim can see out from the meadow but not very far, for tall trees crowd its border, hiding the forest's interior and leaving the life of the meadow to wonder what's happening out there in the dark. Unlike Medusa, whose visage turned men to stone, the Storm Creek meadow and its surroundings turned some men to eternal romance with their mountains. Once discovered, after smelling the breeze from the meadow, hearing the song of the creeks, and feeling the bosom of the valley, there could be no turning away from the sirenlike power of that beautiful land.

The quest for the meadow began one summer during the early 1900s when two teenaged boys, George and Bryan Clarke, ran away from their home in the Bitterroot Valley and began building a cabin in Big Creek Canyon a short ways below the mouth of St. Mary's Creek. By the time they had laid up two rounds of logs, their dad found their hideout and shagged them out of the mountains to tend chores back at the ranch. But the boys returned again and again. By 1909 George (nicknamed "Chink") and Bryan ("Rip") spent more time in the back country than they did on the farm. Their younger brother, Jack, joined them later, and the three brothers often stayed in trapper George Johnson's cabin

The Clarkes posted Storm Creek Meadow as a mining claim but used it mostly as a base for big game hunting and trapping.

near the shore of Big Creek Lake. They built a bigger cabin nearby to serve as a halfway stop and supply base for reaching over the hill into Storm Creek. From the lake they scratched out a trail up a steep slope to the north, thus gaining access to a narrow notch on the crest—their gateway to the land of the Lochsa and to untold opportunities in the forests and valleys beyond.[206]

Big Creek, Storm Creek, Maude Creek, Dan Ridge, and Beaver Ridge formed the centerpiece of their lives. They guided dudes after big game and prospected for gold. Chink Clarke took a partner, Gus Robb—a stalwart mountain man, one of the best in the hills. Each winter Chink and Robb strung traplines deep into the Lochsa's forested basins. Never mind that this was the Selway Game Preserve, closed to hunting and trapping. In their view the closure had nothing to do with the Clarkes' time-proven rights to the Idaho furs. The notch was their entry point; their exit, Maude Creek Pass. Each winter they traveled in with light loads and snowshoed out burdened with furs.

Be it winter or summer, the Clarkes were hooked on the Storm Creek meadow with its tall grass, somber borders, and sparkling brooks. By

Clarke's original route from Big Creek Lake into the Lochsa crossed the crest of the Bitterroots and the Montana-Idaho boundary at the saddle, top center.

the mid-1920s, they had dug a discovery hole and staked a claim. This was the land toward which the dying Indian Isaac had pointed when he said to Jerry Johnson: "See snow." The Clarkes' prospecting found only economically worthless black sand and mica, but they had plenty of other forest treasures—the wildlife, the streams, and the call of the mountains. They loved that land so much that they wanted to claim it for their own.

So they began building a headquarters at the meadow. Master axman Gus Robb framed logs, hewed puncheons for floors and doors, and split shakes for the roof. The Clarkes hauled windows, nails, tools, kitchen gear, two stoves, and even steel cots by pack train up Big Creek, through their notch, and down to the meadow. After the road over Lolo Pass reached the mouth of Brushy Fork, they packed most of their supplies in from there because the trails were better.

By 1928 a one-room lodge stood on the eastern edge of the meadow, and water was piped from the brook to a bathhouse, where it was heated for showers and washing. A small log barn could be seen in the spruces, and another new cabin stood partly finished near the lodge. The Clarkes' hunting clients no longer lived in tent camps; they had sturdy log quarters. And Robb and his keen axe fashioned more each year.

The Clarkes' hunters, some fifteen or twenty each fall, came to Storm Creek from places near and far. In the tradition of the Carlins and President Roosevelt, some wanted trophies and gloried in the thrill of the chase. But many were hard-working miners from the game-scarce Coeur d'Alene mining district; they needed recreation in wildness and meat for their tables. These miners too loved that land. Redheaded Ray ("Pop") Robinson was one hunter from Wallace, Idaho, who returned again and again until he grew too old to climb the steep mountains of the Lochsa.

With plenty of game in the nearby woods, most hunters killed elk within a day's hunt of the meadow. When the hunters were gone, Chink Clarke and Robb trapped or hunted gold. Both the hunters and packers were happy. By 1930 the Clarkes' life in the mountains seemed secured by their claim on the meadow. But the rangers of the United States Forest Service disagreed.

Storm Creek formed the boundary of the Selway Game Preserve, and ranger Ed Mackay suspected the Clarkes and Robb of hunting and trapping within the preserve. A mineral expert, engaged by Mackay, examined the Clarkes' claim and found no evidence of locatable minerals. Mackay subsequently brought charges in court that the Clarkes and Robb were operating an illegal hunting lodge under the pretense of a fraudulent mining claim.

At the conclusion of their trial in Moscow, Idaho, on May 14, 1934, Judge Charles C. Cavanah ruled in favor of the Forest Service. The report of the regional office of the Forest Service at Missoula, Montana, concluded: "The case involved occupancy in trespass of land of the United States, constituting a part of the Selway National Forest, under the guise of a placer mining claim. The defendants, after digging a so-called discovery hole and filing their notice of location of a placer mining claim proceeded to erect buildings and other structures for the purpose of conducting a hunting lodge for the entertainment of hunters in the big game region across the Bitterroot range from Lolo Hot Springs, Montana."

The Clarkes thus lost their hold on the meadow, but the meadow and its environs never loosened their grip on the Clarkes. Chink Clarke kept trapping until about 1938. Speaking many years later of their departure from the Storm Creek meadows, Jack Clarke said: "The Forest Service didn't make it stick. They didn't run us out. Everybody went broke. There was no use huntin' anymore."[207]

Like the trappers and the prospectors, the packers who guided the hunters roamed free on the land at first. But as their numbers increased so did the conflicts among them and between them and other users of the forests. To prevent over-hunting and maintain the peace, the forest rangers eventually allocated loosely defined territories for each packer and guide.

The Idaho legislature reopened the Selway Game Preserve to elk hunting in the fall of 1935. For the first time in sixteen years, the crack of high-powered rifles and the smell of powder and blood mingled with the bugling of bulls defending their harems. Territory once hunted, then closed, again became available to the packers and hunters. The game preserve was loaded with elk—the result of protection from hunting, the killing of predators, and the creation of excellent game range by forest fires. It was the heyday of the men (and the few women) who guided trophy and meat hunters into the heart of the Lochsa's mountains. They all owned trucks to haul their stock to road ends in the Lochsa, and they used Decker pack saddles on the trails; otherwise, their operations had changed little from the days of Spencer and Wright.

Many hunters coveted the Lochsa's wildlife bounty, and more were coming. Some wanted trophies; others wanted meat; many wanted both. The packers, for a price, offered the hunters mountain comradeship, efficient pack trains, and knowledge of the country and its wildlife. Their love of the land was plain to see. All of them—packers and clients—wanted, indeed needed, to rekindle their spirits by hunting big game in some of the finest wild country left in the whole United States.

16

The Winter of the Blue Snow

Sometime between Christmas 1935 and New Year's Day 1936, I snowshoed from Lolo Hot Springs up the West Branch of the Lolo Fork toward Lolo Pass. Light snow fell from a leaden sky, and as I neared the summit wind whipped the snow in whirls and stung my face until I hunched behind the collar of my woolen stag. A big storm loomed ahead, uncertain weather in exciting times. I had often wandered in and out of the Lochsa country since my crossing from the Lolo Fork to the headwaters of the Brushy in 1930. But this time was different. This time I pulled an eight-foot-long toboggan loaded with 150 pounds of my most important possessions: traps, guns, packs, and bedrolls. This time I was going to stay.

During 1934, I had helped the Forest Service fight a big fire on the Lolo Fork. The government check I received for my work at 35¢ an hour provided more cash than I'd ever seen at once before. While fighting the fire I confirmed what I already suspected: that the people who worked for the Forest Service were the best mountain men of that era. I was entranced by the quality of their woodsmanship, and I wanted to join with them to build trails, fight fires, and in other ways help care for the land of the Lochsa.

My chance came in June 1935 when ranger Ed Mackay signed me on with his Powell district crew. Ed paid $75 per month with board. I worked on trail crews, manned the fire lookout at Hot Springs Point, and fought several fires. My job ended in early fall, yet it seemed certain that Forest Service work, with its fair pay and good grub, would be available every summer. But that solved barely half of the problem. I had to make a living during winter, too, and the only way to do that in

Left to right: Dad (Bill Moore), Mom (Hazel Moore), Grandma (Jessie Wright Ayers), and second Grandpa (Charley Ayers) pose at our second Lolo Creek home in about 1935. —Dorothy Pearl Hughes

the wilds of the Lochsa was by trapping furs. With all available areas outside the game preserve already occupied by trappers, the chances of obtaining trapping rights didn't look good.

Then, near Christmas 1935, I joined my family on the Lolo Fork for the holiday. There at my folks' log cabin home I met Orin Van Hoose, who had been trapping along the Lochsa with his headquarters at Wendover Bar (all flats along the river were called bars). After returning from checking his line one evening, Orin accidentally burned down the cabin built by Bert Wendover in 1911. He saved only his snowshoes and furs, which he carried across Lolo Pass and out of the mountains.

In Orin's misfortune lay my chance to tackle the Lochsa in winter. I bought his trapline for $150 and then began to wonder if I could ever find it. Dad hauled my outfit to Lolo Hot Springs in his Model T Ford, and I began mushing over the hill from there.

It took three days to break trail and haul my loaded toboggan to the cabin at Burned Cedar Bar, where I established headquarters for the rest of the winter. My wintertime home stood on the out turn of a big bend of the Lochsa River in what Bill Bell had called the coldest

The trapper's cabin at Burned Cedar Bar on the Lochsa River after a raid by a big bear in late springtime, ca. 1936.

place on the river. Bill claimed that he froze his ears in bed while sleeping there one night. Blizzard winds would drift snow from the river's ice against the door, and some of it would sift across the threshold and spread over the puncheon floor. But plenty of fire-killed cedar stood nearby to be cut for wood, and clear water from the river was close at hand. I decided that Burned Cedar Bar was a good place—indeed, it was the only place with a cabin available to establish home, while searching out the trapline I had bought.

By early March I had retraced most of the trapline. I found the new cabin built by Orin and his uncle Bill on Wendover Ridge buried in fourteen feet of snow. After discovering cabins at Cayuse Creek and at the Forks of Squaw Creek, I became acquainted with Jay Turner, who shared the Burned Cedar Bar cabin with me and ran his traplines down the river from there. Jay told me that he had made a deal to buy Andrew Erickson's trapline in the spring, so I laid out another $150 and bought Jay's downriver line. Jay's line, plus the old Wendover line, would give me the territory needed to sustain big catches of furs.

Soon after the snow melted from the banks of the river, I began building a new home where the glacier lilies and trilliums bloomed beside the meadow and not far from the ashes of the old cabin at Wendover Bar. I worked in the shadow of Bert Wendover, who said of his twenty

Wildlife biologist Bob Cooney at Bud Moore's Squaw Creek cabin in 1938.

years of life along the Lochsa: "I liked it alone in there. I didn't get lonesome. I spent them twenty years. And they were happy for me too. I enjoyed it all."[208]

Bert had come in 1911 because doctors had given him little time to live and he wanted to spend it all in the wilderness. I came to the same bar twenty-five years later, in 1936, to create a future and to make a living at what I knew best: mountain woodsmanship. We both came alone, and we were both in love with the land of the Lochsa.

Bert chose the site; I followed his logic. When springtime sun melted the snow, the sound of the Lochsa's rising water surged into the forest and welled up the mountainsides. Its tones shifted with wind and sun and rain, hammering relentlessly on my senses and on those of the bears and all the other life in the land. The powerful presence of the new water was awesome. As darkness fell in late evening, I would occasionally rest in its spray on the bank near the meadow's edge, smell its freshness, and feel the great river flow through my mind and soul.

Ancient forests surrounded the meadow. Most of the trees were large-diameter cedar, grand fir, spruce, and whitebark pine. It was hard to find ten- to twelve-inch-diameter logs suited for cabin walls because Bert had long before cut the choice timber available nearby for building and extending his cabin. Bert's cabin was big, and he had used lots of logs. He described its structure this way: "Well sir. It was funny about that cabin. I built it fourteen feet by eighteen feet first. Then every year I needed more room so I built on towards the river until I had three cabins hooked together."[209]

Despite Bert's perennial logging, thorough search disclosed good trees scattered here and there throughout the forest, though none were closer than two hundred yards from the site. Log selection was the first step in assuring the quality of my finished cabin. Each tree had to be straight in both bole and grain, show little taper from trunk to top, and be free of large knots. Since my home was to be fourteen feet by sixteen feet inside, I cut the end logs twenty feet and the side logs twenty-two feet in length to allow plenty of space for notching the corners. I planned to extend the cabin's roof to create a six-foot-long porch, so I cut the sills, caps, purloins, and ridge pole twenty-eight feet long.

That spring, as in every spring, the water, forests, and mountains exuded such life that I understood why Bert "didn't get lonesome." Released from ice and swollen by snowmelt, the river called forth a great awakening. Coyotes howled on the ridge where Lewis and Clark's party had climbed the mountain 131 years before. North from the meadow, elk sipped water and licked minerals at a hidden spot in the cedars, while mergansers skimmed in pairs up and down the Lochsa, the whistle of their wings punctuating the turbulent river's song. Great horned owls talked to each other on moonlit nights, and the bears left tracks in the mud as they watched for big steelhead trout digging nests and laying their spawn in the gravel of the creek that flowed across the bar.

I wanted fish, too. So, like the bears, I watched the creek as I worked. Unlike most bears, however, I had never before seen one of those sea-run steelhead. But the big fish should be near because the snow bridges had melted from the logs spanning the creeks, and Andrew Erickson had told me that the melting of the bridges coincided with the coming of the fish. Armed with a three-pronged spear fashioned in the forge at Powell Ranger Station and attached to a ten-foot-long slender lodge-pole, I waited and checked the creek several times each day. Then one morning I met my first steelhead on the little sand bar where the downriver trail crossed Wendover Creek.

Idling at the base of a pool where eighteen-inch-deep water sparkled in full sunlight, his powerful body barely flicked a fin to hold his place in the swirling riffles. An indistinct silhouette against the pale gravel, he hugged the stream bottom. Suddenly, the churning water parted, and his green, black-spotted back and dorsal fin rose above the surface and

Sparky Moore, my younger brother, carries a nice steelhead from Wendover Creek to the cabin, ca. 1937.

shone in the springtime sun. Then one splash of his eight-inch-wide tail drove him under, and I saw bright red sides tip momentarily toward the sunny Lochsa sky.

With spear in hand I waded into the creek some thirty feet below the steelhead, and then I stalked upstream toward his idling tail. At fifteen feet I paused, dug good footing into the slippery gravel and worked my spear pole out full length toward him. I waited. As snowmelt-cold currents swirled around us, warm sun glinted on the water, and I squinted to dim the reflected rays. An upstream-borne breeze whipped the pool, obscuring the big trout in ripples. Then he lifted from the depths, his back again breaking the surface of the water.

I lunged one stride forward, drove the spear home in a powerful arc, and felt the sharp tines strike heavy flesh. Red blood exploded in the clear water. I held the doomed trout pinned against the stream bottom until I felt each struggle growing weaker as his life ebbed. I forked him out onto the bank where the last of his blood stained the melting snow.

At about fifteen pounds, he provided plenty of fish for me to eat with some left over for making "bunkum," a smelly concoction used by most trappers for luring martens to their sets. Wendover Creek was full of steelhead that morning. To assure plenty of "bunkum" for use during

This poled-in tent at Papoose Saddle furnished overnight shelter while I tended my traplines in the Lochsa's high country during the winter of 1936–37.

next winter's trapping, I speared two more big fish, cut them in chunks, stuffed them in jars, and then hung the jars high in the crown of a tall grand fir tree, where the fish would rot out of reach of the hungry bears.

After tending to the fish, I returned to building the cabin. With the help of a government mule, harness, single tree, and chain loaned by ranger Ed Mackay, I skidded the logs into the meadow. By late May I had them all peeled. I used large, flat rocks as piers for the cabin's foundation. Since the foundation was low, I laid up the first round of walls with larch logs, which resist rot when laid close to the ground. With that done, I resumed work for the Forest Service. I spent the summer working on trail crew, fighting fires, and serving as lookout on McConnell Mountain, then one of the most remote stations in the Lochsa country.

Early September found me back home at Wendover Bar, axe in hand and loaded with determination to finish my cabin before winter closed in on the land. In contrast to its springtime power, the Lochsa had been tamed by summer drought to a pleasant river easily waded across any wide riffle. Big boulders, once hidden under water, stood dry in the streambed. Despite the low water, I decided to raft lumber for the cabin's door, roof, and floor from Powell Ranger Station to Wendover Bar, a distance of about four miles. But the scheme failed because the water

The Cayuse Creek cabin site, one of eleven in the territory, offers all a trapper could want: snug shelter, nearby water, dry wood, and good furbearer habitat.

ran too shallow to float the rafts among the Lochsa's boulders. After one hard day's work I beached the fleet less than one mile below the launch site. When it looked like a dirt floor would have to do for my home, Forest Service packer Heinie Williams chanced along, loaded the boards on his mules, and in less than two hours delivered them to the Wendover Bar. That's when I began to appreciate the value of subsidies conferred by the government of the United States.

Raising the cabin went well at first, but as the walls grew in height I had trouble hoisting the heavy logs into place. Fortunately, Dad's intuition was working as usual. He showed up on the scene, bringing along my sister Clarine, who was about fifteen years old at the time. She was wiry and strong but weighed little more than the combined poundage of the steelheads I'd speared to make "bunkum." Dad called her "Midget." Though small in size, she was big in go. She cooked, nailed roofing, handed up tools, cut wood, and packed shake bolts from the cedar grove behind the licks.

With three of us at it, the woods at Wendover Bar echoed with axe and hammer blows from daylight until dark. By mid-October the new cabin's split-cedar-shake roof shone in contrast to the green forest surrounding the meadow. The ashes of Bert Wendover's cabin lay buried in fresh shavings and chips; my new home had replaced the old.

My brother Ed stands atop Moon Saddle cabin, west of Indian Post Office, and prepares to unplug the stovepipe buried under twelve feet of snow.

While Dad and Clarine installed the windows and the door, I readied the line camps for winter. Wood had to be cut, cabins repaired, one tent camp installed, and grub packed to all the shelters before deep snow buried the landscape. Since the old cabin near Elbow Bend on the Lolo Trail had collapsed, I poled in a ten-by-twelve-foot tent at Papoose Saddle and outfitted the camp with a small sheet-iron stove, a sleeping bag, grub, a few dishes, and a palouser—a candle in a two-pound coffee can—for light.

The line cabin on the bench near where Moss Creek flows into Cayuse Creek was one of my favorite places. Though old, it was still sturdy when I found it. The porch, broken by heavy snows of past winters, could be easily repaired. I cut and stacked wood on the porch and pulled fresh beargrass to fill the pole bunk. With the ashes cleaned out of the Kimmel stove, the coal oil lamp filled, and mouse scat washed from the dishes, the shelter was ready for winter.

In a similar way I repaired an A-frame cabin near Indian Post Office built by some trapper long before. Then I dropped from the high country down to the river and readied the snug cabins at the mouth of Indian Post Office Creek and at Burned Cedar Bar. On returning home I found Dad and Clarine gone. The elk hunters were also gone. The people of the Forest Service were closing Powell station because the nip of late fall harbingered the winter. Everybody was leaving, and I squelched a

Jay Turner built this cabin beside the Lochsa River near the mouth of Indian Post Office Creek about 1931. I used it from 1937 to 1942; it was destroyed by construction of the Lewis and Clark Highway during the early 1960s.

tug of loneliness, for this was no time to be distracted from the work yet to be done.

At daybreak one morning, I hiked past the game licks in the cedars and climbed up a spur ridge extending from Wendover Creek north toward the Lolo Trail. Cold rain fell on the river and dripped down through the cedars and filled the dent in the crown of my sweat-stained hat. Mist hung in the timber. As I climbed, the rain thickened to a mixture of water and snow that piled on my shoulders and soaked into my woolen clothes. Not the slightest cracking twig broke the silence as I moved through the soggy forest. There would be tracking snow higher up. Most important, I should find elk at the snowline. I was after meat for the winter.

Fresh tracks showed in the first skiff of snow. It looked like several cows and calves had been feeding up the ridge, picking mushrooms and nipping the sweet buds of the maples. In such dense forest my encounter, and the kill, would be at close range. I closed in on my prey quickly, yet slowly enough to view each unfolding scene in detail because success would lie in spotting the elk before they saw me. A patch of hair, an antler, a moving ear, a yellow rump: that's all the advantage I would need to consummate the kill.

Bud Moore returns to his home cabin at Wendover Bar after a round on his eighty-mile long trapline.

The pungent smell of elk hung in the cold mountain air. Thirty yards away, a clump of maples rattled where, through swirling snowflakes, I saw a young bull rubbing velvet from his spikelike antlers. He faced toward me. As the Winchester's gold bead settled on his chest, he raised his head and ears in too-late recognition that all was not as it should be for elk on Wendover Ridge that morning. I squeezed the trigger. So intense was my concentration that I and the rifle and the bullet were as one. I heard no sound, felt no recoil as the spike bull dropped. I got at him at once with my knife and hatchet, and it wasn't long until the winter's meat was hanging on the pole.

Cold weather began in October of that year, and all fur-bearing animals wore prime coats by mid-November. At that point priorities changed from preparing for winter to setting traps. Never mind the home cabin's half-chinked walls. Never mind that the wood supply remained too small to last all winter. Never mind that rawhide needed to be soaked and stretched or that more jerky should be dried behind the stove. If you want fur, you go for it when the time's right. And I wanted all the fur I could get. So I set traps, hiking from cabin to cabin in a fifty-mile-long loop that formed the hub of my activity. Three spur lines, each extending into good furbearer habitat outside my loop, completed my eighty-mile-long trapline in the heart of the Lochsa's mountains.

This "cubby" set near Wendover Creek each winter provided several mink, marten, and ermines.

In that plan I followed one of two conservation practices used by early-day Lochsa trappers. Andrew Erickson would never set spur lines inside his loop, reasoning that if the furbearers came out, he would have a chance to catch them when they crossed his line. Those that remained inside served as breeding stock to populate the mountains and assure a sustained catch winter after winter. Spur lines set spokelike outside the hub also increased the likelihood of catching furbearers not surrounded within the cabin-to-cabin circle.

A different but equally successful practice was used by Wes Fales to sustain good yields of furs from his traplines in the Lochsa's mountains and in the Sapphire Range east of the Bitterroot Valley. Like Andrew and most other backcountry trappers of the time, Wes set his traps in a big circle with the trapline connected by several cabins. By alternating between the Lochsa line and the Sapphire line, he allowed the furbearers one undisturbed year to build up their populations before he trapped them again.

Like those early trapper-conservationists, I wanted to sustain good catches of fur because I intended to trap each winter, work for the Forest Service in summer, and spend the rest of my life living at Wendover Bar on the banks of the Lochsa River. Andrew's strategy adapted well to my territory, so that was the plan I used.

Heavily laden with traps and bait, I hit the trail each morning in the dark, my way lighted through the forest by a palouser. I built "cubbies" along the streams and placed traps in them to catch mink. I preferred

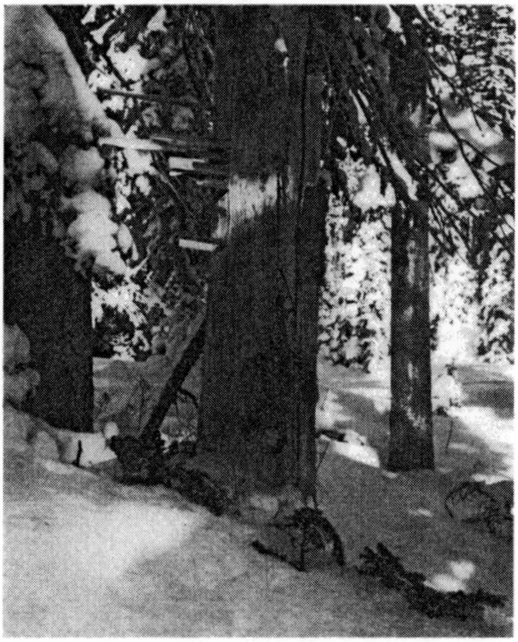

This catch of a prime marten demonstrates the effectiveness of a typical peg set.

notch sets for marten in sheltered forested basins, but peg sets proved more effective on the ridges where blizzard winds might blow the notches full of snow. Here and there I placed special sets at stream junctions for otter or in dense thickets for lynx. Twelve inches of wet snow blanketed the valleys as I extended the trapline from cabin to cabin, while three feet of the fluffy stuff made snowshoeing tough on the high ridges. Each nightfall I'd arrive at a line cabin weary yet satisfied because each day's work placed fifteen to twenty sets in wait for the prowling furbearers.

With fur signs plentiful, prospects for a good catch looked promising. But turning tracks in the snow to fur in the cache is at best an uncertain venture. The outcome, I knew, would depend on timing, weather, trapping skill, my endurance on the trail, perhaps even luck. In late afternoon on the ninth day of travel I placed the last mink set at the mouth of Cold Storage Creek, then legged it for the home cabin on the bar a quarter of a mile up the river. Twilight shaded the land. The squeaky crunch of my boots broke the stillness as I hurried home through the frozen snow. Tired yet impatient, I was in a hurry to get the night behind me and to get on with the morning—when I could run the line, pick up my fur catch, and reset the traps. That night I fried elk steaks and spuds on a crackling fire in the new stove in my new home, with my thoughts on the trails of tomorrow.

Part of the fur catch hangs on my Wendover cabin in December 1936.

I needed to make my trapline pay, to pave my road to economic survival. Nonetheless, anticipation, not economics, is the spice of fur trapping, and its fever ran high at Wendover Bar that cold November night in 1936. Trapping turned out good. The value of the fur I took on that first round would more than repay the $200 in cash I had invested in preparations for the trapline. By late December, 44 marten, 4 foxes, 17 mink, 123 ermines, 7 coyotes, and 3 otters hung in the fur cache. Driven by the spell of trapping the Lochsa's mountains, I kept at it every day and parts of most nights. Christmas Eve passed, I thought, while I slept at Burned Cedar Bar, but I wasn't sure because I had lost track of the days and the dates.

It was about January 1 when powerful storms unleashed their full fury on the Lochsa country. For twenty-one days snow fell with little letup. It piled up seven feet deep on the river, with more than double that depth in the high country. For twenty-one days I mushed each night into line cabins, leaving a deep trail through snow so loose its fluffy crystals looked blue in the wintertime light. For twenty-one mornings I climbed from the cabin's interior up to the snow's surface to find the trails buried by more snow that had fallen in the night.

It was, in mountain-man terms, the winter of the blue snow. Snowshoe trails weren't all that got snowed under. The big snows buried all my traps, and in the high country I moved notch and peg sets up the trees until the marten, ermines, squirrels, and I traveled on snow in places twenty feet above the ground. I had never seen such snow before. The

In contrast to Homer's "ball and chain," snowshoe travel through this well-settled snow at Lolo Pass would be a trapper's "piece of cake."

stuff never settled but instead grew deeper and looser as each wave of storms passed through the mountains. I had heard Homer, whom we've already met in chapter 1, describe it as "slow settlin' snow" (plus several earthier names), and when he was out in the stuff he called his snowshoes "the ball and chain."

One day in January, on the high line between Papoose Saddle and the Cayuse Creek line cabin, I found a slow, steady pace to be the best way to drag my "ball and chain" along the Lolo Trail. Snow had fallen all night at Papoose Camp, and there was no sense of bottom as I plowed westward next morning. As I hauled one snowshoe up and forward, the other would settle slowly until my mittens touched the snow beside the trail. To keep sinking was bad enough but, in the absence of firm foundation, launching the next step seemed a sure road to rapid exhaustion. The harder I plowed, the faster I settled and the deeper I sank. So I throttled back and wallowed forward like a water-logged boat in a storm on the ocean.

At the high point between the two line camps I had found the lowest gear in my forward transmission. Near dark and two hours later I learned that I could go on and on, long after it seemed I had no energy left at all. To discover the end of one's endurance was, I had supposed, a physical experience. But the mind, not the legs, gives up first. I kept moving from the mountain down toward the cabin on Cayuse Creek, but I lost my sense of position in the Lochsa's great space. My world shrank to swirling snow, the blue glint where the webs broke the surface, and the herculean task of moving one snowshoe ahead of the other. All else was instinct. Save for me and the storm, the rest of the world faded from the scope of my benumbed mind.

On into darkness I went, until sometime during the night I felt the solidity of the cabin buried under ten feet of snow. I slid from the snow's surface down under the porch roof, unleashed my boots from the snowshoes, and opened the door. I fumbled in the dark interior until I found the matches and lit the coal oil lamp. Its yellow light showed kindling ready by the sheet-iron stove. I lit the fire, but it wouldn't draw until I had climbed back out into the storm and dug out the buried stove pipe. With the pipe cleared and a fire crackling at last, it didn't take long to boil coffee and macaroni and fry a hunk of frozen elk meat. Frozen marten and ermines caught during the day thawed while I cooked and ate. After supper I skinned and stretched them. Then I blew out the light and crawled between the blankets on the mattress of beargrass, where I slept while the snow piled deeper and the storm roared through the forest above the cabin's roof.

After that storm all hoofed game except mountain goats (they winter on high, wind-swept ridges) wallowed from the ridges to the valley bottoms along the Lochsa River because downhill was the only direction they could go in such deep, loose snow. With the maples and willows, their principal wintertime food, buried in snow, only the strongest escaped starvation. Hungry coyotes and cougar took their toll on the rest.

Nature's way of balancing life is seldom gentle, but during January and February 1937 she seemed especially vicious with the Lochsa's deer, elk, and moose. Once in a while, however, an opportunity could be found to change the odds in favor of the hunted—like that day in January on the river near the Jerry Johnson Bar.

Snow lay deep on the ice, while more fell from a stormy sky, as I snowshoed around a bend and spied a whitetail buck not more than one hundred yards ahead. A large coyote circled the buck at ten paces. The old whitetail kept turning to face him, with hooves ready to strike should the coyote come close. Occasionally, the coyote paused and sat on his

Bud Moore holds a coyote killed on the ice of the Lochsa River about 1937.

haunches. The buck stood with his eyes fixed on the wild canine that would harass him until he weakened and then close in for the kill.

The range was ideal for the .25-.35-caliber carbine I carried. Pushing my left snowshoe forward, I shucked off one mitten and dropped to my right knee. The coyote trotted on in his persistent circle and then sat down. As the gold bead centered in the peep sight I was struck by the wildness of the scene. Central figures in the arena, the coyote and the buck were poised against a backdrop of green cedars and grand firs. At the coyote's slightest movement, the buck's six-point antlers rocked in top-heavy response to the stomp of his hooves. One-inch diameter snowflakes floated down from the gray Lochsa sky. They settled softly on the buck and the coyote and the barrel of my rifle.

I squeezed the trigger. At the carbine's crack the coyote dropped without a sound. But the buck stood statuelike, not believing that his ancient enemy would abandon the chase so suddenly. I snowshoed to within fifty feet of the deer before he quit staring at the fallen coyote, gave me one startled glance, and bounded off down the river. That buck had a new lease on life, and I had a ten-dollar pelt for the fur cache. In a way, I felt like a savior. But only three days later I was to learn that the threat of death in the wilderness applied to me as well.

I emerged molelike that morning from the snowed-under line cabin at Indian Post Office to discover thirty-six inches of new frosting on top of the several feet of snow already on the ground. The new-fallen snow was so loose that I sank above my knees, snowshoes and all. Faced with such traveling, wiser mountain men would have spent the day sheltered in their cabins. But I was young—just turned nineteen—trail-tested, and tough. Eager to reap a still-larger harvest of furs, I shouldered my pack filled with traps and bait and mushed from the high divide to follow the trapline toward the canyon below. As I snowshoed along, the snow settled around me with hollow-sounding "whumps," and occasionally a gob of it slid in a whispering avalanche from the limbs of the burdened trees.

The forest ended about one mile below the ridge top. To continue, I was forced to venture into a narrow canyon upon whose steep, treeless slopes hung tons of loose snow. Sensing danger, I mushed warily into the edge of that great white amphitheater. If I could steal across the half-mile-long expanse without starting a snowslide, I'd be into the safety of the forest beyond. I mushed steadily, cautiously. Ten yards, twenty yards—the canyon slopes menaced like impending storm clouds. My stomach muscles tightened. Suddenly, fifty yards beyond the timber, I triggered a small slide. I was buried waist deep, my snowshoes pinned down. With its foundation cracked by the small avalanche, the whole mountainside began to move. Hopelessly trapped, I watched rivers of snow sweep down upon me from the slopes above. I felt no fear, just resignation, as if I had played my hand and found that the spirits of the Lochsa held all the aces.

As the slide swept over me I covered my face with my arms so that I wouldn't smother in the snow. I remember thinking that no one would ever find me in that isolated place. When the slide stopped, I was buried alive. The weight of the snow was tremendous. Engulfed in darkness but unwilling to surrender life, I thrust both arms upward to make more breathing space. When my mittened hands broke through the slide's surface, I looked up at the most beautiful sky in the world.

My arms free, I dug at the snow packed around me. It took at least an hour to dig down and release my feet from the imprisoned snowshoes. As I crawled out onto the slide, I felt a kinship with the whitetail buck whose life I had spared just three days before. Until the avalanche struck, I had brooked no thoughts that I, like the starving wildlife, might never see the coming spring.

Now I knew better. When it came to preserving life and avoiding death, I held little advantage over my companion creatures in the Lochsa's mountains. I sensed that the buck would outlast the long winter. And having survived the avalanche, I felt sure that I was going to make it, too.

The high country furbearers moved little during the big snows. So sometime in February I sprung all my traps along the big divide, leaving them hanging there on the trees to be reset when I returned to the high line next fall. Trouble was, some of them hung fifteen feet above ground, and I wondered how I'd get them down again after the snow melted. But that is another story.

I kept trapping until late February along the river. The snow had settled enough on the river's ice to make snowshoeing easy compared to dragging the ball and chain through the slow-settling snows of the high line. With the weather warm during daytime and cold at night, the snow packed so hard I could sometimes walk on the crust without snowshoes. In due time the river, long imprisoned beneath the ice, broke free at its rapids, and once again its song began to fill the valley.

One morning at Wendover Bar I heard a woodpecker drum on a snag in the forest. It seemed to me he had picked a day when his territorial challenge would carry especially far and wide. At the hole where I dipped my bucket for water, an ouzel teetered, stuck out his chest, and sang with the abandon of a choirboy on Sunday. Coyotes howled all night long on the ridges behind the cabin. The land was awakening. It was time to bale up my furs and strike out for Lolo Hot Springs, my gateway from the wilderness to the civilized world outside.

But I tarried another day to mingle with the wild creatures, the forest, and the river. I thought of my friends outside in the valleys. "Daniel," some of them called me—the Daniel Boone of the Lochsa, a kind of strange kid who would rather live in the wilderness than enjoy the pleasures of civilized life. As the woodpecker heralded spring, I yearned to see those friends again, but I felt inadequate for the ways of the cities and towns.

There in the shadow of men of the Lochsa's past, I was at home trapping furs, fighting storms, and resting in cabins to regain the energy needed to go out and tackle the storms again. I knew the limits of my strength and how to pace snowshoe travel through the blue snow. But I couldn't do a waltz step, and a square dance scared me far more than crossing thin ice on the river. I could kill game as quick and sure as a cougar, but I could generate no enthusiasm to join in the brawls of the bars and the dancehalls. Although I could drink mountain water a quart at a time, a second beer stuck in my throat halfway down. Pretty girls sure looked good to me, but none of them wanted anything to do with a kid hooked on the call of the wilds.

I belonged to those mountains. And that winter of the blue snow was the beginning of my education in the ecology and spirituality of humankind and earth. My youth had not included the experience needed to prepare me for urban life in America. But the lessons of that great land of the Lochsa were yielding a store of knowledge that I couldn't get anywhere else.

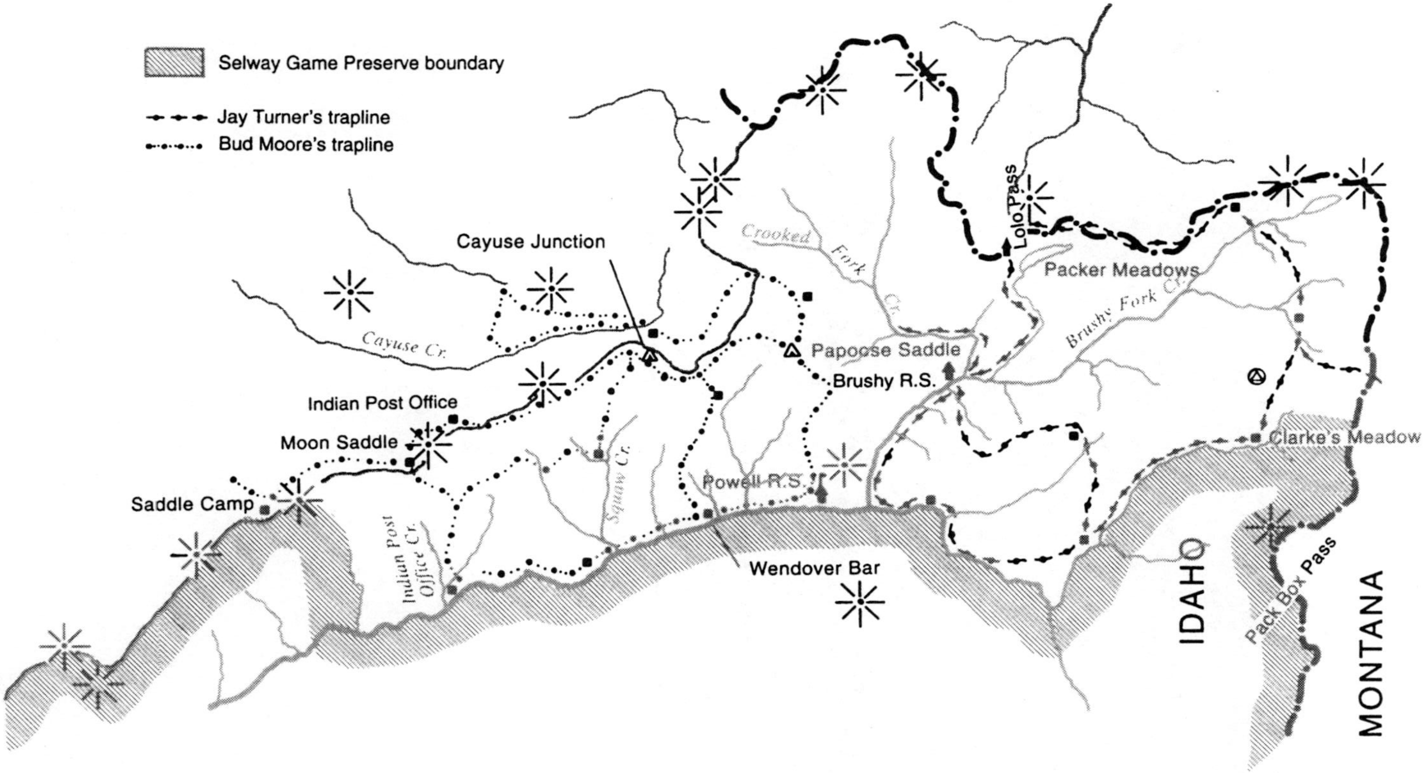

Map 11. *Bud Moore and JayTurner traplines, 1935-1940.*

This grizzly, typical of the silvertips common to the Bitterroot, stands alert to his surroundings. —Chuck Bartlebaugh

17

The Last of the Bitterroot's Grizzlies

M*y enrollment in the Lochsa's university of self-discovery* was not too unlike the practice of the Nez Perce, who, as we saw in chapter 2, sent their young to contemplate alone in the solitude of the mountains in search of a personal "Wyakin." The youth of the Nez Perce found a source of great strength in the spirit of the grizzly bear.[210] Among the animals of the Clearwater country, the grizzly knew no master. Although a male might grow to upwards of one thousand pounds in weight, he was retiring in nature and rarely picked a fight. On the other hand, he never lost one either, except to a larger grizzly bear. He claimed territory by mere presence alone; everything else got out of the way whenever a big grizzly passed through the mountains.

The grizzlies of the Bitterroots were magnificent animals whose seasonal habits varied little from year to year. Each fall found the bears preparing their dens in the high country. Cubs denned with their mothers the first winter following birth; after that they either denned alone or, during their second winter, with one or more grizzlies of their age. Old males always denned by themselves. The grizzlies dug out of their dens in late March or early April. Adult females were often followed by two to four cubs, each about the size of a large house cat.

Hungry following hibernation, the grizzlies grazed early-spring vegetation available on south-facing slopes, and then headed down the west slopes of the Bitterroot mountains to the valleys where salmon or steelhead would be spawning in the upper tributaries of several forks of the Clearwater. Steelhead, known locally in early times as red salmon, reached the headwaters in late April or early May and finished spawning by mid-June. Since the streams flowed bank-full at that time of year, the bears had to work hard. But their fishing paid off because each fish weighed from eight to twenty pounds.

After catching red salmon for a month or so, the bears turned to hunting ants, grubs, and insect larvae on the ridges and mountainsides. They ate several species of tuberous plants as well. The bears lived near the berry patches from early July, when huckleberries began to ripen, until sometime in August, when big fish again splashed in the creeks. Those latecomers were chinooks, also known as dog salmon. Upon leaving the Pacific Ocean and heading back to the Clearwater country, they weighed up to fifty pounds. They were easy prey for bears in the low, clear water of late summer. A grizzly that spotted a chinook in a riffle simply rushed in and seized the fish in its jaws or, with the sweep of a forepaw, scooped the fish out onto the bank. Favored fishing spots might be frequented by several bears at once. As a result, the bears wore trails in the earth by traveling back and forth between their streamside picnicking spots and resting places in the nearby forests. When the fish run was over, the bears went back to the hills for more grubs, ants, and frost-sweetened berries. By mid-October the grizzlies had returned to the high alpine country, where they dug for ground squirrels and marmots until winter storms forced them to hole up again in their dens. That's how a typical grizzly spent each year in the Bitterroot Range before their habitat and their numbers were changed by modern Americans.

It was, of course, inevitable that early settlers and grizzlies would clash in populated areas on the periphery of the Bitterroots. As related in chapter 5, trapper Lawrence, the first known Euro-American resident of the Lolo Fork, was killed by a big grizzly in 1852. Later on, according to trapper–fur buyer Lawrence Humble, homesteaders in the upper Bitterroot Valley had plenty of problems with grizzlies, too. "You see, in those days there was lots of grizzlies. Old Johnnie Richie caught nine in two weeks in the West Fork for my Uncle Fay Humble. That was in the 1870s. One weighed 950 pounds. One hide covered the whole cabin wall."[211]

To secure safe space for their farming and ranching operations, those pioneers waged an aggressive war of extermination against the grizzlies. Nonetheless, the little-explored interior retained the habitat and isolation needed by the bears. But many settlers had their eyes on the resources of that land, as well. The trappers came first. From the time Lawrence was killed by the grizzly, they combed the mountains, killing grizzlies for their pelts soon after the bears left their dens in the spring. The following account of spring bear trapping by Wes Fales is typical.

During early March 1908 Wes lugged his winter's catch of marten, lynx, mink, and ermines from his home cabin at Big Sand Lake over Blodgett Pass and out of the mountains to Hamilton, Montana. He sold his furs and in late April returned to Big Sand Lake, where he began setting traps for bears. Each trap, a No. 5 Newhouse, weighed seventeen pounds. In six days he placed ten sets at promising locations in the surrounding mountains.

Wes caught both black bears and grizzlies in the Big Sand Lake Basin. He described the difference between the two species as follows:

> According to the best authorities there are but two species of bears in the United States, the grizzly and the black, but there are great variations in size and color in both species in different locations. In the black species I have seen all shades of color, from a deep glossy black, to a buckskin. A black she-bear will sometimes have a black and brown cub at the same time. A grizzly will vary from a black to a brown under coat, that is, aside from the long white hairs which give it the name of "silvertip." The silver hairs are sometimes so thick that the bear will seem almost white in some lights. In other specimens they are so few and scattered that the bear will seem almost of a solid color.[212]

Some days Wes caught one bear, some days none, and three times he caught two bears in the same day. He skinned the bears where he caught them, packed the heavy hides to his home cabin at the lake, and then laced them with thongs to a pole frame made slightly larger than the taut bear skin. He skinned the feet out to the last toe joint and then severed the joint so as to leave the claws attached to the hide. He rubbed salt into the feet to aid the curing and sprinkled red pepper on the nose and ears to keep away blowflies. It took him a half day to stretch and flesh a bear skin of average size. Hides of the big grizzlies took longer.

During late May, on the last round of his trapline, Wes caught a large female grizzly in one of his traps below the Hidden Fork of Big Sand Creek. He wanted a photograph. While he waited for good light a cub jumped up on a log, followed by another and another. Then all three ran along the log to their mother, who fought for freedom from the trap. He photographed the trapped mother and her cubs. As he leveled his rifle, the cubs, born in the den during the winter just ended, stood erect, straight as picket pins in a mountain meadow. The old bear dropped at the crack of the rifle, and Wes jumped over her body and grabbed one of the cubs. The cub bit, squalled, tore Wes's shirt, and chomped his thumb. It took

Bert Wendover (left) and Dad McCann (right) display at Lolo Hot Springs some of Bert's bear and lynx pelts taken from the Lochsa in about 1915. —Louise Gerber Gilbert

ten minutes of wrestling to get him tied up. Meanwhile, the remaining two cubs escaped into the forests of the valley of the Big Sand.

By the time Wes had finished skinning the sow grizzly it was late afternoon. Then he had to carry the hide and live cub, together a ninety-pound load, across twelve miles of rough country to reach the cabin at Big Sand Lake. Here's how Wes described his hike through the night:

> It was dark when I reached the timber and the cub on my back began to holler with nearly every breath. He would give a long drawn out o-o-o-wah, o-o-o-wah, accent on the last note, till I thought he would call every bear in the country. As I had been obliged to leave my rifle and camera at the set, I didn't feel any too safe. It was after ten o'clock when I reached the cabin and I was all in.[213]

After stretching the grizzly hide and resting a day, Wes tucked the cub into a wooden coal oil case and carried him over the pass to his cabin on Blodgett Creek. One trap in that basin held a black bear and another a big grizzly, which had dragged the toggle so far that it took three days to find him. Wes also wounded another grizzly in the timber below Blodgett Pass. While Wes was trailing the blood on the snow, the bear charged him. Wes killed it with one shot at a range of twenty feet. All that action, plus three bear skins to flesh and cure, kept Wes and the cub in the heart of the best grizzly country in the Bitterroot mountains for seven more days. Finally, he hiked out to Hamilton. He intended to return after the snow melted with horses to pack out the hides, which would then be shipped to market somewhere in the East.

Wes described killing five black bears and four grizzlies during that spring of 1908. But he implied that he killed several more. And he was but one of six to ten trappers who took to the Bitterroot mountains each spring after bears. The trappers struck when the bears, especially new cubs and their mothers, were under stress to survive in their environment. A conservative estimate is that trappers operating around the turn of the century probably killed twenty-five to forty grizzlies in the Bitterroots each year.

Though they held forth in the most inaccessible places, the grizzlies had little respite from pursuit by man. To kill a grizzly was the trophy hunter's ultimate achievement; thus, soon after the trappers left in the spring, the hunters took over the chase. William Wright, one of the best known of the early-day hunters and guides, himself killed more than one hundred grizzlies, many of them in the Bitterroot mountains.

In his book *The Grizzly Bear*, Wright says that the grizzlies of the Bitterroots were most vulnerable to hunters when fishing at their favored spots for dog salmon. He said of the typical hunter's reaction to killing bears in the creeks: "It is true that in the fishing season his pelt is valueless, as at that time of year he has no fur and but very little hair, but the man who has come out to get a grizzly is apt to look upon this circumstance as, indeed, a misfortune, but one to be taken philosophically."[214]

Wright once watched four grizzlies catch fifteen or twenty salmon in a riffle. After one bear got his fill of fish and disappeared into the brush, Wright decided to kill the remaining three. He carried a .45-100 single-shot Winchester rifle, and by holding two spare cartridges between the fingers of his right hand, he could fire three sure shots in twelve seconds. While two of the bears fished from a log, the third stood on Wright's side of the stream. He shot the first bear square through the shoulders, and it fell from the log into the pool. Before the second fisher on the log knew what was happening, Wright had nailed him, too. But the third ran away, leaving Wright with only two out of three.

Though he made many multiple kills of grizzlies, including five at one shooting, these were the first that Wright had shot during fishing time. Upon close examination he found the hides not worth taking off: "It had been a useless slaughter and I was sorry that I had killed. I took the large teeth and long claws of the dead bears, but since then I have never, but once, shot a grizzly when it was fishing."[215]

Construction in 1927 of the Inland Power and Light Company dam at Lewiston, Idaho, restricted salmon and steelhead swimming upstream to spawn in tributaries of the Clearwater River. —Nez Perce County Historical Society

Another quote from Wright's book describes how the hunters went after the grizzlies: "Late in the fall of 1891 I took Dr. C. S. Penfield and James H. Adams of Spokane into the Bitterroot region after big game. I had just returned from a bear hunt in which our party had killed thirteen grizzlies, and as neither of these gentlemen had at that time killed a bear, this made them particularly anxious to get some."[216]

Bear losses due to trapping and hunting were compounded by the grazing of thousands of sheep after the forests were opened up by the big fires of 1910. Homesteaders from the Selway, the Middle Fork of the Clearwater, and the Bitterroot Valley grazed cattle on mountain meadows in grizzly country, too. These stockmen feared bears, especially the grizzlies, and killed every one they saw near their bands.

Creation in about 1919 of the Selway Game Preserve on the west slope of the Bitterroots didn't help the bears much. The closure kept out most of the hunters, but to protect legal game the State of Idaho allowed the killing of predatory varmints, including all kinds of bears. Thus, although better off than before, bears in the preserve were still not safe from pursuit and killing by people.

In the early part of the twentieth century, then, the Bitterroot's grizzlies, though greatly pressed by mankind, were surviving as a species. But the course of outside industrialization would soon demonstrate that everything in those mountains, even grizzlies, depended in some way or other on everything else.

In 1927, to generate electricity and create a pond to boom logs for the Potlatch Mill, the Inland Power and Light Company constructed a dam across the Clearwater River at Lewiston, Idaho. Fish ladders were included in the design but were ineffective at some water levels. As a consequence, the thirty-five-foot-high obstruction reduced the run of red salmon and eliminated the dog salmon from the entire drainage of the Clearwater River. Visualize the few remaining grizzlies coming down from their dens to find no fish in the creeks. Those bears had to have food, and they had always had salmon. The dam had done more than transform East Lewiston "from a residential area of vegetable gardens and orchards into the valley's most important industrial center."[217] It had struck a fatal blow to the Lochsa's once-abundant grizzlies, a population long under siege and reduced to a remnant, but which had thus far managed to survive the onslaught of homesteaders, trappers, trophy hunters, and ranchers.

The hungry grizzlies left the empty creeks, wandered afar in search of food, and confronted people in places where bears hadn't been seen for years. In contrast to their domination of the natural world, the grizzlies usually lost in those encounters. For example, in 1929 a big bear showed up near the place where trapper Lawrence met his fate in 1852. Rancher Ted Williams, who had lived on the Lolo Fork since 1898, had never before seen a grizzly in the valley. In his words: "One day I heard some growlin' up there by the sheep and there was this big bear. He had a 200-pound ewe and was draggin' her off by the neck. When he drug her through the fence I shot. That son-of-a-gun growled there for an hour."[218]

Besides killing livestock, after the obliteration of their fish source, the bears sometimes broke into Forest Service cabins and camps. For example, in the fall of 1932 Heinie Williams loaded his pack train at Elk Summit one morning and headed east along the trail to deliver supplies to the cabin at Big Sand Lake. Six inches of fresh snow covered the ground, and with each step the hooves of the horses and mules flung globs of mud and snow into the brush beside the trail. At the

Diablo Mountain junction, about half a mile out, Heinie saw tracks where a big bear had entered the trail from the south. The grizzly never left the trail for the next eight miles. When Heinie arrived at Big Sand the bear had already moved on, but it had left the cabin's interior in shambles. Telling the story later, Heinie said: "He walked up on that porch and hit that door one lick and that door was a settin' right up agin the back end of the cabin. That was one helluva bear."[219] It was hard to catch the grizzlies in the act, but the government took its toll of these cabin-busting bears.

Nor did the bears' reproductive capacity favor their survival. Beginning at about age six, a healthy female would give birth to two to four cubs every other year. That may sound like a heap of offsprings. But the Bitterroot grizzlies, among the largest omnivores in North America, weighed only about eighteen ounces when born in the den at midwinter, and when the cubs emerged from the den in spring they weighed only ten to fifteen pounds. Those little bears were subjected to many hazards before reaching maturity at six to seven years. A good population of adult bears was needed if the birth rate was to match the decline from natural tragedies, not to mention the killings inflicted by humans.

Their numbers dwindled. Making matters worse, in 1931 the Western Montana Livestock Association trailed sheep from the Bitterroot Valley to graze the Elk Meadows and other nearby grasslands. The boss, Louis Undem, gave me a job at $15 per month, and thus I became part of the first invasion by the sheep industry into the place where I had met the big grizzly one year before. The herder and camp tender quit in late August, leaving me alone with the mountains, the bears, and some two thousand sheep. I was thirteen years old at the time. When Dad learned about my situation, he hiked into Elk Meadows to spend a few days with me. This turned out to be the only time we worked together at length in the wilds of the Bitterroot mountains.

One day while moving the band, night fell before we reached the new grazing site and the sheep bedded down in dense blown-down trees and brush. We could not camp as close to the band as usual. And that night a big bear raided the band and killed thirty sheep. After eating the hearts and livers of several, he vanished into the forest. Next morning we gathered the scattered band together. While the dogs and I guarded the sheep, Dad saddled two horses, rode out of the mountains, and brought in a bear trap from our homestead on the Lolo Fork.

Dad set the trap. One or the other or both of us checked the set each day for five days with no sign of the bear. On the sixth day, while the sheep were bedded at midday, we hiked to the set. There we found the woods in a shambles.

"We got him," Dad said, his rifle at ready. I opened the breech of my .30-30 Winchester to be sure it was loaded, then turned full attention to spotting the bear. Sheep carcasses had been flung in all directions, a thicket of lodgepole pines was flattened, and tree roots had been ripped from the ground and bitten in two.

Excitement swelled in the pit of my stomach. The dogs—we had three good sheep dogs—wanted to go, but Dad held them back. We circled the trap site but lost the bear's trail at the edge of a long meadow.

"Where is he?" I asked.

"Damned if I know," Dad said, listening to the sounds of the forest.

"Get him," he said to the dogs. They ran down the meadow, the black collie-cross in the lead, with the two smaller curs doing their best to keep up, barking and bawling as they went. We followed the dogs.

Suddenly, we heard the grizzly roaring. He had tangled the toggle in a pile of boulders flanked by big spruce trees. Caught by one front paw, he stood half upright, holding the trap, chain, and toggle off the ground with one foreleg while he swung at the dogs with the other. He was black, and, like the bear I had met on the game trail, long, gray hairs peppered his shoulders, front legs, and neck. Whenever the dogs backed off he dropped to all fours, but he never stopped growling or snapping his teeth, and his head kept swinging from side to side.

Dad's voice cut through the yapping and growling. "Do you want to shoot him?"

To kill him quick I'd have to shoot for the head that never held still. My insides shook, and my arms quivered. Trailing and finding the grizzly had shaken my composure. At that moment there on the Brushy Fork I was not ready to clash with this sheep-killing bear.

In a way I had failed, but at least I was honest. I looked at the bear and then turned to Dad and said, "No. You go ahead." I thought I saw a gleam of understanding in his eyes.

His arms weren't shaking. The bear collapsed at the crack of his rifle, and the dogs closed in to tug at his fur. I shot him once behind his ear to be sure he was dead. His massive size confirmed the legends of Bitterroot bears. Dad said, "He must weigh at least a thousand pounds."

Both black and grizzly bears followed the bleating and smells to sheep grazing at Packer Meadows in 1932.

That grizzly was the only bear killed at our band during the summer of 1931. But sheep kept coming into those mountains. After the 1932 grazing season, I found nine bear scalps nailed on a tree at Packer Meadows; some of those scalps had been lifted from grizzlies. From the late twenties to the mid-thirties the blatting of sheep lured many grizzlies to their doom at the hands of the herders. So far as I know, we never lost a herder to the grizzlies of the Bitterroots, but in the wake of each band's passing lay the ruins of the finest of bears.

Judging from the reports, the grizzlies made their last stand around the northern end of the main ridge of the range, that is, from the headwaters of the most northern forks of the Selway River across the upper basins of the Lochsa River and in the heads of the creeks flowing eastward from the crest of the range into the Bitterroot Valley.

Except where the bears gathered near bands of sheep, human-grizzly confrontations, even observations, were uncommon during the late years of the bear's decline. Taken together, however, those isolated incidents explain in part what happened to the last of the Bitterroot grizzlies. Ranger Bill Bell killed a big male at Elk Summit in early fall, about 1924. In the fall of 1925, while hiking up Blodgett Canyon to a forest fire, ranger Charley Powell met a grizzly in the trail in the

This grizzly was killed at Wallow Mountain, North Fork of the Clearwater drainage, during the mid-1920s. —Les Van Airsdale collection, U.S. Forest Service

This freshly skinned hide shows the characteristic long claws of the large male grizzly.

A grizzly bear treed wilderness activist Bob Marshall near Grave Peak in 1930.

moonlight—"all silver and eight feet high." Joe Alkire trapped a grizzly at Big Sand Lake in 1929, and the bear swam across the lake towing the trap and toggle. Sometime in the early thirties, trapper Stearns Reed saw fresh tracks fifteen inches long in springtime snow at Clark's Pass on the Bitterroot crest. That same year Ed Blake met one "big as a roan horse" in the trail at Big Creek Lake. Trapper Bob Boyd saw several grizzlies in East Moose Creek and adjacent forks of the Selway River during the early thirties. Wilderness crusader Bob Marshall was treed by a grizzly with cubs in the Grave Mountains in 1930. Lawrence Humble, trapper and fur buyer from Hamilton, Montana, saw his last grizzly track in Big Creek Canyon in 1939. In 1934 a big grizzly came down the valley of the White Sand to near Powell Ranger Station, possibly to look at the government headquarters of the varmints who were killing him out of his last domain.[220]

The Forest Service in 1929 was responsible for creating a legend that outlived the last of the bears. A trap set by Homer McClain, whom we met in chapter 1, caught a grizzly that had been tearing up the fire lookout cabin at Beaver Ridge on the western slope of the Bitterroots. By skillful tracking, veteran woodsman Heinie Williams followed the trapped bear's trail deep into the head of Shoot Creek, where the bear had tangled the toggle and wrung off his foot. The grizzly was gone, but his front foot "filled the whole bear trap." So began the legend of

"Peg Leg," a big, seldom-seen bear whose three-footed tracks would stir the imagination of men and women of the Bitterroots for years to come.[221]

Uncertainty clouds the demise of Peg Leg. According to mountain man Frank Bustard, the old bear chased trapper George Johnson into his cabin at Big Creek Lake, and Johnson shot him on the doorstep. Johnson did kill a big grizzly in the Big Creek area, but that was too long ago to have been Peg Leg. Trapper Earl Smith says that Peg Leg was never killed but died of old age somewhere in the mountains. Jack Clarke says that his brother, Chink, found Peg Leg's den in Spruce Creek in the fall of 1932. While hunting in the area one day, Peg Leg rose up out of the brush and Chink shot him. Jack said: "Peg Leg was an old bear. Real white."[222]

While we may be unsure of the circumstances surrounding his death, there remains little doubt that Peg Leg was among the last of his kind to dig for ground squirrels or den near the crest of the Bitterroot Range. Jack Parsell, U.S. forest ranger on the Selway in the twenties and again in the forties, sums up the fate of the bears: "In the 1920s there was grizzlies up in East Moose, over in the Paradise branch of Bear Creek. And Spruce Creek too. On my last hitch in there, '45 to '55, I saw no grizzly sign."[223]

In his book, William Wright sounded an early warning that the bears were threatened: "This is an animal much talked about but little studied.

Here at Beaver Ridge Lookout, Forest Service personnel in 1929 trapped a large male grizzly that sacrificed his foot and escaped to create the legend of old "Peg Leg."

It is now well on its way toward extinction."[224] That was back in 1906, yet when I met the bear on the Brushy Fork in 1930, I hadn't heard that the grizzlies were on the way out. The last track I saw was along the Spruce Creek Fork of the Brushy in 1946. There was no life in its wake. The mud had dried around the imprint of the big paw and its long claws in what seemed to me an attempt by nature to preserve some sign of the last of the great bear's passing. That year the Idaho Fish and Game Department, for the first time, closed the season for hunting grizzlies. But it was already too late.

By the mid-1940s, that most noble animal had disappeared. I sensed, from experience and from my own killing, that everything in those mountains was, indeed, linked to everything else. All life in the land of the Lochsa would thus shift in some way or other in reaction to the bears' passing. One could but wonder how the "Wyakin" could continue to give strength with the grizzlies gone from the mountains. The Bitterroots had become a lesser place than they were when the grizzlies flourished. Those silvertips, you see, were a special part of the mountain's wildness. And, so far as I was concerned, no conceivable change short of their return could replace the emptiness left behind by last of the great bears.

Exploring grizzly habitat near the crest of the Bitterroots.

18

Prelude to Management

M***ajor Kelley wasn't talking about restoring*** the Bitterroot's grizzlies when, after the Lochsa-Selway fires of 1934, he announced that the ordinary work we could do right away but the impossible was going to take a little while longer. He spoke instead of protecting from forest fires the great expanse of unburned timber situated in the upper reaches of the Lochsa River and several of its major tributaries on the Lochsa Ranger District. Beginning with Lieberg's survey in 1897, the commercial potential of those forests had been scouted, and the volume of available sawtimber estimated and reestimated, several times by 1934. Trees are like farm crops, the foresters said. If not harvested in due time, they'll die and be wasted. Even with part of the land declared wilderness, several million board feet of sawlogs could be cut each year. The principal improvements needed to reap this harvest were better fire protection, more motorized access, improved communications, and additional professional personnel.

The Forest Service (of which I was a part) considered the administration of those protection and development activities to be custodial work. That is to say, we were protecting the resources so that they would be available for management and use at some future time. Thus, the Forest Service viewed remote geographical units, like the Powell and Lochsa, as custodial ranger districts; more accessible units, primarily those with timber cutting and logging underway, were considered managerial ranger districts, requiring a higher degree of professional supervision. Although the mid-thirties were custodial times for the Lochsa's rangers, the men were preparing for a future of management that included using people and bulldozers to get the needed work done.

Looking back later on his tenure in the Lochsa, ranger Ed Mackay said: "That Powell crew was the pride of my life." And well they should have been. Ed Miller, a two-fisted high-climber from the West Coast, had charge of Elk Summit. Frank Brot, master powder man, could set off a string of dynamite shots timed so that they sounded like a machine gun working on the Marne. Andy Kuznik and Frank Poulliot bossed the trail crews. Swede lumberjack John Bachman worked with anybody who had stamina to keep up with him. Tom Barker drove the truck, and his commitment to its engine and gears transcended all else in his life. The district's master carpenter, Evan Williams, supervised the building of all manner of structures. Roy Bates cooked for the crew. And Heinie, Homer, and Mansley Brown could, with their government pack trains, move more gear in less time than anyone else in those mountains. Dispatcher Hank Viche took care of the office, while alternate ranger Roy Daniels, the cool head, helped Ranger Mackay line us out so that we got the right jobs done first.

Ed Mackay's crew included other veteran woodsmen and a few kids who, like me, learned how to work from those masters of their trades. Known in the bunkhouse banter as "Settin' Bull," Ranger Mackay's crew was just the kind needed to achieve Major Kelley's "impossible" in the shortest possible time. Together with similar forces stationed on the Lochsa district and on neighboring districts of the Selway, we had, by the end of the thirties, built a wealth of "custodial" facilities for developing and protecting the land.

The Powell district alone boasted more than 600 miles of pack trails, 230 miles of telephone lines, and nearly 150 miles of roads. Fire lookout stations had been established on twenty-three peaks, eighteen of which included permanent living structures. Five sturdy log cabins stood at key locations in the back country. The Elk Summit Ranger Station, built by Adolph Weholt and Bill Bell, continued to serve as a work center, while the Powell Ranger Station had become the central location for government activities in the entire upper Lochsa. Charley Powell's cabin was gone, and a new, shake-sided ranger dwelling stood in its place. The station built in 1911 by Frank Smith and his crew had been converted to a cook house and dining hall. In addition, a big barn, saddle shed, and sleeping cabin for the packers stood down by the river. Forest visitors and we workers met our government in an attractive log office. Three warehouses—one for grub, one for fire tools, and one for miscellaneous storage—stood on Powell's Flat. The big bunkhouse had a bathhouse

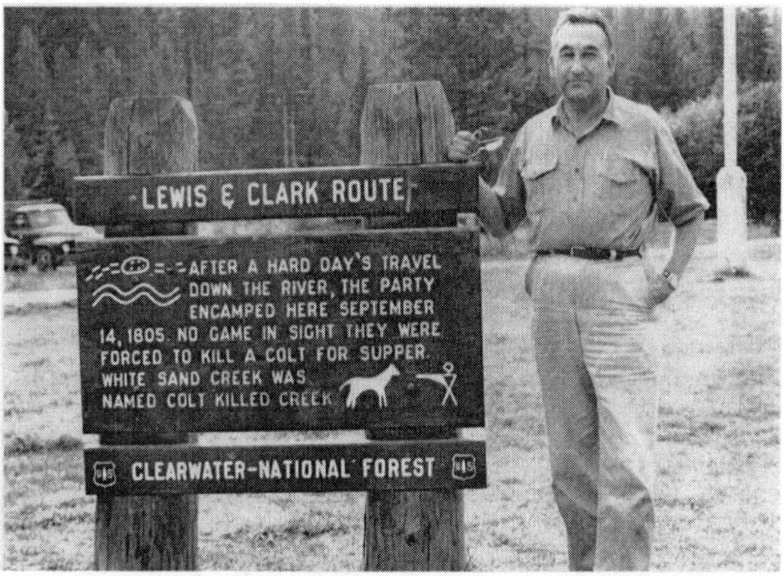

Forest officer and historian Ralph Space poses in 1960 at the sign commemorating Lewis and Clark's campsite near present-day Powell Ranger Station. —Ralph Space

nearby, which included an indoor flush toilet. The Civilian Conservation Corps had built two large frame shop and storage buildings and dug a root cellar into the foothills. In the middle of all this, an attractive sign reminded us that Lewis and Clark and their party had camped there in September 1805 and had killed and eaten a colt. Cook Bates would point to that sign whenever fresh meat became scarce at the station.

Ranger Mackay had strengthened the Forest Service's presence in the Lochsa a great deal since he rode his black horse from Lolo Hot Springs over the hill in June of 1920. Fires would have to be fought forever. But the job of the pioneer builder was over. Ed accepted a new job as supervisor of the Nine Mile Remount Station. So big Ed and his dainty wife, Laura, packed up in the fall of 1939 and left what Laura called "our big ranch at Powell." They would miss the Lochsa. The Powell district crew and the spirits of the Lochsa's mountains would miss Ed and Laura, too.

Thus it was that an old crew with a new ranger snowshoed over the hill in early April 1940 to reopen the Powell Ranger Station and begin the summer's work. In contrast to 225-pound Ed, whose stamina and competence we had learned to respect, bespectacled ranger Ray Ferguson, a man unknown to us, would spring the scales at about 150 pounds; it looked like one snort of a mean mule would flatten him against

Ed and Laura Mackay's new home at Powell Ranger Station in 1932. —K. D. Swan, U.S. Forest Service

the bars of the corral. Nonetheless, "Fergy's" warm personality made him easier to approach than Ed. It was rumored that he had resigned from a top staff job on the Flathead forest to take the Powell district; thus, we figured that there must be considerable good in his heart.

In taking charge at Powell, Fergy found what he was looking for, a place where the spell of the mountains transcended the ego of man. In his words: "My first impression of the Powell district was, it's unbelievable. The vastness of the area and its very ruggedness. The first time I got up where I could look around, I actually prayed 'may I always keep it green.'"[225]

Like rangers of the past, Ranger Fergy brought great reverence for the earth to the Lochsa. He also brought his family—four kids and his pretty, energetic wife, Edna—the likes of which few mountain men had ever seen. Before long, Edna's contagious enthusiasm, as much as Fergy's official direction, drew us together. In this way the Powell crew and the Ferguson family united in the no-nonsense mission of caring for the land of the Lochsa.

Still, a lighter side of our association prevailed at times. For example, young mischiefs, Pat and Clyde, delighted in locking the door of the fire warehouse from the outside while I worked inside. That left me no choice

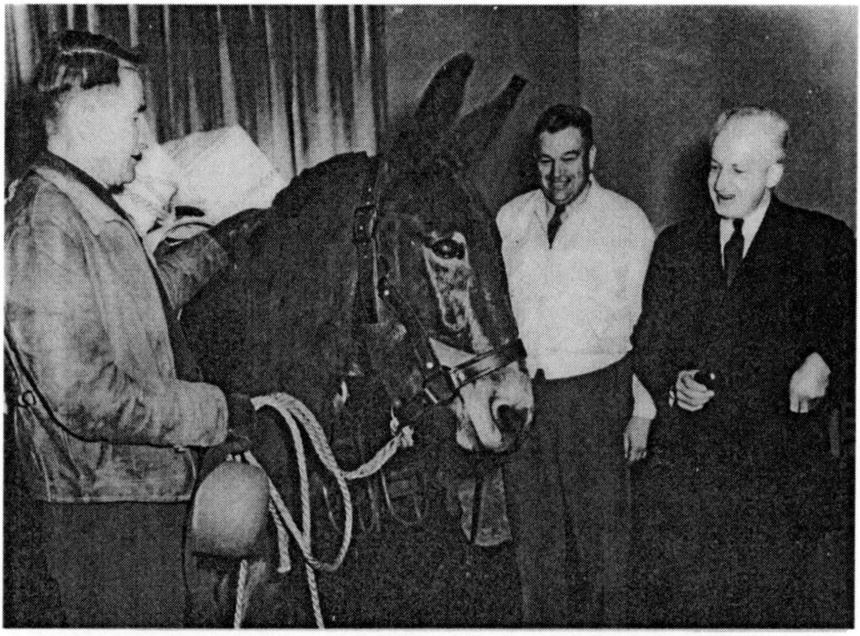

Bill Bell (left) and Ed Mackay (center) present the mule Queenie to Major Kelley (right) during his retirement party at Missoula's Florence Hotel, February 17, 1944. —U.S. Forest Service

Ray Ferguson, Middle Fork district ranger, ca. 1926; Powell district ranger, 1940–1942. —Patricia Stewart

but to crawl out the window. I loved them both just the same. On cool summer evenings, the two beautiful teenagers, Irene and Jackie, would join the boys on the bunkhouse porch. The rowdy talk of the old timers would stall, but the young men loved the girls' feminine charm and the effect it had on the lumberjack crew. I was drawn to Jackie, the older, with her dark eyes, black hair, and the same outgoing spirit of her mother, Edna. For me there was something awesome about this beautiful daughter of our ranger in charge, the same kind of beyond-reach sensation I felt in my trapping days when tempted to poach a few extra pelts from the game preserve. Jackie seemed so very young—then one day she up and married the headquarters guard.

With the coming of Fergy and his family, women were beginning to join men in shaping that land whose mountains and waters had, in many ways, long served as their feminine partners. Now the old ways were fading. Most of us were glad that, so far as human occupation was concerned, the land of the Lochsa could never be the same again.

Land ownership in the Lochsa was changing as well. Government surveyors had established the locations of the railroad grant lands during 1914, 1915, and 1916.[226] In February 1923 President Warren G. Harding approved Patent No. 132, granting approximately 131,970 acres of the Lochsa's public domain to the Northern Pacific Railway Company (formerly Northern Pacific Railroad Company).[227] The company was then and remained interested in disposing of lands that they considered unprofitable to hold. During the late 1930s and early 1940s, the Forest Service saw public advantage in trading for or purchasing private lands intermingled with public forest lands to promote more efficient management of the forest and to obtain needed public recreation and wildlife resources.

The Northern Pacific originally offered to sell to the Forest Service 68,000 acres of their land in the Lochsa, retaining the remainder, the most accessible and best timbered lands, for themselves. After a series of negotiations the Forest Service in 1945 bought 89,989.74 acres of the primary grant lands and paid for them with an equal value of timber from the Nez Perce, Clearwater, and St. Joe National Forests. That purchase returned to public ownership most of the grant lands situated within the Selway-Bitterroot Primitive Area plus considerable acreage outside as well. During later negotiations with the company, the Forest Service obtained title to 160 acres at Powell's Flat, the site of the Powell Ranger Station.[228]

Johnson Flying Service's Ford Tri-Motor positions to drop supplies to firefighters in the Storm Creek drainage, Powell Ranger District.

Meanwhile, the threat from forest fires remained the rangers' greatest concern. Even with prompt discovery, it took smoke chasers so long to hike into remote places that fires sometimes developed into major conflagrations before attack forces could reach the scene. New methods and strategies were needed to attack fires faster. By the mid-1930s supplies had been successfully dropped to fires by air. Ranger Mackay and I received the Powell district's first air drop to a fire at Clarke's Meadow on May 31, 1936. With that delivery of fire rations, tools, and sleeping bags, we became part of a pioneering partnership between the Forest Service and Johnson Flying Service to speed delivery of equipment and supplies. But we still needed to shorten the time required for smoke chasers to hike through the mountains and attack the fires.

An astounding innovation in fire control debuted on July 12, 1940, when a Johnson Flying Service Travelair airplane circled above a fire in the Martin Creek drainage a few miles to the south of the Lochsa country. Like all fires at first, this fire was small, crackling in the dry forest, ready for time and fuels and weather to send its flames into the tree crowns and off across the mountains. Of fuels and weather the rangers had no control, but at Martin Creek they were in command of the time factor. Instead of dispatching smoke chasers on foot from the nearest station several miles away, they loaded two smoke jumpers, Rufus Robinson and Earl Cooley, into an airplane at Moose Creek Ranger Station. In a very few minutes they were looking down at the Martin Creek fire.[229]

Robinson jumped first, followed by Cooley. Spotter Merle Lundrigan and pilot Dick Johnson watched the chutes string out and then blossom

Rufus Robinson, left and Earl Cooley, right, the first smoke jumpers to attack a wildfire from the air, pose with parachute technician, Frank Derry, center.
—Earl Cooley

over the mountains. Drifting down into the timber, pioneers Robinson and Cooley became the first men ever to attack a forest fire from the air,[230] far surpassing the grandest expectations of the slogan printed on the ration sack: "Minutes count—let's go."

That year, 1940, seven smoke jumpers stationed at Moose Creek attacked nine fires in the Bitterroot mountains from the air. In 1941 the smoke jumpers increased their numbers to twenty-six and moved their base from Moose Creek to Missoula, Montana, a more central location for attacking fires anywhere in the northern Rockies. As their numbers grew, so did the Lochsa rangers' dependence upon them. With each jumper added, however, some ranger gave up one or two positions from his district in order to pay for the smoke jumper's salary and operation of their base.

Although smoke jumping was easily the most significant innovation in fire control since Ed Mackay led the retreat of the Lochsa, we at Powell soon learned it wasn't the whole answer, either. When fire-starting lightning clouds hammered across the mountains from the west, the smoke jumpers were often already fighting fires elsewhere by the time the storms reached the Powell district. Furthermore, lightning would sometimes ignite fires so late in the day that jumpers could not be dropped safely before dark. So smoke jumpers were dispatched to fires when

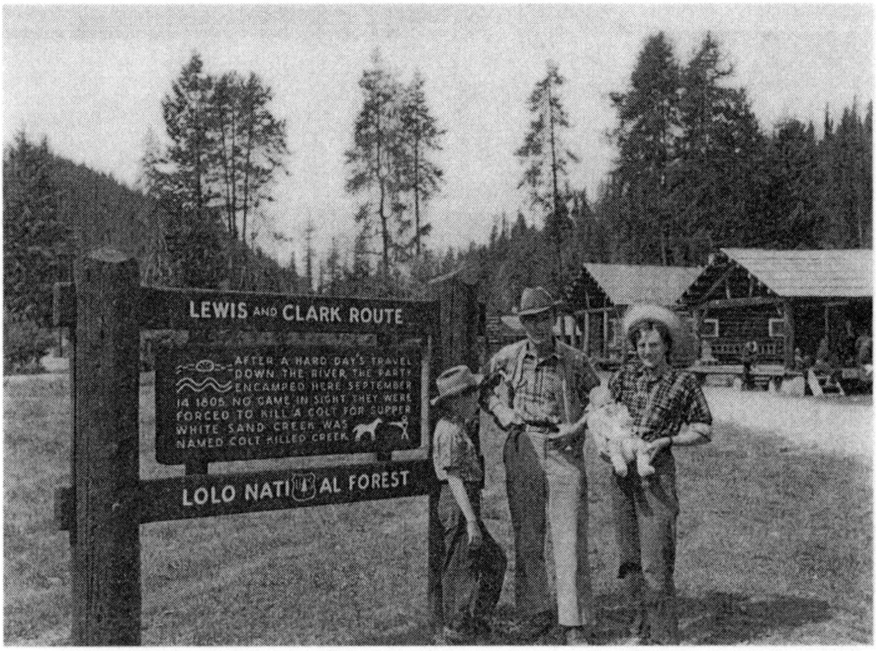

Ranger Bud Moore, his first wife, Jane Moore, son Bill, and daughter Vicki at Powell Ranger Station in 1953. —Ray Acheson

appropriate, but we never grew fully dependent upon them. Day or night, no matter how remote the fire, if the rangers were in doubt about jumper delivery, Powell district smoke chasers would hike through the mountains, alone or in groups as the situation demanded, to battle the blaze.

World War II scrambled the futures of many people who lived or worked in the Lochsa. By that time I had married Jane Buckhouse, a homesteader's daughter from the Bitterroot Valley, and our first-born was coming when I left Missoula for duty with the United States Marines. With the young and able at war, the work of the Forest Service was done, and done well, by old-timers, fifteen- to seventeen-year-old youths, and a few women whose presence on the government payroll was something new in the upper reaches of the Lochsa. By superb fire fighting, they kept the Lochsa's waters running clear in green forests. Coming home became most important to those of us hooked on the Lochsa. When I returned from the foxholes, Fergy was gone. An old friend, Hank Viche, was running the Powell district with unmatched efficiency in the tradition of the mountain man most admired by him, our former ranger Ed Mackay.

Clarine Moore manned Jay Point Lookout for several summers during World War II. —Henry J. Viche, U.S. Forest Service

There were other changes as well. Elk had been plentiful in the Lochsa country when we went to war, thriving in the excellent forage that had sprouted in the wakes of the big fires of 1929 and 1934. During the war, the best hunters in the West were enrolled in military service and therefore unavailable for shooting elk. This wartime respite from being hunted, plus favorable habitat conditions, allowed elk to increase. By the time we turned in our military rifles and machine guns, the Bitterroot mountains, including the Lochsa region, probably hosted more elk than at any other time in history. Elk trails, many worn deeper than the Road to the Buffalo, crisscrossed the mountains, and any day in springtime hundreds of elk could be seen licking minerals at Warm Springs Creek, Weir Creek, the licks near Colgate's grave, and similar places farther west and south. Big herd bulls assembled harems in early September and few, if any, subalpine basins failed to ring with the wild challenge of their bugling.

One morning, after a skiff of snow had freshened the earth, Heinie Williams and I rode saddle horses over Otters Hump and down Eagle Ridge to the river. For the entire distance—about ten miles—bulls were challenging bulls. Wet snow kept falling. Heinie led the pack train while I rode ahead, snug and dry in black leather chaps, hunched under an

Elk increased many fold during World War II, and every September the bugles of herd bulls like this one resound throughout the Lochsa's mountains.

old slicker, with the dents in my hat crown pushed out so that water would drain off and not soak through and run down the back of my neck.

Approaching a small clearing I puckered my lips and uttered a fair imitation of a love-mad elk. A bull promptly answered with a squeal followed by a grunt, leaving no doubt of his intention to fight any bull who dared compete for his harem of cows. Bursting from the brush into the clearing, the bull laid back his heavy rack, opened his mouth, let out another squeal and grunt from deep in his throat, and then headed straight for me and my bay-colored horse. Steam rose from the long black hair on his neck, which was soaked by snow and wet brush. When only forty feet separated us, my horse reared and pranced sideways, and the bull squealed again. It looked certain that we would tangle, until Heinie pulled into the clearing leading his whole string of eight mules. The bull looked us over for a minute or two, and when he realized his mistake his hostility dissipated like the snowflakes melting on the tips of his hair. The mane dropped on his neck. As he walked away, we sensed his resentment at gearing up for a fight only to discover that the enemy had no antlers. We could hear him grunting in the forest as we rode on toward the river.

Hunting was good. Working cooperatively with Idaho's chief conservation officer, Harry Palmer, we established a station at Lolo Pass to check the hunters in and out. Harry set up another station on the Lolo

It takes a lot of energy for elk to plow through the deep snow of the Lochsa in wintertim searching for food.
—Henry J. Viche, U.S. Forest Service

Trail road to contact hunters entering the mountains from the west. At least five thousand elk lived in the Lochsa drainage, and each fall hunters by the thousands came after them from all over the country. Spud farmers from southern Idaho joined miners from Wallace. Lumberjacks from the Idaho panhandle camped alongside businessmen from Spokane. Pilgrims from California and elsewhere came in search of trophy bulls, and even the Forest Service crewmen took to the woods in the fall with their rifles. All dreamed of the kind of encounter that Heinie and I had experienced on Eagle Ridge.

In 1948, 1,965 hunters checked in through the Lolo Pass station.[231] They killed 705 elk, plus a few deer, bear, and two or three illegal moose. Rumor had it that one hunter checked out a mule, neatly quartered with iron shoes still nailed to its feet. More hunters checked in through the Lolo Trail station, and they killed more elk than the entrants through Lolo Pass. In that year, in the same land where Lewis and Clark's party nearly starved to death back in 1805, the most mediocre of hunters could have supplied those explorers with ample red meat.

While the hunters harvested their bounty, rangers Viche at Powell and Hartig at Lochsa station and conservation officer Harry Palmer worried about long-term management of the elk. Were the hunters killing too many too fast? Should they close a few sanctuaries to hunting? Should more elk be taken? Perhaps most significant, could the narrow corridors of edible brush along the stream bottoms continue to carry, say, five thousand elk through winters of deep snow and subzero cold?

A study conducted under Ranger Mackay's direction in the mid-thirties had already shown that the elk population was straining the

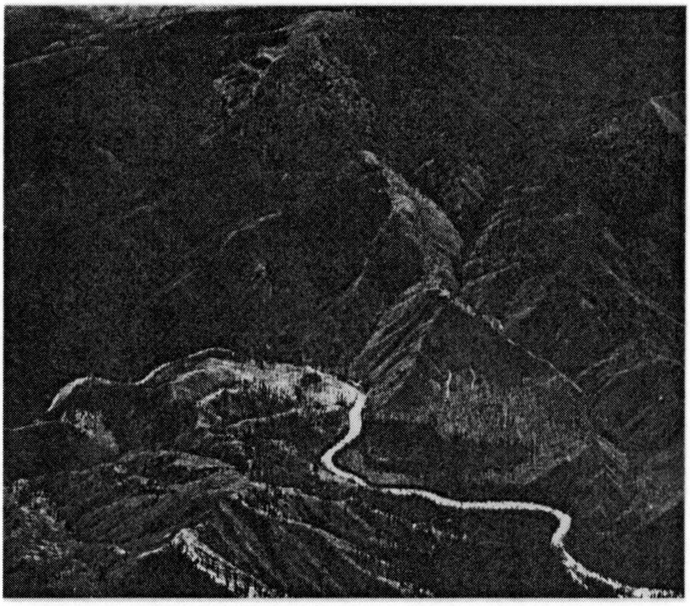

By the mid-1930s, the areas burned along the Lochsa in 1929 produced excellent forage for elk.
—Washington National Guard

capacity of the winter range available on the Powell district. Despite straight shooting by hunters, elk numbers were growing while the food available on the range declined. The edible brush, which had sprouted after the fires of 1929 and 1934, had by 1948 grown so tall that the elk couldn't reach the new growth at the twig tips, which provided the most nourishing forage.

Elk are, in government terms, a renewable resource. The elk situation demanded more than custodial treatment; it required management. The land and resource managers had to do something. Ironically, it was our perceived failures of the past—the runaway fires of 1929 and 1934—that had created thousands of acres of excellent habitat by opening the dense, mature forests and encouraging great fields of willow, maple, ceanothus, and associated shrubs to sprout and grow. Even so, by 1948—the time of our most intense fire control efforts—the elk again needed fires on their range to assure their survival in winter. Fred Johnson, then the top wildlife biologist in the Forest Service's Northern Region, wanted us to touch off a few controlled burns or, at a minimum, chop down some of the brush by hand so that new sprouts would spring from the stumps and provide succulent forage for the elk.

But our custodial mindset was too ingrained for us to accept Fred's management ideas. We decided instead to help the State of Idaho keep the elk population in tune with the varying capacity of the habitat. This left the improvement of elk range, for the time being, in the hands of

Forest Service packer Lennie Smith crosses the Lochsa River with his mule train loaded with salt for the elk.

smoke chasers who might let a fire escape, resulting in incidental forage for the animals.

Historical practice had divided the responsibility for managing wildlife between the State of Idaho, which was accountable for the animals, and the U.S. Forest Service, which was in charge of the habitat. Under the leadership of Harry Palmer and his wardens Springston and Richardson, the Lochsa's rangers drew up their plans. On the Powell district the strategy went something like this:

- encourage the state to increase to 1,000 the hunting permits in the Selway Game Preserve;
- deliver 20,000 pounds of salt, furnished by the state, annually to key locations in the high country;
- urge packers and guides to get more hunters into the back country; and
- begin intensive studies of the winter range.

In sum, the plan was to kill all the elk we could, use salt to lure the remainder from their winter range in early spring, and monitor the condition of the range to see how we were doing.

At first we packed the salt into the mountains by mule train, but we found it impossible to deliver enough salt to the high country early enough to draw the elk up from the lowlands. To hasten the springtime departure of elk from their winter ranges, in 1948 we began delivering some of the salt to the high country by airplane.

Powell ranger Casey Streed, Ted Biladeau from the Idaho Fish and Game Department, and I dropped the first salt on March 27, 1948.[232] The Ford Trimotor departed from the airport at Missoula, Montana, piloted by a man named Ellison. Air service owner and aviation pioneer Bob Johnson rode copilot and coached Ellison, who, I took it, was new to Johnson's organization. I remember Johnson telling Ellison that most pilots in trouble quit flying too soon. When the chips are down, he said, you keep flying all the way into the timber.

We built a chute to hold four fifty-pound salt blocks and hinged the chute in the opening where the cargo door had been removed from the airplane. Because I knew the habits of the Lochsa's elk, I picked the drop spots—usually on the point of a ridge, at the head of a basin, or in an opening in the forest. Ellison always circled the airplane into position for a down-terrain approach so that we could glide away from the mountain should an engine misfire. When the tin bird with the big wings crossed the target at two hundred to four hundred feet above the ground, Ellison pushed the button, the dropper hoisted the back end of the chute, and the salt plummeted into the forest below.

When he felt the salt go, Ellison would open the throttles, and all three engines roared to gain elevation. As the airplane climbed, saliva sank from our throats to the pits of our stomachs while buffeting drafts from the Lochsa's canyons bounced the aircraft around and caused us to stagger like drunks. In three trips lasting two hours each we dropped 8,000 pounds of salt. Now it was up to the Lochsa's elk to find it on the forest floor.

Flying home after dropping the last load, we had time to look around and see long shadows darkening the canyons. To the east, past the tip of the plane's right wing, the sun gleamed on the near-white granite of Ranger Peak's crest. I could see the notch where the Clarkes had crossed the mountains en route to their meadow, which lay indistinct in the shadows in the valley of Storm Creek down below. The Beaver Ridge lookout cabin slid past underneath. Then there was the saddle at the head of the Brushy Fork and the forested valley where in 1930 I had met the big grizzly bear.

At forest supervisor Eldon Myrick's request, I left Powell Ranger Station on April 2, 1948. "It's good to get off your own dung hill," Myrick

Bud Moore and packer Charles Snook Jr. (young Charles) talk business in the Lochsa at Powell Ranger Station. —W. E. Steuerwald, U.S. Forest Service

said. Change to a managerial district would enhance my career. Besides that, freed of my entrenched influence, the new ranger, Casey Streed, would have more latitude to get on with his mission of overseeing the land.

Consequently, I began work for Otto York as assistant ranger on the Missoula district. But that assignment didn't last long. On August 16 that same year, Supervisor Myrick called me at home that evening and put me in charge of the Powell district; Streed had quit. I shall be eternally grateful that this turn of events gave me the opportunity to return as ranger in charge of the land I loved best. It didn't take long to get back into the business of looking after the Lochsa's elk.

A study was needed to map the game ranges, count the elk, and examine the relation between browsing by elk and available forage. On January 11, 1949, Ranger Hartig, assistant ranger Jack Godwin, and conservation officers Cecil Sanford and Frank Keough left the road's end at Bimerick Creek and headed up the Lochsa River to begin their part of the study. On that same day Bill Evers, Hubert Hansen, Walt Hahn, conservation officer Floyd Springston, and I traveled over the hill from Lolo Hot Springs to Powell Ranger Station. Crossing Lolo

Louis Hartig, Lochsa district ranger, 1943–1967.
—U.S. Forest Service

A distant forerunner of modern snowmobiles, this machine hauled game range surveyors into the Lochsa in January 1949.

The Powell district game study crew poses at Lake Creek Cabin near the Lochsa River, January 1949. Left to right: Bill Evers, Floyd Springston, Walt Hahn, Hubert Hansen.

Pass was easy—Idaho Fish and Game Department officers Mike Throckmorton and Cecil Hansen hauled us across in one of our first successful trips by an over-snow machine.

Our plan was to snowshoe from Powell some thirty miles downriver to Lost Creek—Hartig and his crew would come upriver that far—and then examine the range systematically all the way back up to Powell station. After a day's preparation we headed out, mushing through forty-inch-deep snow on the ice of the river. Our packs were heavy. Upon arriving at my cabin on Wendover Bar we dragged the toboggan—the same one I had hauled over Lolo Pass twelve years before—from storage on the porch. We loaded our packs on the toboggan and continued down the river, snowshoeing single file and pulling it behind in our trail.

To travel safely in winter on the ice of the Lochsa takes intuition, experience, and luck. Two elk had misjudged the river at the head of one rapid; their ice-locked carcasses, half-eaten by coyotes, showed that the penalty for error could be severe. Because we reached Jerry Johnson Bar on the wrong side of the river, we too had to cross bad ice over swift currents to get to the cabin. I crossed first, tapping the ice with my snowshoe pole as I went. The taps sounded hollow, and I could hear water rushing underneath. Hubert crossed next, pulling the toboggan across safely. But when Bill followed, a chunk of ice about twelve-foot-

This Forest Service cabin at Jerry Johnson Bar served as a fire-guard station in summer and as a shelter for game range surveyors during winter.

square broke loose and left him hanging on the edge of the hole, the rumbling water yanking at his snowshoes. Hubert grabbed Bill and hauled him out, saving him from the fate of the frozen elk.

A cabin built by the Forest Service during the 1920s stood under the grand firs near the spot where Jerry Johnson's original cabin had long before rotted to earth. That's where we dried Bill out and spent the night. Since the cabin had been built for summertime use, cold air crept past its chinking, heat escaped through the cedar shakes on the roof, and wet boots froze to the floor.

Conditions were tough enough for us, but the odds of survival that year for the Lochsa's many elk and few deer were the poorest I'd seen since the winter of the blue snow. Because there are no grasses or forbs available after the first snows of winter, deer and elk in the Lochsa browse the young growth from edible trees and shrubs. But that winter early, wet snows, followed by cold temperatures, had lopped, buried, and frozen all shrubs. Then big storms had dumped more snow on top of the ice-bound forage. As a result, the elk simply couldn't get at it. Many animals seemed destined to die unless the winter grew milder. And that wasn't apt to happen in this land where the worst storms usually strike in late January, February, and early March.

Following our plan, we began at Lost Creek and worked upriver toward Powell Ranger Station. Besides counting the elk, deer, and moose,

Weak from starvation and exposure to bitter cold, this elk died a few hours later.

we mapped the extent of the winter range and measured the amount of forage used by the elk. Utilization was to be recorded as the percentage (from 0 to 100 percent) of the current year's growth eaten by browsers. The trouble was, in many places the elk had eaten all of the current year's growth plus some of the old. This was just the entree. Then they chomped on down into the trunks of the brush for dessert, licking their ivories after devouring, in some places, 300 percent. Elk even ate parts of themselves. At the mouth of Lake Creek they had dragged the antlers of a dead bull out onto the ice and eaten them from the tips clear down to the brow tines. Those elk were not only hungry, they were starving to death. Yet the most severe winter survival test still lay ahead.

Fifty-one inches of snow covered the brush along the river at the mouth of Indian Grave Creek, where we got acquainted with an old bull who had made his stand under the cedars. There were no thaws, only Arctic-cold days and nights broken from time to time by blizzards that delivered more snow. The situation was natural—and brutal. You could find bands of elk by the crying of the calves. In the wake of a blizzard one morning we found that the old bull of the cedars had died during the night.

I helped the crew until January 18 and then left them to finish the Powell district's share of the Lochsa elk study. No better crew ever tackled a more worthy task in those mountains. They were all good woodsmen, and their actions and banter revealed that they knew how to get along with each other's individuality. Walt Hahn would say to Floyd Springston, the crew's elder: "If you freeze, freeze straight so we can drive you. It's too damn cold to dig a hole." They all soon learned that Hahn was meaner than a wolverine 'til he had his morning cup of coffee, the blacker the better. To sustain his strength on the trail, Hahn carried raisins mixed loosely in his pocket with grit, dust, and miscellaneous possibles. I liked that crew, and I hated to leave them alone out there with the starving elk.[233]

Meanwhile Hartig's crew found the elk on the Lochsa district in even worse straits than those on the Powell. There were too many elk and not enough food. From Bimerick Creek to the Lochsa Ranger Station, the men hiked in trails packed hard by the hooves of hundreds of elk. At several places they saw groups of antlers, eight to ten sets in a group, sticking up through the ice where elk had drowned. No telling how many remained unseen beneath the ice.

Hartig's crew counted 1,488 live elk on the Lochsa winter range between Bimerick Creek and Lost Creek. The Powell crew counted 1,120 elk. Neither crew came close to seeing them all. From April 11 to April 14 Ranger Hartig and Conservation Officers Springston and Richardson rechecked conditions on the lower end of the Lochsa. Browse on the range had taken a beating, and more than half of the elk counted earlier had died.[234]

Too many elk on too little range was part, but not all, of the problem. More elk died on the lower Lochsa, where fires had created the best forage, than on the upper Lochsa, where mature forests shaded much of the land and intercepted the snow, thereby allowing the elk more freedom to travel. Up there in the old growth the land grew less forage per acre, but more of it was available to the elk because they could move around under the trees. There was also some strength in numbers: the elk did best in the upper Lochsa where they could band together to break trail from one clump of browse to another. After 1949 (and before, for that matter) the idea prevailed that we must reduce elk populations drastically to get their numbers in balance with their winter range. That gave us a simple, single objective for managing elk. Nonetheless, even if only five hundred elk had occupied the entire Lochsa country in a

Advanced clearing like this, followed by construction each summer, extended the Lewis and Clark Highway farther down the Lochsa from Powell Ranger Station during the 1950s and early 1960s.

winter like 1948–49, it is certain that the calves would have been crying and all of the weak and some of the strongest would have died.

In the late 1940s, and indeed since the time of Lieberg and Riley, the custodians of the Lochsa country believed that improving access was prerequisite to managing the area's natural resources. The idea prevailed that once we had access we could get everything done. The elk could be cared for. Natural stream fisheries could be improved. Log jams could be moved from the outlet of lakes to create more room for fish to spawn. The timber could be harvested properly, with vigorous, young stands replacing the old. Insect epidemics could be forestalled. Even water would become more abundant and the timing of its runoff controlled to enhance human interests downstream.

The most immediate need was to complete the replacement of the Nez Perce's old Road to the Buffalo with the Lewis and Clark Highway (US 12), which promised to become a road to new opportunities for the people of both Idaho and Montana. Each summer crews pushed the road farther up the Lochsa from the west. At the same time road construction progressed downriver from Powell. As it did, so did the good trout fishing: hundreds of fishermen followed the bulldozers to the hideouts of the west-slope cutthroat trout.

As explained in earlier chapters, the road over Lolo Pass already provided motorized access for recreationists, and sawtimber could be trucked from the upper Lochsa region into Montana. But the Lochsa's rangers and their supervisors believed that the people of Kooskia, Kamiah, Orofino, Lewiston, and other Idaho towns to the west deserved a share of the Lochsa's bounty, too. So our policy at the time was to hook up the highway before getting on with the cutting of timber, which was deemed a most important ingredient in managing the land. When the highway was completed, the Powell and Lochsa would become managerial rather than custodial districts, rangers and their staffs would be better paid, and people could drive cars and trucks to (or nearer) the resources and the fishing holes. Everybody would be happier and better off.

To make ready the way of management required planning. That's why, in January 1949, I left the crew to finish the Powell district game survey and snowshoed back out of the mountains. A timber management plan was needed before the loggers arrived. Since we had made no detailed cruises of timber on the Powell district, I used, as the plan's base, data from the Forest Economic Survey, a compilation of generalized timber statistics available in the regional office at Missoula. Timber planning was a first-time adventure for me. Fortunately, I got excellent help from a young forester, Merle Hofferber, and sage advice from forest staff officer Ed Shults. I calculated the acreage by forest types; then, using the average volume per acre shown in the survey, I compiled the sawtimber volumes available in each type. Hofferber and I estimated that, on the average, it would take 140 years to grow a tree from sprout to sawlog size on the Powell district. By applying that growth rate to the age and characteristics of the various stands, I calculated the potential yield—about thirteen million to fourteen million board feet of sawtimber—that could be harvested each year, forever, from government-owned lands excluding those in the Selway-Bitterroot Primitive Area. Sustaining that yield would, of course, require restocking the land with new trees within a short time after the cutting.[235]

Despite destruction by recent and historical fires, nature had already done a fair job of managing the forests of the Powell district. My projection of the total potential yield over the 140-year period was little different than the estimated sawtimber volumes standing in 1949; that is, the land, when brought under management, could produce little, if any, more sawtimber than it had when left to nature's devices. On April 19, 1949, I finished the first plan ever available for managing the timber on the Powell district portion of the Lochsa, a much-needed step toward readiness for the management era ahead.

Bud Moore, Powell district ranger, 1949–1956.
—University of Montana, School of Forestry

But we needed other plans, too. Commercial timber, after all, wasn't the only resource of value in the Lochsa, although in the Forest Service culture of the times one could easily believe that once you got to cutting timber, all other values would fall into their appropriate place. The elk portion of our wildlife plans was well developed and included habitat mapping, carrying capacity, potential winter range improvement, animal harvest control, interagency cooperation, game salting, and annual monitoring of populations and habitat conditions. But we had done little work on other mammals, birds, or the fisheries. We knew little of geology and nothing of soils, and to protect the land's beautiful water presented problems and opportunities beyond our capability to fully understand. In addition, much of the Lochsa's mystique, even outside the wilderness, was treasured by recreationists seeking a variety of contacts with nature. We would have to plan for all of those resources and uses as well as for managing the forest for timber production.

Moreover, even with such plans in hand, the mandates of one would sometimes cancel out the intent of another. To establish priorities and reconcile conflicts among the various resource uses, we needed a plan for the land, and that plan should come first. Therein lay the beginning of wisdom. Armed with advice from visionary staff officers Ray Harmon and Vic Linthacum of the regional office and forest supervisor Hy Lyman, we did our best to prepare land use plans.

As a first step we divided the land of the upper Lochsa into three zones. The high ridges and basins were called water-producing zones. Sustained yield of high-quality water would have priority there. The foothills and stream bottoms were special zones, where protection of streams and their riparian areas, water, fish, game winter range, and recreational opportunities would have priority over other activities. The forested mountainsides and ridge tops between the special and water-producing zones were called the general forest zone, where management of the forest for timber and other commercial wood products would receive high priority. Though generalized, this planning forced us to consider the consequences of individual decisions on all the land's inherent values as we perceived them at the time.

The status of land and resources in the Lochsa country, at the start of the 1950s, could be described thus: Much of the land south of the upper Lochsa River was classified as wilderness. Where elk once thrived in brush fields produced by big fires, they had died by the thousands because their numbers had increased beyond the capacity of available range to feed them through tough winters. Over forty miles of difficult construction in the Lochsa's canyons remained to be completed to connect the eastern and western ends of the Lewis and Clark Highway. The Powell Ranger District, where much of the Lochsa's commercially valuable timber stood, had adequate road access to Missoula, Montana, but not to the towns on the Idaho side of the Bitterroot mountains. In the oldest forests more wood was dying than growing; thus, from the viewpoint of using trees for economic benefit, this old growth should have been cut and hauled to the sawmills. Our plan was to postpone logging, though, until completion of the highway gave Montanans and Idahoans equal opportunities to harvest the Lochsa's timber. As usual, however, nature had a say in the matter.

These trees fallen across the Lolo Trail motorway are examples of widespread forest blown down by strong winds during the winter of 1949–50 and called the '49 Blow.

19

Trial by Bulldozer

D*uring mid-April 1950,* our Powell district crew snowshoed over the hill from Lolo Hot Springs, reopened the ranger station as usual, and began to repair trails, roads, and telephone lines—first along the river and then, following the receding snow, into the high country. Work progressed routinely until late June, when Herb Erickson's crew discovered that the winds of winter had flattened much of the forest near Papoose Saddle along the Lolo Trail. By mid-July we found that the entire district, except the southern two-thirds of the wilderness, had been struck in varying degrees of severity by the demon winds. Hundreds of thousands of trees lay broken, uprooted, and souring on the ground. Indeed, before the end of summer we learned that the big wind had toppled trees in many places throughout the entire northern Rocky Mountains. We called that mess in the woods "the '49 Blow."

It seemed a shame to waste the potential lumber in all that blown-down wood. But we weren't ready to log, nor were the wood products industries pressing anyone to cut the trees. They had plenty of timber available in more accessible forests located outside the remote Lochsa country. Furthermore, we were as yet unaware of the magnitude of the problem. Except for occasional patches ranging from five to thirty acres, where all the forest had blown down, the many trees remaining upright in the forests hid the full extent of the windthrow from casual observation. We didn't yet know that in the souring trees lay a threat to our policy of delaying the harvest of timber. Nor could we see that an enemy lurked there in the woods, previously held in check mostly by the health of the forest but potentially more dangerous than fire, and, like fire, waiting for ideal conditions to make its appearance.

It took us nearly two years to learn that disease stalked our land. The first alarm came not from the forests surrounding our station but from northern Montana, where insects were killing spruce trees on the Kootenai National Forest. The Northern Region's chief of timber management, Axel Lindh, along with entomologist Jim Evenden and others with regional perspective, feared the worst: that the epidemic on the Kootenai might erupt wherever the '49 Blow had struck.

They assembled Forest Service representatives from the spruce country throughout the northern Rockies to learn how to locate and control the spruce-killing bugs. On July 31, 1952, in company with many others, I attended a class conducted by entomologist Evenden in the courthouse at Libby, Montana. We learned that spruce bark beetles (*Dendroctonus engelmannii*) were crawling out of the trees devastated by the '49 Blow and taking to the air in search of more trees to attack. They flew in June. For each host tree left behind, they attacked two to four live spruce, depending on the numbers of beetles and the health of the trees. Vigorous spruce, like healthy people, were less vulnerable to disease and to insects. In but one day of training the threat became clear. A fourfold or even twofold annual multiplication of infested spruce trees would, if left unchecked, in a very few years reduce the region's spruce forests from expanses of green to sick shades of brown, followed by thousands of acres of rotting snags.

The Kootenai's cruisers—Forest Service and private alike—were finding and marking the beetle-hit trees. Before a new batch of beetles had time to hatch, loggers hauled the logs from the marked trees out of the woods. I sensed the destiny of the Lochsa's land in the dust swirling behind their loaded trucks. Driving home in my green pickup with the pine tree shield on its sides, I reflected on the situation. I had no doubt that logging was already underway in the widespread spruce forests of the Lochsa, and that the bull of the woods was not a broad-shouldered lumberjack but a beetle only one-eighth inch long.

I looked for beetles first at Bear Camp, a place along the Lolo Trail road about four miles north of Powell Ranger Station where a small brook flowed through a forest of giant spruces. Late-day breezes of August 2 stirred the smells of ferns and water and resin as I walked up to a monarch whose sixty-five-inch-diameter bole had caught my attention years before. From a distance the old tree looked healthy. But upon closer inspection, neither shade nor evening dusk could conceal the reddish brown sawdust held in the scales of the bark and suspended midair on the spiderwebs hooked to the trunk.

The tiny sawyers cast dust out onto the tree's bole from their workings under the bark. I chopped out a piece of bark about six inches square and found the tree's lifeline, the cambium, riddled with beetle galleries. As the bark split from the trunk at the blow of my axe, beetles and eggs tumbled onto the floor of the forest, damp, even in August, from moisture exhaled by the murmuring stream. That spruce was doomed. And so were our plans to delay logging until the Lewis and Clark Highway could connect Montana and Idaho.

Before the August night could hide the tragedy, I found half of the spruce forest at Bear Camp crawling with beetles. That left no doubt that the race with the beetles for the timber was on. If we were to save enough live spruce for future management, we'd have to cut those sick trees and haul them, bugs and all, out of the woods to the sawmills. And that would take bulldozers, roads, trucks, and a breed of men and women the likes of which the people of the Lochsa had never seen before.

Close observation of even the most vigorous spruce forest will disclose a tree here and there occupied by spruce bark beetles, but their spread is usually held in check by several competitors for space in the forest environment. There is, for example, a parasite—a white, wormy-looking beast—that lives off bark beetle eggs and thereby curtails the beetles' ability to multiply. Woodpeckers feast on beetles, eggs, and larvae alike. Extremely cold weather will kill larvae in winter. Healthy spruce repel light beetle attacks by sealing beetle galleries with resin (called pitch outs). All these factors, together with others not understood, weaken the capacity of the beetles to invade live trees in mass numbers. With their army thus undermanned, the beetles normally kill only the weaker trees of the forests.

The '49 Blow, however, changed all that in the Lochsa. Those fallen spruces rotting in the forest attracted bark beetles like wild hollyhock blooms draw bees after honey. While we sawed through fallen timber to clear roads and trails, the bark beetles bored into the blowdown. Because their larvae were buried in snow during the winter, they suffered little mortality from cold. Parasites had no time to increase. Because at least one third of the bugs lived in the cambium on the underside of the fallen trees, woodpeckers couldn't get at them. To make matters worse, nature designed woodpeckers, certainly most of the Lochsa's woodpeckers, to do their best pecking while hanging upright on the bole of a

Alternate ranger John E. Wilson supervised the first operation survey to control the spruce bark beetle infestation in the upper Lochsa. He poses here with his children, Dave, Penny, and Johna, after fishing for steelhead trout in the Lochsa River.

standing tree. With claws hooked firmly into the bark, the woodpecker braces his tail against the trunk and, using his tail as a spring, hammers at the bark in quest of his lunch. In this vertical stance and in the spring of his tail lie the strength of his peck. In contrast, he is nearly ineffectual on fallen logs. No matter the lure of bugs gnawing beneath the bark, when sitting like a wood thrush on a wind-thrown trunk, all but the largest woodpeckers lose their torque and can peck only feebly, if at all.

With these odds in their favor, no wonder the bark beetles, during each June, attacked about four live spruce for each dying host tree left behind. We quickly deduced that the wintertime insulation from cold, the scarcity of parasites, and the neutralization of the woodpeckers would have to be countered somehow. To be effective, we would have to know how many trees were infested and where they were located.

Finding the bugs, mapping the perimeters of their infestations, and calculating their potential spread would be a big job. Accordingly, I assigned Johnny Wilson, one of our most talented assistant rangers, to supervise the program. All the participants trained together at Bear Camp; then, under Johnny's guidance, they began examining the forest by road, by horseback, and afoot. By late September our reconnaissance showed

Lochsa Lodge owner and logger Steve Russell hauls Forest Service and Northern Pacific Railway Company cruisers over deep snow during February 1953.

beetle infestations wherever the '49 Blow had downed spruce—in other words, nearly everywhere outside the wilderness and quite a few places inside as well.

We now knew generally where the bugs were, but we needed more precise information. We organized intensive surveys in the Crooked Fork and Brushy Fork drainages, where we thought it most feasible to begin controlling the beetles by logging. The Northern Pacific Railway Company owned several odd-numbered sections in that area, and its spokesman, Dutch Kincaid, agreed that the company would participate in the survey. In mid-February 1953, having contracted with Lochsa Lodge owner Steve Russell to provide his army-surplus "weasel" for over-snow transportation, we set out again to spy on the bugs. We conducted no broad survey this time, but a systematic examination of the spruce forests, drainage by drainage, from Lolo Pass west to Powell Ranger Station.

Ours was a crew of top woodsmen. It seemed to me that entomologists Dave Scott, Galen Trostle, and Tom Terrill knew more about spruce bark beetles than the bugs knew themselves. I was especially impressed with Terrill, who would eat the beetle larvae. He said they tasted like coconut. I took his word for it. Even on the longest days, I never grew

A Powell district bark beetle survey camp stands on twelve feet of snow near Roundtop Lookout, mid-March 1954.

hungry enough to compete with Tom or the woodpeckers. Long, lean Jimmy Papke represented the Northern Pacific Railway Company with good humor and steady snowshoe strides through the forests. Mick Koppang had youthful strength for tough going, while Horace Godfrey was probably the best woodsman in the crew. Steve Russell drove the weasel, and alternate ranger Louis Normand volunteered to cook. When we finished the survey on February 23, 1953, we knew in detail where the bugs were and what we had to do.

Since most beetles clustered in patches near the blowdowns, we would use logging to cut out the infestations. Lolo Forest supervisor Lyman and timber staff man Shults agreed to release from their contract commitments on non-spruce sales loggers who were then operating outside the Lochsa so that capital outlays, machines, and men could concentrate on logging the beetle-killed spruce. To speed up our attack, we would immediately combine our beetle reconnaissance with timber cruises. In that way we would find the bugs and evaluate their rate of spread while assembling information on road and bridge construction, skidding costs, volumes to be cut, slash disposal requirements, and reforestation possibilities—data we would need for appraising, selling, and logging the timber and restoring the forest after the loggers left.

Our appraisals of the timber's value on the stump would include substantial allowances for profit and risk because, within a year after their death from the beetles, spruce trees begin to split open from sapwood to the heart. In three years most of the trees would be no good for lumber because numerous splits would cause the boards to fall apart when sawed. That problem, plus uncertainty about the bark beetle's rate of spread, rendered the volumes to be cut uncertain. Thus, allowing timber purchasers a good margin for profit and risk seemed reasonable.

Trap trees would be used to slow the spread of the beetles in spruce forests that could not be logged in less than two years. The trap tree method involved the felling of green trees among or near infested spruce; in effect, we would create miniature blowdowns to attract the beetles taking flight each June. The beetles would attack the trap trees, because of their souring wood, instead of live trees in the vicinity. By the following June they would be ready to emerge from the trap trees and fly again. During that year we would haul the trap trees—beetles, larvae, and all—out of the woods if the loggers could reach them. If the trees were inaccessible we would kill the bugs in the trap trees with poisonous chemicals, delivered by men using backpack sprayers.

The logging industry within reasonable distance of the Lochsa country was made up mostly of medium- and small-sized operators. Therefore, we decided to advertise the bug-killed timber in sales of about one million to ten million board feet each. That kind of program would, we thought, be manageable for us to administer, best for the local lumber industry, and worst for the bugs.

Such were our plans to win the race for the upper Lochsa's spruce timber. We would haul the beetle-infested trees out of the woods (or chemically destroy the insects) before the beetle larvae could develop and fly. In that way we would save enough healthy trees to ensure the future of the Lochsa's spruce forests. Because the volume of timber scheduled to be cut would exceed the land's capacity to grow trees, the program, like so many logging operations elsewhere in the past, would be a "boom then bust" show. Nevertheless, I was glad that we had a timber management plan for the Powell district. Although we would have to exceed the allowable cut of thirteen million to fourteen million board feet per year, the plan's direction would help us return to an even-flow harvest of timber after the spruce bark beetles had surrendered to the dozers, trucks, sprayers, and saws.

Members of the beetle survey crew plan their work at Powell Ranger Station, February 1952.

At stake was the future of an estimated six hundred million board feet of commercial-sized spruce timber growing in the upper Lochsa country. Except for our plans for the flats alongside the Lochsa River, our approach lacked the detail needed to guide the land use revolution that was sure to be generated by our decision to log the beetle-killed timber as fast as possible. The fate of the land of the Lochsa, outside the wilderness, would for the most part be determined by the wisdom of the people of the Forest Service, the Northern Pacific Railway Company, the loggers, and the road builders. Such immense responsibility for so humble a band.

During late March we began cruising timber at Packer Meadows on six feet of snow. By developing new methods, we gathered accurate data far faster than could have been done using standard procedures of the times. Perimeters of forest types were identified on aerial photographs and then transferred to four-inch-to-the-mile scale base maps. Cruise strips, laid out to assure a ten percent sample in each forest type, were then drawn on the map, showing the compass bearing that the cruiser must use to follow the strip. Guided by this map, the cruiser ran the strip, sampling one-fifth-acre plots at two-chain (one chain equals sixty-six feet) intervals. At each plot he recorded volume, age, and rate

Veteran woodsman Frank Gummer cruises timber in the Brushy Fork of the Lochsa, March 1953.

of growth for each species. Since the quality of lumber to be sawed has much to do with its value, the cruiser graded the quality of one tree of each species nearest the center of each plot. Perimeters of bark beetle infestations, steepness of slope, and the rate of fall of the streams were also recorded on the map. At the end of each day the cruiser gave all these data to the compiler, who assembled them in a form usable for appraising and advertising the timber for sale.

Stricken stringers of spruce forests led the cruisers all over the district. We air-dropped a four-man cruising camp on Doe Ridge; then, using the same logic I used when spacing trapper line cabins, we air-dropped camps at Cayuse Creek, Indian Post Office, and in the saddle west of the Devil's Chair on the Lolo Trail. Meanwhile, we dropped camps and supplies in five locations for Jim Evenden's crews who were checking infestations in the Brushy Fork, Spruce Creek, and Storm Creek drainages.

By the end of July 1953 we not only knew where the spruce bark beetles were (outside the wilderness), we also knew a great deal about how many there were, how fast they were spreading, and where it was necessary to log for control. Furthermore, we had the data we needed to sell the timber and send in the loggers. In less than a year from the time I chopped bugs from the big spruce at Bear Camp, we had examined spruce stands on thousands of acres and laid plans to outflank the beetles.

This sign nailed above the door of the sale compiler's cabin served notice that custodial days were waning and forest management was coming to the Powell district of the Lochsa.

But the pace of the race was outstripping our knowledge of the land. What would logging and road building do to the soils, water, wildlife, trout, and salmon so vital to the spirit of place in the land of the Lochsa? Our land ethic was growing but not yet mature. None of us had the wisdom to foresee the consequences of the program we had devised. We had no Leopolds to give us advice. That we were moving too fast and with too little knowledge seemed obvious, but the bugs wouldn't wait and we couldn't either. With timber-marking axe and road-locating level in hand, we prepared to get on with the logging show.

Frank Lara, our chief compiler, became the center of attention as our plans to sell timber took shape. To provide Frank and his helpers room to work, we converted a warehouse, once called the "Dish Wanagin," into the compiler's headquarters and nailed a professional-looking "Timber Management" sign over the door. (It was our vague hope that some member of the United States Civil Service Commission would chance that way, take note that our activities had progressed from dishes to management, and allocate all of us a raise in pay.) All data gathered by the cruisers went in through the door of "Timber Management" and came out assembled logically according to our plan to advertise the timber in small- and medium-sized sales.

With a great deal of optimism, we advertised in early June 1953 our first two sale areas: Packer Meadows and Swede Cut. Tree Farmers, Inc., Rother, Inc., and Hamilton Lumber Company, all of Missoula, were interested. While prospective bidders examined the sale areas, the timber management gang hardly looked up from their maps and appraisal sheets as they prepared more bug-infested timber for auction. Bear Camp would be next, followed by Roundtop and Crooked Fork, and then the program would move west of Powell station into Papoose, Squaw, and Doe Creek drainages. Meanwhile, we would watch the progress of infestations in the upper Brushy Fork and Spruce Creek and advertise timber for sale there if it looked like the beetles would spread.

After advertising for thirty days, our first two sales were submitted for oral bidding on July 6, 1953. No one from the forest products industry submitted a bid for the timber.

When that happened, all those working in the timber management shack looked up from their maps and papers. If industry was unwilling to purchase our most accessible timber, the chances of selling and logging the more remote spruce forests of the Lochsa looked slim indeed. Our whole plan was in jeopardy. I asked Bill Hodge of Tree Farmers, Inc., the largest company that had initially expressed interest, why he didn't bid on the timber. Bill said that our appraisal had not allowed enough profit margin to cover the risk of volume loss due to splitting of the beetle-killed trees. When I asked the owner of a small lumber company the same question, he answered: "When the big boys say don't bid, you don't bid if you want to survive in this game."

During the next week, Steve Russell expressed interest in the Swede Cut timber, and we sold it, without further advertising, to him. After negotiating with Tree Farmers, Inc., we awarded it the Packer Meadows sale. The bugs had to be hauled out of the woods, so we gave some ground to get started. The local wood products industries had demonstrated by their silence at the bidding table that we couldn't count on them alone as our major allies in controlling the spruce bark beetle epidemic in the Lochsa.

We had to remedy our sole dependence on the local sawmills in nearby Montana. The best way to do that was to put up for sale a block of timber large enough to attract the interest of industries from more distant locales. With that objective in mind, we began reassembling cruise information into a single large sale. The volumes of spruce timber to be cut in the rough country west of Powell, even with a taxpayer subsidy to help build main-haul roads, wouldn't carry development costs and still leave the purchaser a reasonable margin of profit. So, in addition to offering the beetle-killed spruce, we planned to sell enough other species to make the sale a profitable venture. We would advertise one hundred forty million board feet, with the provision that the beetle-hit spruce had to be logged first. The purchaser of the timber would be allowed ten years to complete his contract, and, except for infested spruce, his annual cut would be limited to sustained yield as reported in the timber management plan.

To log beetle-killed spruce from Idaho into Montana was one thing; to tie up choice timber for ten years with access only to Montanans quite another. Since we needed to know how the people of Idaho felt about the matter, forest supervisor Lyman and staff officer Shults held a public meeting in the Clearwater County Courthouse at Orofino, Idaho, on July 20, 1953. Despite our concerns, no opposition to our plan developed at the meeting, which was attended by representatives of the Grangeville Chamber of Commerce, Tree Farmers, Inc., Potlatch Forests, Lochsa Timber Salvage Committee, and several additional people.

Interest in logging the Lochsa grew as word of the big sale spread. In January 1954 the Oregon-based Nettleton Timber Company told us it would buy thirty million to forty million board feet but could not handle the whole block of timber that we proposed to sell. Encouraged by Nettleton's prospect, we split our program into two large sales: Upper Powell, to include forty million board feet in the Crooked Fork and Brushy Fork areas, and Lower Powell, to include seventy-five million board feet west of Powell station. We advertised Upper Powell first. Only Nettleton, Tree Farmers, Inc., and the Great Spirit know what happened behind the auction block, but Tree Farmers bought the sale at appraised prices without competition.

Neither the forest ranger, forest supervisor, nor regional forester could up and sell a block of timber the size of the Lower Powell sale. The chief of the Forest Service reserved authority to do that. Steering our proposal from the Lochsa through the hierarchy of the Forest Service to Washington, D.C., took until August 17, 1954, when Chief McArdle approved our sale prospectus. We advertised immediately. At 2:00 p.m., on September 20, 1954, bidding began in the library of the federal building at Missoula. Bidders were Rother, Inc., of Missoula; Richard Rossignol, of Lolo, Montana; Tree Farmers, Inc., of Missoula; and Nagel Timber Products Company, of Arizona. Rother dropped out when the bidding reached \$675,000; Rossignol left at \$906,000. Nagel Timber Products held on, but after six hours of bidding, Tree Farmers bought the sale for \$1.269 million.[236]

We advertised additional small timber sales wherever bark beetles attacked spruce in unexpected places. But the Upper Powell and Lower

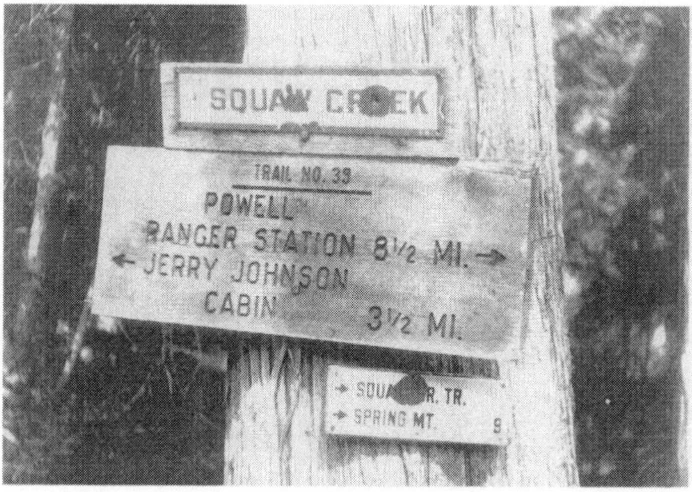

Soon to be displaced by a road, the signs reflect changing times in the Lochsa. At the bottom is the type first used by the Forest Service. The top is second generation, and at center is the style in use during the 1950s.

Powell sales, along with 9.7 million board feet sold later in Spruce Creek and timber sold on intermingled lands owned by the Northern Pacific Railway Company, set the pattern for developing the country outside of the wilderness in the upper Lochsa drainage.

During this time our view of the necessity of access had not waned. Since the advent of the automobile, development in America had been synonymous with the construction of roads. The view prevailed that without roads there could be no serious development of new land nor could there be management or any kind of successful administration by the government. We had to have roads to log out the beetles. Moreover, some of these roads would have to be built with public funds in order to make the logging profitable for the timber industries. Taxpayer-financed roads included progressive extension of the Lewis and Clark Highway down the Lochsa River and main-haul roads into Crooked Fork, Papoose Creek, Squaw Creek, and Doe Creek drainages. Additional roads needed to haul out the timber would be built by the loggers.

Herb Norgaard, in charge of engineers on the Lolo National Forest, recognized that building roads was a far bigger task than our Powell district personnel and his engineers could handle alone. So he borrowed engineers from a neighboring government agency, the Bureau of Public Roads. Those men supervised the surveying, contracting, and construc-

Road construction in 1954 crowds Squaw Creek and its narrow riparian area.

tion of the roads paid for by public funds, while Herb's engineers surveyed and supervised the roads built by the loggers. As ranger in charge, I was responsible to see that the roads were located to get at the beetle-killed timber and to serve other land values in the long term as well.

The location of roads was especially important because roads, more than any other factor, would ordain patterns for the use of the land. Main roads would be permanent. Where the roads went, most people in the future would go also, and those wild things not adaptable to man and machines would perish or leave. For instance, road-building held the potential to degrade the Lochsa's pure water and the fisheries, both sea-run and local, dependent thereon. Depending on where and how they were built, roads could turn out to be either long-term blessings or the means of destroying important land and resource values. I spent many long days in the woods with engineers and road-building loggers, locating control points ahead of construction, trying to avoid needless damage to the land and its variety of life.

It was during reconnaissance of the taxpayer-financed section of the Squaw Creek road that I first recognized the gulf between my philosophy of land values and the views of some engineers. That day, June 10, 1953, engineers Norgaard of the Lolo National Forest, Doug Murphy and Ted Shupert of the Bureau of Public Roads, and I hiked up Squaw Creek to determine the general location of the road prior to surveying and staking. We trudged through the cedars of Squaw Creek's canyon where the trail, carpeted with fallen twig tips and needles, led us among gray trunks, some at least five feet in diameter. Although we saw none, I knew that steelhead trout were spawning in gravel deposited in the eddies of the powerful stream. The sounds and smells of the creek dominated the shaded environment. Here and there trilliums bloomed white in the dusky landscape, and the leaves of bracken ferns were beginning to unroll from their stem-borne balls of green. We all surely sensed some value in these and other creations of nature, but our eyes were not on wild things to be appreciated. Instead, we saw obstacles in the way of the forthcoming road—obstacles to be moved or smashed or circumnavigated.

Nature had been stingy with space when creating Squaw Creek's canyon, leaving barely room between the mountainsides for the creek and its trout and a small cedar grove here and there. Even the two-foot-wide pack trail crossed and recrossed the stream, making its way up the canyon. Now we were planning how to squeeze in still another facility. The fourteen-foot-wide road would be a kind of wedge driven between the creek and the mountains. It would crowd out most of the cedars, shatter timeless rock, and expose the spawning steelhead to view from the road's edge.

The patterns of life in the mountains of the past tore at some consciences as we plotted the land's future. Those of us who had long worked in the Lochsa were creatures of wilderness. To us, the creeks were sources of trout and salmon and ferns and shade and pure water to drink. The engineers and road builders were developers whose mission was to make way for engines and wheels. To them, creeks were obstacles to be bridged and riprapped to protect the roads from damage by water. These disparate views of the Lochsa's earth could not be fully reconciled. For some of us knew the land as God's country, while the newcomers saw opportunity to make its resources more useful to humans.

Inevitably, we collided. The engineers viewed my band of mountain men at times as obstacles in the way of progress. On occasion, when the bulldozers unnecessarily tore at the earth, my resultant loss of temper raised barriers between me, my crew, and the engineers of the Bureau of Public Roads. But BPR engineer Doug Murphy had a way of easing the tension. At the height of some controversy, Doug would say: "They sure look pretty after they're built."

Except for a few cabins at Steve Russell's Lochsa Lodge, the Powell Ranger Station was the only place in the country to eat and sleep. So we housed and boarded the engineers, the cruisers, and all other government-connected workers. Our fifteen-man log bunkhouse soon overflowed with workers, so we pitched tents alongside the buildings for use as additional sleeping quarters. When those facilities filled up, too, we built a camp for the BPR crews at Wendover Bar, across the newly built highway from my old trapping-cabin home, hired them a cook, and trucked in a steady stream of food supplies. Tent camps were established for small groups of engineers surveying roads at Packer Meadows, Doe Creek, Brushy Fork, and upper Papoose Creek. Our packers supplied the remote camps by mule train. As the loggers and road building contractors moved into the Lochsa, we designated locations for their camps in places where they would not conflict with the intent of our land use plans.

Road construction followed close on the heels of the surveyors. For example, on the morning of August 5, 1953, I met Orral Lake of the Bondurant Logging Company at Lolo Pass. Orral had a D-8 cat-and-can (scraper) at the pass prepared to begin building road, staked earlier by the Forest Service survey crew, to the Packer Meadows timber sale. One mark of distinction in the logging business of the times was ability to construct a good road guided only by a centerline blaze. Most equipment operators considered survey stakes insults to their eyeballing aptitude. I knew that. And I also knew that the quality of the roads varied from poor to good according to the capability of the operator of the machine.

"Do you know how to read stakes?" I asked Orral.

"No," he said. "I always just build 'em by eye."

But after we examined the work of the surveyors, Orral conceded: "Those stakes make sense. I can do that." Then he climbed on his cat, cracked the throttle, and with clattering tracks and squeaking cables began the first surveyed and staked logging road ever built in the upper Lochsa.

With skill borne of thousands of hours at the controls, he scraped the dirt from high places to fill in the low. The cat-and-can and the man were like one as both machine and dirt moved back and forth on the roadway. From time to time Orral would stop the cat, get off and read the stakes, then climb on and go again. In less than two hours an eighth of a mile of new road reached out from Lolo Pass toward the stricken spruce forest beyond.

Shortly after that, contractor Morigeau began building the Squaw Creek road, and the Halvorson Construction Company pushed the Lewis and Clark Highway farther downriver. Meanwhile, survey crews located

By 1953 the once-custodial Powell Ranger Station had become headquarters for bustling insect control and timber salvage operations in the upper Lochsa.

roads into Papoose Creek and the Crooked Fork. No longer simply marks on the maps of the planners, roads by 1953 had become centerline flags in the brush, surveyor stakes in the dirt, and land "smoothed and straightened" to accept the wheels of American progress.

The traditional work of protecting the land did not always harmonize with the development of roads and timber sales. Nor did those who treasured the Lochsa's wildness agree that the gouge of the dozer's blade necessarily heralded progress in resource management—or progress of any other sort, for that matter.

To illustrate: On July 10, 1953, Halvorson Construction Company, without warning, blasted a rock bluff from the mountainside into the river, obliterating the pack trail and blocking alternate ranger Frank Gummer and packer Paul White's return from the downriver wilderness to the Powell Ranger Station. During the men's attempt to circumvent the barrier, they injured mules, damaged equipment, and lost their patience with "progress" as well. That same day, a fisherman took on the whole Halvorson construction crew because their bulldozers stood in the way of his travel down the river.

By 1953 Powell's Flat, where once only Charley's hoe scratched the landscape, had become the nerve center of operations for 150 to

200 men and women, their machines, their greed, their joys, and their troubles. Along our journey from custodianship to management, nearly as many hours were spent solving the problems of people as in tending to important resource issues. The agents of the beetle control program hauled the junk of American industrialization into the freshness of the Lochsa's mountains where, like children tired of toys, they dribbled trash whenever their mood changed or their attention shifted to some other interest. Gone were the old habits of carrying lunch wrappers home to be burned, or tucking orange peels under a rock that they might return to earth unseen. Cans, papers, human excrement, used oil, broken cables, and garbage showed up where elk tracks, trilliums, and ferns had once commanded attention. And in August of 1953 we found near the Powell Meadows our first abandoned car—a certain sign that the custodial days were waning and full-fledged management was near at hand.

Happily, some newcomers needed no urging to keep the land clean. Their camps were immaculate; their consideration for the land, its life, and their neighbors, beyond reproach. Nevertheless, we spent considerable time forcing many other pilgrims to clean up after themselves. They not only chose to live in their own filth, but, worse, inconsiderately scattered their rubbish where it would be encountered by others. When it came to cleanliness in the woods, the wildlife of the Lochsa displayed higher standards than many people. The raven would not for long allow a dead elk to pollute the forest. Nor would the coyote leave anything to spoil from the ribs of a fallen deer. When a salmon died in the creek, some alert bear would scoop him up for lunch. Wild creatures cleaned up the forest in many ways, while man littered the landscape. Yet even a starving bear could not clean up a beer can or a puddle of drained crankcase oil. And what were the spirits of the mountains to do with abandoned automobiles?

In the era before progress and development, lawbreaking in the land of the Lochsa had consisted mostly of violations of fish and game codes or an occasional fugitive fleeing to Idaho to escape Montana justice. But during the summer of 1953 somebody stole the wheels off logger Pat Knight's car. Al Fetscher's camp on the Brushy Fork was raided. A party of recreationists reported to the station that someone had stolen cameras and fishing gear from their car. Soon government property began to disappear. In the absence of organized law enforcement, progress was obviously bringing plenty of problems to the mountains. To help reverse

Waters of the 1954 spring snowmelt washed this gravel into the Lochsa River from Squaw Creek, where the streambed had been loosened by road construction in 1953.

the new trend toward lawlessness, I accepted from Idaho County Sheriff Bud Taylor an appointment as Deputy No. 8.

While the bears hibernated in the winter of 1953–54, the snows hid the scars on the land inflicted by the activities of the preceding summer. As they had always done, the steelhead waited far downstream for a burst of fresh water to signal that spring had arrived in the uplands. Clear water and stable streams—those were the hallmarks of springtime in the Lochsa, where the power, the rumble, and the beauty of water transcended, and surrounded, all else.

Spring had always been that way. Nevertheless, the confluence of Squaw Creek and the Lochsa River was a different place in May 1954. A new gravel bar, six feet deep and thirty feet wide, stretched from the creek's mouth seventy-five feet out into the river. That the stones in the bar were new could be told from their light color; their lichen coatings had been ground away by road-building dozers clanking up and down the stream in Squaw Creek's canyon the fall before. Indeed, the gravel bar contained much of upper Squaw Creek's streambed and part of the newly built road as well.

Under natural conditions, stream damage was unheard of in the land of the Lochsa. After all, there was nothing man-made there to damage and human values had to be introduced before even powerful, natural events could be seen as destructive. But with new roads crowding streams in narrow canyons, and with other kinds of human impacts to stream channels and banks, we began seeing—and talking about—damage in 1954. On the evening of May 17 supervisor Hy Lyman and I stood on the banks of Squaw Creek above the new gravel bar; the stream ran bank-full of powerful water. We could hear boulders rolling in its channel as the water tore loose the gravel, further enlarging the bar.

Hy said: "Bud, we can't do this to the land."

The cedars, their shade, and the ferns were gone. The rumbling of boulders and the roar of water filled the canyon. Their protest drained our hearts and souls. The Lochsa belonged to the people, and we were their government agents: ordinary men, a ranger and his boss, with the life of a land in our hands. Only an hour before, Hy had told me that the Powell district ranger position had been upgraded to GS-11, confirming that we had at last attained long-awaited management status. But that achievement paled in the din of the ravaged stream. That night on the banks of Squaw Creek, it seemed that the consequences of bulldozing the earth might be more than the land could bear.

20

Consequences of Logging the Beetle-Killed Spruce

For most of the fourteen miles from Lolo Pass to Powell Ranger Station, the Lewis and Clark road in 1953 clung to steep mountainsides, its single-lane width offering motorists only an occasional chance to pass each other. About one and one-half miles below the pass on the Idaho side of the Bitterroot mountains, however, was one place wide enough for two or three cars to park. A bold spring flowed from the earth at the upper side of the road. In summertime

This roadside spring had, since construction of the Lewis and Clark Highway in 1925, lured motorist to stop, drink, and reflect on the pristine nature of the Lochsa's landscape.

Steve Russell's truck, loaded with spruce logs, leaves Swede Cut—the first advertised commercial national forest timber sale in the upper Lochsa, August 1953.

the spring's clear water trickled almost unseen under the shade of the ferns before passing through a culvert beneath the road on its way to Haskell Creek, a branch of the Crooked Fork. A rusted tin cup hung on the limb of an alder beside the spring, put there by someone when the road was built in the mid-twenties to tempt travelers to sample the fresh mountain water.

That turnout was a beautiful spot, a place for motorists to pause, refresh, and reflect. It was also the only place where a logging spur could branch off the main road for access to the patch of beetle-killed timber sold to Steve Russell in the Swede Cut sale.

We located the spur road's center line above the spring, but when Russell's bulldozer dug out the roadbed, the mud flowed down into the spring, buried the moss, and flattened the ferns. Fed from deep in the earth, the spring kept flowing, but its waters no longer babbled in the culvert; they grated through loaded with silt. Within a week the dust from Russell's logging trucks settled on flattened ferns caked with mud as he hauled bug-laden logs from the Lochsa's woods to the sawmills in Missoula.

The desecration of the spring was irreconcilable. The spring and the cup may have seemed only small pleasantries in a land loaded with water and shade and other bounty. But the potential for accumulation of hundreds of similar misfortunes could seriously degrade the health of the land. And larger threats loomed as well. By 1953 Earl Hall's angle bulldozer had grown from a six-foot-wide blade mounted on a Cletrac 30 to huge D-8s and TD-24s carrying blades fourteen feet wide; and rumors had it that even bigger machines were on their way to the woods from the factories. In the size of the dozers lay an obstacle to thinking small about roads. Some loggers would say: "How in hell can I build a twelve-foot road when the blade on my cat is fourteen feet wide?" But it was the attitude of the man at the controls that caused most of the damage to the land, not the size of his bulldozer.

To appreciate the complexity of building roads and logging without damaging the land's ability to sustain of a variety of resources, one has to understand the organization and practices of the industries that brought logging to the Lochsa. Timber offered for sale was nearly always bought by the companies that owned the sawmills. The larger companies built some main-haul roads, but otherwise the entire job of logging, road construction, felling, skidding, loading, and hauling logs to the mill was contracted ("gyppoed") to the loggers. The mill owners paid the loggers a fee per thousand board feet for logs delivered at the sawmill. A typical gyppo logger owned road-building, skidding, and loading equipment, but most of them subcontracted the felling, bucking, and hauling of the logs to individual sawyers and truckers.

Logging, then, was a series of independent operations at work in a loosely organized team, which required a remarkable degree of initiative, coordination, and accountability among the participants in each of its gyppo jobs. The sawyers had to keep trees felled and bucked ahead of the skidders. Roads had to be built at the right time so that the trucks could get to the skidded logs. No trucker hauled long for an operation if he was forced to wait for the skidders to bring him logs. The objective was to keep a steady stream of logs moving from the stump to the mill. If one link in the chain of gyppo contracts failed, everybody lost.

All gyppos worked by the piece or by board-foot scale; their free personalities would tolerate little thought of working for wages by the hour, by the day, or by any other set schedule. They wanted freedom to work as they chose. Each ruled his own domain but depended on and was responsible for supporting some other link in the logging chain. They were experts at their crafts. Many of them were also expert at passing the buck for shoddy work to some other gyppo and thus confounding

It will take years to heal this damage to the Crooked Fork's waters and streamside by inconsiderate logging road construction during the mid-1950s.

the efforts of the Forest Service officers charged with overseeing the sales. While the word of most of them proved to be a stronger bond than a contract sealed by a notary public, a few were not trustworthy.

The gyppo loggers' concern for the life of land in the Lochsa varied from arrogance to reverence. Sometimes the land was hurt by loggers and rangers alike because we did not understand the consequences of our acts. Surely the people of America can forgive those scars on the earth. But it is not easy to forgive actions defiling the land when we all knew better. We knew that some were quick to seize opportunity for profit regardless of the resulting damage to the land. For example, one day I found a gyppo logger bulldozing an unauthorized road across national forest land and side-casting dirt into the nearby stream. He had no business digging there, and he knew it. But by the time I discovered his clandestine operation, so much damage had been done that only nature, allowed decades of time, could heal the land.

The Northern Pacific Railway Company sold most of its beetle-killed spruce to the Thompson Falls Lumber Company, and we sold most government timber to Tree Farmers, Inc., of Missoula. Though considerable overlap existed between their work forces, each major company contracted its own loggers to bring the spruce to their sawmills. Al

Fetscher Logging Company and Bondurant Logging Company (later known as Huson Logging Company) became the major suppliers of logs for Tree Farmers, Inc., with Ray Fetscher and Steve Russell logging some of the smaller sales. Loggers Russell Oliver, John Oliver, and the Nelson Brothers Logging Company delivered most of the logs from Northern Pacific Railway Company lands in the Lochsa to the rail siding at Lolo, Montana, and the logs were shipped from there to the sawmill at Thompson Falls, Montana.

Since most of the Lochsa's spruce grew in nearly pure stands and the bark beetles killed the spruce in patches, that's the way the Forest Service cruisers marked the trees for cutting. Clear-cut patches ranged in size from one to twenty acres at Packer Meadows and Swede Cut, which were our earliest sales. But it took time to build roads into more remote places, and with time the bark beetles renewed their attacks. The longer it took us to reach an infested spruce forest, then, the bigger the clear-cuts had to be. By the time roads and loggers reached the most remote areas, not only had the beetles killed all the spruce, but sun and weather had split the dead trees, leaving nothing of commercial value to be logged.

We marked trees for cutting with great concern for the land and its forests. But we soon learned that far greater threat to the land lay in road-building than in logging the timber. Where undisturbed soil once absorbed water, packed surfaces collected and ditched water from one road to another until its volume and force eroded the mountains like the sluice boxes used by the gold miners of old. Poorly located roads also diverted streams from their beds, eroding hillsides, silting creeks, and degrading fisheries. It was no easy task to locate, build, and care for hundreds of miles of logging roads and yet avoid erosion, where so much of the land was steep country with water standing, seeping, and babbling almost everywhere.

The hydrology of the mountains was such a complex subject that I thought I should be able to get expert advice from someplace higher in the Forest Service on how to handle matters of water when developing the land. But, alas, when the bulldozers came, plenty of experts on extracting resources from the earth could be found; few, however, could advise on the protection, not to mention enhancement, of water. Ironically, because I had been thinking about water quality, quantity, and the timing of runoff during my land use planning days, I found myself quite knowledgeable about such matters when the threat to the integrity of water ran higher than ever before. Given the culture of the times, the specialists within the Forest Service (with a few notable exceptions) were so fixed on the trees of the forests that they had not given much attention to water and soils, the more basic elements of the land.

The first snows of autumn 1953 fell on elk hunters going into the Lochsa and on log-laden trucks coming out. A variety of vehicles driven by red-coated hunters loaded with horses, mules, camp gear, rifles, and whiskey passed the loggers' big diesels crawling up to Lolo Pass with their transmissions in low gear and the reports of their exhaust stacks reverberating through the mountains. I was glad that we had widened the Lewis and Clark road in many places so that the loggers and hunters could pass; after all, each had a right to his share of the Lochsa's bounty. Many hunters were loggers themselves, taking time from their work elsewhere to rekindle their spirits in a wilder land while laying in meat for the winter. Nevertheless, I wondered how long these two disparate resource uses could coexist.

All roads leading out of the Lochsa at that time converged at Lolo Pass; thus, that's where we scaled the logs. The scaling station stood across the road from the cabin where two men of the Idaho Fish and Game Department checked hunters in and out. By mid-October, Bondurant Logging Company was hauling ninety thousand board feet of infested spruce a day from the Packer Meadows sale and from adjacent lands owned by the Northern Pacific Railway Company. Steve Russell finished the Swede Cut sale on October 19, 1953, thereby eliminating one patch of the infested spruce from the forests of the Lochsa's mountains.

Not far east of Papoose Saddle the beetles had delivered early and devastating attacks in the Crooked Fork drainage on spruce owned by both government and Northern Pacific Railway Company. We planned a main-haul road to reach from the Lewis and Clark road into the Crooked Fork drainage to its confluence with a stream called Shotgun Creek, whose basin hosted millions of board feet of beetle-killed spruce. Since timber owned by both the Northern Pacific Railway Company and the Forest Service would be made accessible, the road was jointly financed by the two entities. In the long term a road would be needed to reach timber on each side of the stream. But because the steep-sided canyon of the Crooked Fork would be difficult to cross and because most of the spruce killed and threatened by the beetles stood west of the Crooked Fork, we decided to build the road on that side first.

Forest technician Warren Patten scales beetle-killed spruce logs at Lolo Pass in 1953.

The plan was workable, but the contractor engaged to build the road had neither the ability nor the zeal to win any race with a one-eighth-inch bug. While the beetles chomped the last fresh spruce cambium left on the Crooked Fork's mountains, the construction company plodded along, its contract obligations almost universally unmet.

Such slow progress wouldn't satisfy the Thompson Falls Lumber Company, however, which had contracted to log the beetle-killed timber for the Northern Pacific Railway Company. Consequently, highly respected construction boss Ernie Gill located a road to access Northern Pacific's lands on the east side of the Crooked Fork. Using an abney level to hold grade, Ernie laid a center line from the Lewis and Clark road, taking off about one-half mile below where Steve Russell had gone west to the Swede Cut sale. Following close on his heels, dozers smashed trees out of the way, sidecast dirt, and even broke through most of the rock to build the logging road. Not far behind came the sawyers, the skidders, the loaders, and the trucks—all after the timber at so many dollars per thousand. These men knew how to build roads and cut trees. It looked like 1954 was going to be a tough summer for bugs killing trees on the railway company's lands.

Gill's road ended at the southwest corner of section 29, directly across the Crooked Fork's canyon from a stand of beetle-killed spruce in Northern Pacific's section 31. This area was scheduled to be tapped by the west side road. Since the contractor's slow rate of progress would never provide access to the timber that year, Gill wanted to cut the timber that stood across the Crooked Fork before it was lost to the weather and sun. The road behind him lay entirely on lands owned by the Northern Pacific. To cross the Crooked Fork, however, he would have to obtain permission to build a short piece of road across the national forest. Furthermore, his road would have to pass through the Blue Slide, an unstable chute of raw earth too steep to host vegetation, a place where the natural mountainside unraveled continually, sending dirt and rocks down into the Crooked Fork at a rate determined by weather and the moisture content of the soil. From the perspective of preventing stream siltation, Gill's road-locating level could not have led him to a worse situation.

Ernie and I examined the proposed crossing on July 15, 1954. Ernie felt that the slide would hold his road, once it was constructed. But it was plain to see that the dirt cast aside during the road's full-bench construction would go down into the Crooked Fork, a stream so clear that trout could be seen in the pools even from a vantage point high on the slide above. At the same time we could also see whole mountainsides turning brown as the dying spruce shed lifeless needles from their limbs.

At the speed Thompson Falls Lumber Company worked, the slide could be crossed, a bridge built, and the stricken timber hauled to market within two weeks. Ernie had located his road with bulldozers close behind, confident that the momentum of his operations would sway events his way when he reached the creek. He had beaten the contractor of the west side road to the spruce by a year, and that year meant the difference in whether the spruce could be used for lumber or would remain a sea of snags, waiting to be cleaned up by lightning and fires.

I told Ernie to cross. He did. And for the first time ever the waters of the Crooked Fork carried mud from a logging road down into the Lochsa, the Clearwater, and beyond. The crossing of the Crooked Fork was no ordinary decision, yet many decisions of similar consequence were made as the lumber companies, the loggers, the road builders, the Northern Pacific Railway Company, and the Forest Service worked together to control the spruce bark beetle epidemic in the Lochsa.

By late summer 1954 Tree Farmers, Inc., began building the main-haul road between Brushy Fork and the crest of Beaver Ridge, an area that became known as Big Basin because of the generous expanse of

The unstable Blue Slide had for years deposited silt into the Crooked Fork of the Lochsa after heavy rains and during springtime snowmelt. Note that the pack trail has been filled by sliding soil.

its well-timbered lands. Al Fetscher, to be joined soon by Ray Bailey as woods boss, began logging spruce from Big Basin in early October.

An impatient, hot-tempered man in the prime of midlife, Fetscher had a keen ability to run a money-making business. He was always on the move. It seemed to me that he worked day and night, or at least stayed awake and thought most of the night. Though we had many spirited clashes of will, all of us who worked for the Forest Service respected Al because he was honest, he never short-cut a joint decision when one was called for, and when his logging was done he took pride in demonstrating that he had met his share of the contract and left the land in good shape.

In contrast, tall, soft-spoken Ray Bailey was a product of life in old-time logging camps where the man who ruled with his fists had the best chance at the job of bull of the woods. Unlike Fetscher, Bailey was slow to anger. But he used to say of conflict with others: "Dammit Bud, a man can only take so much." In his younger days it didn't take much of "so much" before Bailey would stop the talk and start swinging haymakers with both his big hands. By the time Bailey joined Fetscher in the Lochsa, life had tempered his instincts so that reason prevailed over strength—though he still, at about age sixty, had plenty of power to spare. Like Fetscher, he tried to see both sides of the mission, that is, the need to make money for his company and at the same time leave

This bulldozer fords below the new bridge on the Crooked Fork near the Blue Slide, July 1954.

the land of the Lochsa in good shape for the future. Given but small allowance for human frailties, Fetscher and Bailey were the kind of men who earned their rewards in the Lochsa through respect for the integrity of the land.

In those days it didn't take much snow to chase loggers from the high mountains into more arid winter logging shows. Consequently, by early February 1955 all loggers had left the Lochsa, except Fetscher and Bailey who were logging in six feet of snow. They kept the spruce moving out of the woods but not without problems. For one thing, the timber sale contract required that during felling no stumps could be left more than twelve inches high. Bailey furnished shovels to the sawyers so they could dig down and cut the stumps low, but as the snow deepened, felling according to contract became increasingly difficult.

It began to look like discredit from high stumps, not the costs of plowing snow, was going to shut the logging down. Then on February 24 I found, adjacent to Fetscher's logging show, nearly a million board feet of infested spruce whose beetles in the spring could attack live trees at the usual rate of four to one. Better to cut one million board feet early than five million later, even if a few high stumps remained to mar the quality of our logging. So I told Bailey to cut the timber before he pulled out, assuring him that we wouldn't penalize him for high stumps as long

Al Fetscher enjoys a well-earned break from his work of logging spruce from the Big Basin of the Lochsa.
—Bernie Schoenfield, courtesy of Ellen Fetscher

as his sawyers did their best to cut stumps low. Fetscher and Bailey moved out of the Lochsa on March 2, 1955—about the same time of year when the mountain men of old had left for Lolo Hot Springs after trapping furs all winter. They had broken the taboo against logging in deep snow. Henceforth, winter logging would become commonplace in the Lochsa and even preferred in swampy basins because building roads on frozen ground did less damage to the land.

While Fetscher and Bailey logged Big Basin, Tree Farmers, Inc., extended the roads built by the Bureau of Public Roads deeper into the forests of Squaw Creek, Doe Creek, and Papoose Creek. In order to prevent a repeat of the gravel washout in Squaw Creek, we narrowed the logger-built extensions, aligning them to more nearly fit the contours of the mountains. In that way we found room in the canyons for the roads without crowding the creeks or destroying the shade needed to keep the water cool. We were learning from our mistakes.

Our bark beetle control operations attracted the attention of national leaders, including presidential candidate Adlai Stevenson who came to see the logging of the Lochsa in August 1954. I met Adlai's party at Lolo Pass. His traveling companions were regional forester Pete Hanson, Region One chief of information and education Jim Vessey, Dr. Herb

Wintertime logging in the Lochsa controlled the bark beetles with least damage to the moist environment of the spruce forest.

Shrineberg, and noted author Bernard DeVoto. As Adlai got out of their government sedan and climbed into my dusty pickup, I said: "I'm Bud Moore, the ranger in charge." Adlai said, "I'm Adlai Stevenson. I intend to be your next president."

Adlai wanted to see the logging, so we drove to Haskell Creek where part of Russell Oliver's crew was skidding and loading spruce. Curious as a tax assessor, Adlai poked around the skidding jammer, trying to understand the logistics of logging. In his shiny hard hat and new boots he looked like the greenhorn he was, but his faded Levis suggested that he had been in the woods before. I kept him out from under the jammer's boom until the operator shut down his machine to find out the reason for this invasion of government officials into his logging show. As Adlai climbed up onto the big track of the jammer, I was struck by his short stature. All of the campaign photos had made him look like a Paul Bunyan of politics, but there in the Lochsa's woods, reduced from image to reality, Adlai had to scramble to climb from the ground to the door of the big machine's cab.

Adlai shook the operator's hand and told him he'd appreciate his vote; then we got on our way to Bear Camp to see the sawyers felling spruce. The road was narrow where we found the sawyers working, so when we stopped there was no room for another vehicle to pass. As our group piled out of the government rigs, woods boss Alan Nelson's pickup rounded the bend and skidded to a stop, enveloping us in a cloud of dust. Alan was in a hurry. For that matter, Alan was always in a hurry, and anybody, especially government anybodys, who got in his way had better damn well get out of his way so that his logging show could keep going full speed ahead.

Before his pickup rolled to full stop, Alan jumped out in the road to tell our entourage to get out of the way of the next truck coming down. He looked us over for a fraction of a second and then headed for me, the only familiar face in the crowd. He had reached earshot, closing in fast, when I said: "Alan, I want you to meet Adlai Stevenson."

Adlai stuck out his hand, but Alan brushed him aside. Keeping his eyes on me, Alan acknowledged Adlai only as an obstacle to his mission of clearing the cars from the road. But before he could tell me that I should know better than to park in the middle of his logging road, intuition warned him that something out of the ordinary was happening there in the Lochsa's woods.

Abruptly, he turned and looked at Adlai. "Adlai? Adlai?" he said. He seized Adlai's hand and shook it so hard that Adlai staggered around in the dust. Never mind that Adlai wanted to see the sawyers fell the spruce. Never mind that logging trucks stacked up behind our rigs. There on the dusty Bear Camp road it looked like two fellow Democrats were becoming acquainted with each other.

Senator Richard L. "Dick" Neuberger of Oregon was interested in what was happening to the Lochsa country, too. During the summer of 1953 Dick and his charming wife, Maureen, journeyed into the Lochsa to gather information for an article to be published in the *Saturday Evening Post*. After talking with us at Powell, they drove over the Lolo Trail road to visit with Glenn Boy, the ranger at Fenn Ranger Station whose district at that time included the lower end of the Lochsa. The Neubergers, by their writings and their political actions, implored us to take good care of the land, its history, and its resources. To counter the digging of the dozers, Senator Neuberger in July 1955 recommended to Congress that a national monument be established at Indian Post Office commemorating the historical value of the Lolo Trail.

The leaders of the national wilderness movement also worried about where the bulldozers would go and what they would do to the Lochsa's pristine landscapes. At that time, all of the land of the upper Lochsa

These close-spaced roads show the soil disturbance wrought by shovel logging in the upper Lochsa.

south of the river, including most of the White Sand drainage, was part of the primitive area established in 1936. But two roads had already penetrated the area by the time of its establishment: the twelve-mile-long Tom Beall Road and a twenty-four-mile-long road reaching four miles beyond the Elk Summit station, which included about ten miles of secondary roads. Since it was heresy in those days to consider closing a road, we in the Forest Service wanted to move the primitive area boundary back from the river. That would open up these roads and their environs so the forest on the Lochsa's face, across the river from the new Lewis and Clark Highway, could be managed and its timber harvested.

Howard Zahniser, then president of the Wilderness Society, agreed that the roads should be excluded from the wilderness, along with several sections of land owned by the Northern Pacific Railway Company. But he held firmly to the Wilderness Society's position that no land suitable for wilderness should be surrendered to development.

Meanwhile, logging boomed in the Lochsa. As more roads were being built and more beetle-killed trees were being hauled out of the woods, talk of how to keep the land whole also burgeoned. Both the loggers and the Forest Service learned a great deal about care of the land by

Al Fetscher's Bucyrus-Erie shovel drags a log uphill to the boom. The operator will rotate the machine and place the log on the truck.
—A. E. Allen, courtesy of Ellen Fetscher

trial and error or success. For example, when Fetscher and Bailey began logging the steep mountainsides in lower Papoose Creek, they used, as they had in the more gentle topography of the Big Basin, a method called "shovel logging." The technique derived its name from the machine, originally designed for scooping up dirt, which was used for skidding and loading logs. Those shovels were capable of skidding logs about 150 feet uphill and 50 feet downhill; thus, roads had to be constructed on the contour of the mountains at 200-foot intervals in order to reach the logs. In Papoose Creek, much of the terrain was so steep that the dirt discarded from one road on the mountain would tumble down into the road below. Fetscher and Bailey discovered that shovel logging much of Papoose Creek's mountains was too expensive and that building a staircase of roads created unacceptable scars on the land. They didn't like that, and we didn't either. The lesson was costly, but at least we learned from the experience.

We also learned by observing the development of logging equipment outside the Lochsa country. For several years before the Lochsa

Skidding jammers like Sparky's "Old Grunt" could drag logs uphill a thousand feet and thereby widen the road spacing required for shovel logging.

was logged, the shovel-logging industry had centered around Missoula, encouraged by foresters because its use avoided much of the soil damage and erosion caused by the old practice of cat-skidding logs down mountainsides. Consequently, many of the hills in the vicinity of Missoula were corrugated with roads built at close intervals on the contour to accommodate shovel logging. But it wasn't that way everywhere. If you flew from Missoula and looked down on the much-used landscape, the spacing between the roads became wider the farther west you traveled.

In northern Idaho the gyppos used long-line skidders to log their steep ground. Compared to Missoula's modern-day shovels, the Idaho skidding jammers were primitive machines. But they were what we needed in the Lochsa. My brother, Sparky, brought perhaps the first Idaho skidding jammer into the upper Lochsa. He called it "Old Grunt." With Sparky at the controls, and a good hooker in the woods, Old Grunt could reach down the mountain, seize a log, and yank it up from as much as a thousand feet below the road. Using those old machines, we no longer needed to tear down the mountains by building a road within a few yards of every tree.

During the mid-fifties, the gyppos were logging dead and dying spruce from all but the most remote forests in the high basins near the crest of the Bitterroot mountains where the Lochsa's far eastern tributaries began as tiny creeks. During late summer of 1956 I led a band of surveyors into this as yet unroaded spruce country. Camped in a small meadow in the North Fork of Spruce Creek, we gathered close to the fire in the cool of evening after a sudden squall had soaked our clothes. The clang of bells echoed between the peaks, and I could hear their steady chomping as the horses and mules munched grass near the place where I had seen the track of the last grizzly in 1946. This time we were not looking for bears. We were here to scout the location of a logging road to haul out the last of the beetle-killed spruce.

To reach our campsite we had ridden by horseback up Spruce Creek beneath the canopy of one of the most remarkable stands of spruce timber in the northern Rocky Mountains, much of it riddled with bugs. Cutting 5.4 million board feet of timber would control the beetles on national forest land in Spruce Creek. But road-building costs would be high, so we planned to sell 9.7 million board feet to make the logging a profitable venture. All of the bug-killed timber plus some of the green would have to go.

Next day we blazed the location of the road from our campsite northward up the mountainside to the saddle in the ridge between Spruce Creek and the Brushy Fork near Lily Lake. As we ate lunch at the saddle, I looked across the wide basin that held the meadows where I had slept, rolled in my blanket, after meeting the big grizzly twenty-five years before. I could also see the notch in the mountains where a logging road would soon enter from Montana, and I thought of the several pack trips Dad and I had made during my boyhood from the Lolo Fork through that same notch to camp by the big rock at Elk Meadows. I remembered how we had caught red-sided trout from Skookum Lake, packed them in grass coated with the frost of early morning, and carried them out to Mom who considered them a delicacy to be prized above all other fish.

Our scouting completed, we returned as we had come, down the shaded Spruce Creek valley past the noisy falls of the Brushy Fork and the remnants of Big Cabin where Fred Schott had begun trapping furs over fifty years before. We rode quietly most of the way, listening to the farewell song of squeaking saddle leather timed to the rhythm of hoof beats on the trail. This was the last time there would be any reason to walk, or ride a sturdy mountain horse, up that valley into the high basins of Spruce Creek. John Oliver and his bulldozers were coming; the wildness of the land would be leaving.

Several months later, as cold winds of the winter of 1957 blew down from the crest of the Bitterroot mountains, I snowshoed up the South Fork of Spruce Creek searching for the last infestation of spruce bark beetles in the basin. When the sun stood near the zenith of its low arc of travel across the sky, I set fire to a whitebark pine snag, tramped the snow nearby, and then took off my snowshoes and sat on them to eat my lunch. For me, lunchtime on the trail had long been a fulfilling ritual—a half hour of respite from the pragmatic business at hand, a time to reflect upon life and to wonder at the mystery in the surrounding wilds. Smoke from the burning snag drifted near the place where Chink Clarke had killed the bear thought to be Old Peg Leg, one of the last of the Bitterroot's grizzlies. Now Peg Leg's wilderness was gone from Spruce Creek. As I munched sandwiches, I could see the ribbonlike course of John Oliver's road winding through the forest below. John stood tall among the best road builders who ever turned the mantle of the virgin Lochsa's earth. In the grunting of bulldozers, the buzzing of chainsaws, and the creaking of winches under his command lay the end of one era and the beginning of another.

During the five years after the discovery of spruce bark beetles at Bear Camp, we had destroyed a wilderness and opened much of the country to motorized vehicles. By January 1957 main travel patterns, and thus land use patterns outside of the classified wilderness, had been set. Completion of the Spruce Creek road and the logging that followed would pretty well whip the bark beetles. New issues were beginning to overshadow the problems of the past, yet old management questions lingered. Now that the country was opened up, could we of the Forest Service, pressured by people and industries, manage the resources to assure both their sustained yield and the health of the land in the long term? Even more significantly, would the people soon to come treat the Lochsa's earth with reasonable respect?

21

Poisoning the Land and Its Waters

By the fall of 1956, only twenty-four years after rangers Bell and Mackay had rafted across the flood-swollen White Sand Creek, signs of the work of machines showed where the Crooked Fork and White Sand join to form the Lochsa River. The boulders in the Crooked Fork were coated with dark slime caused by dirt cast into tributary creeks by road builders and loggers digging in the uplands. The wilderness-borne waters of the White Sand, on the other hand, looked clean, yet its currents carried invisible residues from another of mankind's activities.

The story of that unseen contamination began in 1946 when I discovered insects chewing needles from the branches of spruce and fir trees growing on the center ridge of the Papoose Creek drainage. July 16 was one of those days when the warmth of the midsummer sun made the woods smell earthy and the waters of the creeks sparkled like they were loaded with something more precious than diamonds, as in truth they are. I studied the landscape from the commanding elevation of the saddle, while my horse picked his way along the trail. About halfway down the center ridge I noticed that the usual fresh green color of the twigs of young fir trees had turned to a sick-looking brown. Close examination showed that all the new growth of needles had been eaten by worms, leaving the ends of the twigs matted with silken webs—a protective cover, I supposed, used by the worms while they chewed up the trees. From the extent of the brown-hued trees on adjacent sidehills, I estimated that the infestation covered about three thousand acres.

Because I had never seen those insects before, I reported their presence to the supervisor's office at Missoula. In a few days Supervisor

Myrick sent out an entomologist who identified them as spruce budworms, a defoliating insect capable of retarding tree growth and, in a persistent epidemic, sure to kill numerous young spruce, alpine firs, grand firs, and douglas firs. Another threat to the health of our forests lurked there on Papoose Ridge, a threat that would have to be watched.

The budworms showed little activity during 1947, however, so we concluded that no control measures were required. But still the insects persisted, dormant some summers, at times reaching out to attack new trees, then receding again to dormancy. At first their threat seemed small compared to the '49 Blow with its ensuing epidemic of bark beetles. Nonetheless, by the early fifties the budworms had spread from Papoose Creek eastward to Lolo Pass and into the tributary basins of the White Sand as far as Storm and Swamp Creeks.

Thus, even as we completed the spruce bark beetle project we had another epidemic on our hands. By 1954 the budworms had defoliated many young trees by repeated attacks. Their eastward spread also left vulnerable large forested areas in adjacent Montana. Furthermore, in 1954 we had planted thousands of young spruce trees in areas logged to control spruce bark beetles, and the tender twigs of those seedlings were threatened by the army of worms. Available management options seemed limited to either no action, other than continued surveillance, or aerial spraying of insect-killing chemicals to halt the spread. Unlike the spruce bark beetle program, control by logging would be impractical because the trees most adversely affected by budworms were young and of small diameter.

Everyone I consulted considered the spray relatively harmless compared to the threat to the woods posed by the budworms. Indeed, it was considered the best approach, if not the only way to go. But neither we of the Lochsa nor the specialists in the Forest Service understood the consequences of drenching the Lochsa's landscapes with DDT. For example, on February 6, 1956,[237] I discussed at length with Fred Johnson, the regional chief of wildlife management, the poison's potential for injuring fish in the streams. Fred, among the best wildlifers in the country, could tell me only that there remained a lot to be learned about the relationship between DDT, water, and fish. Still, Fred was worried because he, like those of us living out there on the land, had felt the surges of life in the powerful streams of the Lochsa.

As ranger in charge of the project, I viewed the collective rationale of Forest Service specialists as follows:

This military surplus airplane prepares to transport the chemical DDT from the airport at Missoula into the Lochsa's forests. —Bob Rehfeld

- The recommended dose—one pound of DDT, dissolved in fuel oil, per acre[238]—wouldn't do any permanent harm.
- There could be minor damage to aquatic life.
- Warm-blooded creatures would not be harmed.
- The spray could be kept away from lakes and major streams.
- If we let those worms kill or retard the forest, the adverse consequences to production of forest resources would be far worse than spraying the poison.

We decided to spray. We had plenty of support, for the inclination to rid the United States of all kinds of pests ran strong in U.S. Department of Agriculture agencies, including the Forest Service. And never before had the killers of insects been blessed with an opportunity comparable to the circumstances following World War II. Airplanes designed to deliver torpedoes and bombs at low elevations could be readily converted to spray insecticides on croplands and forests. Pilots capable of threading a torpedo bomber between the masts of a ship were available and eager to fly. Chemists of wartime laboratories had created deadly potions for use in chemical warfare, and some of these were adaptable for killing bugs as well.

The scientific ingenuity, equipment, and poisons of World War II, then, had much to do with the methods we used to attack spruce budworms in the Lochsa. But our program had much earlier roots. In 1874 a German scientist had synthesized the chemical known as DDT. In 1939 Paul Muller of Switzerland determined that the chemical killed insects,[239] a discovery for which he won the Nobel Prize. By the time we took on the budworms in the Lochsa, chemical industries in the United States were marketing DDT for use in many endeavors of American life. DDT was being aimed at all kinds of insects—by hand sprays in households, gardens, and public places, and from airplanes over communities, fields, swamps, and forests—in widespread efforts to eradicate insects considered detrimental to the welfare or comfort of people.

Before discovery of this country by Europeans, there were no "good bugs" or "bad bugs." For thousands of years insects had increased in the Lochsa's forests whenever conditions favored their multiplication. They ran their course and died out, leaving an opportunity to be seized by some other power in the ever-changing balance of life. No force dominated for long; rather, all forces of nature harmonized, adjusting over centuries of time. But nature's way seemed too slow and wasteful to us. Accordingly, we chose the only control measure known to us at the time, DDT. We would spray it on the land from airplanes designed to kill enemies at war.

We began organizing to spray the worms in the spring of 1955. But the budworms lay dormant that year, as we had observed them to do in the past. Also that spring, entomologists Dave Scott and Tom Terrill discovered that the Lochsa's budworm was a species requiring two years to reach adulthood. Even-numbered years were their time of greatest activity, so we postponed the spraying until 1956.

Spruce budworms are among the most widely distributed forest insects in North America. The moths, which appear in July and August, deposit egg masses on the underside of needles of Engelmann spruce, alpine firs, grand firs, and Douglas firs. The eggs hatch in about ten days, producing tiny larvae. These larvae do not feed during their first year but instead spin silken nets to protect them while hibernating in tree bark, under lichens, in old flower cups, and in similar sheltered places. Emerging from hibernation in the spring when the tree buds begin to expand, they mine into old needles or into the expanding buds, eventually moving to the buds where they dine on the new growth under a protective, silken cover.

The larvae spin loose webs from which they feed on the growing needles. When the new needles have been eaten, they feed on the old. The larvae grow, eating the tree's foliage, until they become wormlike creatures about one inch in length. After that, they undergo a pupal stage before emerging as adult moths, which lay eggs to begin the cycle anew.[240] This life cycle is an annual process except in certain species, like those in the Lochsa, which require two years to reach adulthood.

To assure the success of our control efforts, it was important to strike the budworms during a period of their life cycle when they would be most vulnerable to the poison. If we sprayed too soon, many of the larvae would be inside their mines in the needles and thus shielded from the DDT. If we waited too long, some larvae would have reached adulthood and quit feeding, in which case the moths and their eggs would be unaffected by the poison and the life cycle would continue. In order to kill enough worms to stop their spread, we wanted to spray the forests with DDT when the larvae were on the ends of the twigs eating needles.

Because all major air operations were centralized in the Forest Service's Northern Region, the spraying of the Lochsa's budworms was controlled from the Forest Service Aerial Fire Depot located adjacent to the airport near Missoula. Regional staff officer Clarence Sutliff had overall charge of the project. To assist him, we assigned a forester from the Powell district, Bob Rehfeld, who supervised day-to-day operations as the spray job progressed.

Flight paths were planned on the contours of the mountains and away from lakes and streams. Pilots were to begin flying at daylight and to quit before the sun warmed the slopes sufficiently to create air currents strong enough to scatter the spray. Within a day or two after application, men on the ground would check and record the effectiveness of the spray in killing the worms.

Once we committed to the program, no one questioned the plan's potential to clobber spruce budworms. But we of the Powell district were also concerned about what else we might kill and especially about what might happen to life in those great barometers of land health, the rivers and streams. I dispatched alternate ranger Johnny Wilson and forester Clyde Blake Jr. to check the concentrations of insecticide adjacent to several major streams in the area. They did this by placing absorbent cards on the ground in small openings in the streamside forests before the planes made their runs. By checking the cards after the spray was delivered, they could approximate from the droplets how much poison spray the land at that site had received.

Idaho conservation officer Don Grimes and Idaho fisheries specialist Leon Murphy also observed what happened to the streams in the aftermath of the spraying. Neither these Idaho officers nor the Forest Service personnel had the skills, funds, or time necessary to conduct scientific water monitoring—if, indeed, the procedures or equipment for such monitoring even existed at the time. Our observations, therefore, were unscientific in that we could only monitor the results visually after the spraying and could not specify the amount of invisible poison that the streams might have received.

On June 22 the entomologists checking the woods reported that the larvae were out of their needle mines and would be vulnerable to the DDT. We began spraying promptly at daylight on June 23, 1956.

Forest Service guard Dick Ramberg and I observed the beginning from a vantage point on the Lewis and Clark road near the spring that Steve Russell's dozer had buried with mud. Not long after daylight the first plane burst through Lolo Pass. The pilot flew the single-engine, war-surplus torpedo bomber close to the tree crowns, spraying insecticide from nozzles fastened to a boom beneath the plane's fuselage. Flying down the slopes of Haskell Creek and into the valley of the Crooked Fork, the plane exploded the natural peace and quiet in a great rattle of engine and wings and screaming air. Then the airplane and its noise were gone. In their wake a faint cloud hung like a streak of morning fog clinging to a mountainside after a gentle summer rain. We watched the lethal mist settle into the forest.

Other airplanes followed. Within an hour the forest was full of dangling webs and dying worms. It was also full of a poison that none of us on the Powell Ranger District fully understood.

Finishing the job took several days. Except when rains wet the forests, the planes flew their toxic cargoes each morning at daylight until the entire infested area was thoroughly drenched with DDT. Poison devised by humans fell from the skies onto meadows grazed by the elk and into the forests of the Brushy Fork where I had met the grizzly bear. It settled on the roofs of old cabins at Packer Meadows, in Spruce Creek, on Beaver Ridge, and in the valleys of the Crooked Fork and Storm Creek. It settled into the nests of the birds and into the clear waters. Few crannies of that land escaped its penetration. Its application had to be thorough; to exterminate the spruce

After spraying DDT to kill spruce bud worms near Lolo Pass, the pilot pulls his plane out over the Crooked Fork drainage. —Bob Rehfeld

budworms, the spray needed to saturate the tiniest niches in all of the infested forest.

Mosquito, gnat, and bug spray—that's all it was. Millions of gallons of the stuff were scattered around the United States, packaged for convenient use in sprayers, bottles, cans, barrels, and tanks, available for use to kill any bug that threatened a person, household, garden, field, or forest. Touted by chemical companies, under various trade names, as lethal to pests but (applied properly) harmless to everything else, DDT and its companion poisons constituted a scientific victory over nature in humanity's war against insects. Nevertheless, it wasn't long until the natural systems of the Lochsa—like those elsewhere—began to show that the benefits of DDT were to be had only at a price.

Even before the spruce budworm control project was finished, Don Grimes and Leon Murphy found nearly all the aquatic life dead in Haskell Creek, where the spraying began. Since Haskell Creek is a small, steep stream, it hosted few, if any, trout. But the riffles and barriers in the creek were jammed with dead insects and bloated frogs. Haskell Creek's water was no longer fit to drink, nor could any aquatic life live for long in that poisoned tributary of the Crooked Fork.

My son Bill, Roger Norgaard, and I prepare to camp at Clarke's Meadow shortly after spraying the area with DDT in 1956.

Dead trout floated belly-up at Packer Meadows where the early mountain men had dipped pure water from Pack Creek, which winds serpentlike among the pigmy willows. Johnny Wilson and Clyde Blake found some of the heaviest spray concentrations along major streams, not because the pilots had purposely dumped DDT there, but because some of each successive ribbon of spray released on the contour of the mountains had drifted downslope, accumulating heavy doses of poison in the valley bottoms. In addition to this uncontrollable drift into the valleys, the spray fell into countless tiny brooks that fed the Lochsa's major arteries. There was no way to tell how much poison accumulated in the lakes, Lochsa River itself, or in the Clearwater and mightier rivers to the west.

On July 14, 1956, not long after the spraying was finished, my son, Bill, and I camped at Clarke's Meadow on Storm Creek as we had done several times before. Insects had always thrived in that land in the past, each momentary change of weather or air benefitting a different variety. Buffalo gnats had swarmed at daybreak. Horse flies and deer flies had gone after our horses, mules, and us during the heat of afternoon. When the setting sun cast shade in the valley, mosquitoes would swarm from the meadows like miniature fighter planes forming attack squadrons. And as the cold of the night grounded the mosquitoes, nearly invisible gnats, called no-see-ums, took their place in stalking all warm-blooded animals.

But when we camped in 1956 the leaves of the huckleberry bushes and strawberries were, like Wilson and Blake's check cards, speckled with droplets of poisonous spray, and the horses and mules scarcely switched their tails as they grazed. As cold air settled from the crests of the mountains into the valley in the evening, a faint antiseptic smell, instead of no-see-ums, spread over the land. I missed the airborne insects because, I suppose, they had always been there before.

About three miles southwest of Clarke's Meadow, Siah Lake brightens the dark spruce forest in the shade of Ranger Peak's alpine slopes. The lake is inhabited by cutthroat trout, not transplanted from hatcheries but spawned in the gravel of the uppermost tributaries of the White Sand fork of the Lochsa. Unlike the migratory salmon and trout in the larger tributaries at lower elevations, the cutthroat trout of the high country stay year-round in their lacustrine habitats, moving into the inlet and outlet streams to spawn and feed in summer, then returning to the lake to overwinter.

It is not possible to spray chemicals from fixed-wing aircraft on the forest without poisoning the waters as well. Lily Lake is shown here.

Native trout had thrived in Siah Lake. During July 1956 Jay Turner and his trail crew hiked there, as trail crews camped in the vicinity usually did on Sunday, to enjoy the country and catch a few fish to eat. They found the lake as beautiful as always, its twenty-acre surface rippled by a brisk afternoon breeze. They also found the trout abundant and easy to catch. But the protective slime on the trout's bodies near the tail was gone, and any mucous remaining on the fish stuck to the fishermen's hands like weak glue. Not wanting to eat fish that they feared had been affected by poison, they returned their catch to the lake, hoping that the fish would recover.

To men on foot, like Jay and his crew, the land was big and wild, and Siah Lake was a centerpiece that took two hours of hiking to reach from their camp, and that camp was a long day's walk from Powell Ranger Station. In contrast, the speed of the spray plane compressed the pilot's perception of the landscape. Siah Lake and its pristine environs were but a speck in a cosmos of mountains that appeared in the pilot's vision so briefly that there wasn't time to shut off the spray. Even if time had allowed him to take precautions, the poison would, in any event, settle into myriad tiny watercourses, and then ride their currents down into the lake. Viewed in retrospect, it was plain to see that there was no way to spray DDT on a land like the Lochsa without poisoning the waters and killing the fish.

Sick and dying fish weren't the only tragedies of the Lochsa's poisoned lakes and streams. After finishing the work of the Forest Service in the fall, Earl Smith, one of our foremen, planned to trap mink along the Lochsa River. I told him that when I trapped I had always caught twenty to forty mink each winter. Because no one had trapped along the river for years, mink had been even more numerous in recent times than they were in those early days.

Earl Smith, a keen observer of wild animal signs, scouted the streamsides in October but found no mink tracks. No discarded crayfish shells littered their traditional feeding places, suggesting that mink were no longer combing the beaches. Smith's optimism was not easily destroyed; like the trappers of old, he believed that some undiscovered habitat must surely hold a bonanza of fur. But Smith soon packed up his traps and left, convinced that the spray had killed the mink.

Had the Lochsa mink, which feed heavily on crayfish from beneath the rocks of the river, died like the frogs of Haskell Creek? What, then, of the otter whose feeding habits are similar? Nobody knew for sure.

In late summer, the Lochsa River upstream from the mouth of Papoose Creek was always a good place to catch a mess of trout.

We knew only that the dead frogs in Haskell Creek, the belly-up fish at Packer Meadows, the sticky fish in Siah Lake, and the vanishing mink had no precedent in that land, at least in our lifetimes. We had achieved our objectives, for the spruce budworms were killed in untold numbers. But because we had no scientific means of monitoring the DDT spread through the waters, the side effects of poisoning the land could not be proven. Moreover, there was no one to prove anything to except me—the ranger in charge, responsible for protecting the people's land and its resources.

One afternoon about two and one-half months after the spraying I was jointing my fly rod and studying the big pool in the Lochsa River near the mouth of Papoose Creek. Summer was yielding to fall. The leaves of the cottonwoods had not yet turned, but their color was fading. Water in the river ran low and clear, and the current split on the nose of a big boulder at the head of the pool. That's the place to hook a few trout for supper, I thought, as I whipped the fly back and forth a few times to get the feel of the line and the rod. Then, in a long cast, I dropped the gray-hackled fly into the eddy close to the boulder.

A trout struck, and I set the hook. He came in without the usual energetic leaps of the Lochsa's rainbows. I shortened the line, worked him close to the bank, and then, holding the rod high in my left hand, seized him firmly behind the pectoral fins and lifted him out of the water. He didn't feel slippery. The slime on his body stuck like glue to my hand. I unhooked him and put him back into the river. But I should have rapped his head on a rock, for he was dying.

In sick fish and in sandbars untraveled by mink lay for me the beginning of ecological wisdom in managing land. Everything in the ecosystem was, indeed, hooked to everything else. This was no casual attachment of creatures to water and earth, but a delivery system capable of transporting poisons from land through its water and food chains to injure or kill all forms of life—insects, carnivores, herbivores, omnivores, and perhaps people as well.

And I learned still more. There on the banks of the Lochsa River I reaffirmed what Frank Smith, Bill Bell, and Ed Mackay had known long before me—for better or worse, in the business of protecting the health of the people's national forests, the buck began and stopped with the forest ranger. In addition to supervising the harvest of forest products, by 1956 rangers had to sustain the land's ability to produce a variety of resources in the face of threats from natural forces, such as fire, disease, and insects, as well as overuse, misuse, and even poisoning by man. No matter their good intent, a ranger's superiors could not possibly understand the many factors with which he had to deal. Nor could the ranger expect much reverence for the earth from the industrial agents of free enterprise, for they were too often inclined to profit at the expense of land health. Professional experts could supply valuable information, but they had few answers to complex problems; with rare exceptions, they viewed the land through the narrow window of their respective specialties. And at that time the ranger got little support from the general public; whether nature or human action threatened the land of the Lochsa, the public's voice generally remained silent.

On that day in 1956, surrounded by the great mountains of the Lochsa, I felt very much alone. I thought of the Indians and of the trailblazers, from the European explorers to the early-day rangers who were my predecessors. More so than ever, people seemed to be everywhere, and more—both within and outside of government—were on their way. As I unjointed my fly rod, I wondered what we, purposely or unintentionally, would try to do to the country next.

22

The Turning of America

Six years after we poisoned the Lochsa with DDT, author-scientist Rachel Carson wrote *Silent Spring*, warning of the adverse consequences of spreading chemical poisons on the earth. During that time I left the Lochsa country, in body if not in spirit, working at Forest Service assignments in Missoula, Utah, and Washington, D.C. Meanwhile, all across America, it was becoming clear that the way we extracted natural resources to feed industry, amass wealth, and create jobs exacted a price from the parent land. As timber sales, roads, dams, power lines, mines, resorts, and miscellaneous activities gnawed at the last of America's wild places, doubts began to shadow the long-held belief that what was good for industry was also in the public's interest. Conviction grew that the government was allied with industry to do in the last frontier. Heedless of the old cliché, "You can't fight city hall," the people began to defend their interests and their lands.

Frontier days were gone, as was any opportunity to discover new land. Trappers, prospectors, railroaders, road builders, loggers, hunters, fishermen, naturalists, wilderness enthusiasts, and others had found and begun taking nature's bounty from much of America's lands. Nearly all known, profitable supplies of nonrenewable resources were being used; and renewable resources, like forests, water, range, and wildlife, were sought after by a variety of competing interests.

The days of extravagant harvesting from nature's once-full storehouses was nearing an end in the land of the Lochsa as in America generally. As Gifford Pinchot had said many years before, "There are just two things on this material earth of ours, people and natural resources."[241] People were beginning to realize that neither their economical nor their

Constructed to haul sawtimber from the Lochsa's forests, this road will later serve recreationists who enjoy exploring by automobile.

spiritual well-being could be nourished for long by extracting more resources than the land could sustainably produce.

Maintaining programs to supply the wants of all seemed certain to damage the productivity of the earth. There weren't sufficient resources to satisfy everyone, and many resources could not be used fully for one purpose without destroying or degrading their usefulness for one or several other benefits. Miners, for example, wanted to dig up mountain meadows that were also needed as natural reservoirs for water. Mature forests prized by loggers provided homes for wildlife, and the same woods helped regulate the flow of water from the mountains. Recreationists seeking solitude clashed with those who would rather explore by auto from the bed of a new access road. Preserving wild places helped wildlife and water quality but deprived loggers and miners of the resources they coveted.

Plainly, learning to live within the resource budget of the land would not come easy on the national forests. Indeed, constraints on extracting natural resources flew in the face of the American dream; forest rangers, industries, and the consuming public were used to getting what they wanted from the woods. As the assets shrank, each special interest battled to get its share—or more—from nature's bank of dwindling resources.

Preservation of wild places protects wildlife security, water quality, and solitude cherished by many people while it denies road-building, mechanization, and extraction of resources.

As we have already seen, the Organic Administration Act was passed in 1897 to describe the basic purposes of the forest reserves (later, the national forests). Secretary of Agriculture Tama Jim's 1905 letter, which directed that the dominant industries would be considered first, went on to instruct that, "where conflicting interests must be reconciled, the question will always be decided from the standpoint of the greatest good of the greatest number in the long run."[242] These instructions contained broad guidance for resolving conflicts among competing uses of the land, but at least through the fifties neither Tama Jim nor Congress had assigned priorities among the many uses possible on any given tract of land. Those decisions, potentially far-reaching, were left to the ranger in charge of the land.

Since the Forest Service tended to support the dominant industries, and industrial exploitation of natural resources had long been an American way of life, it is not surprising that the counter idea of creating and protecting wilderness became the catalyst for deciding, in the sixties, how the remaining undeveloped public lands would be used. In response to public concern that the Forest Service could not be relied

A thoughtful ranger, Jack Puckett tends his camp near the shore of Big Creek Lake.

upon to protect the wildness of areas so designated under their administrative regulations, Senator Humphrey, on February 11, 1957, introduced a bill authorizing the United States Congress to designate and require protection of wilderness areas. Chief of the Forest Service Richard McArdle opposed the bill because he considered its precedent a threat to the multiple-use concept practiced by the Forest Service. He countered with a bill that would place the authority to designate wildernesses with the president of the United States, would empower the secretary of agriculture to change the boundaries and acreage of designated wilderness by up to one fourth of their original size, and would allow temporary roads and timber cutting to control pests.

The national leadership of the Forest Service (myself included) did not want *uses* of national forest lands to be allocated legislatively; we wanted to continue to do that ourselves. So the Forest Service sought and obtained passage in 1960 of the Multiple Use–Sustained Yield Act, which directed that the national forests "are established and shall be administered for outdoor recreation, range, timber, watershed, and wildlife and fish purposes." The act further provided: "The establishment and maintenance of areas of wilderness are consistent with the purposes and provisions of this act."[243]

With the practice of multiple use thus protected (indeed required) by law, the Forest Service withdrew its opposition to the federal Wilderness Act, which became law on September 3, 1964. The new law "established a National Wilderness Preservation System to be composed of federally owned areas to be designated by Congress as 'wilderness areas.'" It further directed that these areas "shall be administered for the use and enjoyment of the American people in such manner as will leave them unimpaired for future use and enjoyment as wilderness, and so as to provide for the protection of these areas, the preservation of their wilderness character, and for the gathering and dissemination of information regarding their use and enjoyment as wilderness."[244]

Passage of the Wilderness Act gave the people more clout by providing a direct avenue to Congress in creating wilderness. The Forest Service could be dealt with or bypassed in decisions concerning wilderness designations, depending on the agency's receptivity to proposals by citizens. This new law, for the first time, established priorities for managing designated areas of the national forests based on the attributes of the land.

Once a wilderness area was established, the first objective of management was to maintain the area in its natural state, that is, to allow nature and natural forces to continue to govern the landscapes. Game could be hunted, fish caught, and furbearers trapped, and people could recreate in solitude, as long as those activities did not impair the natural processes at work on the land. These wildernesses would be places of many uses, but where the preservation of naturalness had first priority.

The Multiple Use–Sustained Yield Act of 1960, on the other hand, designated no specific priorities for managing resources outside of official wilderness areas. (Congress had intentionally listed the resources in alphabetical order.) According to the act, "'Multiple use' means: The management of all the various renewable surface resources of the national forests so that they are utilized in the combination that will best meet the needs of the American people."

The act defined sustained yield as "the achievement and maintenance in perpetuity of a high-level annual or regular periodic output of the various renewable resources of the national forests without impairment of the productivity of the land."[245] These definitions promised an interesting future for the rangers in charge of the national forests.

Because we had long practiced multiple use and sustained yield, the 1960 act seemed redundant to many of us then working for the Forest Service who followed Gifford Pinchot's creed of forestry. After all, Pinchot had coined the idea of conservation back in 1907, and in his view conservation and multiple use were one and the same. Since the

Forest Service timber management of the 1960s is demonstrated here in the Lochsa's companion drainage, the North Fork of the Clearwater River.

days of Pinchot, the growth and harvest of timber had come first wherever trees could be grown in commercial quantities; other uses, such as hunting, fishing, recreation, and wildlife, were subordinate in the scheme of managing the forests, incorporated wherever possible. In other words, despite the absence of any statutorily mandated priorities, the culture of the Forest Service included an unstated but undeniable preference for managing forest lands outside of wilderness areas.

Most of us in the Forest Service at the time did not recognize any difference between the supposed intent of the Multiple Use–Sustained Yield Act and the kind of multiple use we had been practicing for a long time before the act was passed. Furthermore, the passage of the Wilderness Act left Forest Service personnel and wilderness advocates alike thinking that the wilderness issue was settled and that all that remained to be done was to reexamine and reclassify those areas already established administratively. All other national forest lands would, therefore, be available for multiple use, whatever that might turn out to be. We didn't foresee the great conflict between the Forest

This Lochsa clear-cut has produced a high yield of sawlogs, but many values other than timber are degraded or lost until a new forest is established.

Service and the citizenry over how to manage some 180 million acres of national forest land.

During the sixties the practice of clear-cutting timber was often prescribed by foresters in charge of timber sales. These cuts left large areas denuded of trees, creating a temporary wasteland exposed to the sun and inhospitable to both people and most wildlife. There were many economic and silvicultural justifications for clear-cutting, but in the aftermath benefits could seldom be shown for the other resources described in the Multiple Use–Sustained Yield Act. In fact, values other than timber were almost universally degraded, at least until the land could be reforested. Although small clear-cuts seldom detracted from the multiple resource-producing value of natural systems, the big cuts, some several hundred acres in size, caused ecological impacts of a magnitude not seen since the forests established themselves after the last ice age. (Later, in 1975, a federal appeals court held that these clear-cuts also violated the Organic Administration Act of 1897.) Large forest fires, of course, wrought similar changes. But fires left a more natural aftermath: Thousands of snags remained to shade the earth and provide hosts for the birds, insects, small mammals, and fungi needed to renew the forest. The soil was not compacted by skidding machines, nor did roads collect water and generate erosion. Ash and rotting timber released nutrients needed to sustain the productivity of the site.

The aftermath of a forest fire presents a far different environment than that left by a logged-over clear-cut.

So far as the recreation users of the western forests were concerned, it was not very important to distinguish between classified wilderness or primitive areas and those areas that remained wild simply because they had not been breached by timber sales and access roads. But once the wilderness issue was supposedly settled, wild landscapes were subjected to management, timber sale by timber sale. Forest Service timber plans and sales forged ahead of general land use plans. Many citizens, resentful of both timber harvest practices and intrusions into natural areas, became convinced that the Forest Service's definition of multiple use was synonymous with clear-cut logging and road construction. Some even coined a new term: "multiple abuse."

Aroused citizens and their elected representatives raised protests on the Bitterroot National Forest in Montana, the Monongahela in West Virginia, the Bridger in Wyoming, and in some areas of Alaska. Although widely dispersed geographically, these outcries projected a common theme: timber sale and road construction practices, especially clear-cutting and terracing, ignored and degraded other important resources of the land including much of the land's potential productivity. Said another way, multiple use, as defined by law, was not, in fact, being practiced on those national forest lands.

St. Mary Peak (distant center) provides a majestic background for the diverse landscape of Montana's Bitterroot Valley, 1952.

As public protests mounted, the Forest Service reacted by assigning in-service multidisciplinary teams to study the problems. Both citizen critics and their legislators objected that allowing the Forest Service to review its own actions was like assigning the proverbial fox to guard the chickens. And the fox's appetite for chickens (or, in this case, logs) would surely overcome any inclination to champion other basic resources. Mistrust deepened. As a result, several independent investigations probed into management practices on the national forests.

Foremost among these investigations was a study of the Bitterroot National Forest, the site of the first ranger station in the United States and situated just east of the Lochsa country. Flanked by the Bitterroot Range on the west and the Sapphire Range on the east, the Bitterroot is one of Montana's most fertile and beautiful valleys. The character and well-being of its people have for centuries been shaped by the waters, the soil, the mountains, and the forests. Living close to the land in small towns, on farms, or in rural homes scattered throughout the valley's wide floor, the people daily see the forested ridges leading from the foothills to the nearly treeless peaks of the uplands. Farmers, ranchers, lumbermen, scientists, retirees, resort operators, merchants, and a host of others have settled there because of the diversity and richness of the region's natural resources and because of the mystique of the wild country deep in the wilderness beyond the visible face of the Bitterroot Range.

History reveals that the peoples of the Bitterroot have cared deeply about their land and valued the privilege to use its resources. For example, Maj. John Owen, on April 11, 1861, wrote: "The chiefs were down and we had quite a talk. They seem quite uneasy fearing that they may be forced to remove to the Jocko reservation. They the Flatheads do not consider by the Treaty of '55 that they have disposed of the Bitter Root Valley to the U.S. They will never leave here of their own free will."[246]

And logger Ernie Townsend was reported in 1970 to have said: "Most people working in the woods feel that the Forest Service is setting the forest back 150 years. We could have gone on sustained yield and continued to have our jobs and homes and families. Now this will be gone when the trees are gone."[247]

Gordon Robinson, Forester for the Sierra Club, charged: "It is my conclusion that this tragedy of the Bitterroot will illustrate the national tragedy of our once glorious Forest Service . . . and how it abandoned multiple use as a basic principle of management."[248]

When the clear-cuts of the Forest Service began to show on the mountains, when once-stable streams peaked in spring and parched in summer, when logging roads industrialized once-pristine hunting and fishing areas, and when perceived overharvesting of timber threatened their livelihoods, the people of the valley began to question the management practices of the Bitterroot National Forest.

The consequences of logging and terracing the Bitterroot stood out in the Forest Service's Northern Region for at least two reasons. First, it is a forest of many diverse values that have to be considered in any scheme for managing land. Second, and perhaps most important, the inhabitants included many people who understood the land and its resources and who did not hesitate to remind the agency of perceived mismanagement. The Forest Service, they said, had long been a captive of the timber industry, and that's why logging was thwarting the goals of multiple use and sustained yield of all resources. Capturing Gifford Pinchot's self-described concept of management, concerned citizens of the Bitterroot called themselves "conservationists" and pressured their elected representatives to intervene.

In May 1969, Regional Forester Neal Rahm responded by appointing a task force, headed by William A. Worf, to study the management practices on the Bitterroot. The task force submitted their completed report to Rahm on April 15, 1970, and, among other findings, the team concluded:

> There is an implicit attitude among people on the staff of the Bitterroot National Forest that resource production goals come first and that land management considerations take second place.
>
> Multiple use plans on the Bitterroot National Forest must become the controlling management documents in fact as well as in principle. This will require strengthening these multiple use plans so they clearly establish the goals and direction of management on individual areas.

They went on to say: "The Bitterroot National Forest should seek better ways to involve the public in its multiple use planning and in developing subsequent resource plans."[249]

Also, in December 1969, Senator Lee Metcalf commissioned the University of Montana's School of Forestry to study Forest Service practices on the Bitterroot. In his letter to Dean of the Forestry School Arnold Bolle, Senator Metcalf said: "I am especially concerned, as are my constituents, over the long-range effects of clear-cutting, and the dominant role of timber production in Forest Service policy, to the detriment of other uses of these natural resources."

The resultant report, entitled "A University View of the Forest Service" but referred to commonly as the Bolle Report, was submitted to the U.S. Senate Committee on Interior and Insular Affairs on November 18, 1970. It had this to say about cutting timber in the Bitterroot:

> It appears inconceivable and incongruous to our Committee that at this time, with great emphasis on a broad multiple-use approach to our natural resources—especially those remaining in public ownership—that any representative group or institution in our society would advocate a dominant-use philosophy with respect to our natural resources. Yet it is our judgment that this is precisely what is occurring through the federal appropriation process, via executive order and in the Public Land Law Review Commissions Report.
>
> "Productivity" we learned time and again, meant maximum physical production of saw logs. . . . The idea that a scraggy stand of over-mature timber could and does provide other values was alien and largely absent from the thinking of most professional foresters we encountered: This in spite of their lip service to "multiple-use."
>
> If "productivity" is held to mean simply saw logs at any cost then much of what we observed was wholly rational. . . . If "productivity" includes

recreation, watershed, wildlife and aesthetic values, then much of what we saw cannot be rationalized at all.

The select committee summarized fourteen findings, including their conclusion that "multiple use management, in fact, does not exist as the governing principle on the Bitterroot National Forest."[250] Tough words, those, directed by a respected academic institution at the policies and practices of the federal agency whose personnel were considered the nation's leaders in forestry and conservation.

But the people of the Forest Service did not intend the ruination of the national forests. Nor were we captives of the industries that sought only to profit from the forest's bounty. True, the leaders of the forest industries and the foresters in charge of the land attended the same schools of forestry, belonged to the same professional organizations, and held many similar personal values. It is also true that the forestry profession monopolized the management and industrial use of forested lands in the United States. Nonetheless, forest rangers, forest supervisors, and their staffs were dedicated public servants who believed that they were doing the right things for the people and their lands. If captured by anything, we were captive to the commercial values that Pinchot and others had built into the early definitions of conservation.

By the 1960s and 1970s, the United States Congress and the people of the Bitterroot and elsewhere had accorded new meaning to the terms "multiple use" and "the greatest good of the greatest number." As is probably best and surely inevitable in a free democracy, the people were trying to lead the government, and Pinchot's brand of multiple-use conservation was becoming inadequate for managing the lands and resources of the national forests.

We of the Forest Service had been so preoccupied with use, especially commercial timber use, that even after sixty-five years of stewardship we could not specify all the values in the forest, the relationships of those values to each other, or the capabilities of different lands to sustain production of those values. We had lost much of the people's trust in our ability as stewards of national forest lands. As a result, we were in transition. Once convinced that our discretion was unchallengeable, we were beginning to realize that fundamental changes had to be made. But the ingrained Forest Service culture, which traced to Pinchot, could not easily adjust to new times. Nor did United States political policy necessarily follow the will of the people of the Bitterroot Valley. In testimony to how difficult change was to be, on January 25, 1971, President Richard Nixon directed the Forest Service to cut more timber to increase the supply of lumber and thereby slow the rising cost of building family homes.

The sixties and early seventies brought great change to all of America. Many people, young and old, turned away from materialism and back to the land whose scars showed the price we had paid, and had yet to pay, for amassing the greatest material wealth the world had ever seen. In a setting of renewed reverence for land and natural life, citizen groups across the nation proclaimed Earth Day, 1970. They celebrated, protested, cleaned up towns, and in other ways dramatized and decried poor land practices. They marched through the streets of Missoula, Montana, rallying at Forest Service Regional Headquarters, the big stone building at Spruce and Alder, which housed the offices of the regional forester and his staff. The ethics of the people toward the use of their land were changing, and it looked like we agents of government were going to have to do some changing, too.

Cattle from the Lolo Fork graze Elk Meadows in 1967.

23

Using and Misusing the Lochsa's Treasures

O***ne morning in August 1967,*** my son Bill and I drove up the middle ridge of the south branch of the Lolo Fork where Dad and I had, in earlier times, led our pack train on the way to fish at Skookum Lake. We crossed the pass into Idaho and then descended to the valley of the Brushy Fork of the Lochsa. Our car rattled up to Elk Meadows in the early morning of a clear day. The car doors thudded shut, echoing in the basin where thirty-seven years before I had awakened to the drumming of a pileated woodpecker. Steam rose from the winding stream as it had each summer morning for ages. But now cattle, not elk, grazed on the meadow, and a barnyard smell hung in air dampened by evaporating dew. A family cooked breakfast over a small fire near the camp rock. Smells of coffee and cows and summer-cured woods rode the lazy smoke of their fire down along the Brushy Fork, across the road, and into the forest. An old geological friend, the rocky crest of the Bitterroot mountains, overshadowed the meadow from the east. But the great bear, the grizzly, was gone from those mountains. And so was much of the wildness of that once-pristine landscape.

I wanted Bill to see the place where I had first crossed over the hill from the south branch of the Lolo Fork, so we hiked to the small lake at the upper end of the Brushy Fork's basin. On this trip skid trails, not moose trails, led us through the once-mysterious valley where much of the old forest had been cut and hauled to the sawmills. Where once signs of historic and prehistoric human activities could be seen in the forest, the only traces of the past were the aftermath of logging—fresh-cut stumps, debris, and broken land. Standing there in the clear-cut, it seemed to me that such logging severed all ties with the natural history of land and heralded a new era of domination by humans and machines.

After eating lunch at the lake, we climbed to the saddle where I first crossed the crest of the Bitterroots to get an expansive view of the Lochsa country. In some ways the land looked the same as it had in 1930. A breeze danced on the surface of the lake, its rippling tracks sparkling in the midday sun. From our perspective, the mountains were timeless, their familiar outlines reassuring us that the topography of the Lochsa remained unchanged.

But the foreground forest of spruce had been logged from the valley below the lake, and in the distance more clear-cuts broke the expanse of forest green. Ribbonlike roads crossed some of the clear-cuts and disappeared into forests of uncut timber; here and there plumes of dust rising above the tree tops suggested that people and machines worked busily below.

The day was hot; the woods, dry. We could see forest fires burning in the Crooked Fork basin and farther west along Warm Springs Creek. Their smoke spread out across the land, mingling with the dust from the roads. The haze deepened as the sun dropped toward the western horizon, closing off our view of details, leaving visible only the darkness of the valleys and the shape of the mountains on the skyline. Bill and I enjoyed an impressive view, to be sure. But the land harbored many secrets obscured by the haze and the dust or hidden behind ridges and submerged in the swamp of history already made or then in the making.

Logging and road building in the Lochsa had received far less scrutiny by local citizens than in the Bitterroot, the Monongahela, or the Bridger National Forests. We have already seen in chapter 18 that the national forests of the Lochsa include all lands except approximately forty-two thousand acres of railroad grant lands. These national forests belong to all the people of the United States. Yet local populations depend upon them for livelihood, economy, recreation, and quality of life. Because of their localized sense of ownership, these people usually speak first and loudest to protect or use the land. The people of Montana enjoyed the best access. But, until the Lewis and Clark Highway was finished, it had been a long way around or through the mountains for the people of Idaho to get to the upper Lochsa and observe what was going on in "their" forests.

Nonetheless, a few defenders of the Lochsa had long been at work from the western gateway at Kooskia, Idaho, and the several gateways

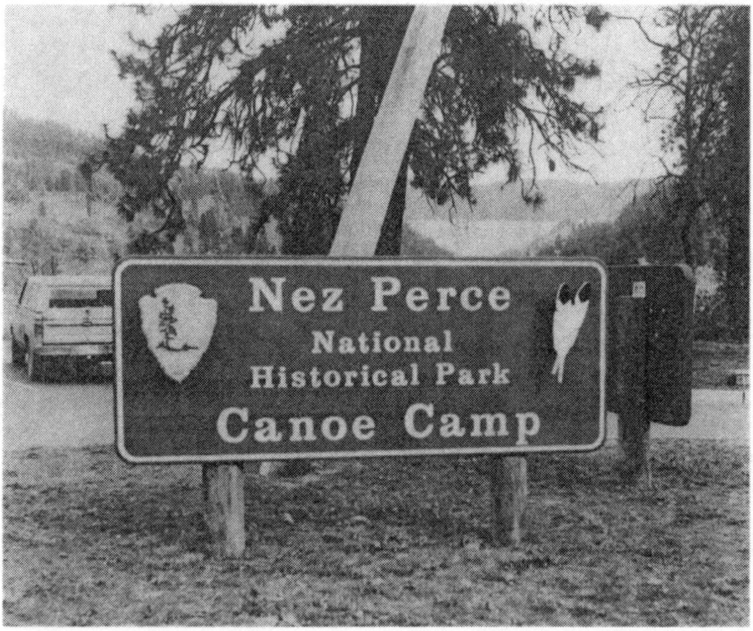

When Lewis and Clark built canoes here, the Clearwater River hosted numerous anadromous fish, but their access to hundreds of miles of spawning streams up the North Fork was eliminated by construction of the Dworshak Dam, shown in the background.

to the Lochsa from Montana. One of the earliest threats to the land and resources came during the early fifties when the U.S. Army Corps of Engineers proposed to construct dams on both the North and Middle Forks of the Clearwater River. As discussed earlier, the stated benefits of those high dams were to control floods, generate power, and provide water-based transportation for hauling logs. But they would also stop upstream migration of salmon and steelhead to spawning grounds, inundate thousands of acres of winter range needed by big game, and destroy water-related recreation on many miles of rivers and streams. Most distressing, the reservoirs behind the proposed dams would forever change the character of the land, which many people valued as it was. The reaction of citizen conservationist and engineer Mort Brigham of Lewiston, Idaho, was typical: "I could never see how we could have a major impoundment or a highway along the North Fork or the Lochsa and still have wildlife."[251]

People from Montana and elsewhere joined with Idaho conservationists to protest the inevitable loss of the public lands' natural values, and they stalled the construction of dams for five years. But in the end

Governors Tim Babcock, of Montana, and Robert Smylie, of Idaho, saw a log to begin the ceremony at Lolo Pass, officially opening the Lewis and Clark Highway in 1962. —U.S. Forest Service

the corps built the giant Dworshak Dam, which impounded some fifty miles of the Clearwater's North Fork and thus eliminated sea-run fish from the upstream river and hundreds of miles of tributary spawning streams. To offset the loss of spawning grounds for steelhead and salmon, the corps built a hatchery—claimed to be the largest of its kind in the world—on the Clearwater River below the dam. In the conservationists' view, however, the hatchery was a mere consolation prize; the dam builders had won, and destroyed, the free-flowing North Fork. The conservationists were successful in thwarting plans to dam the Clearwater River at Penny Cliffs. That reservoir would have flooded portions of both the Lochsa and Selway Rivers, backing water deep into the Selway-Bitterroot Wilderness and inundating Selway Falls.

The long-delayed hookup of the east and west links of the Lewis and Clark Highway brought mixed blessings to the Lochsa. Construction contractors, working upriver from Kooskia and downstream from the Powell Ranger Station, connected the highway in 1960 and completed paving its surface in 1962. People and organizations in villages and cities along the route rejoiced, heralding the opportunities for economic growth created by the new road across the mountains. In recognition of the contributions of people and industries from both states, a dedication celebration was held on the Montana-Idaho border at Lolo Pass. In a special edition commemorating the highway, the *Lewiston Morning Tribune* reported:

> It took almost a hundred years to do it, but the Lewis and Clark Highway has been completed at last. Blasting powder and jack hammers have breached the Black Canyon of the Lochsa, where William Clark and Meriwether Lewis tried in vain to find a passage west. Under the shoulders of ridges trod by Indian ponies, modern engineering has laid down one of the finest scenic highways in the nation. The construction of some sections of the highway was hazardous and difficult, but actual construction was only part of what was needed to get the highway built; it also required the patient labors of a great many men and women who had never tamped a charge of powder or handled a drill. These were the people who contributed years of persuasion, pulled many a political string, and camped on the doorstep of the Bureau of Public Roads. After many years and many disappointments, they prevailed.[252]

After being scouted but rejected by Capt. John Mullan, then surveyed but never built by competing railroads, the Nez Perce's Road to the Buffalo was (following some construction in 1866 by Wellington Bird), at last, replaced by a modern highway. The destruction of obstacles by blasting powder and machines was touted as a conquest of man over nature. "Big game herds abound," the promoters said, and travelers could now get to the wilderness more easily. The Clearwater National Forest reminded the newcomers that the resource treasures made available by the highway were "water, timber, range land, wildlife and recreation." "Timber," a forest spokesman said, "remains the greatest commercial asset" to be had from the Lochsa's land. He went on to say, as so many had said so often in the past, "But, by and large, an adequate road system is today still the greatest single need of the forest outside the primitive area."[253]

A group of merchants from Lewiston, Idaho, sponsored a page in the newspaper. Their message included the following:

> Progress is a vital part of our American way of life. From the sailboat and covered wagon to the moon rocket, progress has constantly accelerated. We move forward at unprecedented speed into an era that seems to place no limit on the scope of man's achievement. The final development of the link between two great states, Montana and Idaho, certainly is an accomplishment of which the Lewiston merchants are proud."

The First Security Bank of Lewiston, Idaho, said:

> This great land, rich in minerals, timber, wildlife, beef and wheat is awakening to the thunder of new growth. The final completion of the Lewis-Clark Highway opens an artery of transportation bringing producer and consumer closer in miles and minutes.
>
> Development in the near future of our waterways will be the final step in this era of progress.[254]

At the dedication nothing was said about the limits of the land's capacity to host this accelerated invasion or the need for restraint in removing the Lochsa's natural resources. The road was a success; its promoters had achieved their dream. But there was another, less prevalent point of view.

Looking back on it from a perspective in the 1980s, Mort Brigham said:

> That road wrecked the best fishin' holes up along that river. The history of road building on the Lochsa is a history of failure to protect wildlife as far as I'm concerned and as far as the Lochsa is concerned. I got to Elk Summit after they got the highway done. It's too beautiful an area. White Sand Creek is a gem of nature.[255]

Completion of the Lewis and Clark Highway meant that big truck engines would soon echo in the canyons where, but a few years before, only the creak of trappers' snowshoes and the howl of coyotes had broken the silence of wildness. Produce could now be hauled from Montana across the mountains to water transportation at Lewiston, Idaho. Great stands of timber could be cut from the Lochsa's basins, and people could drive quickly and close to the fishing holes and the sanctuaries of deer, elk, bear, and moose. The road unleashed another wave of "progress" to smite the land, but it also opened the way for an army of pilgrims who would fight to protect the Lochsa country's spirit of place.

As we have already seen, the early sixties found the Forest Service proposing to reclassify the Selway-Bitterroot Primitive Area to wilderness status in order to give it better protection under regulation U-2. Some acreage was to be added, much deleted. The Forest Service proposed several small additions in the Lochsa region, but it also recommended that the boundary be moved south from the Lochsa River to the crest of the ridges, thus placing the new highway out of sight from

Part of the "Lochsa Face" as seen from the Lochsa Lodge in 1995.

the wilderness, making more land in the canyon available for access roads and campgrounds, and releasing from wilderness constraints the management of big game winter range. Furthermore, some of Major Kelley's truck trails (discussed in chapter 12) had disqualified for wilderness a portion of the area south of Powell Ranger Station. Known as the "Lochsa Face," this proposed exclusion drew support from lumbermen and opposition from conservationists.

To assess the concerns of the public, the Forest Service held hearings in Lewiston, Idaho; Grangeville, Idaho; and Missoula, Montana. Other than a joint memorial passed by the Idaho legislature, opposing designation of any more wilderness in Idaho, few or no objections to the proposed reclassification, in concept, were heard at the hearings. Lumbermen, miners, road builders, and individual and organized conservationists alike could support, or at least tolerate, a wilderness of some kind or another. Hearing participants displayed considerable differences of opinion, however, on the questions of how big and where the wilderness ought to be.

Much of the discussion centered on a large exclusion from wilderness consideration known as the Magruder Corridor. Its purpose was to allow timber harvest and other multiple use activities in the Selway drainage south of the Lochsa country. In a statement typical of the lumber industries' point of view, Ed Shults, manager of Tree Farmers, Inc., said:

> The logical route for the removal of the timber from Area E (Magruder Corridor) is down the Selway River. This route would develop a large area of commercial forest land with some recreational but very little wilderness area value. The area of commercial forest land along this corridor would be approximately a quarter of a million acres. This commercial forest land is critical to local and national economics and should not be included in the wilderness area.

In contrast, the testimony of Guy M. Brandborg, retired supervisor of the Bitterroot National Forest, typified the views of citizen conservationists:

> The large exclusion of 310,000 acres . . . in the upper Selway River Basin should be avoided at all cost. . . . The proposal for exclusion of 71,000 acres of the Lochsa Face should be reconsidered because of the great value this area would have as a buffer for wilderness to the south. . . . For the present, at least, we should preserve this area in its entirety, with only minor adjustments in boundaries.

Two old friends of the mountains and creators of "Lapland," trappers Charley Powell and Earl Malone, spoke in favor of wilderness. Referring to a statement made by the president of the United States, Charley ended his testimony: "Let's not tear down that fence until we know what it was put there for."[256]

Secretary of Agriculture Orville L. Freeman rendered his decision after hearing all the testimony. "Since timber harvesting or the development of roadside recreation is incompatible with wilderness," he stated,

> a multiple use decision of major importance is here involved. In this case it has been decided on the basis of all available facts that wilderness is the predominant public value in some 1.212 million acres designated as the Selway-Bitterroot Wilderness plus some 28,000 acres adjacent to it and that other resource utilization not compatible with wilderness must give way. On the other hand, as to those areas not included in the Selway-Bitterroot Wilderness, it has been decided that other resources are more important than the wilderness resource.[257]

The Forest Service had proposed, the people had had their say, and the secretary of agriculture had decided the destiny of much of the Bitterroot Mountains. Over 28,000 acres of new land were added and 446,906 acres subtracted to create a new wilderness of 1,239,840 acres.

Subtractions included the Lochsa Face and the Magruder Corridor. But strong citizen protest, backed by a committee of scientists appointed by the secretary of agriculture, subsequently caused the Forest Service to withdraw plans to build roads and log in the Magruder Corridor. Furthermore, in one of the first formal recognitions of priority among natural resources, part of the Lochsa Face was designated by the secretary for management on a "recreation key value" basis. The secretary left the Elk Summit area open for commercial exploitation of resources, but time would show that many people remained unwilling to submit that land to the road or saw.[258]

Mort Brigham described the outcome thus: "The biggest fight we had was in the upper Selway. There wasn't time to concentrate on everything. We lost the Lochsa Face and lost Elk Summit. But we won in the Selway. Doris Milner's the gal that saved the Selway."[259] (Doris Milner chaired the Save-the-Selway citizens group. She continued working on similar causes and was later recognized as a national leader in natural resource conservation.)

By excluding the Lochsa Face and the Elk Summit area from the wilderness, the allowable timber cut on federal lands in the Powell district could be increased from thirteen or fourteen million to twenty-four mil-

Bud Moore cooking breakfast somewhere in the Selway-Bitterroot Wilderness.

Where rangers Bell and Mackay crossed by primitive ferry in 1922, the Crooked and White Sand Forks of the Lochsa are now spanned by two steel and concrete bridges built primarily to haul timber from the Lochsa Face and Elk Summit areas.

lion board feet per year. Thus, we now had a wilderness instead of a mere primitive area and an additional ten million board feet of timber harvestable annually from the forested slopes at the upper end of the Lochsa (see map 12).

During the late sixties the Forest Service built two concrete and steel bridges to serve roads leading into this new timber. One bridge spanned the Crooked Fork and the other spanned the Lochsa River; both were near the spot where rangers Bell and Mackay had rafted their men, mules, and cargo across the high water of 1922. These big, permanent bridges demonstrated that engineering of stream crossings had advanced a great deal since Joe Alkire had tossed his dog in the water to test the speed of the Lochsa's current. Timber from several tributaries of White Sand Creek would be hauled across the new Crooked Fork bridge. A main-haul road using the bridge across the Lochsa was intended to lead loggers and trucks to the pristine Elk Summit basin, which had been opened in 1934 to automobiles and light trucks by twenty miles of Major Kelley's truck trails.

Elk Summit's landscapes, however, were better suited as a setting for the trails of elk, moose, and other wildlife. The gouging of main-haul roads into the mountainsides threatened the stability of the land. Even Major Kelley's energetic builders of truck trails had had difficulty making their way to Elk Summit by road. Always in a hurry, the bulldozers dug

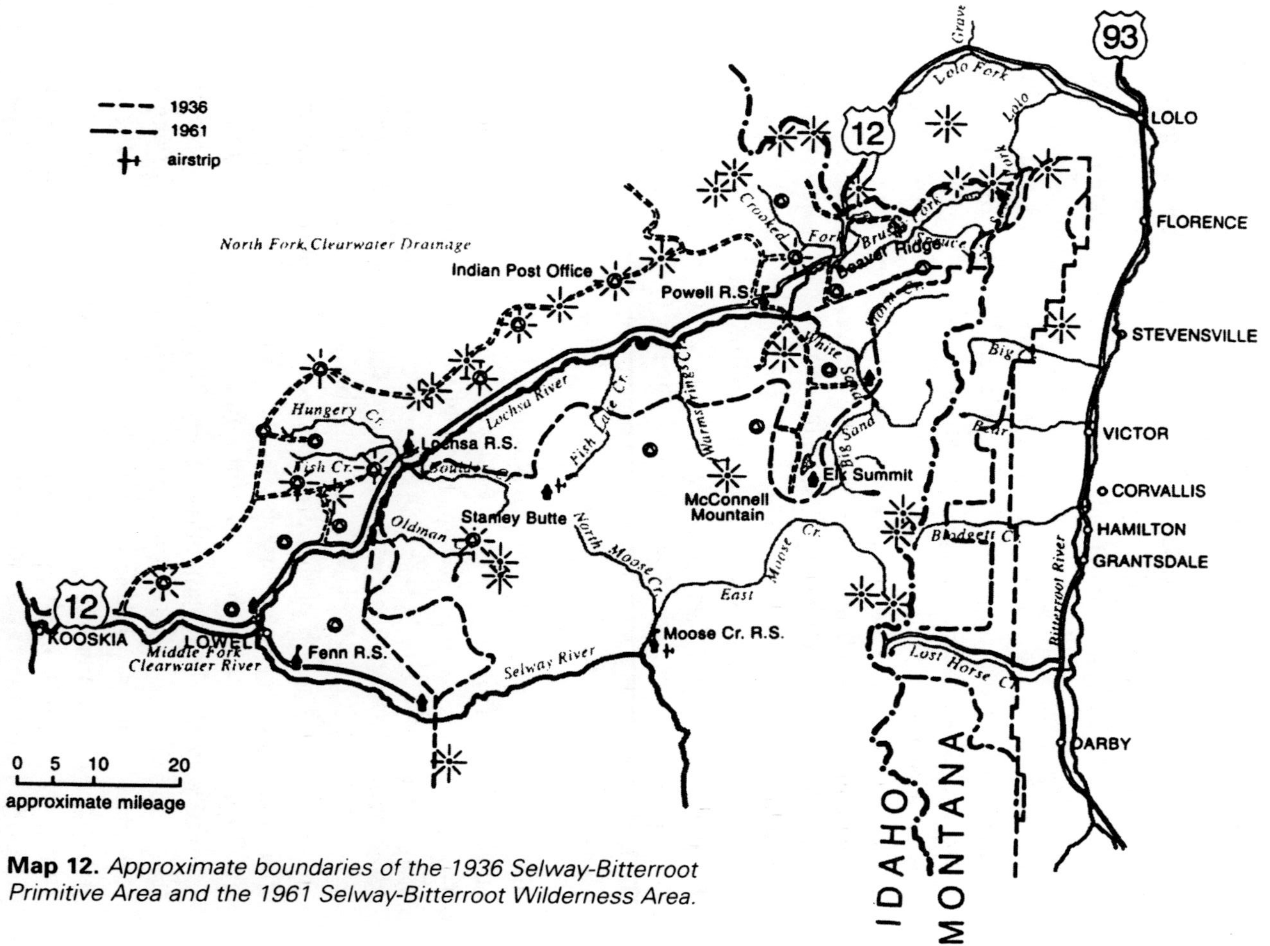

Map 12. *Approximate boundaries of the 1936 Selway-Bitterroot Primitive Area and the 1961 Selway-Bitterroot Wilderness Area.*

close on the heels of the early-day road locators. About halfway between the Lochsa River and Savage Pass, Kelley's crews built a mile of road out onto a spur ridge before realizing that they were lost in the Lochsa's woods. This mistake wasted dollars and time and unnecessarily damaged the environment. The people of the Powell district had appropriately named the mistake the "engineering crime."

The locators of the new road leading from the concrete bridge on the Lochsa toward Elk Summit also committed a crime of road misplacement on the same mountainside where the truck-trail builders had lost their way more than thirty years before. This time the dozer operators followed the stakes of the locators, but their bigger bulldozers dug a far wider road through the forests that held the steep slope in place. It looked for a time like the heavy hand of the machine age would extend highway-grade roads into the largest area in the upper Lochsa left unprotected by wilderness designation. But when spring snowmelt soaked the severed earth, the mountainside slid down and blocked the new road, leaving no apparent way to stabilize the massive movement of soil. The hydrology and geology of the Lochsa's mountains had, for at least awhile, foreclosed the plan to cut the forests of Elk Summit and haul the logs to the mills beyond the mountains.

By the 1970s the Lochsa had become truly a land of many uses, including an impressive share of abuses inflicted by man. Wilderness had been designated, and the persistent quest for road access largely achieved. The frontiers of geographical discovery and initial exploitation behind us, we were deeply involved in harvesting the resources. The workings of the Forest Service's aging bureaucracy increasingly drew rangers away from the land to spend time in the office, governing their districts through plans, programs, budgets, and the direction of subordinates. The job of the forest ranger had become more complex than the job of forest supervisor had been in the fifties.

From our vista on the crest of the Bitterroot mountains, Bill and I viewed a land whose capability to produce valuable resources had changed very little since its discovery by Europeans. But human perception of what is valuable had changed a great deal during the same period. Already the Lochsa's resources had been reassessed several times in response to the expanding demands of the United States' burgeoning population. Though they seemed not to know it, the people's consumption had reached, perhaps even surpassed, what that portion of the earth could sustain.

A dozer trail crosses the big dirt slide that buried the new Elk Summit road in the late 1960s.

In the Lochsa, and perhaps elsewhere, too many of us were taking too much from the land too fast. Many people worried about the degradation of wildlife habitat and the destructive methods of cutting forests. Evolution in the Lochsa had created a balanced community of organisms dependent on the land's natural processes. But logging and road building showed too little consideration for the web of life and physical conditions needed to perpetuate the forest. The "greatest good of the greatest number in the long run" looked in the woods like maximum timber production in the short run.[260]

As we have seen, the people spoke out. And their outcry moved Congress to pass new laws that for the first time since 1897 placed substantial constraints on the management of the national forests by the Forest Service. We have already seen that the Wilderness Act of 1964 provided statutory basis for protecting wild country and that the Multiple Use–Sustained Yield Act cemented the existing discretion of the Forest Service to give equal consideration to all resources. In addition, the National Environmental Policy Act of 1969 (NEPA) established a national goal of environmental protection and required an environmental impact statement with public involvement for major federal agency decisions. In practice, it operated as a quality control device for Forest Service operations. The Endangered Species Act of 1973 imposed constraints on all land use decisions that might adversely affect the habitat of any threatened or endangered species of wildlife. The Forest and Rangeland Renewable Resources Planning Act of 1974 (RPA) required the Forest Service to:

1. prepare an assessment every ten years describing the renewable resources of all the nation's forest and range lands;
2. prepare a program every five years proposing long-range objectives, with a planning horizon of at least forty-five years, for all Forest Service activities;
3. prepare an annual report evaluating Forest Service activities according to the objectives proposed in the program.

The National Forest Management Act of 1976 expanded the RPA's directive by requiring the agency to prepare local land and resource management plans. The act imposed limitations on timber harvesting, including clear-cutting; and subsequent regulations issued by the agency set forth planning requirements for each resource. The act established the national forest as the basic unit for planning purposes.[261]

Prompted by citizen criticism of Forest Service timber harvesting practices on the Bitterroot National Forest, the Monongahela National Forest in West Virginia, the Bridger National Forest in Wyoming, and elsewhere (see chapter 22), the National Forest Management Act in particular set new direction for managing lands throughout the national forest system, including those in the Lochsa.

But the presence of new laws doesn't guarantee change in a self-reliant culture like that of the Forest Service. Nor can the momentum of ongoing programs that entwine personal dreams, family livelihoods, industrial ambitions, institutional power, professional commitment, and land ethics be redirected by memorandum. It takes tolerance and co-operation by stakeholders both in and out of government to do that. And it takes time. Only time would tell whether the new legislative mandates would lead to a better shake for the public, or for the land.

24

Ending the Illusion of Superabundance

The staff of the Clearwater National Forest responded to the Forest and Rangeland Renewable Resources Planning Act of 1974 and the National Forest Management Act of 1976 by preparing a new plan for managing the forest. They began work in 1980 and finished in 1987. The stated purpose of the plan was to guide all natural resource management activities and establish management standards for the next ten to fifteen years.[262] Although appealed by diverse public interests, this plan deserves both credit and responsibility for much of the Lochsa's land stewardship record since the plan was prepared. No plan, however, can fully encompass the historical evolution of a place like the Lochsa. What has happened on the Lochsa, then, was directed partly by the plan, partly by the momentum of past practices, and largely by the convictions of dedicated land managers and interested citizens working on the ground, in the courts, and in the political arena. This modern era is a fascinating one, distinguished by citizen appeals of proposed Forest Service actions that led to extensive interpretation by the courts of the environmental and land laws passed during the 1960s and 1970s.

The forest plan divides the Lochsa's landscapes into sixteen different types for management purposes. Each type is displayed on a map and described; overall goals are established, and specific goals and standards are set for each resource available within the type.[263] In this regard, the plan is too detailed to be useful here for describing the contemporary land-management situation in the Lochsa. However, I have clustered the plan's diverse types into geographic categories for describing the situation in the Lochsa in 1994. This categorization, more useful for our purposes, is as follows: (1) wilderness and potential wilderness,

The Hungery Creek watershed, shown here from right center to upper left, includes the only remaining undeveloped section of Lewis and Clark's route through the Lochsa country.

(2) the Lolo Trail corridor, (3) the Lewis and Clark Highway/Lochsa Wild and Scenic River corridor, and (4) general forest lands, that is, lands hosting a wider variety of resources and uses. Each category and its current management situation are described below (see also map 13).

1. Wilderness and Potential Wilderness

The Clearwater forest's share (259,165 acres) of the Selway-Bitterroot Wilderness forms most of the south and east boundaries of the land of the Lochsa. The forest plan recommends adding 18,500 acres to this wilderness area, plus 23,680 acres in the headwaters of the Crooked Fork as part of the proposed Great Burn Wilderness. The status of wilderness and roadless areas in Idaho, as of December 31, 1992, is explained in Report No. 10 of the Idaho Forest, Wildlife, and Range Policy Analysis Group. A more recent wilderness bill by former Idaho congressman Larry LaRocco would increase the Selway-Bitterroot addition to 38,000 acres and establish a new Lewis and Clark Wilderness of 43,000 acres in the Hungery and Fish Creek tributaries of the Lochsa. These drainages contain the only remaining undeveloped section of the Lewis and Clark Trail.[264]

The wilderness rangers taking care of these areas apply unobtrusive, light-on-the-land stewardship intended to protect the land's natural conditions and minimize intrusion into the freedom of visitors who seek recreation in the solitude of the wilderness. The rangers respect the integrity of that wild land. Their commitment reminds me of early-day

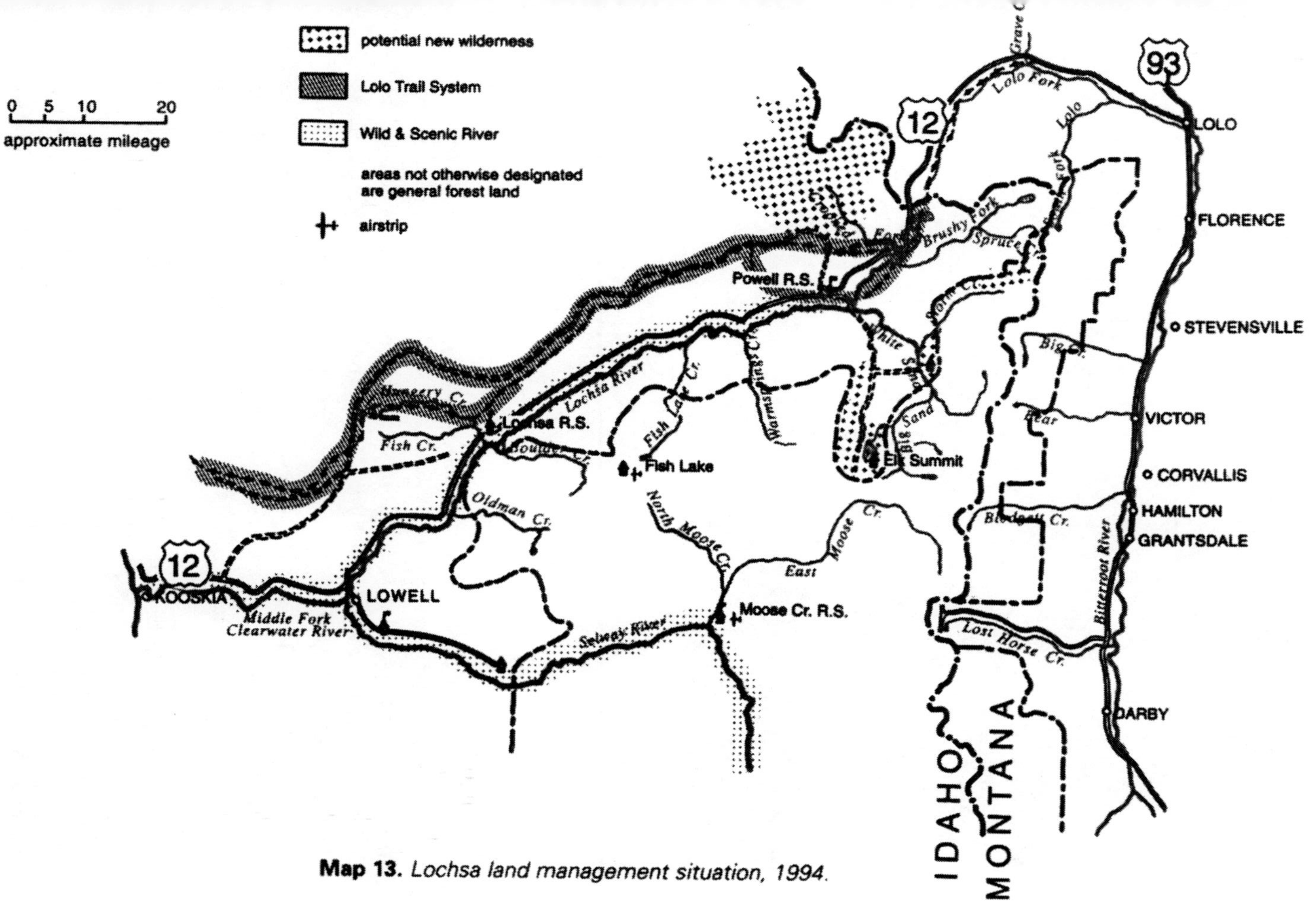

potential new wilderness
Lolo Trail System
Wild & Scenic River
areas not otherwise designated are general forest land
airstrip
0 5 10 20
approximate mileage
93
12
12
LOLO
FLORENCE
STEVENSVILLE
VICTOR
CORVALLIS
HAMILTON
GRANTSDALE
DARBY
Powell R.S.
Fish Lake
Elk Summit
Moose Cr. R.S.
LOWELL
KOOSKIA
Middle Fork Clearwater River
Selway River
Lochsa River
Fish Cr.
Oldman Cr.
North Moose Cr.
East Moose Cr.
Lost Horse Cr.
Bitterroot River
Lolo Fork
Brushy Fork
Spruce Cr.
Big Sand
IDAHO
MONTANA

Map 13. *Lochsa land management situation, 1994.*

The awesome force of free nature at work as seen from Diablo Mountain. An uncontrolled fire burns in the wilderness. —Dennis Elliott

ranger Bill Bell, who so loved the country that he couldn't understand why anyone would want to leave the mountains and go to town for any reason except an emergency. Take wilderness ranger Pete Kola, for example, who was enjoying his weekend somewhere in the wilds of the upper Big Sand when I visited Elk Summit in 1982. That weekend, I also found ranger Gary Oye, who, with the help of a government mule, was packing wire out of the wilderness from an abandoned telephone line that once provided communication to Maple Lake Lookout. Gary and others were clearing the signs of mankind from some of America's finest wild places. They also were rediscovering the old trails, traces of cabins, and similar artifacts, so that they could pass on the history of the land and its people to those who came to explore the wilderness.

Because solitude is among the rare treasures of the wilderness, the rangers try not to intrude on the privacy of wilderness users. Instead of controlling people or their activities, they strive to educate people in how to use the wilderness without damaging its natural values. The premise is that the more people understand and respect the wilderness, the more likely they are to take care of the land. If the strategy succeeds, the rangers are actually left with less work to do. Referring to the Elk

Summit Ranger Station, Gary put it this way: "I'd like to see the station stay right here and the wilderness to become an area we didn't have to do much with."[265] Unlike the early-day rangers who carried instructions from Washington, D.C., in their *Use Book*, wilderness rangers had little supervisory instructions in 1982. They were feeling their way, pioneering new concepts of land stewardship.

The wilderness rangers had also made a truce with fire, once the common enemy of all who worked for the Forest Service. The wilderness is to be a natural place, the rangers said. It follows that extinguishing all fires in the forest, which is a most unnatural condition, is contrary to the wilderness laws of the land. Consequently, after studying the topography and fuels, the rangers were allowing lightning fires to burn so long as they did not threaten human safety or develop the potential to escape from the wilderness and damage resources outside.

Gary Oye offered an example of this policy put into practice. He observed two fires in 1981: one burned several hundred acres of old forests between Big Sand Lake and Blodgett Pass; the other consumed a block of old forest in Hidden Creek. Of the latter fire, he said, "That thing was not a slow, creeping fire. When I went up to Hidden Peak it was just amazing. There was a great mushroom cloud of smoke over Hidden Creek. The sun was yellow on the land. It was great to see that natural thing take its course."[266] Returning natural fires to wilderness takes knowledge and guts. Gary and other men and women of the Forest Service were pioneering a venture as exciting as the work of those who, in earlier times, had tried to banish fire from the forests.

The thousands of acres of ghostlike snags left in the wake of the great burns since 1910 have since been replaced by vigorous forests, and random fires each summer continue to create the diverse landscapes needed to keep the wilderness healthy and whole. And the Lochsa's wilderness is nearly whole and people are a natural part of that whole. Yet the absence of grizzly bears and wolves leaves an unnatural gap in an otherwise near-natural place.

Restoring grizzlies to the wilderness is a controversial idea. According to Clearwater Forest supervisor Jim Caswell: "There's overwhelming response against reintroduction of grizzlies." Yet there is also considerable support. Twenty-six-year veteran of Nez Perce tribal government Allen Slickpoo, Sr., puts it this way: "Our people coexisted with grizzlies years ago. And I don't think it would be much of a problem existing with them today." Timber-related industries in the Clearwater

Reintroduced in central Idaho in January 1995, wolves will likely soon return to their natural role in the wilds of the Lochsa. —Stephen J. Krasemann

area also support bear introduction, but only if it is in the Selway-Bitterroot Wilderness. Dan Johnson of Resource Organization on Timber Supply explains his group's position in support of reintroducing the bears: "We're breaking new ground. We don't want the bear, but we know it's coming so we'll take the lead." Johnson's organization has worked with other groups on a plan to handle the bears if they leave the wilderness. Though there is some disagreement on this, studies have shown that if the grizzlies return, the wilderness can support them. A recovery plan is now under consideration by the Interagency Grizzly Bear Committee. Former acting Clearwater Forest supervisor Orville Daniels adds: "The grizzly is a national treasure, which means it will take priority over things that are not national treasures."[267]

Like the grizzly, wolves are also protected by the federal Endangered Species Act of 1973. Whereas grizzlies in the Rocky Mountains are listed as threatened, wolves in the northern Rocky Mountains are endangered. There is no recent evidence of wolves breeding in Idaho.[268] But unverified sightings since 1967 suggest that lone wolves occasionally pass through or near the Lochsa's wilderness.[269] And in about 1992 one radio-collared wolf from a northern Montana pack was located in the vicinity of Lolo Pass.

The Endangered Species Act, as amended, requires federal agencies to try to establish viable populations of wolves in the area unless they met certain exceptions in the act. Accordingly, during January 1995, the U.S. Fish and Wildlife Service in cooperation with the Idaho Fish and Game Department, land management agencies, and the public, introduced an experimental population in central Idaho. Four wolves captured near Hinton, Alberta, were released near Corn Creek on the Salmon River; eleven, in the vicinity of Indian and Thomas Creeks on the Middle Fork of the Salmon.

Although present, some of the other life forms that are part of the natural system of the wilderness are troubled. Anadromous fish, in particular, are declining. The summer runs of chinook salmon have been declared an endangered species. Still, those few that succeed in negotiating the network of downstream dams to reach the gravel bars of the wilderness streams can spawn in an environment little changed since Euro-Americans reached the Lochsa's headwaters.[270]

Several factors have contributed to a wilderness that is in many ways wilder now than it was, say, sixty years ago. Fire has been restored to a more nearly natural role; many trails built for fire protection have been abandoned; several administrative cabins and fire lookouts have been destroyed (let's keep one or two for historical purposes); phone lines have been discontinued; commercial grazing eliminated; old garbage dumps cleaned up; and a pack-in–pack-out trash policy implemented. The main task now, which requires concerted effort both within and outside wilderness, is to restore the missing links that degrade the wilderness's wholeness. Still, the wilderness rangers, often in partnership with wilderness users, work hard to prevent or restore land degradation caused by human use, most of which shows in overused camping areas, substandard trails, overgrazing by pack and saddle stock, and invasion of exotic plants and grasses.[271]

2. The Lolo Trail Corridor

Somewhat like the Selway-Bitterroot Wilderness to the south, the Lolo Trail corridor straddles the northern edge of the Lochsa watershed. Its historical significance has long been recognized, but attention in the past twenty years has grown from persistent interest by a few individuals to high-priority consideration by management agencies and historical organizations. The Clearwater Forest Plan designates for management purposes a corridor approximately one-half mile wide (a quarter of a mile on either side), which encompasses the historic Lolo Trail System. The system consists of the Lolo Trail, Nee-me-poo Trail, Nez Perce National Historic Trail, Lewis and Clark National Historic Trail, Bird-Traux Wagon Road, and Lolo motorway. Designated sites within the Nez Perce National Historic Park are also included.[272] These historic routes through the mountains, along or near the Nez Perce Road to the Buffalo, collectively constitute an area of uncommon interest and a major management challenge for the Clearwater Forest and the Lochsa's rangers.

The current objective is to study the corridor to determine what's there. Then, with a good inventory in hand, forest staff will prepare a detailed plan for protecting, using, and managing the system's resources. Within the corridor, a variety of relics testify to the ancient and historical use by people. Examples include old traplines and associated cabins, early-day Forest Service structures and phone lines, Indian ceremonial locations and campsites, and historical trails branching off to fisheries on the river, to the Blacklead Mining District, and to Indian camping and hunting sites along the Montana-Idaho divide to the north. The searches necessary to compile such an inventory have brought diverse people together in a common effort to understand and preserve their shared history.

This long-dead lodgepole pine was scarred by historic travelers who removed the cambium and fed it to their pack and saddle stock.

Bud Moore hiking the Lolo Trail near Lost Lakes junction, ca. 1975.

The Nez Perce Tribe has been an active participant in the process. Tribal Council member Allen Pinkham explains his concern: "There are a lot of sites up there that haven't been found. Forest Service biologists are tied in with us. We want the tribe involved in any archaeological sites." Allen Slickpoo adds, "The tribe is now concerned about potential development resulting from recent congressional designation of the Nez Perce National Historic Trail. That could cause a lot of impact." Long-time Lochsa district ranger Jon Bledsoe values the friendship generated by working with the tribes: "Working with the Nez Perce on the Lolo Trail has been an enjoyable and fulfilling part of my life."[273]

Bypassed by the Lewis and Clark Highway, itself a major corridor, the Lolo Trail System is no longer needed as a Road to the Buffalo or as a road to the salmon in the upper Lochsa. Yet these trails are part of the national heritage of all Americans. They were once significant transportation links both regionally and nationally, and they still offer a connection between the past and the present. As mentioned above, the corridor also includes the last remaining undeveloped section of the Lewis and Clark Trail, which is being considered for wilderness designation. And commercial outfitters already operate summertime tours of the corridor for tourists. Treasured by many for many reasons, the Lolo Trail System now seems to be getting the considerate management it deserves.

Lochsa district ranger Jon Bledsoe and his wife, Hergart, pose at the Lochsa Historical Ranger Station in 1992. —Jon Bledsoe

The Lochsa River (left) joins the Selway River (right) to form the Middle Fork of the Clearwater River at Lowell, Idaho.

Historic Forest Service buildings were moved to Lolo Pass to create this modern information center.

3. The Lewis and Clark Highway/ Lochsa Wild and Scenic River Corridor

Taken together, the Lewis and Clark Highway and the Lochsa Wild and Scenic River create another corridor of national significance crossing near the heart of the land of the Lochsa.[274] The highway enters Idaho from Montana at Lolo Pass and follows the Crooked Fork drainage to the vicinity of Powell Ranger Station. From there it parallels the designated wild and scenic portion of the Lochsa River westward sixty-five miles to Lowell, Idaho, where the Lochsa joins the Selway River to form the Middle Fork of the Clearwater. It is within the Lochsa's canyon that the highway and its traffic, a long-sought achievement for the purpose of commerce, coexist with the natural river. Federal law protects the river's free-flowing conditions and immediate environs for the benefit and enjoyment of future generations.

The scenic corridor from Powell Ranger Station to Lowell displays some of the Lochsa's most pristine lands, outside of the Selway-Bitterroot Wilderness Area or lands being considered for wilderness classification. Visitor facilities include a rustic information center at Lolo Pass where exhibits and representatives of the Forest Service explain historical and contemporary highlights of the Lochsa country. Each of the several major campgrounds in the corridor is supervised by a volunteer host who greets visitors and provides information in an unobtrusive way. George Colgate is honored with a historical site and nature

Construction of the Lewis and Clark Highway in the early 1960s destroyed part of the cedar grove where Colgate's ill-fated raft voyage began. Work has begun on the historical memorial and nature trail. —U.S. Forest Service

trail near his grave. And the giant trees unofficially known as the Big Cedar Grove along the Crooked Fork is now a memorial dedicated to Bernard DeVoto, who chose the streamside shaded by those cedars as one of his favorite places to think and write. Its once-bustling activities relocated to a new headquarters in Kooskia, the old Lochsa Ranger Station has been converted to a historical museum, displaying the early-day equipment and activities of the Forest Service. Public services—gas, meals, and lodging—are available at the Lochsa Lodge near Powell Ranger Station and at the villages of Syringa and Lowell near the confluence of the Lochsa and Selway Rivers.

The highway's roadside scenery has been well protected over the years, but the results of extensive logging can now be seen on intermediate and distant mountainsides. Such views are inevitable, as land managers and loggers harvest the timber from lands devoted entirely or in part to the production of commercial wood products. If these harvests are sustainable, as the law defines that term, and if they will assure the continued wholeness of the land without permanent adverse impacts on adjacent landscapes or connecting links between landscapes,

A vigorous forest now obscures the Lochsa Historical Ranger Station where in 1934 some 250 men fought to save the station and their lives from fire.

then these logged-over areas should be seen not as destruction of the scenery but as examples of a positive interaction of people with nature. I applaud the new display at the Lolo Pass Visitor Information Center, which attempts to educate visitors concerning this perspective.

The Forest Service message at the center now contains three parts: Early Days, The Fire Years, and The Present. Here's how it describes the present:

> The completion of the Lewis and Clark Highway over Lolo Pass in 1962 achieved what the old trail could not, it provided an all-weather route across the Bitterroot Mountains with good access. The Forest Service job has changed once again, from simply protecting the forests, to managing the wise use of rich natural resources.
>
> Old fire trails now provide recreation access and new roads sprout from the Highway to rich timber in the hidden drainages of the Lochsa. The vast expanse of Wilderness in the Bitterroot Mountains has become a place reserved for escape and spiritual recovery, rather than a fearsome impediment to man's endeavours.

Although I find it impossible to think of wilderness as ever being fearful, or of the fire years as being simple, I like this statement because,

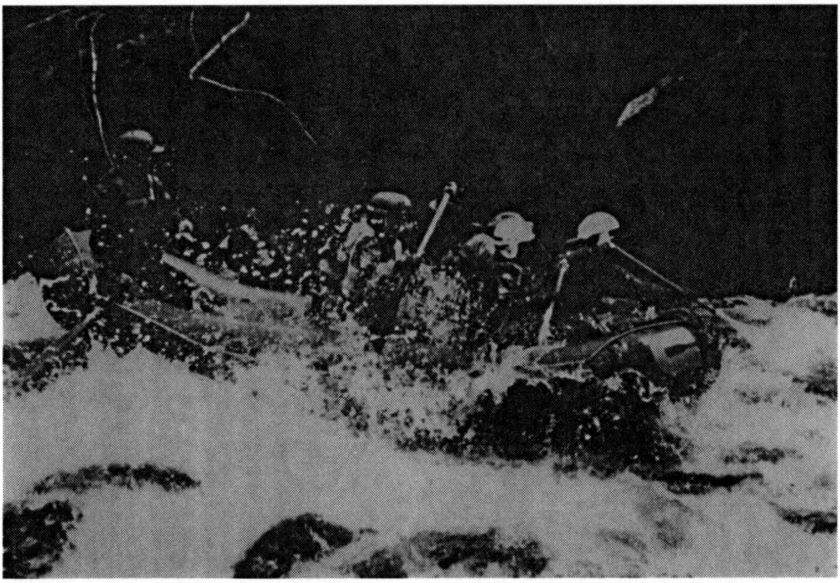

These rafters revel in the power of the Lochsa's springtime water.
—Dennis Elliott, U.S. Forest Service

in contrast to past recreation-oriented displays, it recognizes a more diverse array of resources and uses including the tremendous contribution to the public welfare of timber production in the Lochsa. After reading it, any pilgrim traveling the highway would expect to see evidence of logging and might even wave at the trucker hauling a load of logs from the forest to the sawmills.

The Lochsa River remains a popular place for people to fish, camp, and in other ways recharge their spirits in the spell of the water. Moreover, the awesome power of the Lochsa's spring and early-summer torrent now draws throngs of boaters. Rafters and kayakers delight in the same rapids that in 1893 wrecked the wooden rafts of the Carlin party, forcing them to leave George Colgate to die on the beach while the rest escaped on foot from the Lochsa's mountains. True to its Indian name (*lochsa* means rough water),[275] running the river safely during high water requires proper equipment and, in many stretches, advanced boating skills. In addition to the many enthusiastic individuals and private parties, five commercial boating outfitters have permits from the Forest Service to guide recreational clients down the river. To accommodate this use, the Forest Service has constructed several access sites on the highway at locations where boaters can safely launch their crafts or take them out at the end of a run.

The Lochsa is a water-based recreational resource, accessible, heavily used, and of the highest quality. Retired ranger Jon Bledsoe calls the Lochsa "a remarkable river in terms of white water boating difficulty." I must add that its spirit of place is also good for the heart and soul.

With a modern highway in its center, the corridor bustles with activity, yet to the average motorist it no doubt seems a pleasant place where people live, work, and play in harmony with nature and each other. But as I discovered one night in August while camping beneath the cedars in a public campground a few yards from the site of my old home cabin on Wendover Bar, conflicts still exist among the varied users of the corridor.

As I pitched my tent, a small boy named Jason rode over from a nearby camp on his bicycle, inquiring whether I was lonesome and needed somebody to talk to. He helped me unload supplies from my pickup before returning to his family's camp. He returned later to report that a moose was feeding near their camp. It was a cow, he said, and he asked me to go with him to see it. Because I wanted to make camp before dark, however, I declined. I told him that if a bull with large antlers showed up to let me know and I would go with him. I liked those moose, and I liked Jason, too. It felt good to know that moose and people were getting along together.

After dark, great horned owls began talking back and forth across the river as they had done years before when fresh chips from the notched logs of my new cabin's walls littered the earth at Wendover Bar. I hoped that the owls and the murmur of the river would lull me to sleep, but every three to five minutes all natural sounds were overwhelmed by the noise of trucks passing through on the nearby highway. The approach of each big truck began with a feeling of pressure welling up in the Lochsa's canyon, something like the static in the hush preceding a summer thunderstorm. Suspense hung in the air, gnawed at the pit of my stomach, and then broke in a great blast of shattered air, roaring engine, and rattling chassis and wheels. Each disturbance diminished quickly, as the big engine hauled its driver, truck, and trailer up or down the Lewis and Clark Highway, only to be followed shortly by another and another. Restful sleep eluded me. Although I missed the serenity that the highway had destroyed, the moose and the owls had, by constant association, adapted to "progress" long before.

The crooked highway brought motorized access to the Lochsa canyon, but safe driving demands low speeds from automobiles and trucks.
—U.S. Forest Service

As many as three hundred trucks, some up to eighty-five feet long including their trailers, with a gross weight of 106,000 pounds, each day haul loads of grain from the Dakotas, Montana, and eastern Idaho over the Lewis and Clark Highway to water transportation at the port of Lewiston, Idaho. Those big commercial rigs mingle with motoring tourists and bicyclists, both of whose eyes are distracted from the highway's center by the scenery of the Lochsa. The canyon is crooked; hence, the road is crooked. The top speed allowed is fifty miles per hour, and many curves are posted at much slower speeds. Recreationists enjoy the meandering highway, but commercial truckers want fast transport. Those conflicting needs have created what Idaho State Police officer Bob Shepard once called "the most dangerous road in Idaho."[276]

The Lewis and Clark Highway was not built to serve this kind of trucking, and commercial trucking interests want the road widened. But widening and straightening would crowd the river and degrade the purposes and land values set forth in the Wild and Scenic Rivers Act. Jon Bledsoe says, "The time will come when something will have to give between commercial and recreational use of the highway."[277]

Lurking in the woods is a management problem less dramatic yet more complex than the highway and its associated conflicts. Trees are dying in the old forests along much of the corridor upstream from Colgate

Warm Springs. In areas north of the river and accessible to the highway, dead, dying, and high-risk trees have been cut for lumber. This logging has enhanced scenic and recreational values by removing dangerous trees, opening vistas, and creating space for young trees to sprout and grow. In marked contrast, no salvage logging has been done on the slopes to the south and across the river from the highway. Trees useful for lumber are dying there by the thousands.

Care of the forests in the corridor is the subject of debate between those who treasure the wildness of pristine surroundings and others who do not resent humans meddling in nature's scheme or even expect them to improve on nature's works. Since the last ice age, fire has been the tool used by nature to cleanse the forest, destroy the old and dying trees, recycle nutrients to the earth, and begin life anew. Fires in the corridor's old growth have been suppressed for so long, however, that many of the forests south of the river are ecologically overdue to burn. To many, myself included, it seems a shame to let the trees die unused, when we know that some of them could be carefully harvested within the constraints of the Wild and Scenic Rivers Act.

The Lochsa's corridor, then, is a place of contrasts, a near-natural strip of land about one mile wide and eighty miles long, split lengthwise down its center by a most unnatural highway loaded with the noise and vehicles of both tourists and commerce. Although aided in the task by other agencies, the people of the Forest Service are primarily responsible for restraining the relentless pressure for more economic development of the corridor's land and resources. As the host at Wilderness Gateway Campground, Bob Dammarell said, "This country would go down the tube if it wasn't for the Forest Service."[278] True to the conflict- and contrast-ridden character of the land, others of course would absolutely disagree.

4. General Forest Lands

The general forest lands are adjacent to the above-described wilderness and potential wilderness, the Lolo Trail corridor, and the Lewis and Clark Highway/Lochsa Wild and Scenic River corridor. They are also intermingled in the upper Lochsa with some forty-two thousand acres of railroad land grant sections owned by Plum Creek Timber Company and managed for commercial timber production. These general forest lands are used by the people for a variety of activities and are the primary source of commercial saw timber and other wood products harvested from the Lochsa.

These general forest lands adjacent to White Sand Creek are managed by Plum Creek Timber Company.

The eventual certainty of departing from an even annual flow of raw materials from these general forest lands was beginning to show by the early 1980s. Even then, it looked from Rocky Point Lookout like half of the land north of the Lochsa River had been (or was being) logged. I could see roads leading from the highway into clear-cuts—some old and greened by a dense cover of brush, others new with slash from fresh logging cured brown by the summer sun. So much had been cut that I wondered if the loggers would run out of wood before old trees could be replaced with new trees of sawlog size.

I'm not sure the foresters or loggers were doing right on lands north of the corridor, where the practice of clear-cutting was almost universally used to harvest timber. But what they had done had been largely accepted in the past, given the culture of those times. All marketable wood had been removed from the clear-cuts on well-built roads, usually oiled to prevent dust from coating the vegetation along the roads and smothering the tourists. Remaining debris had been burned to reduce the threat from forest fires and to prepare a bed for new seedlings to sprout. On close examination, such logging looked professional because the work of skillful and conscientious men and women showed in so much of the logged-over land.

But viewed from the standpoint of sustained yield and "the greatest good of the greatest number in the long run," it became clear that the loggers and foresters were getting boxed in. Since the lands out-

Clear-cuts like those in the background are play areas for snowmobilers rallying at Lolo Hot Springs in winter 1994.

side of the wilderness and south of the river remained in the timber supply base, or inventory, the rate of logging on lands north of the river had proceeded on the assumption that the timber to the south would soon be made available for cutting. But the issue of logging south of the Lochsa was far from settled. The massive slide near the "engineering crime" had so undermined the credibility of the Forest Service that many people believed the agency incapable of roading and logging without causing permanent damage to the fragile land. Whether the upper basins in the Elk Summit area should be logged at all was also the subject of much disagreement. Hence, the Forest Service had been counting on a full yield of wood from land that might never be logged or, if logged, harvested at a rate far less than the maximum sustainable yield.

Timber management assistant Tom Geouge showed concern about that when he said to me, "Tying up areas like the Elk Summit Unit and continuing to cut elsewhere as though they were open has caused us to do things in the available areas that we wouldn't have done otherwise."[279] Sustaining the historical supply of commercial timber from the upper Lochsa had become even more uncertain because, despite much effort by foresters and others, many clear-cuts remained less than fully stocked with young trees. Lumber industries located in both Idaho and Montana depended upon those lands to grow enough trees to sustain the present flow of wood to their mills. Meanwhile, the Forest Service was

This landscape shows how logging began to diversify the upper Lochsa country by the mid-1960s. Rocky Point Lookout is in the center foreground. —U.S. Forest Service

selling its full quota of timber as though the lands both north and south of the river were available and fully productive.

Powell district ranger Dick Ferrar was aware of the problem of future timber supply. Using the potential Turkey Track Sale in the Papoose Creek drainage as an example, he said, "There's no way in hell I can go there, build a road, log, then regenerate that in five years. We could go in there on a one-time shot, but no way could we reforest that in five years." (Ferrar was referring to the National Forest Management Act's requirement that logged areas be restocked within five years.) He summed up the commercial timber supply situation in his district: "I can't sustain twenty-four million [board] feet here unless I go into Elk Summit. If I had a cut of fifteen million, maybe, and could do a good job in Elk Summit, then I might buy time to come back to some of the old cutover areas."[280]

So in the early 1980s it looked like the short-term solution for continuing a reasonable flow of timber from the upper Lochsa depended on logging the Elk Summit Unit and the Lochsa Face south of the river. These are both pristine areas and are, like the whole Lochsa prior to

By 1994 the same southeast view from Rocky Point reveals an ecosystem changed a great deal by logging.

the 1950s, susceptible to considerate stewardship yet vulnerable to damage by careless road building and logging.

Now, to supply the expected demand for timber, the ranger needed to bring logging to those lands across the river, and it was prudent to ask: What lessons of the past suggest that he can manage that land for "the greatest good of the greatest number in the long run" and according to the contemporary laws that govern activities of the Forest Service? His entry into virgin territory would provide a new chance to study all the values in each unique unit of land and then to maintain each unit's wholeness, health, and productivity. By an understanding of and respect for natural processes, he could work more with nature and less against nature. He could assume human understanding of ecological processes to be limited and proceed conservatively, learning more as the results of his work unfolded. And he could listen to the wisdom of one-time Powell district ranger Larry Cron who said, "A lot of timber stands back in the Elk Summit unit are different, even though they fit a silvicultural type. They're not typical commercial forest stands. The stands are there because of some unique event that we can't duplicate."[281] The option

Timber harvest and regeneration on national forest lands, looking northeast from Walde Mountain in 1994.

was also available to postpone logging on lands south of the river and reduce his district's timber cut accordingly.

Adherence to the requirement of the new laws described in chapter 23 would also help the ranger accomplish high-quality land management across the river. For instance, clear-cutting could be used only if it were the "optimum" method of timber harvesting. Protection of streams, soil, watershed, wildlife, and recreational resources must be assured. And he must be able to regenerate the cutover stands within five years. These helpful laws establish the legal framework within which the ranger must operate.

When Tom Geouge talked about the future of managing the lands of the upper Lochsa, there was danger as well as hope for change in his words. "In the past," he said, "the highest priority was to meet that cut. That's something we'll do. But in Badger Creek the highest priority is to stock understocked areas previously logged."[282]

"[M]eet that cut. That's something we'll do." Therein lay the greatest threat to the national forest lands of the Lochsa. And we should never log the Elk Summit unit on the Lochsa Face until *manage and care* has replaced "meet that cut" in the minds of those in charge. That's the way I saw the situation in the general forest lands of the Lochsa in 1982.

Timber harvest on national forest lands in the Lochsa came close to "meeting that cut" until the late 1980s. During that time, Plum Creek logged extensively; its objectives were to harvest timber, regenerate its

A young stand of future commercial timber grows on this Lochsa land logged earlier by Plum Creek Timber Company.

forests to correct problems caused by spruce bark beetle logging in the fifties, and improve future timber productivity of the company's lands.[283] So much land has been cutover on Plum Creek ownership and the national forest that logging and associated road building have to a great extent replaced forest fires as the agents of diversity outside of the classified wilderness. Thanks to early-day fire protection, however, we have in recent times enjoyed a rich bounty in wood products from the Lochsa. Yet the collision of this generous harvest with growing demands for other values from the forest gives rise to the most serious present-day land management problems.

Taken together, the Powell district's projected sustainable yield of 24 million board feet of timber and the Lochsa district's 20 million board feet created an expected 44 million-board-foot annual flow of commercial wood products from national forest lands of the Lochsa.[284] Public resistance and, to a lesser extent, immaturity of the forest's restocking after the burns of 1929 and 1934, have prevented access to national forest timber in the Elk Summit area and elsewhere south of the river. The inevitable decline in timber production from national forest lands began in 1989. And the volume of timber sold from the Powell and Lochsa

Northwest from Rocky Point, the magnitude of logging the Lochsa's landscapes shows in 1994.

districts dropped from 38.7 million board feet in 1989 to 7.6 million board feet in 1993.[285]

Acting district ranger Gerald Beard explains the situation on the Lochsa district:

> We are constrained by our past activities. Appeals kept us from entering the roadless areas, and we tried to take up the slack in already developed areas. Our forest plan gave us standards and technology to more accurately measure the consequences of logging and roading on stream quality. We find that sediment from logging hasn't flushed out of important streams and watersheds haven't recovered. Cutting of old-growth forests is restricted due to scarcity. We'll stay out of the upper Fish Creek area due to the Lewis and Clark wilderness proposal. The areas burned in 1934 are not yet mature enough for commercial timber. From the point of producing wood products we have no place to go except roadless areas.[286]

Powell district ranger Margaret Gorski adds, "We are faced with the realization that we can't take care of other values and produce timber supply at the rate we used to. We have been trying to meet the requirements of all laws, provide a high output of other values, and at the same time, on the same land, furnish the timber that fuels the market we created."[287]

Similar reductions in other districts of the Clearwater National Forest and elsewhere suggest that throughout the northern Rocky Mountains our national forest lands cannot sustain the timber supply promised by historic practice and in the national forest plans.

The Lochsa's interested and dependent publics are deeply concerned over this situation. Bill Mulligan, resource manager for Weyerhaeuser's Kamiah operations, says, "Forest Service ability to manage resources is at a complete breakdown. Their attempts to manage for the National Forest Management Act haven't worked. How they can get back on track is of deep concern." Dan Johnson, of Resource Organization on Timber Supply, speaks on behalf of organized labor and the Clearwater's timber industries. "In the short term," he says, "we need wood. And we have to get some from the national forests. In the medium term, we have to change the process to consider dependent communities. If we can't produce paper and wood products here, today, then where can we in the Lochsas of the world?"[288]

The Nez Perce people are concerned about the future of their hunting and fishing in the Lochsa country. Tribal Council member Allen Pinkham explains: "A major issue is how to get the Forest Service to preserve and protect the rights spelled out in our Treaty of 1855. If they're not taking care of the habitat for fish and game, then they're not doing their job and are violating the treaty."[289]

Dennis Baird, Sierra Club representative in Moscow, Idaho, who loves the Lochsa's wild country, says, "We don't always agree with the timber people, but we respect each other. While we value wilderness, we know people have to eat, too. If the only players were the Idaho people, we could work something out. We have a strong sense of community."[290]

Mike Bader, leader of the Missoula-based Alliance for the Wild Rockies, says of the Forest Service:

> They're an agency that's in transition and floundering around a bit. The thing that did them in was ignoring what the rangers wanted. The Forest Service has been shot through by political pressures and overcutting. They did a good job of telling the people what they wanted. Then when they couldn't deliver, they got shot down. I see them headed in a new direction. They've got a good crew. I think it will come out for the best.[291]

The foregoing comments express the concerns of diverse interests, each seeking different ways of using and protecting the resources of the

Lochsa's general forest lands. They also show a hint of willingness to work together to sustain the long-term productivity of the national forests. That's something worthwhile to rally around because sustaining our forests has much to do with each individual's welfare and the prosperity of our communities.

Since their first coming, people have been drawn to the Lochsa's natural spirit of place, which, according to early-day woodsman and modern-day writer the late Norman Maclean, "comes right out of the duff." Its power is reflected in timber sawyer David Hatfield's enthusiasm. "I like the country. Seems so virgin. The work. There's always a challenge. Always something that could kill you. I'm here by choice, not by chance." And part of the Lochsa's appeal is the kind of people it attracts. As forester Cheryl Holman put it in 1982 at Rocky Point Lookout: "I love the Lochsa. The grandeur. People who come to Powell tend to stay here. The people are the ones who make any job. People here, all in all, are real good."[292]

It seems to me that, as in the past, there remains in the Lochsa a great union of the land and the people. In the spirit of today and the hope of the future lies conviction that wise use of land no longer depends on more access, more government money, more commerce, or more jobs, but is instead a matter of attitudes and time. It's like René Dubos wrote: "Man can manipulate nature to his own best interests only if he first loves her for her own sake."[293] I was thinking about that when I fell asleep in my tent that night at Wendover Bar.

25

A New Look at Conservation and Multiple Use

In 1907, two years after establishment of the Forest Service, Chief Gifford Pinchot published a small government manual entitled "Use of the National Forests." In it, he wrote: "National Forests are made for and owned by the people. They should also be managed by the people. . . . What the people want as a whole will be done."[294]

To be sure, its first chief's instructions set the newly formed Forest Service on a course in line with the principles of American democracy. Few save the most self-centered interests could fault their intent because, for perhaps the first time in world history, Pinchot's manual applied to the land the idea of government of the people, by the people, and for the people. But, except in times of extreme national emergency, the people of the United States had never wanted anything "as a whole"—nor did they in the 1980s, nor would they in the future. Their wants were expressed instead in a variety of self-centered, business-centered, or community-centered interests, usually expressed in the short term. Perhaps as a result, the Forest Service's interpretation of what the people wanted "as a whole" did not, by the 1980s, look like wise use of the land and resources of the nation's national forests.

Such was the situation in the forests of the Lochsa where the long-sought access, finally attained, had delivered opportunity for management to the rangers in charge. With the land's resources coveted by a variety of oftentimes conflicting interests, rangers had to enlarge the scope of their responsibilities. The conceptual requirements of that change—from custodial care of the country to the professional management of land—descended on the Lochsa's rangers with the force of an avalanche loosed from the Bitterroot crest. Protecting forests, building more ac-

This view looking north from Beaver Ridge contains both national forests and land owned by Plum Creek Timber Company.

cess, even marketing timber, though still needed, were no longer adequate by themselves for managing land. In addition to those traditional activities, Forest Service employees had to define the capacity of the land to sustain production of resources and to allocate their time, finances, and equipment to the demands according to priority. And all of this had to be done in the spirit of "what the people want as a whole."

It is a gross understatement to say that the complexity of managing the Lochsa had come to demand the utmost professional capability from its rangers. It must have been a sobering experience for them to view the results of their decisions from a place like Beaver Ridge Lookout, where two great concepts of land use can be seen, each contributing a variety of values to the welfare of the people.

There at the spot where a No. 6 Newhouse bear trap set by Homer launched Peg Leg on his way to becoming a legend, the ranger could see the landscapes of the natural wilderness to the south. From a nearby observation point, he or she could look northward at lands brought under management by the hands and machines of men and women. Comparison by an observant person of the results of the management schemes, north and south, would surely disclose fundamental truths about how well we have lived with the land in the past and what we should do in the future to sustain the array of earth's renewable resources.

Management of the national forests has so long been synonymous with commercial use of resources that many people, even in the nineties, would describe the landscapes to the north as managed and the wilderness to the south as unroaded, undeveloped, and therefore unmanaged lands. However, in the early exploitation of the Lochsa's resources and the subsequent recovery, or lack of recovery, of land productivity lies a humbling truth—that there is little, if any, opportunity for "managing" to improve either the productivity or the quality of multiple resources produced on lands in their natural state. If multiple use means, as I think it does, managing land to produce a sustained yield of multiple resources, then nature has, by centuries of trial and adjustment, developed an excellent scheme.

Bounty from the Lochsa's once-natural lands to the north had been rich enough to allow industries to harvest a single resource, primarily trees for sawtimber, and to make it pay despite heavy expenditure of both industry and federal money and energy. But this initial entry to exploit resources in the Lochsa, as elsewhere, has almost always been followed by decline in the quantity and quality of some resource values originally present in the site. After long reflection upon my own experiences in a lifetime of work with the public's lands, I have to say that I've never seen an intrusion of humankind and high-impact technology improve the productivity of multiple values in any natural place. Improvement of one or two values is often achieved but always at the expense of several other resources that had been thriving naturally before "development" took hold of the land.

What makes our current management activities appear successful is not so much the wisdom of people as it is the contrast between the land's natural condition and the degradation that occurred during first entry into natural places. So much damage had to be fixed in the wake of those bulldozing pioneers that it was easy for professional managers to show improvement. Erosion had to be checked, forests restocked, slash and debris disposed of, and related activities accomplished to nurse the wounded natural system back to health. The manager's emphasis necessarily shifted from exploitation to restoration, and he or she usually found that the potential for production of some resources had been degraded or, in some cases, even lost for all time.

Various stages of Plum Creek and Forest Service timber harvest and regeneration are seen from near Beaver Meadow. Powell Ranger Station is behind the knob in the upper center.

Reflecting on the wild landscape south of Beaver Ridge, it seems to me that the most competent professionals must realize that there is no such thing as managing to *improve* a place like the Selway-Bitterroot Wilderness. Since nature takes care of resource restoration, the place needs only sensitive stewardship, not expensive programs, machines, or roads. But to the north, where much of the land is allocated to the production of commodity resources, initial entry followed by reentry over good roads is needed for road-oriented recreation or for recreationists to access large remote areas, for periodic timber harvest, and for management activities associated with these and similar uses. Those entries, including their associated impacts on land and resources, should not be considered a triumph of mankind over nature. If properly conducted, they should be viewed as a partnership with nature where understanding of and respect for the functioning of natural systems should underlie every management decision and action.

Management in the Forest Service is a culture to which I have long belonged and still believe in. But there is a danger in its worship, and people both in and out of the Forest Service will further the public good by critical examination of the tenets of management from time to time. For example, I believe that a richer *mix* of resources has been and is now being produced in the Lochsa's natural systems than on those lands that have been converted to management. Since human memory is so cluttered with advertisements of special interests, it would be easy to lose sight of this truth and lapse into thinking that management is responsible for all the bounty available from the land. That's what the public relations programs of many business organizations and government agencies would have us believe. And without contrasts like those displayed in the landscapes north and south of Beaver Ridge, people would, in a very few years, have little reason to question them.

With the frontiers of discovery and first entry largely behind us, our society would now do well to limit its demands for renewable natural resources of all kinds to the capability of our nation's lands to sustain a yield. As for the national forests of the Lochsa, we can no longer assume that a bounty of the magnitude created by nature and enjoyed by people of the frontier period will continue to be available. An ethical resource budget has to constrain the appetite of the people to the supply of resources that can be produced sustainably, in partnership with nature, on the managed lands.

As we look forward to depending on our capability to interact wisely with nature, it is helpful to place future human use temporarily in the background while we try to understand the natural processes working on each unique tract of land. In the past we might have been too eager to inventory and plan the useable resources with too little attention to understand those natural linkages that sustain the land's wholeness, health, and productivity. With this basic land ecology understood as best we can, we are ready, as a second step in our deliberations, to use that knowledge (together with information about social and cultural preferences, economics, and other factors) to decide how and at what rate the resources could be used sustainably by the people.

The interdependence, potential productivity, and output of resources are thus susceptible to management. No single resource stands alone in its quality, vigor, or production quantity. Each complements the other, depending on the characteristics of a given unit of land. The resource of trees, for example, contributes both quality and quantity to other resources like wildlife, wildness, and water. It is a dangerous oversimplification of natural laws to describe for management purposes, much less attempt to harvest, any resource without considering its relationship to all others.

It is widely thought that multiple use management, if well done, can achieve a whole output greater than the sum of the productivity of each of the land's individual resources. But the Lochsa's experience suggests that this output cannot be attained or sustained by management based solely on inventory and productivity projections of individual resources. There is more promise in examining the natural processes necessary for a unit of land to thrive, identifying the several resources that can be sustained, determining their relationships to one another, and then deciding what has to be left to keep the land thriving and whole.

Though the Multiple Use–Sustained Yield Act does not specifically say so, it implicitly establishes goals that cannot be achieved without detailed knowledge of the capacity, complexity, and limitations of unique units of land. The act also requires "making the most judicious use of the land for some or all of these resources . . . and harmonious and coordinated management of the various resources, each with the other, without impairment of the productivity of the land."[295] Thus, to apply fully the *multiple use* and *sustained yield* concepts to the national forests, the ecology of the whole of each area has to be understood.

I believe that the framers of the act respected the workings of natural systems; the managers and specialists of today and tomorrow should do no less. In *A God Within*, René Dubos wrote, "Instead of imposing our will on nature for the sake of exploitation, we should attempt to discover the qualities inherent in each particular place so as to foster their development. Human life should grow, not quantitatively through the conquest of nature, but qualitatively in cooperation with nature."[296] Dubos published those words in 1972. His advice is still good. And it provides a prerequisite for managing land to produce multiple values to be used by people in a variety of ways.

There is, of course, much more to land management than a statement of philosophy. And to "discover the qualities" of a place, as Dubos would have us do, is not a matter of digging a road in the mountains with a bulldozer like we did on some of the Lochsa's lands. Such methods, typical of the frontier ethics that dominated our past culture, prevent us from avoiding damage—indeed, often cause damage—to sometimes irreplaceable land values.

The Lochsa's varied land forms, climate, hydrology, soils, and associated biological factors have, during thousands of years of natural evolution, created on the land a host of varied "placeanalities" not unlike the personalities that make each human being different from all others. The Horse Heaven Meadows near the base of Diablo Mountain, for example, are far different from the forested lands along the Lochsa River. Likewise, the forested lands on the north slopes of the river bear scant resemblance to those on the south, and an alert observer can find many

Geology, hydrology, climate, exposure, soils, small creatures and organisms, plus a host of lesser understood factors—each linked to the others to form a functional whole—create unique local environments in this landscape.

unique natural subdivisions within the lands both north and south. The beginning of wisdom is to identify each unique place, study what forces of nature brought the land to its present condition, and predict what will happen to it if nature is left alone. As a foundation for management, this approach recognizes the evolutionary movement in nature, thus opening the way to predict the consequences, over time, of the chosen management scheme.

Implementing the Multiple Use–Sustained Yield Act demands recognition, stewardship, and sustainability of multiple values useful to humans. To decide how these values can be used and sustained requires study of the biotic and abiotic linkages (that is, all of the land's natural parts) that keep the land whole and healthy and its ecology functioning. It is important here to remember that nature does not *extract*—it displaces, replaces, and recycles. That's why our approach to managing national forest lands should focus more on what to leave to keep the land whole in the long term than on the bounty to be harvested for immediate use. The challenge is to relegate the idea of individual resource management to an honored place in history and replace it with management of land as a whole, where resources are viewed as the multiple outputs resulting from considerate and professional husbandry of the earth. This involves studying each unit of land, unlike but connected to all other units, a piece of earth to be treasured and examined in preparation for thoughtful management and care. And when considering the land's values, there is no substitute for detailed, on-site examination of each of these unique places.

Protecting or enhancing the factors that keep the land whole deserves first priority in management. A variety of ways to use the land and its values, without detracting from management's first priority of wholeness, will surface in turn. A choice may then be made among this array of sustainable options. A more ecological foundation for management will better assure land health and sustainability, but it will not by itself settle historic disputes about how to use the many resources of the national forests. That still remains a task to be undertaken by the people and the government reasoning together. I would like to see the responsible forest land managers develop these sustainable ways to use the land and present them to the public much earlier in their information and decision processes. That would tend to focus public Forest Service discussions more on *sustainable uses*, less on uses alone. It would also recognize the responsibility of public land managers to understand and communicate to the people the ecology and best sustainable options for use of each unique tract of land in their charge.

The land is a whole. But divisive forces from within both the general public and government tend to splinter, not protect, that wholeness. The Forest Service itself reflects that tendency. Except for certain support services, each level of the administrative organization is partitioned according to functions, like minerals, range, wildlife, recreation, timber, water, and fire. Appropriation of funds to the Forest Service follows a similar piecemeal pattern. In my days, it was even hard to find a place in the files to store records dealing with the qualities of a given piece of earth. And the leaders in charge of this array of functional divisions tend to emphasize their respective specialties on the same tracts of land.

Achieving responsible husbandry of land amid such organizational splintering requires a great deal of coordination among the people working within the Forest Service. Indeed, it is surprising that the agency's land management programs come out as well as they do. Much of their success is due to forthright cooperation among specialists, but the primary responsibility for keeping the appetites of both public and in-service interests in balance with land capability has long been centered in the line officers of the Forest Service. These persons form a four-level hierarchy within the organization: (1) chief of the Forest Service, (2) regional foresters, (3) forest supervisors, and (4) district rangers.

Henry J. Viche, Powell district ranger, 1943–1947.

These officers have long needed more detailed land-based information to help them protect the wholeness of earth and make reliable decisions. Consequently, in 1980 the Forest Service launched a nationwide program to "discover the qualities" in each unique place in every national forest and to prepare plans intended to help balance the needs of the people with the capacity of the earth to provide resources. This was an important step in the right direction. But these plans have, for a variety of reasons, fallen far short of achieving their concurrent goals of delivering expected raw materials from the forests, sustaining the productivity of the land, and meeting growing demands by the public for wildness and primitive recreation.

Within the Forest Service, then, the deep-rooted factors tending to oppose the integrated management of land are countered by land management plans and the authority assigned to line officers, the most significant being the practice of assigning a ranger to take charge of a district of land. When Adolph Weholt found Elk Summit and Frank Smith camped at Powell's Flat, they became the Forest Service's anchor men, responsible for preserving the quality of the upper Lochsa, their individual portions of the earth. Since then the land ethics of the Forest Service have been rooted in the concept of ranger districts, and those roots are as essential today as they were in 1909. Unlike Smith and Weholt and others who pioneered government rule of the national forests, today's rangers of the Lochsa and elsewhere have to blend lessons from the past with the knowledge of modern times while they look to the future as stewards of the earth.

In the words of the Lochsa's loggers, it takes a special kind of ranger to run "a damn good show." Writing during the 1860s of man's impact on land, George Perkins Marsh set forth timeless advice applicable to the forest rangers of today. "This exercise of the eye I desire to promote, and next to moral and religious doctrine, I know of no more important practical lessons in this earthly life of ours—which, to the wise man, is a school from the cradle to the grave—than those related to the employment of the sense of vision in the study of nature."[297]

Ted Williams, long-time rancher from the Lolo Fork, put Marsh's wisdom another way when he said: "The best rangers was them that knew their country."[298] Today's ranger has to be able to see the land despite the trees. He or she has to understand the values in each unique place, the association of those values with each other, the relationship of each place to all other places, and the workings of important connecting links to landscapes beyond his jurisdiction. Such an ecological view of the earth is necessary to comprehend the natural energy sustaining the land's productivity, identify the multiple values needed by people and communities, then manage the land and govern land use accordingly.

René Dubos extended Marsh's advice about using one's sense of vision when he wrote: "[Man] changes the environment by his very presence and his only options in his dealing with the earth are to be destructive or constructive. To be creative, man must relate to nature with his senses as much as with his common sense, with his heart as much as with knowledge. He must read the book of external nature and the book of his own nature, to discern the common patterns and harmonies. . . . Reverence for nature is compatible with willingness to accept responsibility for a creative stewardship of earth."[299] Every ranger, every specialist, and, for that matter, every land user ought to read Dubos's advice often and then go out on the land and practice what it says.

Among other things, Dubos's words mean that forest rangers, like all land managers, must never cease their attempts to understand each natural system in their charge, that is, how it evolved to its present condition and where and how it is going in the future. The effects of trends in land use are important, too. For example, the implications of the mud in the spring near Swede Cut are as important to the Lochsa's rangers today as they were in 1953. The story of the spraying of DDT on the landscapes ought to be required reading for every man, woman, and child living in or involved with the Lochsa. Success stories are also part of the trends that make up the ranger's "show," and there is a great lesson in Powell district ranger Puckett's decision of the mid-1950s to keep roads out of the canyon of the White Sand. Here and there, examples of logged-over areas supporting stable streams and land well stocked with new forests suggest that somebody treated nature's systems right. Be it happenstance or good management, the red-bellied trout at Fish Lake remain unthreatened by man-imported exotics. Today's ranger should thank his predecessors—and luck—for that and vow to keep this native cutthroat population pure. To be sure, familiarity with the history of people and land is necessary for land managers to build on the strengths and avoid repeating mistakes of the past.

Contemporary rangers also deal with paperwork, which has progressively drawn their attention away from the land. In 1904, after work any evening, Ranger Stuart could read the entire text of his five-by-eight-inch, ninety-seven-page manual of instructions. When ranger Frank Smith quit in 1914, he said of his boss, "If Howell can't take my word for it, I ain't writin' any papers for him." As Forest Service work grew more complicated, both administration and associated paperwork necessarily increased. In marked contrast, today's multivolume Forest Service Manual takes several feet of library shelf to store its voluminous instructions. Its contents could not likely be mastered by any one person. If today's rangers felt like Frank Smith did about paperwork, they would quit en masse.

From an old ranger's point of view, I am tempted to call the old days simpler times, but that wouldn't be true. Instead, the Lochsa experience displays a series of *different* times, each with unique complexity and challenges to be met by the rangers and their crews. Passage of new laws that require detailed documentation, legal interpretations of old laws, conflicting demands for use of forest lands, failure of past practices to assure sustainability, lack of public trust in the Forest Service, and the need to implement a more ecological approach to managing forest land: these are the conditions that characterize the complexity of the district ranger's job today.

But rangers, you may say, are delegated limited authority, and they can do only what they've been authorized to do. That's basically true. There are, however, few limits on the ranger's authority to carry out his or her most professional task, which, as we have already seen, is not managing resources; it is instead stewardship—to protect and, where needed, to restore land health and assure a sustainable flow of resources needed by the people and their communities. In this context, the only constraints are the limitations of science, the ranger's personal land ethics, and the viewpoints and needs of the interested public. The work environment of rangers has been that way since establishment of the national forests. As the first chief forester, Gifford Pinchot, said: "I hold it to be the first duty of a public officer to obey the law. But I hold it to be his second duty, and a close second, to do everything the law will let him do for the public good, and not merely what the law compels or directs him to do."[300]

The law imposes relatively few substantive limits on Forest Service rangers when it comes to on-site management of the land, and there is no one else in government to do that job. Since day-to-day land management is seldom a dramatic issue, neither the rangers nor their staffs will often become heroes. But there is a touch of greatness in those men and women who decide issues based on their knowledge of the land, their country's needs, and the effects of human action on the earth.

Establishment of ranger districts in 1909 has proven to be an effective way to organize integrated, hands-on management of the national forests. Since then, district rangers have been and should remain the key people in the Forest Service responsible for discovering "the qualities inherent in each particular place so as to foster their development" and, further, for sustaining the wholeness and productivity of the earth. Their job has in recent times grown a great deal in size and complexity. Modern technology, however, hastens communications, expedites the paperwork, and in other ways saves time so the Lochsa's rangers and their staffs can focus more on land management and the people who use their districts.

Today's rangers need (and all those I know possess) a strong blend of professional knowledge, empathy with people, and respect for the details of the earth. Add to that Pinchot's conviction that "the greatest of all luxuries is to work yourself to your very limit in a cause in which you believe with your whole soul,"[301] and we have the profile for a most-wanted land manager, capable of understanding people, the earth, and their sustained interaction with each other.

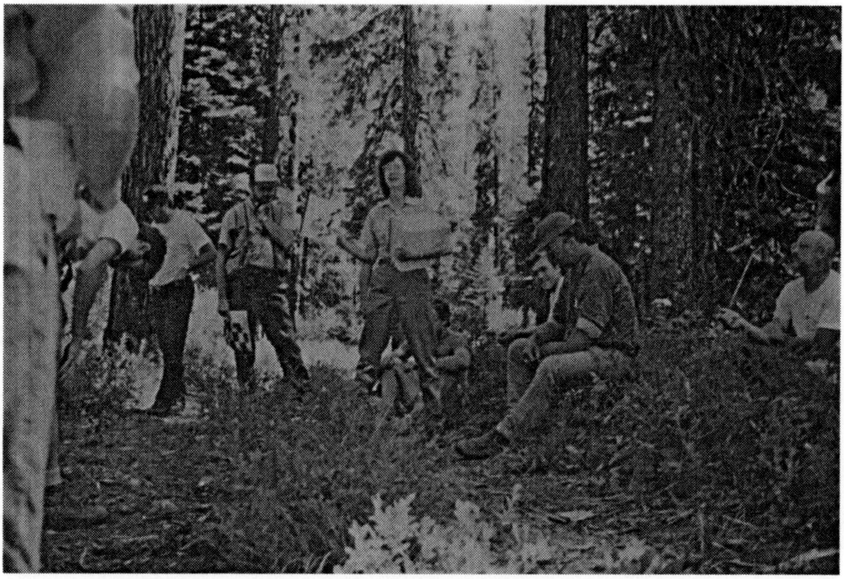

Powell district ranger Margaret Gorski explains the White Sand Ecosystem Management Project to concerned citizens in 1994. —Margaret Gorski

26

The Land, the People, and Tomorrow

Logging, prescribing fire, leaving the land alone so natural processes can work, and a combination of these are the organic tools available to the Lochsa's managers joined in partnership with nature to care for the land of the Lochsa. Together with modern technology, these tools provide the means for accountable men and women to deal positively with the earth. The thoughts, convictions, and hopes of people of the past two centuries are carved on the Lochsa's landscapes in both constructive and destructive ways, depending on how the tools were used. We can all learn from this biotic map of human intervention.

For example, timber harvesting in several drainages, especially on intermingled Forest Service–Plum Creek Timber Company ownership in the upper Lochsa, has opened up so much area in such a short time that cumulative effects have increased siltation and warmed stream temperatures to limits that threaten the health of fish populations.[302] There is little hint of naturalness in what is going on; as a result, the Lochsa's general forest lands have become a far different place than they were when humans first arrived here. Perhaps we have gained economically, that is, in the quantity of commercial wood products available, by harvesting the old and restoring the forest anew. But we have lost something, too.

I will try to illustrate by sharing my thoughts while visiting the headwaters of the Brushy Fork on June 21, 1994. On that day I drove from Lolo Pass through the low gap and down into the Brushy Fork valley. Except that some spruce bark beetle control sites logged in the fifties had not been fully restocked, the land looked good—that is, until I found a huge clear-cut extending from near Lily Lake to Elk Meadows

This clear-cut near Elk Meadows is well stocked with young trees, but total removal of the forest on such a large scale has left the ecosystem no longer whole.

and on, out of sight, into the uplands. The big spruce were gone, as was much of the life dependent on old-growth forests. In their place an emptiness spread over the once-vibrant land. The great forest had been cut to the meadow's edge. At the big rock campsite I found that recent campers had left their cans and spoiled food in the fire pits. When I first saw Elk Meadows the mystique of the grizzly prevailed. Then came bands of sheep followed by cattle, and now it's big clear-cuts and cans. So far as maintaining a degree of wildness goes, that's the deficit side of the legacy of our occupation of one of the gems of the Bitterroot mountains.

I hiked up the meadow to where I had first camped alone in the Lochsa sixty-four years before. To verify the location, I searched above the meadow for traces of the old Middle Ridge Trail, but logging, both old and new, had left no clues of the trail's whereabouts. The bones of a dead horse lay where I thought my campsite must have been. I photographed the meadow and the clear-cut mountains beyond. I felt no anger, only disappointment that the course of America had brought the Lochsa to such circumstances. To some, this was commercial forestry at its finest. To me, it represented a great loss of natural values that didn't have to happen in order to harvest and perpetuate the forest.

This 1994 view of Elk Meadows and vicinity from near my campsite of 1930 no longer includes the mystery of the great forest or the mystique of the grizzly bear.

Most of Elk Meadows and adjacent lands are owned by Plum Creek, and I respect the company's right to do what it wants with its land so long as it obeys state and federal laws and does not degrade neighboring lands of the national forests. Plum Creek's professionals have restocked their clear-cuts with vigorous young trees. The land is not ruined from a commercial silvicultural point of view. But from an ecological point of view, the Brushy Fork's landscapes are no longer whole. Combined operations of Plum Creek and the Forest Service have changed, and are still changing, this once-ecologically diverse land to a utilitarian tree farm.

Having known this land in its natural state, the magnitude of change created by logging is overwhelming. It seems to me that the principles of forestry brought back from France by Gifford Pinchot in 1890, and since then refined by research and experience, should have been applied more conservatively. Yet, what I am feeling is not so much disappointment at the application of science as a wish that ethical matters of the heart and soul were more connected with science by those who manage the Lochsa's lands. I am not troubled here about Plum Creek alone. Its land management objectives are far more commercially oriented than those of the Forest Service, and I respect that. I have drawn this example because it is the place where I began this story and where I first entered into close association with the land of the Lochsa.

The intrusion of humans into wild areas is certain to generate change, some positive, some negative, depending on how change happens and on the values of both those who effect the change and the beholders of it. As viewed by this beholder, the uplands of the Brushy Fork do not display the more conservative and diverse management I had in mind in the early 1950s when I located the control points for the road from Packer Meadows into Spruce Creek, past Lily Lake and Elk Meadows to the Montana-Idaho line. And I remain convinced that we could sustain a brisk flow of wood products from the Lochsa's forests and still keep intact the wholeness of the land (all of its parts) and most of its natural spirit as well.[303]

The history of protection and management in the Lochsa parallels in many ways the state of the Forest Service throughout the northern Rockies and, to a lesser extent, nationwide. The loss of grizzlies and wolves and the steady decline of anadromous fish shouted early warnings that the wholeness of the land was disintegrating. Where we once considered motorized access as key to successful land management, we are now closing roads to prevent overuse or damage to resources. Roadless areas have become scarce treasures in themselves, and attempts by the rangers of the Lochsa to enter roadless areas and harvest commodities have been rebuffed by successful appeals. Yet the rangers kept logging elsewhere at a rate that could be sustained, on a forest-wide basis, only if the roadless lands were eventually logged. Most appeals were won on the charge that, in a desperate attempt to keep selling timber, the Forest Service had broken its own laws and regulations. Many people lost trust as the shelves emptied in the resources-for-sale store of the Forest Service.

That's not a pleasant story. And it seems to me that we of the Lochsa, of the Clearwater, and perhaps as a nation have become willing victims of political, industrial, and technological expansion of the same Manifest Destiny that shouldered the Indians out of the way of European domination of the West. But this time it's not just the Native Americans who are in the way of somebody else. Because we have reached or exceeded the capacity of our land to provide the wants of all of us, we all now seem to be in the way of each other. We have become a divided people with respect to the use of the public commons. Yet we—the government and the people together—brought ourselves to this situation. And we should hold much closer together to work our way out of it. We need a new vision for the future to unite us and speed us toward a manifest destiny of respect for each other, wholeness of earth, and sustainable ways of using our land and its resources.

The people in charge of the Lochsa's national forests realize that their past ways of doing things are inadequate for today and tomorrow. They are beginning what could become the most significant change in the Lochsa's Forest Service since Charley Powell welcomed Ranger Smith to Powell Flat in 1909. They are being directed by Forest Service Chief Jack Ward Thomas to manage ecosystems, which entails understanding the processes of nature, working constructively within the limits imposed by nature, and giving first priority to keeping the land whole and able, in the long run, to sustain its contribution to people and communities. In contrast to past practices, the processes that keep the ecosystems healthy will get more attention, as will interaction among life forms within each ecosystem and among ecosystems that make up the larger landscapes. Along the lines of what I described in chapter 25, we will begin to manage land with resources viewed not as the primary focus of management but instead as the side benefits of considerate stewardship of the earth.[304]

Professor Eugene P. Odum further described this idea:

> Ecology has emerged from its roots in biology to become a separate discipline that integrates organisms, the physical environment and humans. From this point of view the ecosystem level becomes the major focus. Populations are considered as ecosystem components and landscapes as associations of interacting ecosystems. This view is now generally accepted.[305]

Thinking about transferring Odum's concept to management actions on the varied ecosystems of the Clearwater National Forest, Supervisor Caswell says, "We would look at sustainable ecosystem health over the long haul as first priority. All critters would be there in the right proportion if the system is in balance. I feel good about the process we got in motion."[306]

As one of the "humans" in Odum's description, I too feel good about "the process we got in motion." It is as much a way of thinking as it is a practice, more a cultural evolution than a quick change in forest management. Everyone interested in, associated with, or dependent on national forest and adjacent lands will be affected. Few will encounter tougher change than the people who work for the Forest Service. They have to simultaneously set new direction for themselves, overcome public distrust, convince people that ecosystem management is not just a new package to perpetuate old ways of doing things, and involve people in defining the idea and putting it to work. Public relations programs alone won't do this job. Nor will the common practice of developing programs and then subjecting them to public scrutiny get very far.

The Forest Service needs local public guidance in this matter. We who make up the dependent communities are not sideline observers in a government process but responsible stakeholders with a role to play in shaping our own destiny. As such, we need to form accountable partnerships with government as the ecosystem management concept unfolds. Civil wars among special interests won't promote this job. It is no longer possible for the Forest Service, an agency charged with stewardship of multiple values for multiple uses, to ably manage the national forests with so many citizens polarized against each other, each seeking different bounty from the same acre of land. Surely we can "want as a whole" when it comes to sustainable land health and community prosperity—which plainly go hand in hand.

We of the Lochsa and adjacent communities are part of the ecosystem. As everything in an ecosystem is "hitched" to everything else, we are, no matter our individual or collective activities, linked to each other and to the land by similar invisible bonds. Chief Thomas has directed that ecosystem management replace traditional resource management throughout the national forests. Northern regional forester Dave Jolly, by memo of June 28, 1993, told his folks to get on with it. Forest supervisor Caswell likes it. And the Lochsa's rangers are starting to try it on the land. (The White Sand ecosystem on the Powell district is the Clearwater forest's lead project.)[307] It remains now for the Lochsa's public to unite in common endeavor and join in partnership with their government to help get ecosystem management working on the land.

To do that will take time. I don't think we can assure sustainability on the Lochsa's lands by passing more laws. Sufficient legal tools are available. Nor can we achieve a stable future by confrontational politics. The essential ingredients for implementing ecosystem management are largely present—public knowledge, capable citizen advocates, well-meaning industrialists, an agency receptive to citizen input. What isn't fully there yet is determination to work together, with respect for each other, for the good of our land and communities.

This is not a matter of applied science versus human emotions. We need both. Chief Thomas has made it plain that people must be included in ecosystem management. Contemporary scientific knowledge, important as it is, represents but a small fraction of the enlightenment needed to fully understand and appreciate the biotic and abiotic workings of any place.[308] There is plenty of room for, indeed an absolute need for, insights from the heart and soul and for that feeling that comes from intimate association with whole and healthy land. Many problems, both past and present, in the Lochsa were not caused by lack of knowledge but instead resulted from an illusion that we knew much more than we did about the land. There is so much we still don't know scientifically. And that suggests to me, as it has many times before, that we should be conservative when entering new lands in the Lochsa to harvest resources, to ensure that we don't degrade the land's productivity.

Return with me now to my camp near the banks of the Lochsa River:

Daylight broke late because the canopies of the cedars wouldn't let light from the cloudy sky into my camp below. Awakened by the crackling of another camper's fire, I unzipped my sleeping bag and felt the damp cool of morning air along the Lochsa. I built a fire. I appreciated the companionship of the flames as well as their warmth. After breakfast I sat by the fire, sipped coffee, and listened to the Lochsa until its sounds created a kind of mental impasse where, for a few minutes, I stopped my search for truth in the world. I let the spirit of that great land seize me as it had so many times in so many ways before. Hear the river. Smell the cedars. Honor silence. Feel the valley. Cleanse the mind. Relax. I am part of, not apart from, the unknown beyond eternity. Let it go. Listen hard, lest I miss the message when the mountains speak. It felt good to be home again, near the shores of the Lochsa River at Wendover Bar.

A slammed car door broke the spell of the fire and the land. I packed lunch and left for Indian Post Office, so that I might see the Lochsa's landscapes from high on the mountains. There was no breeze or sun as I drove down the highway along the river. Except for the water, the land stood still, as though its many lives had also paused, like I had by the fire, to reflect a moment on their relations with each other. Driving through the gorge that had thwarted Lewis and Clark's passage rekindled memories of scrambling among the snow-covered boulders in the fall to set traps for mink and otter. The head and shoulders of a fisherman disappeared from view behind the banks of the highway as he headed toward a deep pool in the river near Badger Creek. As the landscape across the river slid past the frame of my pickup window, the many dead and dying white pines demonstrated the inevitability of life and death

From Indian Post Office, where Ranger Smith in 1909 saw a near-pristine landscape, the workings of modern people now dominate much of the Lochsa's topography.

and the futility of trying to hold nature still in order to preserve some desired situation on the landscape.

I turned off the highway at Squaw Creek. A half-mile farther on I turned left on the Doe Creek road and began climbing to the high country. I remembered how the torn earth looked when we built that road and gave thanks that the Lochsa's wet climate and nutritious soils had returned new trees, brush, and smaller plants to the once-raw roadside. At one place a traveler had parked his camper near the stream and slept, immersed in the sounds of Doe Creek. Here and there, cropped twigs on the young trees showed that moose or elk, or perhaps both, still sought shelter beneath the cedars during the deep snows of winter.

I saw the place where the stream-hugging road built by the Bureau of Public Roads ended, and where our logger-built road began its narrower way high enough on the mountainside to leave a few trees between itself and the creek. I liked our road better then, and I still do. The great spruce forest where I had caught so many marten fifty-eight years before had been converted by logging to a huge field of brush. The forested site of my trapline camp at Deep Saddle had been replaced by an old logging landing. I stopped there and pondered the past. For a moment I again felt the pressure of the big storm on that night before the avalanche buried me in the canyon down below. I had almost forgotten the alpine hemlocks, but the first one I saw along the road rekindled memories of the Lochsa's northern high country. I drank clear water from the spring in the basin below the divide where bloodred Indian paintbrush contrasted with white-plumed beargrass.

I drove on through the pines, the firs, and the hemlocks to Indian Post Office. There, near noonday, I rested near the spot where Ranger Smith got his first expansive look at the land he was to rule. Thin clouds obscured the sun, cast a haze across the mountains, and darkened the Lochsa's many steep-walled canyons. The warm air on the mountain stood still; its inertia seemed to signal a pending storm. The lake in the basin mirrored the surrounding forest in its waters.

Despite the haze, I could identify the valleys, ridges, and peaks in this land I knew so well. A Clark's nutcracker flew past me and landed in a whitebark pine backdropped by the long ridges where the Nez Perce Indians had traveled from their Road to the Buffalo to the hot springs now called Jerry Johnson. An ant bit my wrist, and I brushed him off. The life, the beauty, and the mystery of the land welled up on the mountain. I could feel its power just as Ranger Smith and his crew must have, eighty-five years before.

Since its discovery by white men the Lochsa region has done more than its share to feed the resource wants of private and corporate America. To the south the wilderness remains wild, but elsewhere clear-cuts scar landscapes barely marked in Smith's time by the scorch of scattered fires. Black bears still thrive here, but the grizzly is gone, and few salmon run upriver to spawn in the creeks. More common fish are still here, however, as are the elk and deer and moose. And the land, with all its inherent productive potential, still evolves in ways not yet fully understood by either the managers or the users of the Lochsa country.

Ranger Smith and those who followed came to rule the land. They sometimes planted pine where fir trees ought to grow, built roads where the trails of elk once laced the landscape, controlled fires in woods that cannot live without the flames, and took the land's bounty, thinking they knew how to replenish as they reaped. But now our talk of sustained yield echoes across such logged-over expanses that it seems impossible for the land to sustain the flow of resources taken from the Lochsa since we began building roads and logging the beetle-killed spruce.

Not many have touched the Lochsa and escaped the land's great spirit of place, and realization is growing that nature's ways have to be respected if we are to prosper very long. The quest for understanding nature can never end, for humans will never fully solve the mystery of it all. Everything in this land, including ourselves, is so intricately connected to everything else. The important thing is that while we continue to harvest the land's bounty, as we must, we keep on learning as we go.

We must take time now to deepen our understanding of the consequences of what we have done and are doing to the land. Within our reach lies untapped knowledge whose exploration, together with lessons drawn from the successes and failures of the past, offers us a remarkable opportunity to draw closer to the earth. By doing so, we of the Lochsa—and people everywhere, for that matter—can continue to live and prosper in harmony with the land.

Three young ground squirrels chased each other among the boulders. The clouds darkened. I saw a glint of lightning behind the crest of the Grave Mountains, far to the south. The land oozed life, and its fresh breath rippled the surface of the lake. I suppressed an urge to hike out along the ridge and beyond, into the depths of a new frontier. To do that takes more than one lifetime. A raindrop fell. I looked around at that great expanse, feeling the natural power that had shaped so much of what I am and what many others are. Then I lay down in the beargrass and listened to the wind.

Notes

Chapter 1 *Over the Hill, That's God's Country*

1. U.S. Department of the Interior, *Twentieth Annual Report of U.S. Geological Survey, 1898–99,* by John B. Lieberg (Washington, D.C.: GPO, 1900), 319 (hereafter *USGS Twentieth Annual Report*).

Chapter 2 *The Nez Perce Indian's Ethic*

2. Display at the old headquarters of Nez Perce National Park, Spalding, Idaho.
3. Alvin M. Josephy Jr., *The Nez Perce Indians and the Opening of the Northwest,* Yale Western Americana Series, no. 10, abridged ed. (Lincoln: University of Nebraska Press, 1971), 22.
4. Kate C. McBeth, *The Nez Perces Since Lewis and Clark* (New York: Flaming H. Revell Co., 1908), 10.
5. Josephy, *The Nez Perce Indians,* 15.
6. L. V. McWhorter, *Hear Me My Chiefs!* (Caldwell, Idaho: The Caxton Printers, 1952), 4.
7. Josephy, *The Nez Perce Indians,* 24–27.
8. Alan Slickpoo Sr., interview by author, Kamiah, Idaho, 19 February 1994.
9. Josephy, *The Nez Perce Indians,* 22.
10. Sister M. Alfreda Elsensohn (St. Gertrude's Convent, Cottonwood, Idaho), *Pioneer Days in Idaho County,* vol. 2 (Caldwell, Idaho: The Caxton Printers, 1951), 240.
11. Ibid., 368.
12. Sister M. Alfreda Elsensohn (St. Gertrude's Convent, Cottonwood, Idaho), *Pioneer Days in Idaho County,* vol. 1 (Caldwell, Idaho: The Caxton Printers, 1947), 12–13.
13. Because it sits apart from the Bitterroot crest, the early pioneers of the Lochsa commonly referred to the extensive high-alpine terrain surrounding Grave Peak as the "Grave Mountains"; only Grave Peak, however, is shown on modern maps.
14. L. V. McWhorter, *Yellow Wolf: His Own Story* (Caldwell, Idaho: The Caxton Printers, 1948), 297–300.
15. McWhorter, *Hear Me My Chiefs!,* 67–68.
16. Ibid., 77–86.

Chapter 3 *A Tough Trip for Lewis and Clark*

17. Bernard DeVoto, ed., *The Journals of Lewis and Clark* (Boston: Houghton Mifflin Co., 1953), xxv–xxvi.
18. Ibid., 236.
19. Ibid., xxiii–xxvi.
20. Ibid., xxxvii.

21. Gary E. Moulton, ed., and Thomas W. Dunlay, asst. ed., vol. 5 of *The Journals of the Lewis and Clark Expedition, July 28–November 1, 1805* (Lincoln: University of Nebraska Press, 1986), 196.
22. DeVoto, *Journals of Lewis and Clark*, 237.
23. Ibid., 237–38.
24. Ibid., 238–39.
25. Patrick Gass, *Journal of the Voyages and Travels of A Corps of Discovery* (Philadelphia: Printer for Matthew Carey, 1811), 138.
26. Moulton and Dunlay, *The Journals of the Lewis and Clark Expedition*, 206, 207.
27. DeVoto, *Journals of Lewis and Clark*, 239.
28. Ibid., 240.
29. Gass, *Journal*, 138.
30. Moulton and Dunlay, *The Journals of the Lewis and Clark Expedition*, 211, 213.
31. Ibid., 215.
32. Gass, *Journal*, 138.
33. Eva Emery Dye, *The Conquest*, 3d ed. (Chicago: A. C. McClurg & Co., 1903), 233, 234.
34. Josephy, *The Nez Perce Indians*, 12.
35. Gary E. Moulton, ed., and Thomas W. Dunlay, asst. ed., vol. 8 of *The Journals of the Lewis and Clark Expedition, June 10–September 26, 1806*, A Project of the Center for Great Plains Studies, (Lincoln: University of Nebraska Press, 1986), 24.
36. Ibid., 32.
37. Ibid., 51.
38. Ibid., 56.
39. Ibid.
40. DeVoto, *Journals of Lewis and Clark*, 415.
41. K. Ross Toole, *Montana, An Uncommon Land* (Norman: University of Oklahoma Press, 1959), 41.

Chapter 4 *Pioneer Occupation of the Indian's West*

42. H. M. Chittenden, *American Fur Trade of the Far West*, vol. 1, pt. 2 (Stanford, Calif.: Academic Reproduction, 1954), 119; John Work, *Journal of John Work*, ed. William S. Lewis and Paul C. Phillips, Early Western Journals, no. 1 (Cleveland: Arthur H. Clark Co., 1923), 24; Catherine M. White, *Journals of David Thompson, Relating to Montana and Adjacent Regions, 1808-1812*, vol. 1 (Missoula: Montana State University Press, 1956), cii–civ; Work, *Journal of John Work*, 28.
43. David Lavender, *The American Heritage History of the Great West*, ed. Alvin M. Josephy Jr. (New York: American Heritage Publishing Co., 1965), 107.
44. H. M. Chittenden, "The Fur Trade," *American Fur Trade of the Far West*, vol. 1 (Stanford, Calif.: Academic Reproduction, 1954), preface to part 1.
45. Reuben Gold Thwaites, *Early Western Travels 1748–1846*, vol. 27 (Cleveland: Arthur H. Clark Co., 1906), 229, 230; Josephy, *The Nez Perce Indians*, 77–81, 85–90.
46. Ibid., 125–29.
47. Ibid., 144–51.
48. Ibid., 188–92.
49. McWhorter, *Hear Me My Chiefs!*, 65–67.
50. Josephy, *The Nez Perce Indians*, 152–58.
51. Ibid., 193–97, 237–40.
52. Toole, *Montana, An Uncommon Land*, 59–60.
53. Thwaites, *Early Western Travels*, 292–94.
54. Josephy, *The Nez Perce Indians*, 243–52.

55. Isaac Ingalls Stevens, *A True Copy of the Record of the Official Proceedings at the Council in the Walla Walla Valley 1855*, ed. Darrell Scott (Fairfield, Wash.: Ye Galleon Press, 1985).
56. McWhorter, *Hear Me My Chiefs!*, 97, 98; Josephy, *The Nez Perce Indians*, 383–88.
57. Gen. 1:28.
58. McWhorter, *Hear Me My Chiefs!*, 106–14.
59. William S. Shiach assisted by Harry B. Averill, *An Illustrated History of North Idaho Embracing Nez Perce, Idaho, Latah, Kootenai, and Shoshone Counties* (Western Historical Publishing Co., 1903), 76. This is a collection of histories written by several authors. Shiach, assisted by Averill, wrote the north Idaho general history and special histories of Nez Perce, Idaho, and Shoshone counties.
60. Captain John Mullan, *Report on the Construction of a Military Road, Fort Walla Walla to Fort Benton* (Washington, D.C.: GPO, 1863), 2–7.
61. Toole, *Montana, An Uncommon Land*, 69, 88.
62. Shiach, *An Illustrated History of North Idaho*, 21; Public Land Law Review Commission, *History of Public Land Law Development*, by Paul W. Gates with a chapter by Robert W. Swenson (Washington, D.C.: GPO, 1968), 374.
63. Toole, Montana, *An Uncommon Land*, 140–42.
64. Paul C. Phillips, *Journals and Letters of Major John Owen, Pioneer of the Northwest, 1850–1871*, vol. 2 (New York: Edward Eberstadt, 1927), 314–16.
65. Josephy, *The Nez Perce Indians*, 480, 485–92; McWhorter, *Yellow Wolf*, 40.
66. Josephy, *The Nez Perce Indians*, 494–507.
67. Ibid., 511–15.
68. Ibid., 534–39, 542–44.
69. McWhorter, *Hear Me My Chiefs!*, 496–99.

Chapter 5 *Fur Trappers Claim the Lochsa*

70. Ralph S. Space, *The Lolo Trail* (Lewiston, Idaho: Printcraft Printing, 1970), 2.
71. McWhorter, *Hear Me My Chiefs!*, 343.
72. Victor J. Miller, interview by author, Lolo, Montana, 26 April 1969.
73. Author's field notes, 26 July 1974.
74. Jay Turner, interview by author, Spokane, Washington, 24 May 1975.
75. Elsensohn, *Pioneer Days in Idaho County*, 1:394, 412–15.
76. DeVoto, *Journals of Lewis and Clark*, 413.
77. Louise Gerber Gilbert, interview by author, Stevensville, Montana, 5 May 1975.
78. Bert Wendover, interview by author, Missoula, Montana, 10 May 1969.

Chapter 6 *The Legend of Isaac's Gold*

79. A. L. A. Himmelwright, *In the Heart of the Bitter-root Mountains: The Story of "The Carlin Hunting Party,"* (New York: G. P. Putnam's Sons, 1895), 37–42.
80. U.S. Department of the Interior, *USGS Twentieth Annual Report*, 373.
81. Ibid., 325.
82. U.S. Department of Agriculture, Forest Service, *The Clearwater Story: A History of the Clearwater National Forest*, by Ralph S. Space (Missoula: USFS Northern Region, ca. 1980), 133.
83. Ibid., 134.
84. Author's field notes, 10 August 1975.
85. Ed and Myrtle Gilroy, interview by author, Kooskia, Idaho, 16 May 1976; Gilbert interview.
86. Ernest Hansen, interview by author, Cayuse Creek, Idaho, 19 July 1956.

87. Ibid.
88. Ibid.
89. Gilbert interview.
90. Ibid.
91. Fred Schott and Frank Smith, as told to author on individual occasions about 1927.
92. Gilbert interview.
93. Schott and Smith, as told to author.
94. Bob Boyd, interview by author, Hamilton, Montana, 1 April 1976.

Chapter 7 *The Government Stakes Its Claims*

95. Gifford Pinchot, *Breaking New Ground* (New York: Harcourt, Brace & Co., 1947), 84.
96. *An Act to repeal timber-culture laws and for other purposes*. *U.S. Statutes at Large* 26 (1891): 1095–1103.
97. *An Act making appropriations for sundry civil expenses of the Government for the fiscal year ending June thirtieth, eighteen hundred and ninety-eight, and for other purposes. U.S. Statutes at Large* 30 (1897): 11, 31–36.
98. U.S. Department of the Interior, *USGS Twentieth Annual Report*, 274.
99. Ibid., 388.
100. Ibid., 392.
101. Than Wilkerson (unpublished historical paper written for Bitterroot National Forest, 1938).
102. Elsensohn, *Pioneer Days in Idaho County*, 2:349.
103. U.S. Department of the Interior, General Land Office, *Forest Reserve Manual for the Information and Use of Forest Officers* (Washington, D.C.: GPO, 1902), 3.
104. Ibid.
105. Elsensohn, *Pioneer Days in Idaho County*, 2:354.
106. Louis Hartig, *Lochsa*, ed. Shirley Moore, The Pacific Northwest National Parks & Forest Association (Dubuque, Iowa: Kendall/Hunt Publishing Co., 1989), 2–6.
107. Pinchot, *Breaking New Ground*, 11, 22.
108. Ibid., 140.
109. Ibid., 167.
110. Ibid., 190.
111. U.S. Department of Agriculture, *The Use Book: Regulations and Instructions for Use of the National Forest Reserves* (Washington, D.C.: GPO, 1906), 16, 17.
112. Ibid., 148.
113. U.S. Department of Agriculture, Forest Service, *Report on the Bitter Root (Idaho) Reserve*, by Smith Riley, Forest Inspector (Denver, 5 February 1907). I have never found the maps referred to in this report showing the boundaries of the original fourteen districts within the reserve.

Chapter 8 *The Coming of the District-Based Rangers*

114. Carl Weholt, interview by author, Harpster, Idaho, 26 May 1975.
115. Ibid.
116. U.S. Department of Agriculture, Forest Service, *The Nez Perce Story: A History of the Nez Perce National Forest*, by Albert N. Cochrell (Missoula: USFS Northern Region, 1960), 107. (This publication was revised in 1963 and 1970.)
117. Public Land Law Review Commission, *History of Public Land Law*, 356–77.

Chapter 9 *The War of the Railroads*

118. Ralph S. Space, *The Lolo Trail*, (Lewiston, Idaho: Printcraft Printing, 1970), 42.
119. O. O. Howard, *Nez Perce Joseph*, (New York: Boston, Lee & Shepard Publishers, 1881), 189–90.
120. Schiach, *An Illustrated History of North Idaho*, 77–81.
121. Ibid.
122. Ibid.
123. Lewis Tuck Renz, *The History of the Northern Pacific Railroad* (Fairfield, Wash.: Ye Galleon Press, 1980), 94, 119.
124. U.S. Department of Agriculture, Forest Service, *Early Days in the Forest Service*, vol. 3 (Missoula: USFS Northern Region, 1962), 111–14.
125. Ibid.
126. Ibid.
127. Victor J. Miller, interview by author, Lolo, Montana, 26 April 1969.
128. Interesting background information on the Parry family can be found in "Major Fenn's Country," by Neal Parsell (Kooskia, Idaho: Upper Clearwater-Lochsa-Selway Chamber of Commerce, 1986), 3.
129. U.S. Department of Agriculture, Forest Service, *Early Days in the Forest Service*, 3:114.
130. Ralph S. Space, interview by author, Orofino, Idaho, 3 June 1976.
131. Elsensohn, *Pioneer Days in Idaho County*, 2:62.
132. U.S. Department of Agriculture, Forest Service, *The Clearwater Story*, 95.

Chapter 10 *Their Common Enemy Was Fire*

133. Ed Thenon, "The Adventures of Three Men in the Great Forest Fires of 1910," (Kooskia, Idaho: n.d.).
134. U.S. Department of Agriculture, Forest Service, *The Nez Perce Story*, 74–76.
135. C. H. Shattuck, *Preliminary Report of the Forestal Conditions and Possibilities of the Clearwater National Forest, June, July, August, 1910* (Moscow: University of Idaho, Department of Forestry, 1910), 33.
136. Ibid., 68.
137. Elers Koch, "Unpublished History of the 1910 Forest Fires in Idaho and Western Montana" (n.d.).
138. U.S. Department of Agriculture, Forest Service, *The Nez Perce Story*, 74–76.

Chapter 11 *Expanding the Indian Trails*

139. Turner interview.
140. Loyd Rupe, interview by author, Harpster, Idaho, 26 May 1975.
141. Ibid.
142. Ibid.
143. Miller interview.
144. Gilroy interview.
145. Gilbert interview.

Chapter 12 *Testing the Ranger's Resolve*

146. Ed Mackay, interview by author, Darby, Montana, 7 June 1969; William K. (Bill) Samsel, interview by author, Missoula, Montana, 15 April 1975.
147. U.S. Department of Agriculture, Forest Service, *The Clearwater Story*, 207; Hartig, *Lochsa*, 58, 59.
148. U.S. Department of Agriculture, Forest Service, "The First Ten Years Were the Toughest," by Ralph L. Hand, in *Early Days in the Forest Service*, 3:79.

149. Henry G. (Heinie) Williams, interview by author, Hamilton, Montana, 6 May 1975.
150. Elsensohn, *Pioneer Days in Idaho County*, 2:412; Miller interview.
151. U.S. Department of Agriculture, Forest Service, *The Clearwater Story*, 76.
152. Jack Parsell, interview by author, Hamilton, Montana, 13 June 1975; Samsel interview; Williams interview.
153. Pearl Bell McKee, interview by author, Missoula, Montana, 17 April 1975.
154. U.S. Department of Agriculture, Forest Service, "The First Ten Years," 97.
155. U.S. Department of Agriculture, Forest Service, "The Lochsa River Fire," by Elers Koch, in *Early Days in the Forest Service*, vol. 1 (Missoula: USFS Northern Region, 1962), 114.
156. U.S. Department of Agriculture, Forest Service: *The Bulldozer, A Pioneer Step in Development of Machines for Forest Road Construction* (Missoula: USFS Northern Region, 1930.
157. U.S. Federal Security Agency, *Final Report of the Director of the Civilian Conservation Corps, April, 1933, through June 30, 1942*, by J. J. McEntee (n.d.).
158. U.S. Department of Agriculture, Forest Service, *History of Selway Fires(1934*, by C. B. Sutliff (Missoula: USFS Northern Region, 29 December 1934).
159. C. K. Lyman, interview by author, Condon, Montana, 22 June 1978.
160. U.S. Department of Agriculture, Forest Service, *History of Selway Fires*.
161. Roy Lewis, interview by author, Hamilton, Montana, 13 June 1975 (includes notes taken from a tape of his late wife, Mabel's, experience).
162. Ibid.
163. U.S. Department of Agriculture, Forest Service, *History of Selway Fires*.

Chapter 13 *Lapland and the Fur Poachers*

164. Fay Burrell, interview by author, Hamilton, Montana, 7 May 1975.
165. Charley Powell, interview by author, Spokane, Washington, 24 May 1975.
166. Earl Malone, interview by author, Hamilton, Montana, 6 May 1975.
167. Powell interview.
168. Ibid.
169. Ibid; Malone interview.
170. Burrell interview.
171. Mackay interview.
172. Ibid.
173. Ibid.
174. Lewis interview; Powell interview.

Chapter 14 *The Wilderness Ethic*

175. Malone interview.
176. Gen. 1:28; Gen. 3:23.
177. Roderick Nash, *Wilderness and the American Mind* (New Haven: Yale University Press, 1967), 24.
178. Brooks Atkinson, *Walden and Other Writings of Henry David Thoreau* (New York: Modern Library, 1950), 613.
179. Nash, *Wilderness and the American Mind*, 123.
180. Ibid., 108.
181. Ibid., 132–33.
182. Ibid., 134–35.
183. Ibid., 137.
184. Ibid., 140.
185. Pinchot, *Breaking New Ground*, 322.

186. *Creation of the National Park Service Act. U.S. Statutes at Large* 39 (1916): 535.
187. Nash, *Wilderness and the American Mind*, 187, 191.
188. George Marshall, "Adirondacks to Alaska: A Biographical Sketch of Robert Marshall," *The Ad-i-ron-dac*, May–June 1951, 44–45, 59.
189. Robert Marshall, "The Problem of Wilderness, " *The Scientific Monthly*, February 1930, 141–48.
190. Roderick Nash, "The Strenuous Life of Bob Marshall," *Forest History*, October 1966, 18.
191. Robert Marshall, "Impressions from Wilderness," *The Living Wilderness*, (Autumn 1961): 10–11.
192. U.S. Department of Agriculture, Forest Service, *A Study of the Bitterroot-Selway Primitive Area, Bitterroot, Clearwater, Lolo and Nez Perce Forests* (Missoula: USFS Northern Region, n.d.).
193. Burrell interview.

Chapter 15 *Hunters and Packers*

194. Theodore Roosevelt, *The Works of Theodore Roosevelt: Hunting the Grisly and Other Sketches* (New York: P. F. Collier & Sons Publishers, 1893), Preface.
195. Montana Fish and Game Department, *Game Management in Montana*, ed. Thomas W. Mussell and F. W. Howell, Federal Aid Project W-3-C, (Helena, Mont.: 1971), 9–11.
196. William T. Hornaday, *Our Vanishing Wildlife: Its Extermination and Preservation* (New York: New York Zoological Society, 1913), preface.
197. Ibid., 165, 167.
198. William H. Wright, *The Grizzly Bear* (New York: Charles Scribner's Sons, 1910), 5–6.
199. Ibid., 59–61. Their travel route suggests that Wright's encounter with this grizzly took place at present-day Jerry Johnson Hot Springs.
200. Ibid., 11.
201. Theodore Roosevelt, *The Works of Theodore Roosevelt: The Wilderness Hunter* (New York: P. F. Collier & Sons Publishers, 1893), preface.
202. Himmelwright, *"The Carlin Hunting Party,"* 34–36.
203. This stream is Warm Springs Creek, and the lick is now called Jerry Johnson Hot Springs.
204. Himmelwright, *"The Carlin Hunting Party,"* 65, 66.
205. Ibid., 160.
206. John and Dorothy Buker, interview by author, Bukers' ranch near Victor, Montana, 6 May 1979.
207. Jack Clarke, telephone interview by author, Mullan, Idaho, 16 March 1979.

Chapter 16 *The Winter of the Blue Snow*

208. Wendover interview.
209. Ibid.

Chapter 17 *The Last of the Bitterroot's Grizzlies*

210. McWhorter, *Yellow Wolf*, 297–300.
211. McWhorter, *Hear Me My Chiefs!*, 343; Lawrence Humble, interview by author, Hamilton, Montana, 6 June 1975.
212. Elsensohn, *Pioneer Days in Idaho County*, 2:225–31.
213. Ibid.
214. Wright, *The Grizzly Bear*, 69.

215. Ibid., 74.
216. Ibid., 95.
217. Nez Perce County Historical Society, Reflections of East Lewiston, 1925. Exhibit at Luna House Museum, Lewiston, Idaho.
218. Ted and Lil Williams, interview by author, Williams's ranch near Lolo, Montana, 11 June 1975.
219. Williams interview.
220. McKee interview; Powell interview; Lawrence Alkire, interview by author, south of Hamilton, Montana, 1 April 1976; Stearns Reed, interview by author, Victor, Montana, 13 June 1975; Bob Boyd, interview by author, Hamilton, Montana, 1 April 1976; Marshall, "Impressions from Wilderness," 13; Humble interview; Williams interview.
221. Ibid.
222. Frank Bustard, interview by author, Missoula, Montana, 14 April 1975; Earl Smith, interview by author, Missoula, Montana, 4 July 1978; Clarke, telephone interview.
223. Parsell interview.
224. Wright, *The Grizzly Bear*, 3.

Chapter 18 *Prelude to Management*

225. Ray S. Ferguson, letter to author, 7 September 1968.
226. Field notes approved by the United States Surveyor General, 29 April 1916.
227. See county records at Orofino and Grangeville, Idaho.
228. Ibid.
229. Earl E. Cooley, *Trimotor and Trail* (Missoula: Mountain Press Publishing Co., 1984), 22–23.
230. U.S. Department of Agriculture, Forest Service, *History of Smokejumping* (Missoula: USFS Northern Region, 1974).
231. Author's official diary, 1 December 1948.
232. Ibid., 27 March 1948.
233. Margie E. Hahn, *Mules and Mountains: Walt Hahn, Forest Service Packer* (Stevensville, Mont.: Stoneydale Press Publishing Co., 1993), chap. 17.
234. Hartig, *Lochsa*, 191-94.
235. I drew the 13–14 million board feet annual sustainable yield of saw timber from memory because I could not find a copy of my 1949 timber management plan in the files of the Forest Service.

Chapter 19 *Trial by Bulldozer*

236. Author's official diary, 20–21 September 1954.

Chapter 21 *Poisoning the Land and Its Waters*

237. Author's official diary, 6 February 1956.
238. U.S. Department of Agriculture, Forest Service, *Spruce Budworm Control Program Report* (Lolo National Forest: Powell Control Unit, 1956).
239. Rachel Carson, *Silent Spring* (Greenwich, Conn.: Fawcett Books, 1962), 28–29.
240. Canada Department of Forestry and Rural Development, *Important Forest Insects and Diseases of Mutual Concern to Canada, the United States, and Mexico* (1967), 76–77.

Chapter 22 *The Turning of America*

241. Pinchot, *Breaking New Ground*, 325.
242. U.S. Department of Agriculture, *The Use Book*, 16, 17.
243. *Multiple Use–Sustained Yield Act, U.S. Code*, vol. 16, secs. 528–31 (1960).

244. *Wilderness Act*, sec. 2(a), *U.S. Code*, vol. 16, sec. 1131(a) (1964).
245. *Multiple Use–Sustained Yield Act*, *U.S. Code*, vol. 16, secs. 528–31 (1960).
246. John Owen, *Journals and Letters of Major John Owen*, vol. 1 (New York: Edward Eberstadt, 1927), 236.
247. Dale A. Burk, *The Clearcut Crisis* (Great Falls, Mont.: Jursnick Printing, 1970), 13.
248. Ibid., 97.
249. U.S. Department of Agriculture, Forest Service, *Management Practices on the Bitterroot National Forest, A Task Force Appraisal* (Missoula: USFS Northern Region, 1970).
250. *A University View of the Forest Service, Prepared for the Committee on Interior and Insular Affairs, United States Senate by a Select Committee of the University of Montana* (Washington, D.C.: GPO, 1970).

Chapter 23 *Using and Misusing the Lochsa's Treasures*

251. Mort Brigham, interview by author, Lewiston, Idaho, 23 April 1982.
252. *Lewiston (Idaho) Morning Tribune*, Lewis and Clark Highway Edition, 19 August 1962.
253. Ibid.
254. Ibid.
255. Brigham interview.
256. U.S. Department of Agriculture, Forest Service, *Record of Hearings held at Missoula, Montana, March 7, 1961, and at Grangeville, Idaho, March 14, 1961.*
257. Orville L. Freeman, Secretary of Agriculture, *Establishment of Selway Bitterroot Wilderness Area* (Washington, D.C.: 1963).
258. Ibid.
259. Brigham interview.
260. Arnold W. Bolle, foreword to *Land and Resource Planning in the National Forests*, by Charles F. Wilkinson and H. Michael Anderson (Washington, D.C.: Island Press, 1987), 1–6.
261. Ibid., 36–45.

Chapter 24 *Ending the Illusion of Superabundance*

262. U.S. Department of Agriculture, Forest Service, *Clearwater National Forest Plan* (Orofino, Idaho: USFS, 1987). More specifically, the plan (1) describes management practices, (2) provides for multiple use and a sustained yield of goods and services to maximize long-term benefits, and (3) sets forth prescriptions for using various tracts of land and special areas.
263. Ibid. For a typical example see Management Area E-1, chapter 3, 57–60.
264. Ibid., 32, 36; James G. MacCracken, Jay O'Laughlin, and Troy Merrill, *Idaho Roadless Areas and Wilderness Proposals* (Moscow, Idaho: University of Idaho, Idaho Forest, Wildlife, and Range Experiment Station, 1993); *The Idaho Wilderness, Sustainable Forests, and Communities Act of 1994*, 103rd Congress, second session, H. R. 3722.
265. Gary Oye, interview by author, Elk Summit, Idaho, 4 August 1982.
266. Ibid.
267. James L. Caswell, interview by author, Orofino, Idaho, 15 February 1994; Slickpoo interview; Daniel G. Johnson, interview by author, Konkolville, Idaho, 3 March 1994; Orville L. Daniels, interview by author, Missoula, Montana, 3 March 1994.
268. Carla Wise et al., *Wolf Recovery in Central Idaho: Alternative Strategies and Impacts* (Moscow: University of Idaho, Idaho Forest, Wildlife, and Range Experiment Station, 1991).

269. Harlan Opdahl, interview by author, Mire Creek Camp, Powell Ranger District, Idaho, 13 August 1994.
270. Charles F. Wilkinson, *The Eagle Bird* (New York: Random House, 1993), 91–96.
271. U.S. Department of Agriculture, Forest Service, "Monitoring and Evaluation Report, Fiscal Year 1992," in *Clearwater National Forest Plan* (Orofino, Idaho: USFS, 1993), 120–36.
272. U.S. Department of Agriculture, Forest Service, *Clearwater National Forest Plan*, Chapter 3, 19.
273. Allen V. Pinkham, interview by author, Orofino, Idaho, 15 February 1994; Slickpoo interview; Jon Bledsoe, interview by author, Orofino, Idaho, 13 January 1994.
274. *Wild and Scenic Rivers Act. U.S. Statutes at Large* 82 (1968): 906–18, designates, as the first river of the national wild and scenic rivers system, the (1) Clearwater, Middle Fork, Idaho—The Middle Fork from the town of Kooskia upstream to the town of Lowell; the Lochsa River from its junction with the Selway at Lowell forming the Middle Fork, upstream to the Powell Ranger Station; and the Selway River from Lowell upstream to its origin; to be administered by the Secretary of Agriculture.
275. Elsensohn, *Pioneer Days in Idaho County*, 2:44.
276. Bob Shepard, interview by author, Powell, Idaho, 6 August 1982.
277. Bledsoe interview.
278. Bob and Margaret Dammarell, interview by author, Wilderness Gateway Campground, Idaho, 7 August 1982.
279. Tom Geouge, interview by author, Powell, Idaho, 6 August 1982.
280. Dick Ferrar, interview by author, Powell, Idaho, 6 August 1982.
281. Larry Cron, interview by author, Coeur d'Alene, Idaho, 22 April 1982.
282. Geouge interview.
283. Denzil B. Sigars II, interview by author, Missoula, Montana, 14 March 1994.
284. Ferrar interview; Bledsoe interview.
285. A memo from Ken Hotchkiss to the author, dated 15 April 1994, contained the following table, showing the volume of timber sold, by ranger district, on the Clearwater National Forest during the last five years. Figures represent thousand board feet (mbf).

Year	Pierce	Palouse	North Fork	Lochsa	Powell	Total Forest
1993	8,872	18,047	8,173	6,836	785	42,712
1992	2,049	6,985	4,837	3,216	7,440	24,527
1991	34,916	36,125	29,353	18,957	6,654	126,004
1990	42,776	24,612	31,325	12,438	16,991	128,141
1989	40,989	27,227	43,964	17,847	20,885	150,911

286. Gerald Beard, interview by author, Kooskia, Idaho, 23 June 1994.
287. Margaret Gorski, interview by author, Powell, Idaho, 11 January 1994.
288. Bill Mulligan, interview by author, Kamiah, Idaho, 18 February 1994; Johnson interview.
289. Pinkham interview. See also *State v. McConville*, 65 Idaho 46, 139 P. 2d 485 (1943), and *State v. Arthur*, 261 P. 2d 135 (1953), concerning the establishment of the Nez Perce Indians' hunting and fishing rights within the boundaries of the 1855 treaty area.
290. Dennis Baird, telephone interview by author, Moscow, Idaho, 13 June 1994.

291. Mike Bader, interview by author, Missoula, Montana, 9 March 1994.
292. David Hatfield Jr., interview by author, Powell, Idaho, 5 August 1982; Cheryl Holman, interview by author, Rocky Point Lookout near Powell, Idaho, 7 August 1982.
293. René Dubos, *A God Within* (New York: Charles Scribner's Sons, 1972), 45.

Chapter 25 *A New Look at Conservation and Multiple Use*

294. Gifford Pinchot, *The Use of the National Forests,* U.S. Department of Agriculture, Forest Service, *by Gifford Pinchot* (Washington, D.C.: 1907), 25.
295. *Multiple Use–Sustained Yield Act, U.S. Code,* vol. 16, secs. 528–31 (1960).
296. Dubos, *A God Within,* 12.
297. George P. Marsh, *The Earth as Modified by Human Action: A Last Revision of "Man and Nature,"* (New York: Scribner, Armstrong & Co., 1874), 12.
298. Ted and Lil Williams interview.
299. Dubos, *A God Within,* 173.
300. Pinchot, *Breaking New Ground,* 441.
301. Ibid., 379.

Chapter 26 *The Land, the People, and Tomorrow*

302. U.S. Department of Agriculture, Forest Service, "Clearwater Monitoring and Evaluation Report," 25–47, 85–97. See page 97 for stream segments of concern in the Lochsa and Powell ranger districts and page 41 for water temperature problems in White Sand and Brushy Fork Creeks.
303. William R. Moore, "Land Management Responsibilities Unseen or Ignored," *Western Wildlands* (Winter 1978): 34–39.
304. Hal Salwasser, "The Challenge of New Perspectives," in *Proceedings of a Regional Workshop,* U.S. Department of Agriculture, Forest Service (Denver: General Technical Report RM-220, September 1992); Jerry F. Franklin, "Toward a New Forestry," *American Forests* 95 (November/December 1989): 37–44; Norman Meyers, "The Question of Linkages in Environment and Development," *Bio Science* 43 (May 1993): 302–10; Chris Maser, "New Forestry, New Questions: A New Future?," *Western Wildlands* (Winter 1992): 21.
305. Eugene P. Odum, "Great Ideas in Ecology for the 1990s," *Bio Science* 42 (July/August 1992): 542.
306. Jay O'Laughlin et al., *Forest Health Conditions in Idaho, Executive Summary,* (Moscow, Idaho: University of Idaho, Idaho Forest, Wildlife and Range Experiment Station, 1993); Caswell interview.
307. U.S. Department of Agriculture, Forest Service, *White Sand Landscape Level Integrated Resource and Ecosystem Analysis* (Clearwater National Forest, Powell Ranger District: 1993).
308. Aldo Leopold, *A Sand County Almanac,* 2d ed. (New York: Oxford University Press, 1966), 220.

Selected Bibliography

Atkinson, Brooks. *Walden and Other Writings of Henry David Thoreau*. New York: Modern Library, 1950.

Burk, Dale A. *The Clearcut Crisis*. Great Falls, Mont.: Jursnick Printing, 1970.

Carson, Rachel. *Silent Spring*. Greenwich, Conn.: Fawcett Books, 1962.

Chittenden, H. M. *American Fur Trade of the Far West*. Vol. 1, pt. 1, *The Fur Trade*. Stanford, Calif.: Academic Reproduction, 1954.

———. *American Fur Trade of the Far West*. Vol. 1, pt. 2, *Historical*. Stanford, Calif.: Academic Reproduction, 1954.

Cockrell, Albert N. *The Nez Perce Story: A History of the Nez Perce National Forest*. Missoula, Mont.: U.S. Department of Agriculture, Forest Service, Northern Region, 1960, and rev. eds. 1963, 1970.

DeVoto, Bernard. *The Journals of Lewis and Clark*. Boston: Houghton Mifflin Co., 1953.

Dubos, René. *A God Within*. New York: Charles Scribner's Sons, 1972.

Elsensohn, Sister M. Alfreda (St. Gertrude's Convent, Cottonwood, Idaho). *Pioneer Days in Idaho County*. 2 vols. Caldwell, Idaho: Caxton Printers, 1947–51.

Franklin, Jerry F. "Toward a New Forestry." *American Forests*. Vol. 95 (November/December 1989): 37–44.

Hahn, Margie E. *Mules and Mountains: Walt Hahn, Forest Service Packer*. Stevensville, Mont.: Stoneydale Press Publishing Co., 1993.

Hartig, Louis. *Lochsa*. Edited by Shirley Moore, Pacific Northwest National Parks and Forest Association. Dubuque, Iowa: Kendall/Hunt Publishing Co., 1989.

Himmelwright, A. L. A. *In the Heart of the Bitter-root Mountains: The Story of the "Carlin Hunting Party."* New York: G. P. Putnam's Sons, 1895.

Hornaday, William T. *Our Vanishing Wildlife: Its Extermination and Preservation*. New York: New York Zoological Society, 1913.

Howard, O. O. *Nez Perce Joseph*. New York: Boston, Lee & Shepard Publishers, 1881.

Josephy, Alvin M., Jr. *The Nez Perce Indians and the Opening of the Northwest*. Yale Western Americana Series no. 10, abridged ed. Lincoln and London: University of Nebraska Press, 1971.

Leopold, Aldo. *A Sand County Almanac*. 2d ed. New York: Oxford University Press, 1966.

MacCracken, James G., Jay O'Laughlin, and Troy Merrill. *Idaho Roadless Areas and Wilderness Proposals*. Moscow: University of Idaho, Idaho Forest, Wildlife, and Range Experiement Station, 1993.

Marsh, George P. *The Earth as Modified by Human Action*, final rev. of *Man and Nature*. New York: Scribner, Armstrong & Co., 1874.

Maser, Chris. "New Forestry, New Questions: A New Future?" *Western Wildlands*. Vol. 17 (Winter 1992): 21.

McBeth, Kate C. *The Nez Perces Since Lewis and Clark*. New York: Flaming H. Revell Co., 1908.
McWhorter, L. V. *Hear Me My Chiefs!* Caldwell, Idaho: Caxton Printers, 1952.
———. *Yellow Wolf: His Own Story*. Caldwell, Idaho: Caxton Printers, 1948.
Meyers, Norman. "The Question of Linkages in Environment and Development." *Bio Science*. Vol. 43 (May 1993): 302–10.
Moore, William R. "Land Management Responsibilities Unseen or Ignored." *Western Wildlands*. Vol. 4 (Winter 1978): 34–39.
Moulton, Gary E., and Thomas M. Dunlay, eds. *The Journals of the Lewis and Clark Expedition, July 28–November 1, 1805*. Vol. 5. Lincoln: University of Nebraska Press, 1986.
———. *The Journals of the Lewis and Clark Expedition, June 10–September 26, 1806*. Vol. 8. Lincoln: University of Nebraska Press, 1986.
Mullan, John. *Report on the Construction of a Military Road: Fort Walla Walla to Fort Benton*. Washington, D.C.: GPO, 1863.
Nash, Roderick. *Wilderness and the American Mind*. Rev. ed. New Haven: Yale University Press, 1967.
Odom, Eugene P. "Great Ideas in Ecology for the 1990s." *Bio Science*. Vol. 42 (July/August 1992): 542.
O'Laughlin, Jay, James G. MacCracken, David L. Adams, Stephen C. Bunting, Keith A. Blatner, and Charles E. Keegan, III. *Forest Health Conditions in Idaho, Executive Sumary*. Moscow: University of Idaho, Idaho Forest, Wildlife, and Range Experiment Station, 1993.
Parsell, Neal. *Major Fenn's Country*. Kooskia, Idaho: Upper Clearwater–Lochsa–Selway Chamber of Commerce, 1986.
Phillips, Paul C. *The Journals and Letters of Major John Owen*. Vols. 1–2. New York: Edward Eberstadt, 1927.
Pinchot, Gifford. *Breaking New Ground*. New York: Harcourt, Brace & Co., 1947.
Public Land Law Review Commission. *History of Public Land Law Development*, by Paul W. Gates and Robert W. Swenson. Washington, D.C.: GPO, 1968.
Renz, Lewis Tuck. *The History of te Northern Pacific Railroad*. Fairfield, Washington: Ye Galleon Press, 1980.
Roosevelt, Theodore. *The Works of Theodore Roosevelt: Hunting the Grisly and Other Sketches*. New York: P. F. Collier & Sons Publishers, 1893.
Shattuck, C. H. *Preliminary Report of Forestal Conditions and Possibilities of the Clearwater National Forest, June, July, August, 1910*. Moscow: University of Idaho, Department of Forestry, 1910.
Shiach, William S. assisted by Harry B. Averill. *An Illustrated History of North Idaho Embracing Nez Perce, Idaho, Latah, Kootenai, and Shoshone Counties*. Spokane, Washington: Western Historical Publishing Co., 1903. Note: This is a collection of histories written by several authors. Shiach, assisted by Averill, wrote the north Idaho general history and special histories of Nez Perce, Idaho, and Shoshone counties.
Space, Ralph S. *The Clearwater Story: A History of the Clearwater National Forest*. Missoula, Montana: U.S. Department of Agriculture, Forest Service, undated but written about 1980.
———. *The Lolo Trail*. Lewiston, Idaho: Printcraft Printing, 1970.
Thwaites, Reuben Gold. *Early Western Travels 1748–1846*. Vol. 27. Cleveland: Arthur H. Clark Co., 1906.
Toole, K. Ross. *Montana, An Uncommon Land*. Norman: University of Oklahoma Press, 1959.

U.S. Department of Agriculture, Forest Service. *Clearwater National Forest Plan*. Orofino, Idaho: USFS, 1987.

———. *The Clearwater Story, A History of the Clearwater National Forest*. Missoula: USFS Northern Region, 1964.

———. *Early Days in the Forest Service*. Vol. 1. Missoula: USFS Northern Region, 1944.

———. *Early Days in the Forest Service*. Vol. 3. Missoula: USFS Northern Region, 1962.

———. *History of the Selway Fires, 1934*, by C. B. Sutliff. Missoula: USFS Northern Region, n.d.

———. *History of Smokejumping*. Missoula: USFS Northern Region, 1974.

———. *The Use Book: Regulations and Instructions for Use of the National Forest Reserves*. Washington, D.C.: GPO, 1906.

U.S. Department of the Interior. *Twentieth Annual Report of U.S. Geological Survey, 1898–99*, by John B. Lieberg. Washington, D.C.: GPO, 1900.

———. *Forest Reserve Manual for the Information and Use of Forest Officers*. Washington, D.C.: GPO, 1902.

White, Catherine M. *Journals of David Thompson, Relating to Montana and Adjacent Regions 1808–1812*. Vol. 1. Missoula: Montana State Univeristy Press, 1956.

Wilkinson, Charles F. *The Eagle Bird*. New York: Random House, 1993.

Wilkinson, Charles F., and Michael H. Anderson. *Land and Resource Planning in the National Forests*. Washington, D.C.: Island Press, 1987.

Wise, Carla, Jeffry J. Yeo, Dale Goble, James M. Peek, and Jay O'Laughlin. *Wolf Recovery in Central Idaho: Alternative Strategies and Impacts*. Moscow: University of Idaho, Idaho Forest, Wildlife, and Range Experiment Station, 1991.

Work, John, *Journal of John Work*. Edited by William S. Lewis and Paul C. Phillips. Cleveland: Arthur H. Clark Co., 1923.

Wright, William H. *The Grizzly Bear*. New York: Charles Scribner's Sons, 1910.

Index

Bud and his wife, Janet, entered Idaho from Montana at Blodgett Pass in the present-day Selway-Bitterroot Wilderness.

In 1971 Bud Moore married Janet Richardson-Fitzgerald, the first professional staff women in the Forest Service's Division of Fire Control in Washington, D.C. Her groundbreaking efforts in fighting socially entrenched discrimination and promoting equality for all has contributed much to the acceptance of women in many fields, especially in national forest firefighting. After marrying Bud and moving to Montana, Janet was elected to the state legislature, where she served from 1985 to 1991.

About the Author

Bud Moore grew up in the shadow of the Bitterroot mountains. He hunted, trapped, and explored the Lolo and Lochsa drainages—east and west of the Bitterroot crest—and knew all the stories local mountain men had to tell about that country by the time he took a job with the U.S. Forest Service in 1934.

During his forty-year career as a forester, he cared for the land and grew even more knowledgeable about and attached to it. He became one of the Forest Service's "greatest fire experts," according to his good friend, the late Norman Maclean, who wrote *Young Men and Fire* and *A River Runs Through It*, and he is the principal architect of its current wilderness fire management policy. In addition, Bud knows a great deal about other forestry issues such as water quality, sustainable use of resources, and the "wholeness" of the land now termed ecosystem management.

Since retiring from the Forest Service in 1974, Bud and his wife, Janet, have turned their attention to managing Coyote Forest, an 80-acre plot of land in Montana's Swan Valley (on which they live) plus another 167 acres farther south, near the town of Ovando. The centerpiece of their operation is a sawmill that produces lumber from their "light-on-the-land" approach to logging in the Swan Valley. They use an "even-flow" system—balancing the rate of harvest with the rate of forest regeneration and growth.

Bud is profoundly dedicated to the forest and all of the natural elements, including people, that make it whole. He believes anyone who works with the land must have a feel for it. "When in doubt, go slow," he advises. "Be humble. Learn from your mistakes."

CPSIA information can be obtained
at www.ICGtesting.com
Printed in the USA
FFOW04n2236070118
44363330-44057FF